ROMANCING DECAY

General Editors' Preface

The European dimension of research in the humanities has come into sharp focus over recent years, producing scholarship which ranges across disciplines and national boundaries. Until now there has been no major channel for such work. This series aims to provide one, and to unite the fields of cultural studies and traditional scholarship. It will publish the most exciting new writing in areas such as European history and literature, art history, archaeology, language and translation studies, political, cultural and gay studies, music, psychology, sociology and philosophy. The emphasis will be explicitly European and interdisciplinary, concentrating attention on the relativity of cultural perspectives, with a particular interest in issues of cultural transition.

Martin Stannard
Greg Walker

University of Leicester

Romancing Decay:
Ideas of Decadence in
European Culture

edited by
Michael St John

Studies in European Cultural Transition

Volume Three

General Editors: Martin Stannard and Greg Walker

Routledge
Taylor & Francis Group

LONDON AND NEW YORK

First published 1999 by Ashgate Publishing

Published 2016 by Routledge
2 Park Square, Milton Park, Abingdon, Oxfordshire OX14 4RN
711 Third Avenue, New York, NY 10017, USA

First issued in paperback 2016

Routledge is an imprint of the Taylor & Francis Group, an informa business

British Library Cataloguing-in-Publication data

Romancing decay: ideas of decadence in European culture. – (Studies in
   European cultural transition; v. 3)
   1.Decadence (Literary movement) – Europe 2.European literature – History
   and criticism
   I. St John, Michael
   809

Library of Congress Cataloging-in-Publication data

Romancing decay: ideas of decadence in European culture / edited by Michael
   St John.
   (Studies in European cultural transition; v. 3)
   Includes bibliographical references and index.
   1.European literature – History and criticism. 2.Decadence (Literary
   movement) – Europe. 3.Decadence in literature.
   I.St John, Michael. II. Series.
   PN56.D45R66   1999
   809'.911—dc21   99–16569
                                CIP

ISBN 13: 978-1-138-26884-5 (pbk)
ISBN 13: 978-1-84014-674-5 (hbk)

Contents

List of Illustrations   vii

Acknowledgements   viii

Introduction   ix

1   Redeeming the Decadent City: Changing Responses to the
     Urban and Wilderness Environments in the *Lives* of St Jerome   1
     David Salter, Leicester University

2   Nature, Venus, and Royal Decadence: Political Theory
     and Political Practice in Chaucer's *Parliament of Fowls*   17
     Michael St John, Leicester University

3   Reading Symptoms of Decadence in Ford's *'Tis Pity She's a Whore*   27
     Carla Dente, University of Pisa

4   'Bawdy in Thoughts, precise in Words': Decadence, Divinity and
     Dissent in the Restoration   39
     Michael Davies, Nottingham Trent University

5   Dickensian Decadents   64
     Vincent Newey, Leicester University

6   Defining Decadence in Nineteenth-century French and
     British Criticism   83
     Julian North, De Montfort University

7   Somewhere there's Music: John Meade Falkner's
     The Lost Stradivarius   95
     Nicholas Daly, Trinity College, Dublin

8   'Squalid Arguments': Decadence, Reform, and the Colonial
     Vision in Kipling's *The Five Nations*   107
     Andrew St John, Leicester University

9   The Metamorphoses of a Fairy-Tale: Quillard, D'Annunzio and
     The Girl With Cut-Off Hands   118
     Julie Dashwood, Lucy Cavendish College, Cambridge

10   A Passion for Dismemberment: Gabriele d'Annunzio's
     Portrayals of Women   128
     Susan Bassnett, University of Warwick

11 The Escape from Decadence: British Travel Literature on the
   Balkans 1900–45   141
   Andrew Hammond

12 Books and Ruins: Abject Decadence in Gide and Mann   154
   Martin Halliwell, De Montfort University

13 Resisting Decadence: Literary Criticism as a Corrective to
   Low Culture and High Science in the Work of I. A. Richards   171
   Daniel Cordle, Nottingham Trent University

14 Blow It Up and Start All Over Again: Second World War
   Apocalypse Fiction and the Decadence of Modernity   183
   Tristram Hooley, Leicester University

15 Decadence and Transition in the Fiction of Antonio Tabucchi:
   a Reading of *Il filo dell'orizzonte*   199
   Marina Spunta, Leicester University

16 Beyond Decadence: Huysmans, Wilde, Baudrillard and
   Postmodern Culture   209
   Nicholas Zurbrugg, De Montfort University

17 Translation: Decadence or Survival of the Original?   223
   Amir Ali Nojoumian, Leicester University

18 The Decadent University: Narratives of Decay and the
   Future of Higher Education   235
   Mark Rawlinson, Leicester University

19 The Lateness of the World, or How to Leave the Twentieth Century 246
   Martin L. Davies, Leicester University

Bibliography   257

Index   273

List of Illustrations

Niccolò Colantonio, *St Jerome and the Lion* (*c.* 1445), Naples: Plate 1
National Museum of Capodimonte

Niccolò Colantonio, *St Francis Distributing the Rule to the First*   Plate 2
and Second Orders (c. 1445), Naples: National Museum of Capodimonte

Acknowledgements

Many thanks to the contributors to this volume for their generosity and patience, especially those who provided essays on particular periods and subjects at my request. I would like to take this opportunity to thank John Parkinson for his crucial encouragement, as well as William Myers and Vincent Newey. Special thanks are also due to Martin Stannard and Greg Walker for their friendship and advice, also to my parents, Costa and Wendy, for their constant support, and, most of all, to Maire, Emma and Clare.

Introduction

This is the third volume in the series *Studies in European Cultural Transition*, the aim of which is to explore identifiable moments of transition in European culture in a fresh and stimulating manner. To begin the series 'decadence' has been chosen as the subject for discussion, as differences in the way in which that particular concept has been defined through time suggest very clearly the forces of cultural transition at work. Yet, along with change, similarities have also emerged, and the value of a collection of essays such as this, dealing with a subject across the periods, is that recurrent patterns relating to the formation of a concept such as decadence can be identified. In this volume it has been the political connotations of any definition of decadence that have proved particularly striking. The ways in which seemingly diverse examples of decadence, even those of an apparently apolitical kind, can be so easily politicized, reveals the extent to which defining anything as decadent is in itself a highly charged and arguably political act. I would like to illustrate the political issues surrounding the idea of decadence with two quite disparate historical examples, in order to suggest how the subject of decadence facilitates interdisciplinary debate across the periods. The first example is an obviously political idea of decadence taken from the twentieth century, the second an apparently apolitical and predominantly psychological definition of decadence made some sixteen centuries earlier.

On 19 July 1937 the National Socialist government of Germany made a dramatic public attempt to define authoritatively the nature of decadent art for the benefit of its citizens. By gathering together hundreds of works thought to be no longer acceptable from thirty-two German museums, an exhibition was assembled illustrating all that was corrupt in contemporary art in Nazi eyes. This exhibition was called *Entartete Kunst* ('Degenerate Art'), and was seen by over two million visitors as it toured Germany and Austria over a period of three years.[1] The word *entartet* had been in use for several years and was semantically implicated in the desire for racial as well as cultural purity that obsessed the exhibition's creators:

> *Entartet*, which has traditionally been translated as 'degenerate' or 'decadent,' is essentially a biological term, defining a plant or animal that has so changed that it no longer belongs to its species. By extension it refers to art that is unclassifiable or so far beyond the confines of what is accepted that it is in essence 'non-art'.[2]

---

[1]   Stephanie Barron, *'Degenerate Art': The Fate of the Avant-Garde in Nazi Germany* (Los Angeles and New York: published jointly by Los Angeles County Museum of Art and Harry N. Abrams, Inc., 1991), p. 9.

[2]   Ibid., p. 11.

The inclusion of works in the exhibition was intended to vilify both the artists themselves and those museum curators who had originally displayed them. It was effectively modern art prior to 1933 which was being censured. The exhibition included works by artists such as August Macke, Ernst Ludwig Kirchner, Emile Nolde, Karl Schmidt-Rottluff, Max Beckmann, George Grosz, and Otto Dix. The fact that only six of the one hundred and twelve artists included in *Entartete Kunst* were Jewish exemplifies that it was the art itself that determined which artists were censured, and that it was a cultural exercise in the classification of a 'species' of art, devised and conceptualized in a manner commensurate with the Third Reich's racist ideology.[3]

The aims of *Entartete Kunst* are given in the programme, written and designed to provide a highly prescriptive interpretation of the material for its visitors. *Entartete Kunst was* meant to signal (and confirm) a specific historical moment of cultural transition. So much is stated in the first of a number of declarations at the beginning of the programme subtitled 'What the "degenerate art" exhibition means to do':

> *It means* to give, at the outset of a new age for the German people, a firsthand [*sic*] survey of the gruesome last chapter of those decades of cultural decadence that preceded the great change.[4]

This 'cultural decadence' is attacked in the programme as an orchestrated act of political subversion. Consequently no allowance is made for the artist to represent reality as he sees it. The artist is, instead, a co-conspirator with other 'political agents' in creating what has *become*, socially as well as culturally:

> *It means* to show that this was no 'necessary ferment' but a deliberate and calculated onslaught upon the very essence and survival of art itself . . . *It means* to show too, how these symptoms of degeneracy spread from the deliberate troublemakers to infect those more or less unwitting acolytes who, in spite of *previous* – and in some cases also *subsequent* – evidence of artistic talent, were so lacking in *scruple, character,* or *common sense* as to join in the general Jewish and Bolshevik furore.[5]

The programme therefore politicizes both the art and the artists in its aim to 'expose the common roots of *political* anarchy and *cultural* anarchy'.[6] The decadent artist, no matter how unwittingly, has, in the view of the Reich, become part of the 'Jewish and Bolshevik' conspiracy, working towards 'anarchy in

---

    3   Ibid., p. 9.
    4   *Guide to the Exhibition Degenerate Art,* p. 2. Quoted from the facsimile of the Entartete Kunst programme reproduced in Barron, *Degenerate Art,* pp. 357–90, with a translation by David Britt.
    5   Ibid., p. 2.
    6   Ibid.

cultural politics'.[7] In order to encourage hostility towards the contents of the exhibition, the programme employs sexual metaphor to draw out the threatening latent energy of the artist and his work:

> Constrained reality is split up and broken open to become a vessel for his accumulated, burning sensual passion, which once inflamed is oblivious of all psychic depths and bursts out – consuming, expanding, copulating with all its parts. There exist for him no resistance and no preordained limits . . .[8]

These words are presented in the programme as an unattributed quotation from a text that originally supported the 'new art', so that the world-view of those who approved of it can be equated with a disruptive and disturbing sexual presence in the minds of people attending the exhibition. They, especially the women, must be protected from such 'abortions' (a much used word in the programme), their own physical and mental purity being covertly played upon as the issue that is really at stake. In this way the organizers are able to capitalize upon established fears and anxieties concerning racial purity. Having invoked the predatory sexual energy latent in the material however, the organizers must then protect those who attend the exhibition, since 'The sheer diversity of the manifestations of degeneracy, as the exhibition seeks to show them, is such as to stun and bewilder any visitor.'[9] This 'containment' is effected by the structure imposed upon the exhibition: 'a clear organizational principle has been adopted whereby the works in each room are classified by tendency and form into a number of groups'.[10] Then, after the experience of so much carefully policed decadence, there is the vision of the non-decadent, the ideal that has emerged despite the destructive effect of such art, and this is described at the end of the programme by the Führer himself.

> Today the new age is shaping a new human type. In countless areas of life huge efforts are being made to exalt the people: to make our men, boys, and youths, our girls and women healthier and thus stronger and more beautiful. And from this strength and this beauty there springs a new lease on life, a new joy in life. Never has mankind been closer to antiquity, in appearance or in feeling, than it is today. Steeled by sport, by competition, and by mock combat, millions of young bodies now appear to us in a form and a condition that have not been seen and have scarcely been imagined for perhaps a thousand years. A glorious and beautiful type of human being is emerging [. . .] This human type, as we saw him in last year's Olympic Games, stepping out before the whole world in all the radiant pride of his

---

7   Ibid., p. 4.
8   Ibid., p. 5.
9   Ibid., p. 6.
10 Ibid., p. 6.

bodily strength and health – this human type, you gentleman of the
prehistoric, spluttering art brigade, is the type of the new age.[11]

It is difficult to imagine a more politicized definition of decadence than that
attempted in the *Entartete Kunst* exhibition. It is also difficult to imagine a more
powerful warning of the dangers involved in defining anyone or anything as
decadent for overtly political reasons. The charge of decadence is now and has
always been a potent weapon in the hands of political *élites*. When that potency
is at the disposal of a totalitarian regime with the capacity to define its
implications definitively, the result is politically as well as culturally catastrophic.
The definition of what is or what is not decadent must thus be open to continuing
debate as a safeguard against its use to oppress or castigate dissenting voices. It
is hoped that this volume might help to stimulate and assist such debate.

The political implications of the above example are striking. I now want to
consider a much earlier definition of decadence by St Augustine that at first sight
seems to be as far removed from issues of a political kind as possible, and which
also introduces the interplay between theology and society that has informed
definitions of decadence in the West, which is studied further in some of the other
essays in this volume.

St Augustine (354–430), Bishop of Hippo, wrote his theological treatise the
City of God (413–26) during one of the most crucial periods of transition in the
history of Western culture. The Emperors had embraced Christianity, but many of
the Roman aristocracy and wealthy land owners had not, and remained deeply
opposed to the idea of abandoning the traditional forms of pagan worship. In the
context of such an opposition Augustine had to defend the Church against the
arguments of those who blamed the ailments and decay of the Roman state upon
the usurpation of the old religious practices by Christianity. Much of the *City of
God* is therefore concerned with demonstrating the absurdities of pagan practice,
as well as the limitations of the pagan writers such as Plato and Cicero. This
meant that Augustine was prepared to attack not only pagan ideology, but also the
social injustices that it served to maintain.

> In regard to justice, the city of God had an obvious bias to the poor.
> Augustine noticed that the most vocal defenders of the old social order
> were in general defenders of the social order in which the poor fawned on
> the rich, and the rich exploited their dependent clients [*City of God* 2.20].
> He realised how inadequate was private almsgiving and the Church chest
> with its register of paupers daily fed from the soup kitchen. The
> dimensions of destitution were too great to be met except by redistributive
> taxation [*City of God* 5.17].[12]

---

[11] Ibid., p. 6.
[12] Henry Chadwick, *Augustine* (Oxford: OUP, 1986), p. 100.

There is, therefore, an obviously political dimension to the *City of God*. However, the legacy of the text has generally been regarded not in terms of its politics, but in terms of its description of the decadence of the human subject as a result of the Fall, which has deeply influenced the course of Western theology, both Catholic and Protestant. It is this that I now want to consider.

In the *City of God* Augustine presents a teleological account of human history that contains his famous description of the decadent subject. According to Augustine, as a result of the expulsion of Satan and his angels from heaven, there was allotted a specified amount of time in which the human race could produce enough people (saints) to fill the spaces vacated by the fallen angels. Then, when this number has been reached, history will have fulfilled its purpose and be brought to a close. This idea, however, creates problems where human sexuality is concerned, because lust, which the early Church regarded as sinful, seems to be integral to the process.[13] How could sinful passions have existed in Eden before Adam and Eve had disobeyed God? Because of this problem other theologians, such as Ambrose, Jerome and John Chrysostom, maintained that there would have been no sexual intercourse in Eden, which only arose as a consequence of the Fall.[14] Augustine begins by addressing those who held this traditional view before developing his own idiosyncratic theory of what sex in Eden would have been like.

> If anyone says that there would have been no intercourse or procreation if the first human beings had not sinned, he is asserting, in effect, that man's sin was necessary to complete the number of the saints. For if they would have remained in solitude by refraining from sin, because, as some may imagine, they could not have bred if they had not sinned, it follows that sin was essential if there were to be a number of righteous people, instead of a single pair.[15]

In opposition to such an idea Augustine proposes an account of pre-lapsarian sexuality that is devoid of the experience of lust which is caused by sin.

> It follows that, if there had been no sin, marriage would have been worthy of the happiness of paradise, and would have given birth to children to be loved, and yet would not have given rise to any lust to be ashamed of; but, as it is, we have no example to show how this could have come about.[16]

---

[13]   Sexual desire is almost always treated negatively by the Church Fathers, despite the fact that St Paul regarded it as a sound reason for entering into marriage, within which the desire can be indulged and satisfied freely (1 Corinthians 7: 1–5).

[14]   See Peter Brown, *The Body And Society: Men, Women and Sexual Renunciation in Early Christianity* (London and Boston: Faber and Faber, 1989), p. 399.

[15]   St Augustine, *Concerning the City of God against the Pagans*, trans. Henry Bettenson (Harmondsworth: Penguin, 1984), Ch. 23, p. 585.

[16]   Ibid.

There is 'no example to show how this could have come about' but Augustine can rationally apprehend how this would have been since parts of the body, hands and feet for example, are still subject to the will. This leads Augustine to ask:

> Then why should we not believe that the sexual organs could have been the obedient servants of mankind, at the bidding of the will, in the same way as the other, if there had been no lust, which came as the retribution for the sin of disobedience?[17]

Augustine proposes a pre-lapsarian sexuality that is devoid of the passions that we naturally associate with reproduction, replacing them instead with purely rational motivations. Because of this he regards some contemporary accounts of the extraordinary control of the will over the body as vestiges of this pre-lapsarian control still remaining in certain individuals.

> We do in fact find among human beings some individuals with natural abilities very different from the rest of mankind and remarkable by their very rarity. Such people can do some things with their body which are for others utterly impossible and well-nigh incredible when they are reported. Some people can even move their ears, either one at a time or both together. Others without moving the head can bring the whole scalp – all the part covered with hair – down towards the forehead and bring it back again at will. Some can swallow an incredible number of various articles and then with a slight contraction of the diaphragm, can produce, as if out of a bag, any thing they please, in perfect condition. There are others who imitate the cries of birds and beasts and the voices of other men, reproducing them so accurately as to be quite indistinguishable from the originals, unless they are seen. A number of people produce at will such *musical sounds from their behind (without any stink) that they seem to be singing from that region* [. . .] We observe then that the body, even under the present conditions, is an obedient servant to some people in a remarkable fashion beyond the normal limitations of nature [. . .] If this is so, is there any reason why we should not believe that before the sin of disobedience and its punishment of corruptibility, the members of a man's body could have been the servants of man's will without any lust, for the procreation of children?[18]

This famous passage strikes the modern reader as bizarre, especially where the breaking of wind in a musical fashion is introduced in order to support a serious theological argument, since it seems at once to be both comical and inappropriate. But this is not apparent to Augustine because he has such a strong sense of the decadence of the human subject where the power of the will is concerned. There

---

[17] Ibid.
[18] Ibid., pp. 588–9.

would have been no aspect of the body that would not have been governed by the sovereign will. In order to maintain the idea of rationally motivated sexual intercourse in Eden he must account for the subsequent decay of the will and dominance of lust over reason, and the examples he gives are intended to provide evidence of a residual dominance of the will over certain bodily functions in certain individuals.

This passage seems to be far removed from the domain of politics and has generally been interpreted in the context of Augustine's own subjective experience as evidenced in his earlier writings, especially the *Confessions* (397–98). John O'Meara writes, for example, that the text is 'founded upon Augustine's own experience' and that 'it is an application of the theme of his own development and conversion, as described in the burning pages of the *Confessions*'.[19] The origins of Augustine's views are easy to trace in his own accounts of his struggle with lust which he describes in great psychological detail in the *Confessions*. Traditionally, scholars such as O'Meara have followed this path (which Augustine surely intended) by relating his theories in the *City of God* to his own subjective experience, thereby emphasizing the highly personal source of his arguments. Others, however, have chosen to draw out what they see as the political implications of Augustine's description of the decadence of the human subject. Elaine Pagels argues that what seems like an analysis born out of introspective reflection, is in fact a suitable vehicle for furthering a political agenda:

> His analysis of internal conflict, indeed, leads directly into his view of social conflict in general. The war within us drives us into war with one another – and no good pagan or Christian, remains exempt. So, he explains, while a good man is progressing to perfection, one part of him can be at war with another of his parts; hence, two good men can be at war with one another.[20]

Pagels claims that Augustine, unlike other theologians such as John Chrysostom, viewed the authority of the state as a necessity in a fallen world, and that Augustine 'acknowledges the emperor's rule however limited (or even brutal), to be nevertheless, as permanent and ineradicable – in this world, at least – as the effects of original sin'.[21] Thus she draws out the political implications of Augustine's account of the post-lapsarian decadent subject who, divided against himself, must be policed by the state.[22]

---

[19]   St Augustine, *City of God*, op. cit., introduction by John O'Mara, p.vii.
[20]   Elaine Pagels, *Adam, Eve, and the Serpent* (London: Penguin Books, 1988), p. 113.
[21]   Ibid., pp. 118–19.
[22]   Peter Brown provides an example of a more 'traditional' approach to Augustine, aware of the political issues but also of the importance of private experience in

It is unclear to what extent Pagels regards Augustine's thinking in the *City of God* as being politically motivated. Certainly she seems to place political issues at least on a par with theological ones when considering his authorial intentions. Her reading, though, is of interest here because she demonstrates the ease with which a description of decadence, no matter how apparently removed from the realm of politics, can be seen to have profound political implications. Describing anything, or anyone, as decadent, involves reference to an ideal from which the subject thus described declines, this in turn implies ways in which that subject might be thought of and treated in society. The decadent subject defined by Augustine must, according to Pagels, be policed in some way, hence she argues that Augustine provides the theoretical support for justifying the Church's relation to the state, and hence the powerful influence that his ideas have exerted upon Western theologians. Contentious as this reading of Augustine is, it demonstrates the ease with which descriptions of decadence can be politicized.

These two examples, then, one from the early Christian era and the other from more recent history, can be associated in discussion when the political significance of decadence is brought to the fore. It is in this way that the subject of decadence affords a unique opportunity, or window, upon European culture, revealing the ideas and values that determine what is, or is not, privileged and how these change. The political implications of decadence are therefore evident in a number of the essays in this volume. Michael Davies for example, examines a tract by Jonathan Swift, drawing out the political agenda that is latent in his argument concerning the decay of the English language. His approach thus reveals the way in which court libertines and religious non-conformists are both allied in the mind of Swift as a combined threat, an unlikely combination and one that has hitherto been little commented upon. Andrew St John locates the poetry of Rudyard Kipling in the domestic political debate concerning the problems posed by social decay in British cities for the effective running of the empire. This reveals Kipling's sympathy with the working classes of England and the colonies, in contrast to the radical policies current at that time and advocated by parties right across the domestic political spectrum. Mark Rawlinson's essay deals with a more contemporary debate and considers the idea of the 'decadent university' as a politically contentious issue of great importance to the future of academia. My essay presents a reading of Chaucer's *Parliament of Fowls* in which political references are identified in the poem and related to the Good Parliament of 1376, where the sexual conduct of Edward III became the subject of both debate and censure.

Augustine's work. Henry Chadwick, *Augustine* (Oxford: OUP, 1986) also cautions against politicizing Augustine's views: 'The *City of God* is treated incorrectly if it is regarded as a statement about political theory [. . .] Augustine offers much more hope to the individual than to the institutions of human society, peculiarly liable to be vehicles of group egotism', p. 106.

The importance of early Christian culture in shaping ideas of decadence is evidenced by two further appearances of Augustine in this volume, in the essays by David Salter and Martin Davies. Salter examines the idea of the decadent city presented in the *City of God*, how influential this was in medieval Europe, and how it came to be altered by the Franciscan mission to redeem the cities. This transformation is examined with reference to two paintings produced in the fifteenth century by Colantonio. Martin Davies's essay reminds us once again of the psychological significance of Augustine's thought, as he considers the very human perception of the present as somehow always less than that which proceeds it. Augustine's famous remark that it is 'in the mind' that time is measured is used to further define Davies's concept of 'lateness'. In Amir Nojoumian's essay, Derrida's views on translation are considered as post-structuralist secularized versions of Walter Benjamin's metaphysically inclined theories, which involved a particular understanding of the Book of Genesis. The importance of the accounts of the Fall and the Tower of Babel for both writers again demonstrates the influence of theological ideas upon concepts of decadence. Tristram Hooley's essay further underlines this influence by looking at the biblical idea of 'Apocalypse' and how this was used in the work of various British novelists in order to engage with the events of the Second World War through what Hooley refers to as 'Apocalypse fiction'.

The European dimension of this volume is supported by Susan Bassnett, Marina Spunta, Julie Dashwood and Andrew Hammond. Bassnett introduces us to the truly decadent world of the Italian writer Gabriele D'Annunzio, offering some useful insights into his disturbing fictions. Marina Spunta explores the work of the contemporary Italian writer Antonio Tabucchi, analysing his very urban descriptions of decay and the description of an isolated individual perspective in his novel *Il filo dell'orizzonte* (*Vanishing Point*). Julie Dashwood's essay considers the use of macabre fairy-tale motifs in the nineteenth-century drama of both Gabriele D'Annunzio and Pierre Quillard. Andrew Hammond's essay considers descriptions of the Balkans by British travel writers in the first half of this century, who held up the Arcadian ideal they found there as a contrast to the decadent reality of their native modern Europe.

Although I have deliberately sought to extend the range of this volume beyond the confines of a traditional treatment of nineteenth-century aesthetic decadence, a number of essays nevertheless touch upon this area in new and stimulating ways. Vincent Newey provides an engaging analysis of Dickensian decadents through incisive close readings of Dickens's work, and suggests ways in which certain characters point towards a fascinating anticipation of the condition of *fin-de-siècle* decadence. Julian North reconsiders the origins of the *fin-de-siècle* concept with special reference to French writers and English criticism from the Romantic to mid-Victorian period. Nicholas Daly examines the parallels between Oscar Wilde's *The Picture of Dorian Gray* and John Meade

Falkner's *The Lost Stradivarius*, in order to engage with the sexual politics of the 'decadent novel'. Some of the issues touched upon by Daly can also be traced in Martin Halliwell's treatment of Thomas Mann's reading of André Gide, though quite different conclusions are reached. Halliwell examines specific works by Gide and Mann in order to contest the idea that aesthetic harmony can be established as a response to moral disorder.

Science and technology also raise important issues where the idea of decadence is concerned in the twentieth century. Daniel Cordle shows how, in the work of I. A. Richards, the threat to society and culture that was in part seen to be the result of the power of science, paradoxically informed Richards' formulation of an 'objective' criticism, designed to bolster the declining influence of high culture through the reading of literature. Finally, Nicholas Zurbrugg identifies the parallels between modern and postmodern decadent mentalities, in order to consider 'technological cultural mutations', which include the perceived decadence of an ever proliferating media culture.

The essays that follow are arranged chronologically according to their subject. This does not of course mean that they must be read in sequence – each essay is self-contained and designed to be read as it stands. And, although contributors have responded to one another's arguments in certain places, it is the reader's prerogative, and, I hope, reward, to make the kind of observations seen above concerning decadence, and to use the concept as a means of appreciating significant changes, and correspondences, in the development (or perhaps even decadence) of European thought. Above all I hope that these essays will provide a starting point, and stimulate further original debate concerning an idea that is arguably central to Western thought.

Chapter 1

Redeeming the Decadent City: Changing Responses to the Urban and Wilderness Environments in the *Lives* of St Jerome*

David Salter

Introduction: decadence and the city

From ancient times, decadence has been seen as a characteristically urban vice. Evidence of the antiquity of the association between decadence and city life can be found in the Book of Genesis, which tells how the first city was established by Cain, the first murderer, on whose forehead – as a sign of his irreparably corrupt and fallen nature – God is said to have placed a mark of shame (Genesis 4: 15–17). Writing at the beginning of the fifth century of the Common Era, and following a tradition of both Jewish and Christian legend which regarded Cain as the founder of a race of degenerate evildoers, St Augustine drew upon the strongly antagonistic view of urban civilization evident in the Book of Genesis when he identified Cain's city with the 'City of Man', an allegorical place whose inhabitants consisted of those men and women whom God had condemned to suffer eternal damnation.[1] However, although Augustine's writings betray a deep distrust of the wickedness and depravity of urban life – for instance, he wryly noted that Rome, like the city of Cain, was founded by a fratricide (*City of God*,

*   I am grateful to Professor Greg Walker and Dr Elaine Treharne of Leicester University for their helpful comments after reading an earlier draft of this essay.

[1]   See St Augustine, *Concerning the City of God against the Pagans*, trans. Henry Bettenson (Harmondsworth: Penguin, 1984), Book XV, Ch. 5, pp. 600–601. A useful introduction to the apocryphal legends of Cain can be found in O.F. Emerson's 'Legends of Cain, Especially in Old and Middle English', *Publications of the Modern Language Association of America*, XXI (1906), pp. 831–929, and John Block Friedman's, *The Monstrous Races in Medieval Art and Thought* (Cambridge, Massachusetts: Harvard University Press, 1981), pp. 94–107.

Book XV, Chapter 5) – his attitude towards cities was nonetheless ambivalent, for not only did he choose to represent Hell and damnation in terms of urban civilization, but he also conceived of the Heavenly kingdom as a city:

> I classify the human race into two branches: the one consists of those who live by human standards, the other of those who live according to God's will. I also call these two classes the two cities, speaking allegorically. By two cities I mean two societies of human beings, one of which is predestined to reign with God for all eternity, the other doomed to undergo eternal punishment with the Devil.[2]

The idea of the City of God – like that of the City of Man – has its origins in the Bible, not least in the new Jerusalem of the Book of Revelation, while Augustine himself indicated that its direct source was Psalm 87: 'Glorious things are spoken of thee, O city of God' (Psalm 87: 3). But Augustine's belief that Heaven could best be understood as a city no doubt also reflects the very great extent to which his cultural and intellectual outlook was moulded by the civic values of classical Greece and Rome. The city stood at the very centre of classical civilization. According to Aristotle: 'man is by nature a political animal', that is, one who participates fully in the life of the city (*polis*).[3] Thus, it is possible to discern both in the work of Augustine, and in the wider cultural milieu from which he drew, two contradictory attitudes towards city life. On the one hand, Augustine saw the city as the arena within which human civilization was best able to flourish, the place where all that was most noble in human nature could be realized, while on the other hand he was profoundly suspicious of the worldliness and hedonism that were so much a part of urban existence.

Of course, each of these two views of the city carries with it a corresponding set of beliefs and assumptions about that which is not the city: the countryside or wilderness. To those who look favourably upon the city, the country can be seen as a rustic backwater that knows nothing of the great cultural achievements of human civilization such as philosophy and art. Alternatively, the country can be viewed as a pastoral idyll that has remained relatively untouched by the decadence and corruption of the city – a place that has thus managed to preserve something of the primal innocence of humanity.[4] In this essay, I shall explore these different responses to the country and the city by examining how urban existence was represented in the *Life* and work of Augustine's great contemporary, St Jerome, both in his writings and in the legendary stories that

---

[2]   See Augustine, *City of God*, Book XV, Ch. 1, p. 595.
[3]   See Aristotle, *The Politics*, trans. T.A. Sinclair and Trevor J. Saunders (Harmondsworth: Penguin, 1981), Book 1, Ch. II, p. 59.
[4]   Raymond Williams has investigated the different ways in which these ideas have been treated in English literature, particularly by authors of the eighteenth, nineteenth and twentieth centuries, in his study: *The Country and the City* (London: Chatto and Windus, 1973).

subsequently came to be told about him. As a point of entry into this material, I shall concentrate upon the painting of *St Jerome and the Lion* that was undertaken in the middle of the fifteenth century by the Neapolitan artist Niccolò Colantonio (Plate 1). By comparing its treatment of the themes of the city and the wilderness with Jerome's professed views on these subjects, it will be possible to reflect upon the ways in which attitudes towards the urban and wilderness environments altered over the course of the Middle Ages.[5]

St Jerome: life and legend

Jerome was born during the middle of the fourth century at Stridon in Dalmatia (the exact date of his birth is unknown, but modern scholars estimate that it was some time between 331 and 347), and his greatest contribution to history, and the achievement for which he was most revered during the ensuing Christian centuries, was his production of a Latin translation of the Bible (which became known as the *editio vulgata*, the Vulgate or popular edition), a text that for almost a thousand years, and throughout the Latin-speaking West, was regarded as the standard version of the Scriptures.[6] However, in addition to his skills as a linguist, scholar, and translator, Jerome was also famed for his advocacy of the monastic life (a life that he himself practised, first in solitude in the Syrian desert, and then as the leader of a community of monks at Bethlehem in Palestine), and it is while

---

5   Very little is known about Colantonio. His artistic education is thought to have taken place under the patronage of René D'Anjou, who reigned in Naples from 1438 to 1442, while his last work was commissioned in 1460 by Queen Isabella Chiaromonte, the wife of King Ferdinand I of Naples. The painting of *St Jerome and the Lion* (which formed the lower section of an altarpiece, the upper panel of which was a depiction of *St Francis Distributing the Rule to the First and Second Franciscan Orders*), was completed near the beginning of Colantonio's career, and although it is not known who commissioned the work, there is documentary evidence to indicate that it was originally housed in a chapel dedicated to St Jerome in the Franciscan church of San Lorenzo, Naples. For a discussion of Colantonio's life and work, see Giovanna Cassese, 'Niccolò Colantonio', in ed. Jane Turner, *The Dictionary of Art*, vol. 7 (London: Macmillan, 1996), pp. 542–4. See also Penny Howell Jolly, 'Jan Van Eyck and St Jerome: A Study of Eyckian Influence on Colantonio and Antonello da Messina in Quattrocento Naples' (University of Pennsylvania, PhD thesis, 1976), pp. 80–151.

6   For an excellent modern biography of Jerome, see J.N.D. Kelly, *Jerome: His Life, Writings, and Controversies* (London: Duckworth, 1975). Useful essays on Jerome, his biblical scholarship, and the medieval history of his translation of the Bible can be found in the first two volumes of the *Cambridge History of the Bible*. See H.F.D. Sparks, 'Jerome as Biblical Scholar' in P. R. Ackroyd and C. F. Evans, eds, *The Cambridge History of the Bible*, vol. 1 (Cambridge: Cambridge University Press, 1970), pp. 510–41: E.F. Sutcliffe, 'Jerome' in ed. G.W.H. Lampe, *The Cambridge History of the Bible*, vol. 2 (Cambridge: CUP, 1969), pp. 80–101; and Raphael Loewe, 'The Medieval History of the Latin Vulgate' in ed. Lampe, *The Cambridge History of the Bible*, vol. 2, pp. 102–54.

1 Niccolò Colantonio, *St Jerome and the Lion* (c. 1445), Naples: National Museum of Capodimonte

he was residing in Bethlehem during the second phase of his monastic career that his miraculous encounter with the lion is supposed to have taken place.[7]

Jerome's extensive writings, and in particular the many letters that he wrote to his friends (and enemies), are full of personal information about his life and work, and these scattered autobiographical references – along with testimonials to his character from such eminent figures as St Augustine, Sulpicius Severus, Gregory the Great, and Isidore of Seville – were the sources from which two ninth-century Latin *Lives* of the saint were compiled. These *Lives*, written independently of one another by anonymous authors, are known as *Hieronymus noster* and *Plerosque nimirum*, and were in turn used as sources for all of the subsequent medieval biographies of Jerome.[8] However, as well as recording the known facts of Jerome's life, the author of *Plerosque nimirum* also included in his narrative the legendary story of the saint's encounter with the lion, a tale that had previously been told in relation to a near-contemporary of Jerome – the Palestinian abbot St Gerasimus – by John Moschus in his seventh-century collection of the lives of the desert fathers, the *Pratum Spirituale*.[9]

Colantonio's *St Jerome and the Lion*

According to the author of *Plerosque nimirum*, the encounter between Jerome and the lion took place one evening while the saint was listening to the sacred lessons with his fellow monks in the monastery that he had established at Bethlehem. A lion suddenly came limping into the building, whereupon everyone fled except for Jerome, who confidently approached the animal as though he were welcoming an honoured guest. The lion showed Jerome his paw, and seeing that the creature was badly injured the saint summoned his brothers and instructed them to wash and bind the wound with care. As the monks were performing this task they observed that the lion's paw had been scratched and torn by thorns, but they washed and dressed the wound so carefully that they were able to restore the

---

7   For an account of Jerome's monasticism, see Kelly, *Jerome: His Life, Writings, and Controversies*, pp. 46–55 and 129–40.

8   See *Hieronymus noster*, in *Patrologia Latina Cursus Completus*, 22: 175–84, ed. Jacques Paul Migne (hereafter referred to as *PL*), and *Plerosque nimirum*, in *PL* 22: 201–14. For a discussion of the sources of these two works, and their influence on the subsequent biographies of St Jerome, see Eugene F. Rice, *Saint Jerome in the Renaissance* (Baltimore: John Hopkins University Press, 1985), pp. 23–48.

9   For the story of St Jerome and the lion, see *Plerosque nimirum*, 209 ff. See also Joannes Moschus, *Vita Abbatis Gerasimi, in Pratum Spirituale*, in *PL* 74: 172–4. Eugene Rice (*Saint Jerome in the Renaissance*, pp. 44–5), has suggested that in all probability the story of Gerasimus's lion became attached to the figure of Jerome some time during the seventh century, after the military invasions of the Arabs had forced many Greek monks who were living in the deserts of the Middle East to seek refuge in Rome.

animal to full health. From then onwards the lion lost all traces of his former wildness, and lived tamely alongside the monks, helping them with their labours.

The story of Jerome and the lion was widely disseminated in the late Middle Ages thanks to its inclusion in two of the most popular and influential books of the thirteenth century; Vincent of Beauvais's *Speculum Historiale*, an account – completed in 1244 – of the history of humanity from the Fall to Vincent's own lifetime, and the *Legenda Aurea*, a collection of saints lives written by Jacobus of Voragine, the Archbishop of Genoa, which dates from about 1260.[10] However, the popularity of the story was not simply confined to the medium of literature; it is also reflected in the field of the visual arts. According to the art historian Grete Ring, Jerome was perhaps 'the most frequently represented saint in art from the fourteenth to the sixteenth century, with the exception of the members of the Holy Family and St John'.[11] Although a number of different episodes from the legend of St Jerome not involving the lion formed the subject of some of these fourteenth-, fifteenth- and sixteenth-century representations, the saint was most commonly shown dressed as a cardinal and seated on a chair in his study (or on a rock in the wilderness), either removing the thorn from the lion's paw, or reading a book with the animal lying quietly at his feet.[12]

The eminent Italian canonist Joannes Andreae, who taught law at the University of Bologna from 1301 until his death in 1348, and who commissioned a number of paintings of Jerome, is usually credited with introducing the motif of

---

[10]   See Vincent of Beauvais, 'De Vita et Actibus Sancti Hieronymi Presbiteri', in *Bibliotheca Mundi. Vincentii Bellovacensis Speculum Quadruplex: Naturale, Doctrinale, Morale, Historiale*, ed. Benedictini Collegii Vedastini, 4 vols. (Douai, 1624), vol. IV, Liber XVI, Cap. XVIII, p. 623, and Jacobus of Voragine, *The Golden Legend of Jacobus de Voragine*, trans. Granger Ryan and Helmut Ripperger (New York: Arno Press, 1969), pp. 587–92. The popularity of the two books is reflected in the large number of manuscripts that has survived from the period. Gregory G. Guzman has compiled a list of 200 manuscripts of the *Speculum Historiale*, while according to Eugene Rice, there are over 500 extant manuscripts of the *Legenda Aurea*. See Gregory G. Guzman, 'A Growing Tabulation of Vincent of Beauvais' Speculum Historiale Manuscripts', *Scriptorium: International Review of Manuscript Studies* 29 (1975), 122–5, and Rice, *St Jerome in the Renaissance*, p. 23.

[11]   Grete Ring, 'St Jerome Removing the Thorn from the Lion's Paw', *Art Bulletin* 27 (1945), p. 190.

[12]   The art historian Herbert Friedman has observed that: 'The lion occurs in the great majority (more than three-quarters) of all paintings, graphics, and sculptures representing Saint Jerome in the wilderness. . . . It also occurs in more than half of all renditions of the saint in his study chamber. The beast is to be found in many, if not the majority, of representations of Jerome's last communion and of his death, as well as in more than half of other compositions in which Jerome is shown, either by himself as a formal, hieratic figure of a great Church Father, or as one of the attendant, lateral figures in conventional altarpieces, especially in those created after the first years of the fifteenth century.' See Herbert Friedmann, *A Bestiary for Saint Jerome: Animal Symbolism in European Religious Art* (Washington DC: Smithsonian Institution, 1980), p. 229.

the lion into the visual arts, and combining it with images of the saint as a scholar and theologian.[13] In his book *Hieronymianus* or *De Laudibus Sancti Hieronymi*, Joannes wrote:

> I have also established the way he should be painted, namely, sitting in a chair, beside him the hat that cardinals wear nowadays (that is, the red hat or *galerus ruber*) and at his feet the tame lion; and I have caused many pictures of this sort to be set up in divers places.[14]

The painting of *St Jerome and the Lion* by Colantonio perfectly accords with Joannes's prescriptions, and is one of the best-known, and most interesting, artistic treatments of the subject. The painting is dominated by the figures of Jerome and the lion, both of whom are situated in the centre of the composition, and Colantonio successfully managed to convey not only a sense of the benevolence of the saint and the pathos of the injured animal, but also a strong feeling of trust and companionship between the two. However, the picture is also remarkable for the extraordinary detail with which it represents the interior of Jerome's cell.[15] The shelves are strewn with books, pens and papers, along with all of the other equipment that one would expect to find in a scholar's study, while the book that is lying open on Jerome's desk, and the general atmosphere of disorderly clutter, gives the impression that the saint had been busy at work when the lion entered his room, seeking his help. Jerome himself is seated on an ornately carved chair. He is dressed in a brown habit and cloak, and is wearing a tightly fitting grey hat, while his tasselled, red cardinal's hat, the *galerus ruber*, is prominently displayed to the left of the lion, on a table in front of his desk. Finally, in the bottom right-hand corner of the painting, behind Jerome's chair, a mouse can be seen eating a scrap of paper.

Amidst all the finely observed detail of Jerome's study, the lion remains a somewhat incongruous, almost enigmatic figure. In spite of the animal's large size and enormously powerful frame, he is stripped of the conventional leonine attributes of wildness and courage, and is pictured instead with a slightly mournful and subdued expression, looking rather ill at ease in the domestic setting of Jerome's book-lined chamber. The lion's former wildness stands in stark contrast to his present domesticity, and the encroachment of the animal into the indoor, human space of Jerome's study seems to blur the traditional opposition between the concepts of 'nature' and 'culture', 'wilderness' and

---

[13] For a discussion of Joannes's role in establishing the iconography of Jerome, see Rice, *Saint Jerome in the Renaissance*, pp. 64–8, and Ring, 'St Jerome Removing the Thorn from the Lion's Paw', p. 190.

[14] Quoted in Rice, *Saint Jerome in the Renaissance*, p. 65.

[15] Penny Howell Jolly ('Jan Van Eyck and St Jerome', p. 103), has suggested that Colantonio's painting 'is the first Italian representation of St Jerome in his study to make the setting of such great importance'.

'civilization', and 'wild' and 'tame'. Moreover, Jerome's evident sympathy for the predicament of the lion, and the proximity and intimacy of the two, threatens to dissolve still further the conventional boundaries separating the human and animal worlds.

It is significant that in contrast to the literary version of the story found in *Plerosque nimirum*, Colantonio chose to locate the action not in one of the monastery's public, communal areas, but in the private space of Jerome's study, a setting that enabled him to depict an impressive array of books and papers in the background of the painting. Furthermore, rather than following *Plerosque nimirum* and portraying a scene in which Jerome at first examined the lion's wound, and then delegated the task of washing and dressing it to his monks, Colantonio showed the saint actually removing the thorn from the animal's paw. (According to *Plerosque nimirum*, the lion did not have a thorn stuck in his paw, but merely a wound that he had received when his paw had been pierced with thorns.) The effect of these two changes was to simplify the narrative while simultaneously amplifying the role that Jerome played in it. By removing the other monks from the scene, and so making Jerome solely responsible for healing the lion, Colantonio eliminated all the superfluous elements of the story that could divert attention from the saint, and reduce not just the dramatic impact of the miracle that he performed, but also the strength of the bond connecting him to the lion. With great narrative economy, then, Colantonio was able in the one painting to convey two quite distinct images or impressions of Jerome. On the one hand, he depicted a popular animal story in which a genuine sense of intimacy and companionship between the human and animal protagonists was conveyed, while at the same time he projected an image of the saint as a great scholar and theologian – reminding his audience of Jerome's reputation for erudition through the expedient of locating the action in his study.

Of course, in addition to these two aspects of Jerome's life and character, Colantonio – following the artistic convention established by Joannes Andreae – also represented the saint as a cardinal, displaying his red cardinal's hat on the table situated in front of his desk. In the same way that the books and papers lining the shelves of Jerome's study lend intellectual weight to the portrait, so the presence of the *galerus ruber* invests the figure of the saint with considerable ecclesiastical authority, denoting as it does the important position that he was thought to have occupied in the governing hierarchy of the Church. However, it is important to note that the institution of the college of cardinals was not actually established until the eleventh century, over six hundred years after Jerome's death, and it was not until the Council of Lyons in 1245 that Pope Innocent IV declared that the red hat should be worn by holders of the office.[16]

---

[16]   For a discussion of the origins of the Cardinalate, see Rice, *Saint Jerome in the Renaissance*, p. 37, and I.S. Robinson, *The Papacy 1073–1198: Continuity and Innovation* (Cambridge: CUP, 1990), pp. 33–120.

The anachronism of granting Jerome the title of cardinal reflects the way in which the writers and artists of the late Middle Ages tended both to visualize and understand historical figures in terms of the customs, fashions and institutions of their own time. Interestingly, Colantonio's painting contains a number of such historical anomalies. For instance, the magnifying glass that is hanging from the shelf above Jerome's desk is clearly a late-medieval detail, as such devices did not come into use until the end of the thirteenth century,[17] while the folded document situated on the bench immediately above the mouse has a papal bull attached to it, which can be identified as late-medieval in origin from the heads of saints Peter and Paul that are visible on its seal.[18] But, even more important than the anachronistic presence of these physical objects (at least from the point of view of the present discussion), is the fact that Jerome's relationship with the lion is also represented in an anachronistic manner. An examination of this aspect of the painting will highlight discrepancies between the attitudes towards city life that were held by Jerome and his monastic contemporaries, and the view that prevailed a thousand years later during Colantonio's lifetime.

Jerome's *Lives* of Paul and Malchus

Alison Goddard Elliott has observed that miraculous encounters with wild beasts are one of the characteristic features of the *Lives* of the early Christian anchorites, and that lions appear much more frequently in these stories than any other animal.[19] Significantly, Jerome himself was the author of three biographies of desert saints, two of whom – Paul the hermit and Malchus the monk – had dramatic encounters with lions in the wilderness. Thus, it is possible to compare Colantonio's late-medieval treatment of the story of Jerome and the lion with two narratives, both involving saints and lions, that were actually written by Jerome himself.[20]

---

[17]   As has been noted by George Sarton in his discussion of the technological developments that occurred in the field of optics during the late Middle Ages. See George Sarton, *Introduction to the History of Science*, vol. II (Baltimore: Williams & Wilkins, 1931), p. 24.

[18]   According to Penny Howell Jolly ('Jan Van Eyck and St Jerome', p. 102), 'the heads of Sts Peter and Paul . . . [were] a commonly used form for the reverse of papal seals in the 14th and 15th centuries'.

[19]   See Alison Goddard Elliott, *Roads to Paradise: Reading the Lives of the Early Saints* (Hanover: Brown University Press, 1987), pp. 144–67.

[20]   See *St Jerome, Life of St Paul the First Hermit*, trans. Sister Marie Liguori Ewald, in ed. Roy J. Deferrari, *Early Christian Biographies, The Fathers of the Church*, vol. 15 (Washington DC: The Fathers of the Church, 1952), pp. 217–38, and *St Jerome, Life of Malchus*, trans. Sister Marie Liguori Ewald, in ed. Deferrari, *Early Christian Biographies*, pp. 281–97.

It is thought that Jerome wrote his *Life of St Paul the First Hermit* some time around 376, while he was living the life of a solitary hermit in the Syrian desert.[21] According to Jerome, contrary to received opinion – which regarded St Anthony as the instigator of the monastic movement – Anthony had merely followed the example of his master, Paul of Thebes, who was in fact the first Christian monk to withdraw into the desert.[22] At the very end of his narrative, Jerome described how – after enduring the privations of the wilderness for almost a century – Paul finally died, leaving his body to be discovered by Anthony, who grieved that he did not have any tools with which to dig a grave. However, two lions suddenly appeared from out of the desert, prostrated themselves before the dead body, wagging their tails and roaring loudly with grief. After communicating their feelings of sorrow in this way, they began to dig a hole in the ground not far from Paul's corpse, and when they had made a space large enough to contain the body, they respectfully approached Anthony, who sent them away with a blessing.[23]

The holy monk, Malchus, the subject of Jerome's second sacred biography, also had a miraculous encounter with a lion in the wilderness. After living in a monastery in the desert for a number of years, Malchus returned home to visit his widowed mother for one last time. On his way he was captured by Ishmaelites and sold into slavery. He eventually managed to escape with a fellow Christian slave, but they were pursued across the desert by their former master, who was accompanied by a servant. Malchus and his Christian companion finally took refuge in a cave, convinced that they were about to be murdered, yet they were miraculously rescued from this fate by a lioness who attacked and killed their assailants, but left them completely unharmed.[24]

As Alison Goddard Elliott has observed, the lions that feature in the *Lives* of the desert saints typically perform a similar function to the 'helpful beasts' of folklore, in that they willingly override or renounce their naturally bestial inclinations in order to grant their assistance to those holy figures whose innocence and sanctity they instinctively recognize.[25] But, as well as using this common folkloric motif as a way of highlighting the holiness of Paul and Malchus, the two stories also share a similar location – a cave in the desert, beyond the boundaries of the civilized, human world. This wilderness setting, far from being incidental to the two narratives, actually reflects the theological concerns and convictions of the desert fathers themselves, for both Paul and

---

[21]   See the comments of Sister Marie Liguori Ewald (p. 221), in her introduction to Jerome's *Life of Paul the First Hermit*. However, J.N.D. Kelly dates the work slightly later, arguing that it was written by Jerome in Antioch, after he had returned from his first sojourn in the wilderness. See Kelly, *Jerome: His Life, Writings, and Controversies*, pp. 60–61.

[22]   See Jerome, *Life of St Paul the First Hermit*, 1, p. 225.

[23]   See Jerome, *Life of St Paul the First Hermit*, 16, p. 236.

[24]   See Jerome, *Life of Malchus*, 9, pp. 296–7.

[25]   See Elliott, *Roads to Paradise*, p. 159.

Malchus chose to forsake the world and lead a solitary existence in the wilderness because they believed that the civic, humanistic values of late-classical society were incompatible with the ascetic ideals proclaimed by Christ in the Gospels.

The inherent sinfulness of human society, and the redemptive, purifying power of the wilderness, is a theme that is given particular prominence in the *Life of Malchus*. According to Jerome, Malchus first went into the desert in order to escape the malign influence of his relatives, who – ignoring his vow of chastity – were trying to force him to marry. Then, having lived as a monk in the wilderness for many years, Malchus decided to visit his widowed mother one last time before she died, only to be told by his abbot that this seemingly innocuous wish was in fact a temptation from the Devil, and that in succumbing to it he would be placing his soul in great jeopardy. The abbot's forebodings proved to be well founded, for Malchus was captured by Ishmaelites on his journey home, and sold by them into slavery. In this captive state his virginity was again imperilled, this time by his new master, who tried to force him to marry a fellow slave, and it was in order to escape this threat to his sexual purity that he once again sought refuge in the desert. For Malchus, then, the harshness of the desert climate, and its general physical inhospitality, made it a place of spiritual safety, a religious haven where on two separate occasions he sought sanctuary from the moral corruption of human society.

Jerome's attitude towards the wilderness was identical to the view that he attributed to Malchus. In a famous letter that he wrote in 384 to Eustochium, the daughter of his friend Paula, he reflected upon his own experiences of the austerities of the desert – with its potential for spiritual salvation – and compared it to the morally corrupt and decadent nature of life in the city:

> Oh, how often, when I was living in the desert, in that lonely waste, scorched by the burning sun, which affords to hermits a savage dwelling place, how often did I fancy myself surrounded by the pleasures of Rome. ... Filled with stiff anger against myself, I would make my way alone into the desert; and when I came upon some hollow valley or rough mountain or precipitous cliff, there I would set up my oratory, and make that spot a place of torture for my unhappy flesh. There sometimes also – the Lord Himself is my witness – after many a tear and straining of my eyes to heaven, I felt myself in the presence of the angelic hosts, and in joy and gladness would sing: 'Because of the savour of thy good ointments we shall run after thee [Song of Solomon 1: 3]'.[26]

Like Malchus, Jerome would seem to have regarded human society in general, and urban existence in particular, as beset with moral dangers; dangers that could best be countered by withdrawing from civic life and retreating into the

---

[26] St Jerome, 'Letter XXII: To Eustochium', in *Select Letters of St Jerome*, ed. and trans. F.A. Wright (London: Heinemann, 1933), pp. 67–9.

desert. Of course, as Eugene Rice has noted, such a complete and absolute rejection of the values and institutions of human society represented a profound political and philosophical break with the traditions of classical antiquity:

> His abandonment of the earthly city for a *civitas nova*, the citizens of which meditate night and day on Scripture and God's law, was . . . explicit. The wilderness and solitude, he thought, are lovelier than any city. Indeed, he believed the civitas incompatible with Christianity: *'quicumque in civitate sunt, Christiani non sunt'* [those who are in the city are not Christians]. From the remotest antiquity, urban living had distinguished the civilized from everything savage, rustic, and barbarous. Jerome's reversal of traditional values could hardly have been sharper.[27]

For Rice, then, the extreme asceticism of Jerome and the desert fathers developed in part as a reaction to the civic values of classical society. Their rejection of pagan religion led to their abandonment of pagan society's social and philosophical underpinnings, which in turn resulted in their withdrawal from urban life. Alison Goddard Elliott has argued that because the lion was regarded in late antiquity as a symbol 'of everything that does not obey man, of savage, non-socialized nature, thicket, and desert',[28] it came to be seen as the antithesis of the civilized, worldly values that Jerome, Paul and Malchus had so emphatically rejected. More than any other creature, then, the lion was thought of as the archetypal representative of the natural, non-human world, and it is perhaps for this reason that the animal was viewed as the ally, as well as the emblem, of the early Christian hermits.

Although Paul and Malchus's lions symbolize the willingness of the two saints to renounce human society and accept the rigours of the desert, the lion that features in Colantonio's painting carries a very different meaning. Whereas both Paul and Malchus encountered their respective lions in a cave in the wilderness – the animal's natural habitat – the story of Jerome and the lion is, as we have seen, located within the walls of the monastery itself, with Colantonio setting the scene in the highly rarefied atmosphere of the saint's book-lined cell. Rather than abandoning human civilization and embracing the natural world in the manner of Paul and Malchus, Colantonio depicted Jerome accommodating the lion, and, by implication, the world of nature, within his private study. Significantly, there is nothing in Colantonio's painting to suggest a desert location. On the contrary, even though the historical Jerome shared the same hostile and distrustful view of the city that he attributed to Paul and Malchus, Colantonio chose to portray the saint surrounded by the kind of cultural artefacts that one would normally associate with a highly sophisticated, urban civilization.

---

[27] Rice, *St Jerome in the Renaissance*, pp. 8–9.
[28] See Elliott, *Roads to Paradise*, pp. 166–7.

It would thus appear that in the thousand years that separate Jerome's *Lives of Paul and Malchus* from Colantonio's painting of *St Jerome and the Lion*, there occurred a fundamental change in the way in which Jerome was thought to have manifested his holiness in relation to the natural world. By the end of the Middle Ages, civic life was no longer associated with classical, pagan civilization, and the urban existence from which the desert fathers had so desperately tried to escape ceased to have exclusively threatening and sinful connotations. While power over wild animals continued to be interpreted as a sign of sanctity, it had become possible for the artists of the late-medieval period to portray miraculous encounters between beasts and saints in an urban, as well as a wilderness setting. Therefore, what for the desert fathers had been a symbol of their rejection of the sinful, urban culture of classical antiquity, had become for Colantonio an emblem of the redemptive capacity of the new, urbanized Christianity of early Renaissance Italy – a faith characterized most pointedly by the Franciscan Order, with its mission to preach to and redeem the towns.

Conclusion: Colantonio, St Francis, and the redemption of the cities

Colantonio's painting of *St Jerome and the Lion* has a strong Franciscan connection. As mentioned above, although the circumstances of the picture's composition are obscure, it is known that the altarpiece of which it originally formed a part was initially housed in the Franciscan church of San Lorenzo, Naples, and this Franciscan association is further suggested by the subject of the altarpiece's upper panel: *St Francis Distributing the Rule to the First and Second Franciscan Orders* (Plate 2).

The emergence of the Franciscan Order in the early years of the thirteenth century under the leadership of its charismatic founder, St Francis of Assisi, constituted a profound break with the traditions of monasticism. For, whereas from the time of Jerome onwards monks had withdrawn into their monasteries in open flight from the world, the Franciscans – along with their fellow Mendicants the Dominicans, Carmelites and Austin Friars – rejected the contemplative life in favour of an active, evangelical ministry, which necessitated their full participation in the life of the towns.[29]

Colantonio's painting of St Francis captures something of the evangelical fervour with which the Franciscan Order embarked on its mission to redeem the cities. The composition is dominated by the figure of St Francis, who is standing in the very centre of the panel. Kneeling before him are representatives of the first two Franciscan Orders; the Friars (to his right), and the Poor Clares (to his left),

---

[29]   For an account of the Mendicant Orders' mission to the towns, see C.H. Lawrence, *The Friars: The Impact of the Early Mendicant Movement on Western Society* (London: Longman, 1994), pp. 102–26.

2 Niccolò Colantonio, *St Francis Distributing the Rule to the First and Second Orders* (c. 1445), Naples: National Museum of Capodimonte

and it is to the foremost member of each group (believed to be St Anthony and St Clare respectively), that Francis is shown handing over a copy of the Franciscan Rule.[30] Two angels with banners bearing biblical quotations are hovering just above the saint. The banner on Francis's right reads: '*Quicumque hanc regulam secuti fuerint pax super illos et misericordia*' ['May peace and mercy be upon those who follow this Rule'] (Galatians 6: 16), while that on his left states: '*Signa thau super frontes virorum genenium*' ['Mark a *Tau* upon the foreheads of the men who grieve] (Ezekiel 9: 4).

It is through the second of these two biblical quotations that Colantonio highlighted the specifically urban nature of the Franciscan ministry. The quotation is taken from the ninth chapter of the Book of Ezekiel – an apocalyptic vision of the destruction of Jerusalem, in which God visits tribulation upon the inhabitants of the city for their sinfulness and corruption. Six men, each with weapons in their hands, are assembled by God to destroy everyone in their wake. But in their midst there is a seventh man, clothed in linen, and with a writing case at his side:

> And the Lord said to him [the man clothed in linen], Go through the midst of the city, through the midst of Jerusalem, and set a mark upon the foreheads [Vulgate: '*et signa Thau super frontes*'] of the men that sigh and that cry for all the abominations that be done in the midst thereof. And to the others he said in mine hearing, Go ye after him through the city, and smite: let not your eye spare, neither have ye pity: Slay utterly old and young, both maids, and little children, and women: but come not near any man upon whom is the mark (Ezekiel 9: 4–6).

The mission of the man in linen, then, was to mark with the sign of the *Tau* – written as a Roman majuscule T – the foreheads of all those who were to be saved from apocalyptic destruction. Now amongst his *followers* it was widely believed that Francis had been sent by God to call sinners to salvation before the coming of the Apocalypse; a role that was thought to have been foreshadowed in the pages of the Bible by the man clothed in linen. Francis thus came to be identified with this biblical figure, and within Franciscan circles the ninth chapter of the Book of Ezekiel was interpreted as a prophecy of their founder's coming. For instance, writing in approximately 1260, Bonaventure – the then Minister General of the Franciscan Order, and Francis's official biographer – identified the saint quite explicitly with the Man in Linen by stating that his ministry: 'was to mark with a *Tau* the foreheads of men who grieve'.[31] Moreover, both Bonaventure and Thomas of Celano, another of Francis's biographers, noted that the *Tau*

---

[30] For a tentative identification of some of the kneeling Franciscan figures, see Jolly, 'Jan Van Eyck and St Jerome', pp. 111–12.

[31] See St Bonaventure, *The Life of St Francis*, trans. Ewert Cousins (New York: Paulist Press, 1978), Prologue, pp. 181–2.

emblem exerted such a powerful hold over his imagination that he habitually used it as the personal mark with which he signed his letters.[32]

However, from the point of the view of the present discussion, what is significant is not so much the supposed apocalyptic nature of the Franciscan mission, but the fact that, like the Man in Linen, the role that Francis was believed to have been divinely appointed to fulfil was that of calling to repentance the sinful inhabitants of the cities. Therefore, in striking contrast to the historical Jerome, instead of taking flight from the city in a state of moral dread, Francis and the members of his Order consciously chose to make their home in the urban environment. For both Francis and Jerome, city life was inherently decadent, and yet in the case of the late-medieval saint this decadence was not something to fear, but was rather a spur to evangelical action.

In her discussion of the overall iconographic design of the San Lorenzo altarpiece, Penny Howell Jolly argues that by juxtaposing the figures of Francis and Jerome, Colantonio was trying to highlight what were, amongst Franciscans, well-established connections between the two saints.[33] Jolly points out that Jerome was held in especially high esteem by Franciscan writers, who regarded him as a figure whose life in many ways anticipated that of their founder. Thus, like Francis, Jerome was thought to have turned his back on the allurements of worldly honours and preferment by adopting the *vita apostolica*, the apostolic life, as a result of which he was believed to have attained such a state of grace and holiness that – once again anticipating the actions of St Francis – he was able to tame and befriend even the wildest of animals. But, as we have seen, this appropriation of St Jerome by the Franciscan Order was anachronistic. To a great extent, Jerome and Francis shared the prevailing beliefs and assumptions of the distinct cultures in which they lived. Despite the obvious parallels between their lives, the two saints differed profoundly not just in terms of their attitudes towards the city, but more generally on their understanding of the role of the Church in the world.

---

[32]   See Bonaventure, *Life of St Francis*, Ch. 4, p. 214, and Thomas de Celano, *Tractatus de Miraculis Beati Francisci*, in *Analecta Franciscana* X, Fasc. IV (Quaracchi: Collegii S. Bonaventurae, 1936), II, 3, p. 273. For a more extended discussion of the strongly apocalyptic tone of many of the early Franciscan writings, see John V. Fleming, *From Bonaventure to Bellini: An Essay on Franciscan Exegesis* (Princeton: Princeton University Press, 1982), pp. 99–128, and Richard K. Emmerson and Ronald B. Herzman, *The Apocalyptic Imagination in Medieval Literature* (Philadelphia: University of Pennsylvania Press, 1992), pp. 36–75.

[33]   See Jolly, 'Jan Van Eyck and St Jerome', pp. 150–51.

Chapter 2

Nature, Venus, and Royal Decadence: Political Theory and Political Practice in Chaucer's *Parliament of Fowls*

Michael St John

Chaucer's *Parliament of Fowls* (*c.* 1380–82) is the third and arguably the most accomplished of his four dream visions. In this essay I shall present a reading of the poem that draws out the political implications of its imagery and design with special reference to the decadence of Edward III and his court, which became a contentious issue in the Good Parliament of 1376. In particular I shall examine the way in which Chaucer uses and modifies his source texts in order to develop scenes that offer a general commentary upon how the sexual desires of the aristocracy relate to the good of society as a whole.

In the *Parliament of Fowls* the narrator falls asleep having read Cicero's *Dream of Scipio*. This Roman civic poem offers advice for the young statesman (Scipio) and introduces from the outset a political frame of reference for the dream that follows. The narrator of the *Parliament* encounters Africanus, Scipio's grandfather, who introduces him to the kind of delightful garden that is typical of many medieval dream visions. In the garden he discovers, *inter alia*, the temple of Venus, a place of unfulfilled and destructive sexual desire, before discovering an assembly of birds gathered around the figure of Nature. This is the parliament of fowls, meeting on Valentine's day, to debate the issue of choosing a suitable mate for a female eagle, after which all the birds of the various lower ranks will find their respective partners under the benevolent guidance of Nature. Three eagles court a single female and this situation threatens deadlock, preventing the other birds, who must wait until the eagles' affairs are dealt with, from being able to find their mates. Fortunately, however, the deadlock is overcome by the three eagles accepting Nature's advice that they wait another year for the female's decision. In order to appreciate the kind of political issues at stake in the poem and how these relate to the subject of decadence, it is necessary to consider in detail how Chaucer uses and alters his source texts, beginning with the figure of Nature.

Nature as she originally appears in Alain De Lille's (1125/30–1203) *Complaint of Nature* is an awesome figure. She is a spiritual being whose authority is not questioned by any element of the natural realm except man. She is not, therefore, a figure that is particularly conducive to political exploration.[1] When she appears before the narrator she does not come to debate but to lecture in order to correct a society that is in an advanced state of decay. Chaucer's Nature, however, presides over a parliament. She encourages the members of that parliament to make free choices concerning the seeking of partners, and to debate when required. She is not so constrained by moral and spiritual concerns that she is unwilling to embrace political ideals of a more democratic kind where the different species are concerned. This creates an impression of a figure who is powerful, but who exerts that power in a select and careful manner, giving freedom to her subjects where that freedom does not compromise the good of the community. She is consequently much less severe than the figure in Alain's poem, who simply rules all creatures except sinful man whom she rebukes. It has been suggested by some that the reason for Chaucer placing Nature at the heart of a recognizable political institution is because of medieval political theories that saw such institutions as the natural outcome of man's nature.[2] Such theories stemmed ultimately from Aristotle, specifically his *Politics*, and were Christianized by a number of medieval thinkers, most importantly Thomas Aquinas. Professor Walter Ulmann stresses the revolutionary change in political thought brought about by the renewed knowledge of Aristotle's *Politics* in western Christendom, and gives a useful summary of the main contributions that the *Politics* made to medieval political thought. Aristotle's political doctrine, according to Ulmann,

---

[1]   By this I mean that her mission is so urgent (because of the extent of social decay) that there is no time for any debate or reconsideration of political systems, or the language and traditions associated with them. Alain De Lille, *De Planctu Naturæ* (*The Complaint of Nature*) trans. Douglas M. Moffat (New York: Henry Holt & Co., 1908). In Metre I Nature attacks homosexuality in particular as evidence of social decay: 'The sex of active nature trembles painfully at the way in which it declines into passive nature. Man is made woman, he blackens the honour of his sex, the craft of magic Venus makes him of double gender' (p. 3).

[2] See for example B.K. Cowgill, 'The Parlement of Foules and the Body Politic', *Journal of English and Germanic Philology* 74 (1975), 315–35, and P.A. Olson, 'The Parlement of Foules: Aristotle's Politics and the Foundations of Human Society', *Chaucer Review* 24 (1990), 53–69. Both offer good accounts of the way in which political theory based on Aristotle can further our understanding of Chaucer's *Parliament of Fowls*. Cowgil attempts a useful explanation of the unity of the poem in terms of political theory, though his interpretation of the royal eagle as being responsible for the breakdown of order in the parliament is questionable. Olson considers the parliament as 'a picture of how people discover civic charity through institutions for "speaking together"', with specific reference to Aristotle's thought, 'and the implications of those institutions for deliberation which existed in Chaucer's own time', p. 56.

culminates in the view of the State, the supreme community, as the product of nature. The State is, according to him, an issue of the law of nature – and not an issue of any convention or agreement. This law of nature that brings forth the State is proper to man himself. Man is born with the natural law which determines him to live in the State; neither civilised life nor the attainment of man's aspirations is possible outside the State.[3]

Ulmann goes on to stress the 'naturalist' dimension of Aristotle's thinking:

> This naturalist feature pervades the whole thinking of Aristotle. 'Nature does nothing in vain'; 'Nature does nothing superfluous'; 'Nature behaves as if it foresaw the future'; and so forth, statements of Aristotle which show the overriding importance he attaches to the working of nature in his system.[4]

These remarks reflect the importance of nature to Aristotelian political thought. The political institutions that man participates in are not inventions, created purely on the basis of a rationality that is divorced from natural sentiment. They are pre-determined by the nature of what man is, a creature with various physical needs that can only be met in a stable and just organic community. It is the rational capacity of man that enables him to discern what nature dictates for him:

> The further essential feature of Aristotelian doctrine is that the thinking and reasoning capacity of man is determined by the law of nature. Blind obedience to the natural proclivities is the hallmark of animalistic creatures and their communities; the reasoned transformation of the laws of nature into a common will is the hallmark of man's State. Conscious willing, the reasoned voluntas of man is the expression of the law of nature.[5]

Reason and language are the tools by which men in discussion with one another are able to discover what nature demands of individuals as part of the community. The human individual, unlike other animals, is able to discover rationally, and consciously acknowledge, that which is naturally expected of him. The socially responsible individual is also capable of rationally informed acts of will, and Ulmann explains this in terms that are particularly relevant to the *Parliament of Fowls*:

---

3   Walter Ulmann, *Principles of Government and Politics in the Middle Ages* (London: Methuen, 1961), pp. 232–4. Ulmann is commenting upon Bk I ii of Aristotle's *Politics* (see Aristotle: *The Politics*, trans. T. A. Sinclair (Harmondsworth: Penguin, 1962), pp. 55–61).

4   Ulmann, *Principles of Government*, pp. 232–4.

5   Ibid., pp. 232–4.

The natural urge of animals to congregate, and the natural urge of men to form the State, stand in the same relation as the uncouth natural sound expressing pleasure and pain to language which expresses good or evil: the fixation of right and wrong is the result of human reasoning capacities, and right and wrong are determined by the human insight into, and understanding of, what nature itself demands. The *voluntas* of man is therefore intrinsically linked with the nature of man.[6]

It is natural for man to congregate and debate in order to determine what is best for the community, just as it is natural for certain animals to group together. This political theory can help us in our understanding of the relation of Nature to the language of the birds in the *Parliament*. Nature is the structuring principle of their language and their debate. First of all she instils in them the desire to mate. Secondly she facilitates their congregation by presiding over their parliament. Thirdly she gives them language that is appropriate to their particular natures. Nature and the birds therefore represent, allegorically, and in broad terms, the relationship of nature to men and how they collectively form the state as defined by Aristotle. These birds are not, however, straightforward substitutes for medieval human subjects, and their debate falls far short of the ideal for man because they are limited by their respective natures. They are, I believe, like the animals depicted upon Nature's robe in Alain's poem:[7] unfallen and obedient to Nature, so that their language is a direct and faithful expression of their inner selves. Nature nevertheless enables some of their language to be elevated: she gives the best language to the birds that clearly represent the best in society according to Chaucer. This is an ideal that is elitist, but which has a democratic function, in that it is something to which all rational subjects should aspire. Nature thus brings what Ulmann calls 'uncouth natural sound expressing pleasure and pain', the 'Kek kek! kokkow! quek quek!' (499) of the lower birds, into a direct contrast with the refined courtly discourse of the higher birds. It is their refined language that contains the best traditions of courtly love, and these traditions, specifically the respect for the free choice of the female and the ideal of long suffering of the suitors, enable the three eagles to act with regard to 'commune profyt'.[8] They consent to wait for another year so that all the other

---

6   Ibid., pp. 232–4.
7   Alain De Lille, *The Complaint of Nature*, Prose I, p. 11.
8   The term 'commune profyt' (47), meaning the good of the community as a whole, contrasts with the idea of 'synguler profit' or personal gain, a term used in Chaucer's previous dream vision, the *House of Fame* (310). The outcome of the parliament is that the royal birds, in conformity with those protocols of courtly love which affirm long-suffering perseverance on the part of the lover, agree to forego the immediate satisfaction of their needs so that all of the other birds can find their mates that day. This is a particularly political adaptation of the ideals of *fin amor* (all references to Chaucer are taken from *The Riverside Chaucer*, ed. Larry D. Benson (Oxford and New York: OUP, 1987), numbers in brackets indicate line numbers of poems).

birds can choose a mate. This is their act of what Ulmann terms 'reasoned
voluntas'.

The *Parliament of Fowls* therefore presents a political lesson by showing how
a parliamentary forum and debate is born out of the government of Nature. To this
extent it demonstrates the influence of Aristotelian political theory: transforming
Alain's Nature from a transcendent Platonic archetype to an immanent caretaker
of the commonwealth, directly involved in the political life of her subjects. Her
direct control is what enables the baser language of the birds ('murmer of the
lewednesse') to be incorporated into a debate, structured along principles of a
democratic kind:

> Nature, which that alwey hadde an ere
> To murmur of the lewednesse behynde,
> With facound voys seyde, 'hold youre tonges there!
> And I shal sone, I hope, a conseyl fynde
> Yow to delyvere, and fro this noyse unbynde:
> I juge, of every folk men shul oon calle
> To seyn the verdit for yow foules alle (519–25).

Political practice: the Good Parliament of 1376

Chaucer's decision to set his debating birds in the context of a parliament can,
then, be seen as a direct reflection of his sense of political theory, drawn from
Aristotle and combined with his reading of Alain's *Complaint and the Dream of
Scipio*. It might also, however, have had a more direct and immediate prompt as
well, in his knowledge of recent events in the English Parliament. Specifically I
want to consider the Good Parliament of 1376, in which issues directly relevant
to Chaucer's poem – including the sexual activity of the monarch – were the
subject of intense debate and negotiation. The impact of this Parliament and its
successful, though temporary, challenge to royal power, was profound, and
signalled the growing strength of the national Parliament in Chaucer's time.

The Good Parliament was called for the usual reason of raising money for war
via taxation. It was the norm for this request to be put before the Commons on
behalf of the Lords, who would wait for the Commons to deliberate and approve
the request as a matter of course. In this Parliament, however, the Commons
decided to deny the request unless certain demands were met. Their principal
contention was that the funds requested would not have been necessary if the king
had not been so badly advised in his military campaigns.[9] Edward III, who was
very ill at this time, was represented by his son, Chaucer's patron, John of Gaunt,
who sat in his place. Sir Peter de la Mare was chosen as spokesman for the

---

[9]   See George Holmes, *The Good Parliament* (Oxford: Clarendon Press, 1975),
pp. 4–6.

Commons and along with other members he was admitted into Gaunt's presence in order to present their objections. These initial meetings were unproductive and Peter de la Mere insisted that the entire Commons be admitted with him at further meetings. In the course of the subsequent meetings the Commons expressed their dissatisfaction with the royal court and its policies. Various courtiers were accused of corruption and of abusing their position and the Commons demanded their dismissal. The King's Chamberlain, William Latimer, and the Steward of the Household, John Neville, were both dismissed from office, and Richard Lyons, a powerful merchant, was imprisoned and stripped of his property. The other important dismissal was that of Alice Perrers, the king's mistress, and it is here that the matters of the Good Parliament impinge upon issues considered in Chaucer's text.

Alice Perrers was perceived by de la Mare and his group to be at the heart of the corruption of the royal court. At this point in his reign the once great Edward III was a shadow of his former self. His death mask, with one side of the mouth turned down, may provide direct evidence that he had suffered from one or more strokes. It seems that for more than a year before he died in 1377 he had a mind not much stronger than 'a boy of eight' and tended 'to agree with whatever those around him suggested'.[10] In this condition Edward was vulnerable to manipulation, and Alice Perrers was allegedly exploiting his weakness for her own gain.

> Since, too, those who needed to make their deeds official needed the King's consent, they can have had no choice but to approach him through the lively and acquisitive Alice. She therefore became not only powerful but rich, intensely unpopular and the subject of every kind of rumour.[11]

In the course of the Good Parliament it was alleged that Perrers' self-aggrandizement was costing the nation three thousand pounds a year. Her influence over the king was common knowledge, and was spoken of in sermons, tracts and other public discourse.[12] In 1374 her pretensions resulted in an outrageous apotheosis. Decked in royal jewels, some of which were Queen Philippa's, she was driven in a chariot as 'Lady of the Sun' from the Tower of London to a tournament at Cheapside. Such a state of affairs was more than the Commons could bear and their request that she be dismissed from the royal court was successful.

The Good Parliament, then, took upon itself unprecedented powers to discuss matters which had hitherto been the personal, and indeed private, concerns of the king. It claimed the right to comment upon, and ultimately to determine, the

---

[10] Michael Packe, *Edward III* (London: Routledge and Keegan Paul, 1983), p. 286.

[11] Ibid., p. 287.

[12] See G.R. Owst, *Literature and Pulpit in Medieval England* (Oxford: Blackwell, 1961), pp. 579–80.

sexual activities of the monarch, if they were perceived to be detrimental to the common good. In so doing it was exploring, in the harsh glare of contemporary politics, the same issues which Chaucer was to discuss in the fictive realm of his avian assembly, in which the 'common' birds took it upon themselves to offer advice to the royal eagle on how he should conduct his courting of the formel. In what sense, then, might Chaucer's poem be connected with the events of the Good Parliament? It may well have been the case that the events of the Good Parliament impressed themselves upon Chaucer, as a court poet, and suggested the form of a debate in which the sexual needs of individuals are measured against a wider social framework. In support of this idea is the fact that Chaucer's father John was directly involved in the controversy surrounding Alice. He was one of a number who stood surety for Richard Lyons who was ordered 'not to harm Alice Perrers, or prevent her going about her own and the King's business'.[13] It is not unreasonable to suppose that the reason for this action revolved around Alice's ability to control the king. Lyons was a powerful merchant who profited from his association with the court, and Alice seems to have become an obstacle to his ambitions, presumably because they conflicted with her own. The details of this case, then, may also have helped to encourage Chaucer's interest in the events of the Good Parliament.

On a universal level the story of Alice Perrers represents a situation common to numerous real governments. Many a king, minister or president has had their ability to govern questioned due to sexual impropriety. This is perhaps why Chaucer gives us the temple of Venus in the middle of the poem. He presents what is, in political terms, the dead end of costly and illicit sexual relations. The temple is an enclosed space of limited possibilities. All desire is self-consuming, running around the interior of the temple in the 'swogh' of 'sykes hot' without end:

> Withinne the temple, of sykes hoote as fyr
> I herde a swogh that gan aboute renne,
> Whiche sikes were engendered with desyr,
> That maden every auter for to brenne
> Of newe flaume; and wel espyed I thenne
> That al the cause of sorwes that they drye
> Cam of the bittere goddesse Jelosye (246–52).

This is a description of a sexual 'desyr' that will not project life into the future, in contrast to the procreative effect of the desire that the fowls of the parliament experience. The figures who succumb to the temptations of Venus are presented as static, such as those who are painted on the temple walls (lines 284–92), and also Priapus.

---

[13]   Derek Pearsall, *The Life of Geoffrey Chaucer* (Oxford: Blackwell, 1992), p. 14.

The god Priapus saw I, as I wente,
Withinne the temple in sovereyn place stonde,
In swich aray as whan the asse hym shente
With cri by nighte, and with hys sceptre in honde.
Ful besyly men gonne assaye and fonde
Upon his hed to sette, of sondry hewe,
Garlondes ful of freshe floures newe (253–59).

In describing Priapus, Chaucer departs from his otherwise faithful translation of Boccaccio's *Teseida*, the source text for the temple scene.[14] Firstly, Chaucer refers to Priapus as a god, which Boccaccio does not. Instead of highest place he says 'sovereyn place' – the word 'sovereyn' introducing connotations of excellence as well as royalty. The euphemistic description of the god 'with hys sceptre in honde' further reinforces this intimation of royalty, at the same time as introducing a comic bawdy dimension that is not found in the *Teseida*. Emerson Brown Jr states that the association of the sceptre with Priapus occurs in some iconographic traditions, but it is, nevertheless, a noteworthy departure from the literary source to which Chaucer is generally faithful.[15] Whatever the reasons for these innovations, the result is that Priapus is a much more significant figure here than in Boccaccio's text.

Venus and her immediate entourage are also stationary, as are the couple that plead on their knees (278). The sighs and the flames they inspire are the only dynamic elements in the temple, along with the activity that surrounds Priapus. All else is arrested, cut off from the flow of life that both surrounds the temple and is very much a part of the avian parliament. Succumb to desire as a political leader and you may well jeopardize the state by negating reason and exposing yourself to public shame: this is the moral of the temple for those who govern, and Paris, Cleopatra and Troylus, who are depicted upon the temple's walls, are all examples of such leadership compromised by desire. In the avian parliament the sexual needs of the royal eagle and his rivals are also in danger of jeopardizing the common good. The three eagles all desire the same mate, a situation that must be resolved in order for the other birds to choose their partners. But, fortunately, they respect both the protocols of courtly love and the government of nature, enabling them to rise above the immediate demands of desire. This is at the very least an endorsement of the idea of parliament: as an institution that facilitates communication between different groups with their respective, and sometimes competing, needs and values.

Another significant variation between the temple description in the *Teseida* and Chaucer's poem is in Chaucer's description of a 'materialistic' Venus who is very much associated with finery.

---

[14]   G. Boccaccio, *Teseida*, trans. S. Battagua (Firenza: Garzanti, 1958), vs. 50–66.
[15]   Emerson Brown, 'Priapus and the Parlement of Foulys', *Studies in Philology* 72 (1975), 258–74.

And in a prive corner in disport
Fond I Venus and hire porter Richesse,
That was ful noble and hautayn of hyre port –
Derk was that place, but afterward lightnesse
I saw a lyte, unnethe it myghte be lesse –
And on a bed of gold she lay to reste,
Til that the hote sonne gan to weste (260–6).

When we initially encounter Venus in Boccaccio's text she is naked, lying on a great bed, and we are told that she is beautiful. He informs us, for example, of Venus's golden hair fastened around her head without any tress. But Chaucer does not focus upon Venus's innate beauty and transfers the word golden to the thread that binds her hair as well as her bed, 'Hyre gilte heres with a golden thred / Ibounden were, untressed as she lay' (267–68). Minnis comments upon Chaucer's transference of the adjective 'golden' to apply to 'inanimate objects'.[16] The effect of this is to make Venus seem more materialistic, especially since she is in much closer proximity to the figure of 'Richesse', and also with the addition of the 'coverchef of Valence' (272). It does not seem very godlike to have such concern for man made luxuries. Specifying 'Valence' as the source of fine French cloth serves to tie Venus into a specific semiology of wealth that would have made her more real to a courtly audience. The nearest Chaucer comes to recognizing anything like the perfect and ideal beauty of Boccaccio's Venus is when he describes her as 'noble' and 'hautayn of porte'. But the word 'noble' also has connotations of rank, and does not necessarily accord with physical perfection. Also it is applied to her porter, which serves to rob her of any unique attributes. Boccaccio in contrast to this stresses that Venus's face is more beautiful by far than anyone else's. The overall effect of these changes is to make Venus more human than godlike, which means that she is less removed from the real world than is Boccaccio's goddess.

Having established that the *Parliament* has a universal applicability to the themes of politics and sex in the real world, it now becomes possible to see how a contemporary courtly audience could have interpreted Chaucer's Priapus and Venus as a direct allusion to Edward III and Alice Perrers. Priapus is a significant figure in Chaucer's poem and the description of Venus herself follows on directly after him. In terms of presence these two are on a par with one another, although Priapus is primarily an image of embarrassment and failure, whereas Venus is a figure of influence in the affairs of erotic love (lines 278–9). Priapus is subject to Venus and her ways just as the decrepit king was, and the use of the words 'sovereyn' and 'sceptre' could be allusions to his royal person. More specifically the reference to crowning with 'Garlondes' could be metaphorical. Chaucer may be referring here to debate over Edward's reputation. This would make some

---

[16] Alastair J. Minnis, *Oxford Guides to Chaucer: The Shorter Poems* (Oxford: OUP, 1995), p. 286.

sense of the words 'assaye' ('try' or 'investigate') and 'fonde' ('strive') in line
257. Rather than being tautological in meaning, this line and the next could be
interpreted as 'they investigated and strove to put the garlands on his head'. The
'Garlondes' which are of 'sondry hewe' would therefore be the different stories
that make up a reputation. This would also establish a thematic continuity with
the *House of Fame*, which is a concerted exploration of the nature of reputation
based on texts. Also, if Chaucer's Venus is interpreted as Alice Perrers (and her
materialistic associations make this possible), the contradiction that lines 265–6
seem to present ('And on a bed of gold she lay to reste, / Til that the hote sonne
gan to weste'), can be resolved.[17] Again the meaning may be metaphorical. We
have already noted that Edward publicly paraded Alice through the streets of
London as 'the Lady of the Sun'. To refer to a monarch as the sun is a common
enough metaphor. Thomas Walsingham does so when writing about the high
point of Edward's reign in the *Historia Anglicana*: 'Then folk thought that a new
sun was rising over England'.[18] What Chaucer may therefore be saying in lines
265–6 is that Alice enjoyed her great privilege – lying on the 'bed of gold', until
Edward's death, signified by 'the hote sun gan to weste'. Certainly the adjective
'hote' is used by Chaucer elsewhere to mean sexual passion (*Knight's Tale* l.
1735, for example, and *Man of Law's Tale* l. 586), and could be a reference to the
passion of the king for his mistress, which he retained right until his death.

Chaucer's *Parliament of Fowls* presents us, I believe, with a fascinating
aesthetic response to the dichotomy that could be observed between medieval
political ideals and real courtly politics. The transcendent figure of Nature, who
appears as a Platonic archetype in Alain's poem, is reworked by Chaucer in order
to facilitate a parliament. This parliament, with its demonstration of ideal courtly
conduct, advocates a beneficial approach to the potentially disruptive effect of
sexual desire. This stands in opposition to the temple of Venus, where sexual
desire is seen to be a destructive force in social terms. By designing his poem in
this way Chaucer is able to describe the decadent sexual conduct of his social
superiors via the temple, whilst affirming the natural quality of sexual desire and
its positive function in society, when governed by the ideal courtly principles
displayed in the parliament of birds.

---

[17]   See R.A. Pratt, 'Chaucer's Use of the Teseida', *Publications of the Modern
Language Association of America*, 62 (1947), 598–621. Pratt says that the idea of Venus
not being able to cope with the 'hote sun' (266) contradicts the earlier statement that there
was never 'grevaunce of hot ne cold' (205) in the garden, as well as the assertion of
perpetual daylight there (209–10).

[18]   Thomas Walsingham, *Historia Anglicana*, ed. H. Riley, 2 vols, Rolls Series,
1863–4. I, p. 272.

Chapter 3

Reading Symptoms of Decadence in Ford's *'Tis Pity She's a Whore*

Carla Dente

The word 'symptom', contained in the title of my paper, opens up a universe of discourse dealing with disease. This seems appropriate because very often decadence is treated as a disease, a situation where an ideal, healthy state has declined, and plague and sickness have taken over. From the 'Theatre Controversy' of the Renaissance through to Artaud and his pervasive concept of 'Cruelty', theatre in particular has been conceived as associated with plague and disease, as Keir Elam has recently remarked.[1] The diseases most commonly associated with the idea of decadence are sensationalism, egocentricity, an insistent search for the bizarre, artificiality, flippancy and sometimes even perversity, with certain critics and playwrights assuming that these tendencies have an artistic quality, marking the 'decadent' state off as better than life, very often larger than life. In epochs when such an ethos becomes dominant, it spreads like a contagious disease, leaving its unmistakable mark on the times.

Literary historians coined the label 'decadent' in reference to the writing of the last decades of the nineteenth century but the term has been applied to plenty of earlier texts, such as Ford's tragedy *'Tis Pity She's a Whore* (1628).[2] In my view it is basically correct to speak of Ford's attitude as 'decadent' because *'Tis Pity* depicts the death-throes of a cultural paradigm, the one canonically termed 'Renaissance', which became Renaissance/baroque by rejecting the lucid rationality and literary realism that had characterized the former period.

---

[1] See Keir Elam, '"In what chapter of his bosom?": Reading Shakespeare's Bodies', in ed. Terry Hawkes, *Alternative Shakespeare* 2 (London: Routledge, 1996), pp. 140–63.

[2] In his lecture on Jacobean playwrights, Hazlitt described Ford's art as immoral and artificial, a view which later became a critical orthodoxy. In the twentieth century this has become a cliché of historical criticism, pointing to the fact that the late Jacobean and Caroline age had lost its moral bearings and indulged in prurient suggestions and sensational incidents.

'*Tis Pity*, then, may be considered as a transitional work, a product of a crisis in the dominant cultural ethos, namely the paradigm of an harmoniously organized universe, both in the macrocosm and in the microcosm. This paradigm is successfully undermined by the search for the subject underway throughout the period,[3] and the subject is thus placed at the very centre of the world picture in a way necessitating a revision of the whole *weltanschaung*, and consequently the search for a new aesthetic and cultural balance. The play makes issues of concepts like deceit and perversion, familial and social transgression. It experiments with inversions almost to the point of celebrating what is deprecated by the *status quo*. In performance it achieves a 'redeeming cruelty' as Artaud put it,[4] through the sensational representation of conventionally outrageous actions, with the ultimate result of attracting those negative ethical judgements from the audience implied in the term 'decadence'. The statement the play inevitably represents is ambiguous and elitist, epitomizing a propositional content which cannot be shared except through a process of inversion.

Like a disease, individual passion grows and spreads, despite the inadequate efforts of society to control it. The outbreak of this disease contaminates everyone. The original passion results in corruption, and, as it spreads, it manifests itself as wounded jealous pride, zeal for revenge and deceit. Passion goes beyond the boundaries of the fictional world and is communicated to the spectator through the contact/contagion provided by language, thus confirming the Puritan contention that the theatre was a pathological phenomenon. But if the acts the main character performs on stage produce negative value judgements in the spectator, these acts simultaneously contradict those produced by his monologues – which supposedly reveal the depth of his psyche. The presentation of incest, for instance, as 'sin' universally condemned, thus renders Ford's argumentational procedure in this tragedy analogous to a *reductio ad absurdum*, making the spectator keenly aware of a process of gradual inversion, while at the same time feeling sympathetic to this inversion.

From a perspective internal to the story, the play reflects the conflict between a young couple (a tersely rational man, Giovanni, in love with beauty, and a passionate young lady, Annabella, endowed with a certain sense of guilt) and the rest of society, portrayed as insensitive, gross and philistine, and from which the young couple in their private universe of uncontaminated love feel wholly removed. From a perspective which takes account of its effect on the spectator, on the other hand, this tragedy capitalizes on a taste for rebellious dissatisfaction with current religious thought, and for the glorification of egocentricity and 'perversion' – represented sensationally on stage – while at the same time it

---

[3]   See C. Belsey, *The Subject of Tragedy: Identity and Difference in Renaissance Drama* (London: Methuen, 1985).

[4]   A. Artaud, 'Theatre and the Plague' in *The Theatre and its Double* (London: Calder and Boyars, 1970), pp. 7–22.

appears morally to sanction both these and the conventional attitudes of the *status quo*.

The main appeal now of Ford's tragedy is, surely, the axiological system it encodes, an aspect of the text's ideology which may be investigated through its use of modality,[5] apt to reveal the special relationship of the speaking subject with the object of utterance. A spectator or a reader can pass judgements on this special relationship on the grounds of modal competence, a complex parameter resulting partly from actual and partly from literary experience.

The study of the modal articulation of this tragedy reveals an authorial strategy aiming at the representation, valorization and transmission of passion, an element itself capable of disrupting the ideological framework of the Renaissance world picture. This textual strategy, which is more marginal in drama of the Elizabethan period, not only highlights the actual cracks in the compact ideological code that had shaped almost a century-and-a-half of speculation without undergoing explicit challenge, but also locates the tragedy at the uncertain perimeters of a system the disintegration of which gives way to negative moral connotations, subsequently revised by historians of ideas.

The essential difference between the conception of evil on the Elizabethan and on the Jacobean stage, however, is that this fascination with evil became a creative impulse, making any judgement passed on it increasingly unstable. Evil in both periods was often represented by characters in a position of power, thus offering the chance for a critique of contemporary social morals. But something else is happening in Jacobean drama, something far more subversive. A moral crisis in the early seventeenth century has been discussed by many historians who see a connection with the regicide concluding the epoch.[6] Molly Smith, for instance, suggests there was a cultural fracture in 1660, focusing on the development of an interest in what she calls 'the darker world':

> These later plays do more than argue with conventional notions of hierarchy; they trace evil through metaphor, allusion and suggestion to the very root of the hierarchical system, the king himself. The potency of the dramatic argument arises therefore, from its united force as criticism of monarchy as it then existed.[7]

This seems to endorse what Greenblatt says when he validates the historically consolidated effect of Jacobean tragedy as one of the agents responsible for the

---

[5]   The term 'modality' is used here in the very limited sense of 'verbal modality'.

[6]   See L. White Jr, 'Death and the Devil', in ed. R. Kinsman, *The Darker Vision of the Renaissance* (Berkeley: University of California Press, 1974), and also Maurice Ashley, *Charles I and Oliver Cromwell: A Study in Contrast* (London: Methuen, 1987).

[7]   M. Smith, *The Darker World Within* (Newark: University of Delaware Press, 1987). Smith's contention is that Jacobean theatre dramatizes 'the darkness within', while Restoration Theatre dramatizes 'social illness' (p. 13).

dissolution of the paradigm of the dominant Renaissance culture.[8] An accelerating factor in this cultural transformation is the representation of psychic evil, even though it would be difficult to say that the end of this tragedy offers an unequivocal 'message'. But that is the essential point: where Elizabethan texts have tended to aim towards closure, Jacobean texts are unerringly open. On the one hand the representation of evil may be conceived as the intensification of a collective cultural experience through a theatrical rite,[9] but on the other, as already mentioned, they may be conceived also as 'a redeeming epidemic'.[10] Essential to this uneasy balance is the metaphor of disease.

'Tis Pity begins in medias res, with a dialogue supposedly begun offstage which can be interpreted as a dispute between the Friar and Giovanni. The two characters are in opposition, while the Friar clearly has the advantage of Giovanni and is the first to speak: 'Dispute no more in this'.[11] The imperative expresses prohibition, implying authority while also indicating something of the Friar's selfless sense of moral responsibility to others. In what follows, this ethical dimension is linguistically expressed through modalities such as permission, prohibition and obligation. Whatever the subject of the characters' discussion, the Friar reacts passionately and instructively, and gives a picture of the world he considers opposed to his own, as one where 'nice philosophy' tolerates 'unlikely arguments' grounded in an excess of dialectical geniality. His own epistemic system – what he knows, does not know, and believes – excludes all the rational arguments against God's existence. The Friar seems to stand as a champion of medieval notions of rationality, according to which reason was conceived as a contradictory force, often in the power of the devil. The Friar is a man of such deeply felt faith that his epistemic and axiological systems coincide: he knows what is good, he does not know what is bad. He honestly believes what the Church tells him to believe, and for this reason he cannot listen to Giovanni's arguments. Giovanni is the diligent disciple who opens his 'burden'd soul' to his spiritual mentor, giving him the keys of his mind: 'all what I ever durst, or think, or know'.[12] What he wants in exchange is permission to love the object of his desire.

At this point, the spectator's interpretation can take two different directions: one could either follow a line of action suggesting prohibition, violation, punishment, the other would follow the scenario Giovanni wishes for himself, a love quest, summarized in the formula lack, acquisition, possession.

---

    [8]   S. Greenblatt, ed., The Forms of Power and the Power of Forms in the English Renaissance (Norman: University of Oklahoma Press, 1982).
    [9]   Note that the rite becomes important when conditions of social uncertainty, impotence and disorder become established in a given historical period.
    [10]   A. Artaud, The Theatre and its Double, p. 22.
    [11]   J. Ford, 'Tis Pity She's a Whore, ed. D. Roper (London: Methuen, 1975), I, 1: 271. All further references cited as 'Tis Pity.
    [12]   'Tis Pity, I, 1: 17.

Intellectually Giovanni sees no obstacles to the fulfilment of his quest because nature itself seems to enforce its legitimacy: he and his beloved are physically alike, they came from the same womb and feel:

> . . . each to the other bound
> So much the more by Nature? by the links
> Of blood, of reason? to be ever one,
> One soul, one flesh, one love, one heart, one all.[13]

This series of close repetitions has an intense emotional impact upon the spectator or reader. But equally passionate is the Friar's indignant reaction which, although unconvincing, remains an effective evocation of damnation in the name of authority. This collision of opposed world views is clearly manifest when Giovanni comes to ask what remedy he could adopt for the disease of his soul, and subsequently obeys the Friar's instruction:

> Repentance, son, and sorrow for this sin:
> For thou hast mov'd a Majesty above,
> With thy unraged (almost) blasphemy.[14]

In this first stage of the drama Giovanni induces himself to accept the contemporary cultural code and rationally decides that he must not yield to his passion. The ease with which he renounces his passion here seems to accord with medieval ideals, when those representing the Church could distinguish good from evil in human behaviour and provide guidance that was applicable to everyone, from the king to the most humble servant. The ethical issues surrounding the ideal of a virtuous life had been explored by classical philosophers, such as Plato and Aristotle, and their teachings had been adapted for Christendom by the Church fathers and other teachers such as Aquinas. Thus, teaching derived in part from Plato was christianized and passed on by the men of the Church with the full force of Divine Authority.[15] In the early fifteenth century, however, this system was questioned and a different attitude began to prevail: the answer to the question of how to live within an ontological system capable of giving life meaning concerned the individual, not the whole of mankind. In the first half of the seventeenth century the process had reached a point where the answer to the same question was grounded in man's (relative) autonomy, in his limited freedom, in

---

13 *'Tis Pity*, I, 1: 30–4.

14 *'Tis Pity*, I, 1: 43–5.

15 Renaissance neo-Platonic philosophy followed Plotinus, adding to the earlier adaptations of Plato's ideas by such thinkers as St Augustine, Boethius and many other influential writers of the medieval period, including, of course, Dante, whose writings drew heavily upon classical philosophy as interpreted by Aquinas. See Michael Haren, *The Western Intellectual Tradition from Antiquity to the 13th Century* (London: Macmillan, 1985).

his conscious choice between alternatives, in his power over the world and himself. The aim of human life was found in a transcendent world in which the relationship between objects was ideal and harmonious and it was thought that through the contemplation of such harmony man could achieve moral virtue and partake of beauty. Morality and aesthetics thus became uncomfortably intertwined for the more straightforward authoritarianism of the medieval and Renaissance minds.

In Ford's tragedy the two main characters seem to engage in this debate, but with different degrees of awareness. Annabella's behaviour is instinctive, non-reflexive. It is remarkable that at their first encounter she does not recognize the man whose appearance inspires such an intense emotive response.

> *Ann.*: But see, Putana see, what blessed shape
> of some celestial creature now appears?
> What a man is he, that with such sad aspect
> walks careless of himself?
> *Put.*: Where?
> *Ann.*: Look below.
> *Put.*: Oh, 'tis your brother, sweet.
> *Ann.*: Ha!
> *Put.*: 'Tis your brother.[16]

In the soliloquy opening the third scene, and occupying the lapse of time necessary for Annabella to come down from the upper stage, Giovanni expresses his despair after the failure of his efforts to accept the Friar's proscription.

> Lost, I am lost, my fates have doom'd my death,
> The more I strive, I love, the more I love,
> The less I hope, I see my ruin, certain.
> What judgement or endevours could apply
> to my incurable and restless wounds
> I thoroughly have examined, but in vain.[17]

This passage not only expresses the tragic hero's awareness of his unequal fight against overwhelming odds, but also implies the realization that judgement is inadequate to oppose passion.

In the Renaissance, Reason was believed to help man to give passion its right measure ('passions of the mind', in Thomas Wright's terms)[18] but here the intensity of passion behind the words is such as to defy the sense of measure and

---

16 *'Tis Pity*, I, 2: 131–5.

17 *'Tis Pity*, I, 2: 144–9.

18 Thomas Wright, *The Passions of the Mind in General, A Critical Edition*, W. Webster Newhold, ed., *The Renaissance Imagination*, vol. 15 (New York and London: Garland Publishing Inc., 1986).

harmony characteristic of the mature Renaissance ethos. Indeed, in the soliloquy the rhetorical figure of hyperbole plays an important part in giving the speech an emphatic tone. To give only a few examples: 'wearied heaven with my pray'rs', 'dried up the spring of my continual tears', 'starved my veins with daily fasts'.[19] This might appear to be no different from any other conventional representation of the Renaissance melancholic type, who generally lives in a state of psychological conflict between reason and passion, and who is often endowed with intellectual and creative inclinations. It is also true that this type is often reputed to suffer from madness; in Giovanni's case an ambiguous madness, given his total deconstruction of morality, which elevates the conventionally anti-heroic figure of the melancholic man to the status of hero of the tragedy. It is interesting, however, that the story ends with the spectacular moral denigration of this type *as hero*.

Giovanni is conscious of the imperative to decide for himself what his line of action should be. This idea of the *rights* of the individual conscience is by far the most revolutionary in the play.[20] He thus comes to the conclusion that he cannot change. Realizing that escape from this Love is impossible, he first accepts it, then proclaims it as a 'fate':

> ... 'Tis not, I know,
> My lust, but 'tis my fate, that leads me on.
> Keep fear and low-faint hearted shame with slaves!
> I'll tell her that I love her, though my heart
> Were rated at a price of that attempt.[21]

To convince Annabella to comply with his wishes, Giovanni uses all the conventional arguments of the lover,[22] and thereby brings the semantic areas of Love and Disease closer together - 'Trust me, but I am sick; I fear so sick / 'Twill cost my life'.[23] To be assured that he is loved by Annabella, Giovanni takes advantage of the fact that the word 'love' can be used to define both the feeling of a brother towards his sister and the sexual feeling experienced by lovers. Even so, she says nothing when he states that he has the approval of the Church.

---

[19] *'Tis Pity*, I, 2: 152–4.
[20] See G.F. Sensabaugh, *The Tragic Muse of John Ford* (New York: Benjamin Blom Inc., 1965) with particular reference to Chapter 3, 'Unbridled Individualism'. He mentions reactions to the cult of the Virgin at court and the debate over Mariolatry and the Sabbatarian conflict as examples of this. What is relevant is the growing consciousness that controversy might in the long run help to solve any problem, provided all sides of the argument were considered.
[21] *'Tis Pity*, I, 2: 158–62.
[22] The allusion here is to the mythical register Giovanni employs, the use of similes consolidated by usage, and the conventional link of love and death.
[23] *'Tis Pity*, I, 2: 185–6.

>   . . . You
> My sister, Annabella; I know this;
> And could afford you instance why to love
> So much the more for this; to which intent
> Wise nature first in your creation meant
> To make you mine: else't had been sin and foul
> To share one beauty to a double soul.
> Nearness in birth and blood doth persuade
> A nearer nearness in affection.
> I have ask'd counsel of the holy Church,
> Who tells me I may love you, and 'tis just
> That since I may, I should, and will, yes will.[24]

At this stage Giovanni has intellectualized his passion, accepted it himself and sought to make others accept it through amoral rationalism and appeal to authority. This route is traceable in the modal chain of the speech just quoted. It starts with the modality of 'possibility' and then passes to that of 'obligation' / 'obliged' to indulge his desires, even against the sanction of authority (the Friar and the Cardinal representing the Church; his father and his sister's husband, Soranzo, representing the family and society at large).

    Elsewhere Giovanni is more explicit with the Friar:

> What I have done, I'll prove both fit and good,
> It is a principle that you have taught,
> When I was yet your scholar, that the frame
> And composition of the mind doth follow
> The frame and composition of the body,
> So, where the body's furniture is beauty,
> The mind must needs be virtue; which allowed,
> Virtue itself is reason but refined,
> And love the quintessence of that; this proves
> My sister's beauty, being rarely fair,
> Is rarely virtuous; chiefly in her love,
> And chiefly in this love, her love to me.[25]

Giovanni's ideological 'career' thus proclaims the equation of beauty and goodness, together with the idea that true love unites like hearts and leads them to heaven through carnal fruition. Love is the most important thing and a sure guide to virtue, more important even than marriage,[26] and the only basis on which liberty of action and thought can be founded. This complex net of reciprocal

---

[24]   *'Tis Pity*, I, 2: 232–53.
[25]   *'Tis Pity*, II, 5: 13–26.
[26]   Marriage is in fact imposed on Annabella by circumstances. It is advised by the Friar and accepted by the lovers when Annabella's pregnancy is discovered.

influences suggests that in Renaissance aesthetics, ethics and politics did not have discrete spheres, with the result that there was no awareness generally of the possible contradictions between the qualities of goodness and beauty, beauty and utility, utility and goodness.[27]

All this is still within the recognized Renaissance cultural code. Yet Ford transgresses it in that Giovanni accepts no rules at all, nothing above and beyond the imperatives of individual judgement. This is indeed to stretch a widely accepted principle to its (unacceptable) limits. The transgression is made even more evident to the reader/spectator in that this ideological position has to do with both gender and sexuality, and with the way in which emotion, which is connected with beauty and passion, is represented – without any sense of restraint and without the celebrated golden 'mean'.

Giovanni perversely overturns the imperative against incest, which in his view becomes the true means to achieve the most perfect Platonic affinity possible in Nature. As to emotion, it is seen as irresistible and far beyond human control. It is expressed in a rich language which produces its effects on Annabella, who in turn is 'infected' by Giovanni's rhetoric:

> For every sigh that thou hast spent for me,
> I have sighed ten: for every tear, shed twenty:
> And not so much for that I loved, as that
> I durst not say I loved; nor scarcely think it.[28]

Later, when she realizes she is pregnant, she accepts the Friar's suggestion that she marry Soranzo in the firm belief that even marriage is unimportant compared with her tie to her brother. After her reason for marrying is discovered, another passion takes possession of Annabella's mind and behaviour as a consequence of the Friar's violent reprimand: the sense of guilt. This feeling manifests itself as a premonition and a ready acceptance of the idea of death.

> Thou precious Time, that swiftly rid'st in post
> Over the world, to finish up the race
> Of my last fate, here stay my restless course,
> And bear for ages that are yet unborn
> A wretched woeful woman's tragedy.
> My conscience now stands up against my lust.[29]

---

[27] There are, of course, occasions during the Renaissance when certain individuals seem to gain insights beyond that of the dominant paradigm, as in Shakespeare's *Sonnets* for example, where some of these categories are explored in a critical manner.

[28] *'Tis Pity*, I, 2: 248–51.

[29] *'Tis Pity*, V, 1: 4–9.

The image of the 'restless course' is reminiscent of Dante's *Inferno*, and in particular of the circle in which he places Paolo and Francesca, and the others carried away by the whirlwind, just as in their lives they were overcome by the winds of passion. From this point, Annabella is comforted by the Friar who now resumes his position of authority and his influence over the events to follow, and expresses the repressive sanction of the Church. Thus Annabella follows a course leading backwards, from actions represented as permitted to actions represented as forbidden, and thereby subjected to moral sanction. The sequence of modals is inverted and the chain of modality may be summarized as 'to be able', 'not to be allowed', 'to be obliged not to do'.

Giovanni's intellectual isolation, his hell, is now complete, even though he is still a part of Annabella's emotive universe:

> Oh would the scourge, due to my black offence,
> Might pass from thee, that I alone might feel
> The torment of an uncontrollable flame![30]

Unaware of his sister's change, he expresses the sense of fulfilment his passion produces in him:

> . . . Oh, the glory
> of two united hearts like hers and mine!
> Let boring book-men dream of the other worlds,
> My world, and all of happiness, is here,
> And I'd not change it for the best to come:
> A life of pleasure in Elysium.[31]

The spectator, of course, knows better than the character and notes the tragic irony, as well as a display of intellectual heroism against subjection to God's authority. Giovanni has now achieved a kind of freedom from the authority of the Church. Our reaction, though, is inevitably ambivalent. This ultimate sin is both an act of extreme individualism, and one which exemplifies an egotistical disregard for others. From this perspective the Renaissance world picture, with its orderly, hierarchical universe – a universe centred on God – collapses into entropy.

When Annabella declares her sense of guilt over her incestuous passion, Giovanni is dismayed at his sister's betrayal, and the logical conclusion of the tragic story is a result of the impossibility of any dialectic between the general ethos and the character's personal ethos. Giovanni feels Annabella's decision to be a revolt (*'Tis Pity*,V, 5: 8), and had she been 'one thought more steady than an ebbing sea' (*'Tis Pity*,V, 5: 14), he could have 'command[ed] the course/ Of

---

30   *'Tis Pity*, V, 1: 21–3.
31   *'Tis Pity*, V, 3: 11–16.

Time's eternal motion' ('*Tis Pity*, V, 5: 12–13). Refusing to modify his ideological position and behaviour, despite the insistence of the figures of authority, he sees his sister's death and the literal appropriation of her heart to be the only possible way of remaining faithful to himself.

In Giovanni's eyes the 'perversion' of incest has been so far intellectualized as to border on celebration. This suggests the phenomenon of carnivalization, in the Bakhtinian sense of the term, an opinion shared by Molly Smith who comments on the different roles played by Giovanni and Annabella during the development of the story and considers them as a sign of constant becoming and serial transformations, which are primary characteristics of the grotesque body.[32]

When Giovanni accepts his passion for Annabella and has the full enjoyment of it, it is self-evident that patriarchal authority is defeated. Indeed it is represented as such in the figure of Florio, Giovanni and Annabella's father, on whom the consequences of the tragic event and of personal and familial defeats ultimately fall. The play thus guides the audience towards a range of festive events which ultimately, however, according to Bakhtinian dynamics, only confirm the necessity of order.

In '*Tis Pity* the death of Annabella is unavoidable because a general situation of crisis has been set up by her power of seduction over Giovanni. The eruption of the crisis is made possible by the weakness of the 'established powers' of patriarchal society, effectively represented only by the isolated, private and stern voice of the friar confessor. In order to set up a form of compensation for the society menaced by the breach, it is necessary to activate a sort of scapegoat mechanism, whereby society victimizes those who are outsiders, those who are marked by the devil through physical deformities, or those who stand for the elemental cultural differences as in the case of sins of parricide and incest. In '*Tis Pity* this is triggered by the process of making evil conscious through and in Annabella. It is a mechanism which also functions as a self-ruling aspect of society. Giovanni's final act, inscribed in a festive and ritualized context, is nevertheless ominous and arouses horror – even if the character represents it linguistically as valiant. This suggests a tension between the conception of an action and its transformation into an act, between word and deed. The audience cannot help but see how Giovanni's emotive manipulation of Annabella, which at a certain stage becomes sexual manipulation, later develops into a manipulation of her body as a fragmented, physical entity. Throughout the play, while the characters are caught between the urge to respect and the urge to demolish social barriers, the audience is equally caught between opposed emotional responses to the play's engagement with 'disease' as decadence. Such concepts, the play

---

[32] Smith, *The Darker World Within*. According to Smith, Giovanni is Annabella's brother first, then her lover, then a father figure, while she experiences phenomena of grotesque bodily transformations by first swallowing Giovanni's body, while making love to him, and then multiplying her own body in pregnancy.

insists, are relative to the point of view of the observer, and we are immediately plunged into a curiously 'modern' world, where authority is arbitrary and where, although beauty may appear to be truth, neither concept is verifiable.

Chapter 4

'Bawdy in Thoughts, precise in Words': Decadence, Divinity and Dissent in the Restoration*

Michael Davies

> The Period wherein the *English* Tongue received most Improvement I take to commence with the Beginning of Queen *Elizabeth*'s Reign, and to conclude with the great Rebellion in Forty-two. [. . .] From that great Rebellion to this present Time I am apt to doubt whether the Corruptions in our Language have not, at least, equalled the Refinements of it; and these Corruptions very few of the best Authors in our Age have wholly escaped. During the Usurpation, such an Infusion of Enthusiastick Jargon prevailed in every Writing, as was not shaken off in many Years after. To this succeeded that Licentiousness which entered with the *Restoration*; and from infecting our Religion and Morals, fell to corrupt our Language.[1]

What this passage affirms is that Jonathan Swift's point in writing his *Proposal for Correcting, Improving and Ascertaining the English Tongue* (1712) is far from just to bewail problems with style, the 'daily Corruptions', 'Abuses and Absurdities' in the language (such as 'that barbarous Custom of abbreviating Words' which not only 'offends against every Part of Grammar' but which also creates 'such harsh unharmonious Sounds, that none but a *Northern* Ear could endure').[2] Rather, as Tony Crowley has recently noted, here Swift aims to present

---

* This essay is part of my ongoing research into liberty of conscience and Restoration literature. I would like to note my gratitude to Professor Bill Myers of Leicester University's Department of English for his industry in reading and commenting upon this essay in its earlier form.

[1] Jonathan Swift, *A Proposal for Correcting, Improving and Ascertaining the English Tongue* (1712), in *The Prose Works of Jonathan Swift*, eds Herbert Davis et al., 14 vols (Oxford: Blackwell, 1939–68), IV, 1–21 (pp. 9–10).

[2] Swift, *Proposal*, pp. 6, 10–11. For Swift's other writings on corruptions in the language and on style more generally see also *Hints towards an Essay on Conversation* (first published 1763) and *A Complete Collection of Genteel and Ingenious Conversation* (1738), both in *Prose Works* IV, pp. 87–95, 99–201, 'On Corruptions of Style' (first published in *Tatler*, no. 230, 26 September 1710) and *A Letter to a Young Gentleman Lately Entered into Holy Orders* (1721), both in *Satires and Personal Writings*, ed. with

'an early example of Tory literary history' under 'the guise of a critique of language' in which the present pollution of both language and society can be rooted firmly in the turbulent years of the Civil War and the more licentious Restoration of Charles II.³ Swift's *Proposal* thus reveals itself to be not so much 'an attempt to reform language' as a means of commenting upon social and political decline.⁴ Swift does this, moreover, using a scrupulously crafted rhetoric of decay which literally re-enacts the fall of the English language upon the page. In the quotation given above, what becomes noticeable is how the reasonable and tentative Swift, who begins by balancing 'Corruptions' against 'Refinements' and who is modestly 'apt to doubt' about such matters, subtly becomes replaced by a far less hesitant spokesman who regards the Civil War and Interregnum as an unqualified 'Usurpation' and for whom the Restoration brings an outright disease upon 'Religion and Morals', a condition which then 'fell' (that most important rhetorical hinge) to affect the language. The sweep of Swift's chronology of corruption is irresistible as it becomes impossible to disentangle the inherent doubleness of his critique of social and linguistic ills.

Despite the fact that literary commentators commonly quote these lines from the *Proposal* in order to confirm how Swift lays the blame for the current decay of language and society solely upon the Interregnum, Swift himself clearly perceives the worst damage as having its epicentre not in the English Civil War but, more significantly and much more pervasively, in the Restoration.⁵ Indeed, Swift's chronicle of decay in the *Proposal* has its culmination not in the 'Usurpation' at all but, rather, in the reign of Charles II, Swift's linguistic criticisms subsequently being directed most emphatically against the supposed 'Refinements' of this period more than any other. It is 'the Poets, from the Time of the Restoration' whom Swift views as having 'contributed very much to the spoiling of the *English* Tongue', and it is Restoration wits and writers whom Swift explicitly castigates for having established the fashion for 'affected

---

an intro. and notes by William Alfred Eddy (London: 1932; repr. 1967), pp. 251–8, 269–93. For Swift's satire on 'Enthusiastick Jargon' see *A Discourse Concerning the Mechanical Operation of the Spirit* (1710), in *A Tale of a Tub and other Satires*, ed. with an intro. by Kathleen Williams (London: Dent, 1975), pp. 167–90 (pp. 182–3, 189).

   ³   Tony Crowley, 'The Return of the Repressed: Saussure and Swift on Language and History', in ed. George Wolf *New Departures in Linguistics* (New York and London: Garland, 1992), pp. 236–49 (pp. 244–5). For readings of Swift's *Proposal* in relation to Robert Harley (the Tory *'prime Minister'* to whom the tract is dedicated) and Swift's partisan politics, see Louis Landa's 'Introduction' to *Prose Works* IV, pp. x–xvi, and Ann Cline Kelly, *Swift and the English Language* (Philadelphia: University of Pennsylvania Press, 1988), pp. 89–103.

   ⁴   Crowley, 'Return of the Repressed', p. 243.

   ⁵   Critics often cite the English Civil War as Swift's sole focus of attack in the *Proposal*. See Crowley, 'Return of the Repressed', p. 244; Kelly, *Swift and the English Language*, pp. 60–2; J. Russell Perkin, 'Religion, Language, and Society: Swift's Anglican Writings', *English Studies in Canada* 15 (1989), 21–34 (p. 25).

Phrases, and new conceited Words', all of which (being the antiquated 'Product of Ignorance and Caprice') are 'now hardly intelligible'.[6] Ultimately, however, Swift asserts that the source of 'this Defect upon our Language' lies in the decadence of the Restoration Court. Because 'the Court of King *Charles* the Second' came to comprise those 'who had been altogether conversant in the Dialect of those *Fanatick Times*' (meaning the Civil War period), Swift bemoans how 'the *Court*, which used to be the Standard of Propriety, and Correctness of Speech, was then, and I think hath ever since continued the worst School in England for that Accomplishment'.[7] With the corrosion of this most important locus of linguistic (and most obviously political) authority, Swift can no longer trust 'illiterate Court-Fops, half-witted Poets, and University-Boys' with the improvement of the language. Instead, he advocates the establishment of an Academy to police linguistic innovation and eject verbal undesirables, one built upon those more sturdy pillars of Anglican Protestantism, 'the *Bible* and *Common-Prayer-Book* in the vulgar Tongue' which, through their '*Simplicity*', have 'proved a kind of Standard for Language, especially to the common People' over the past 'Hundred Years'.[8]

That the *Proposal* should finally become a critique of Restoration language and courtly corruption is, in one way, wholly unsurprising. After all, what Swift's treatise reflects and reinforces at this point is, quite simply, the popular and received view of the Restoration as one of the greatest (and therefore worst) periods of decadence in English history, particularly in relation to the Court. While it is the purpose of this essay to question such a casual reconstruction of the Restoration, nevertheless it is important to note how deeply embedded this vicious view of England under Charles II lies within the broader cultural imagination. In this respect, Swift's view of the reign of Charles II as a time when England's 'Religion and Morals' became infected with sexual and intellectual libertinism (from the King downwards, presumably), as well as with sectarian fanaticism, is wholly at one not only with contemporary accounts of the period but with most historical and literary renderings of it ever since. The high Tory Earl of Clarendon, for example, adopts the same language that we find in Swift's *Proposal* in his own rendition of the Restoration: following the 'total decay' of all order and social structures under Cromwell, post-1660 England is described as a diseased body into which 'corruptions' have been merely 'transplanted, instead of being extinguished'.[9] The Restoration is thus characterized as an era when all 'relations were confounded by the several sects in religion, which

---

6   Swift, *Proposal*, pp. 10–11.
7   Swift, *Proposal*, p. 10.
8   Swift, *Proposal*, pp. 14–15. For similar comments from Swift see *A Complete Collection of Genteel and Ingenious Conversation*, in *Prose Works* IV, pp. 108–9.
9   *Clarendon: Selections from The History of the Rebellion and The Life by Himself*, ed. G. Huehns, with an intro. by Hugh Trevor-Roper (Oxford: OUP, 1978), pp. 374–82 (pp. 381–2).

discountenanced all forms of reverence and respect', when 'young women conversed without any circumspection or modesty, and frequently met at taverns and common eating houses', and when the King himself 'unbent his mind from the knotty and ungrateful [. . .] business' of ruling the realm 'and indulged to his youth and appetite that license and satisfaction that it desired'. The 'time itself', Clarendon states, became 'educated in all the liberty of vice, without reprehension or restraint'.[10]

This is, of course, the Restoration that Macaulay was to reproduce in the nineteenth century and which still grips the imaginative and scholarly interests of novelists such as Rose Tremain and literary historians such as Roger Thompson (among many others) in the late twentieth century.[11] As Thompson himself puts it, 'The England of the Merry Monarch was a heyday for alcoholism, astrology, flogging, gambling, religious paranoia, persecution, and ritualised violence' (not to mention 'pornography, obscenity, and degraded bawdry'): 'The times', he states, 'were out of joint'.[12] The reign of Charles II is thus commonly typified by the kind of moral and religious decay that Swift is keen to emphasize, including a literary decadence which, Macaulay declares, left literature 'deeply tainted by the prevailing licentiousness' and poetry 'the pandar of every low desire'.[13] In the Restoration, 'the nation displayed an astonishing capacity for pleasure', Graham Parry tells us, 'unlike anything experienced before in England', the concept of 'pleasure', here, covering a broad spectrum of indulgences.[14] As early as 1667, in fact, the likes of Samuel Pepys can be found bewailing how 'the King and Court were never in the world so bad as they are now for gaming, swearing, whoring, and drinking, and the most abominable vices that ever were in the world – so that all must come to naught'.[15] In this context, Swift's focusing upon the Restoration

---

[10]   Clarendon, *History of the Great Rebellion*, pp. 378–81.

[11]   See Lord Macaulay, *The History of England from the Ascension of James the Second*, ed. Charles Harding Firth, 6 vols (London: Macmillan, 1913–15), I, pp. 160–5. Rose Tremain's novel *Restoration* (London: Hamish Hamilton, 1989) places great emphasis upon the period as one of sexual libertinism: 'The truth is that, when the King returned', Tremain's protagonist narrates punningly, 'it was as if self-discipline and drudgery had exploded in a clap of laughter. [. . .] Women were cheaper than claret, so I drank women. My thirst for them was, for a time, unquenchable. I tumbled them riotously. Two at a time, I longed to take them . . .' (p. 19).

[12]   Roger Thompson, *Unfit For Modest Ears: A Study of Pornographic, Obscene and Bawdy Works Written or Published in England in the Second Half of the Seventeenth Century* (London: Macmillan, 1979), pp. 214–15, 8–17.

[13]   Macaulay, *History of England*, p. 160.

[14]   Graham Parry, *The Seventeenth Century: The Intellectual and Cultural Context of English Literature, 1603–1700* (London: Longman, 1989), pp. 112–13.

[15]   *The Diary of Samuel Pepys*, eds Robert Latham and William Matthews, 11 vols (Berkeley and Los Angeles: University of California Press, 1970–83), VIII, 355 (27 July 1667), and cited in Stephen N. Zwicker, *Lines of Authority: Politics and English Literary Culture, 1649–1689* (Ithaca and London: Cornell University Press, 1993), p. 119. Zwicker has commented insightfully upon how criticism of Charles II in terms of sexual

as a time of great corruption in practically every sense is, even by the early eighteenth century, nothing less than conventional.

But Swift's choice of target is also unusual, here. That Swift assails the Restoration as the greatest source of linguistic and social abuse in his *Proposal* is not only odd in that he fails to take full advantage of an opportunity to disparage Civil War religious fanaticism (one of Swift's favourite topics) but because he neglects to mention the fact that the Restoration itself produced discourses upon the corruption and decay of the English language which were often much more comprehensive and more polemical than his own. This is evident, of course, in the ubiquity of satirical portraits of fops and town-gallants in Restoration literature whose affectations in clothing and manners are accompanied by matching pretensions in modish swearing and imported *bons mots*. Etherege's Sir Fopling Flutter and Vanbrugh's Lord Foppington (formerly Sir Novelty Fashion) are good examples of such verbal and cultural decadents.[16] At the same time, however, the endeavours of the newly created Royal Society (supported by many prominent reactionary Church of England divines) to establish a 'plain style' of language, scientific or otherwise, are not only prevalent throughout the Restoration but, more importantly, they have their roots in an overtly political desire to stabilize the restored monarchical regime through a distinctly Anglican hegemony, a project that Swift (even given his antipathy to the Royal Society) would wholly support.[17]

---

decadence and excess was firmly established in political satire as early as the mid-1660s. This satirical rendering of Charles and the Court draws, moreover, upon the imagery of 'abundance, liberality, and pleasure' with which the Restoration of the king was inscribed upon his return and in the early years of his reign. See Zwicker, *Lines of Authority*, pp. 35–6, and esp. Ch. 4 'The Politics of Pleasure', pp. 90–129. See also Parry, *The Seventeenth Century*, pp. 107–17, and Pepys's responses to public displays of vice in the following entries of his *Diary*: 1 July 1663, 13 July 1667, 30 July 1667, 1 June 1669, 27 June 1669 (all cited in Thompson, *Unfit for Modest Ears*, p. 17, fn. 44).

    16   These characters appear in Sir George Etherege's *The Man of Mode* (1676) and Sir John Vanbrugh's *The Relapse, or Virtue in Danger* (1696–7). For similar satirical portraits of modish swearers and language users in Restoration society see also Samuel Butler's *Characters*, ed. with an intro. by Charles W. Daves (Cleveland and London: The Press of Case Western Reserve University, 1970), especially the characters of 'A Prater' (pp. 138–9), 'A Complementer' (pp. 167–8), 'A Debauched Man' (pp. 191–2), 'An Affected Man' (p. 193), 'A Swearer' (pp. 202–3), 'A Flatterer' (pp. 238–9), 'A Court-Wit' (pp. 262–3), and 'The Modish Man' (p. 292).

    17   Swift's hostility to the Royal Society is, of course, infamously embodied in his description of the 'Academy of PROJECTORS in Lagado' in *Gulliver's Travels*, ed. Peter Dixon and John Chalker, with an intro. by Michael Foot (Harmondsworth: Penguin, 1967; repr. 1985), pp. 221–37. Central to Swift's satire of the Royal Society is his mocking of its various universal language projects (pp. 230–31), which is curious if only because Swift's *Proposal* has so much in common with them both politically and 'scientifically'. Not only must Swift admit to himself having turned 'Projector' in the *Proposal* but his assertions throughout parallel to a great extent Thomas Sprat's discourse on language and language reform in *The History of the Royal Society* (London: 1667). The latter pre-empts Swift's

But what seems even more curious about Swift's *Proposal* is that, in locating the corruption of the English language specifically in the Restoration, he lays the blame for such decay simultaneously upon two quite disparate groups: enthusiasts (a broad term of abuse for religious radicals and Nonconformists in the seventeenth century) and Court libertines. It is precisely this uncommon union of decadents and Dissenters in Restoration literature and culture that this essay aims to investigate. What Swift quite notably creates, in fact, is something of an unusual (if not an unholy) alliance between the 'Enthusiastick Jargon' of Nonconformists, on the one hand, and the language of Restoration foppery and licentiousness on the other, discourses which, it would seem, have very little in common whatsoever. After all, as the inheritors of a tradition most often referred to as 'Puritan', the strict and godly lifestyles of most Restoration Nonconformists (excluding those of radical antinomians like Lawrence Clarkson and Abiezer Coppe) could not be any further in terms of morality and religion (we can presume) from the legendary excesses of the Hobbist, atheist, materialist, free-thinking Court aristocrat.[18] This initial strangeness of Swift's combination of decadents with anti-decadents is, moreover, exacerbated by the fact that Restoration history, and literary history in particular, has conventionally (unlike Swift) separated these two parties. The canon of Restoration literature has traditionally been presented as reflecting the apparent cultural schizophrenia of

---

Proposal on practically every issue when it comes to the corruption of language, Sprat making the same historical connections as Swift in terms of the decline of empires and the effect of Civil War enthusiasm on the nation's tongue. Like Swift, Sprat outlines the need for an Academy which will regulate the language and, consequently, redeem the state through the hegemonic power of Church, monarch and Royal Society. On the politics of such schemes, see Brian Vickers, 'The Royal Society and English Prose Style: A Reassessment', in *Rhetoric and the Pursuit of Truth: Language Change in the Seventeenth and Eighteenth Centuries* (University of California, Los Angeles: William Andrews Clark Memorial Library, 1985), pp. 1–76, and Joel Reed, 'Restoration and Repression: The Language Projects of the Royal Society', *Studies in Eighteenth-Century Culture* 19 (1989), 399–412. On universal language schemes both within and beyond the Royal Society in the seventeenth century, see Vivian Salmon, *The Works of Francis Lodwick: A Study of his Writings in the Intellectual Context of the Seventeenth Century* (London: Longman, 1972); James Knowlson, *Universal Language Schemes in England and France, 1600–1800* (Toronto: University of Toronto Press, 1975); Umberto Eco, *The Search for the Perfect Language*, trans. by James Fentress (Oxford: Blackwell, 1995; repr. London: HarperCollins, 1997), pp. 228–68.

    [18] The actuality or historical veracity of the supposed excesses of Nonconformists and religious radicals in the seventeenth century is controversial given that, as is shown later in this essay, many dissenting groups were accused falsely of libertinism associated with antinomian Ranterism. On radical religious groups see Christopher Hill, *The World Turned Upside Down: Radical Ideas During the English Revolution* (Harmondsworth: Penguin, 1972; repr. 1991) and J. F. McGregor and B. Reay, *Radical Religion in the English Revolution* (Oxford: OUP, 1984). See also *A Collection of Ranter Writings from the 17th Century*, ed. with an intro. by Nigel Smith (London: Junction Books, 1983).

the period, one which encompasses the rumbustious wit of Restoration drama and satirical poetry at one extreme while, at the other, incorporating the pious writings and spiritual autobiographies of persecuted Dissenters. The literature of this age is typically characterized not only by decadence, therefore, but also by its distinct and irreconcilable opposite: the 'precise [. . .] Words' of Restoration divinity (both Anglican and Nonconformist) are set against a literary ethos of Restoration satirists, playwrights, and poets far more 'Bawdy in thoughts'.[19]

That Swift unites these broadly dichotomous aspects of Restoration culture in the *Proposal*, and that in this combination lies the crux of his attack on linguistic and social decay, may seem (to a modern reader at least) idiosyncratic of Swift if not downright eccentric. However, the reason why Swift deliberately makes this connection between aristocratic libertinism and religious enthusiasm is crucially important not only for an accurate reading of the *Proposal* and of Swift's view of English history in general but, more incisively, for an understanding of the complexity of Restoration literature, politics, and culture more broadly. What will be shown in this essay, in fact, is that Swift's dual identification of decadence within very different groups in Restoration language and society has its roots in a much older discourse about national decay, religious conscience, and the complex concept of 'liberty' (with all its ramifications) which is embedded within so much of the literature of the Restoration as a whole. It is this discourse which, as we shall see, links decadence with divinity and dissent.

In order to illustrate Swift's case, it is perhaps best to begin with two of the Restoration's most famous and most wildly different authors: John Wilmot, Earl of Rochester, Court poet and satirist, and John Bunyan, the Bedfordshire preacher and author of the Christian classic *The Pilgrim's Progress*. That these two writers share anything in common may seem incredible given that they are diametrically opposite in practically every sense – socially, theologically and (presumably) morally and spiritually too. But both can be said to represent fairly accurately Swift's two types of Restoration decadents. As a separating Independent or Congregationalist whose Nonconformist faith relied upon spiritual experience and whose language, as the prefaces to *Grace Abounding* and *The Pilgrim's Progress* both show, relies heavily upon Scriptural models, metaphors, and allegories, Bunyan was indeed considered 'fanatical' by his Anglican counterparts, such as Edward Fowler with whom Bunyan exchanged tracts in a brief doctrinal skirmish. Because of his Nonconformity, Bunyan's type of church and belief could easily be disparaged by his opponents as 'Enthusiastick' and his

---

[19]   These phrases (and hence the title of this essay) are taken from John Wilmot, Earl of Rochester's bawdy poem, 'On Mistress Willis' (line 17), in *The Poems of John Wilmot, Earl of Rochester*, ed. Keith Walker (Oxford: Blackwell, 1984; repr. 1988), pp. 44–5.

style as 'Jargon' or 'Cant'.[20] Equally, as one of the most notorious libertines of the Restoration, the Earl of Rochester hardly needs any qualification to be identified with Swift's decadent 'young Men' of Charles II's Court. Only 'after Buckingham', as one commentator states, is Rochester to be considered 'the most dissolute character of a dissolute age'.[21]

The utter disparity of these two writers' world-views is, moreover, worth dwelling upon, especially when it comes to the more conventional concept of Restoration decadence, the latter being defined here as moral, spiritual and bodily decay brought about through a fixed set of late seventeenth-century vices: drinking, fornication or whoring, swearing and irreligion. Again, Rochester's status as a Restoration libertine in these terms is far too infamous to warrant any introduction, the myths of his propensity for indulgence in all manner of sensuality and illicit consumption being inscribed not only within numerous biographies and apocryphal stories of the Earl but, moreover, in his own poetic presentations of himself. No matter how self-ironizing a poem like 'To the Post Boy' might finally be, nevertheless it presents a portrait of Rochester's decadence which is simultaneously laughable in its outrageousness and horrifying in its depravity. The power of such a poem, however, stems not only from cramming all Restoration vice into just sixteen lines but from the fact that the reader (as is the case with most Rochester poems) is left in doubt as to how to respond to it. We are fundamentally destabilized not by the amoral lifestyle of a Rochester looking for 'the Readyest way to Hell' but by a more profound uncertainty as to whether this account should be taken as historically accurate or just mythical and playful. Despite the fact that there is some biographical corroboration for such a portrait, nevertheless it is only with profound discomfort that we can contemplate the former option: confirming his decadent status by opening with profanities ('Son of A whore God dam you'), this poem's speaker recalls how he has 'out swilld Baccus', out sworn the 'furies', 'bravely' enjoyed his own cowardice, 'swived more whores more ways than Sodoms walls', threatened 'murder' over

---

[20] Bunyan's attack upon Edward Fowler's *The Design of Christianity* (London: 1671) and its doctrine of rational moralism in *A Defence of the Doctrine of Justification by Faith* (London: 1672) provoked the response of an author on Fowler's behalf in a tract entitled *Dirt Wipt Off* (London: 1672). In the latter, Bunyan is rebuked as 'a very Pestilent Schismatick' and his language the 'brutish barkings' of an 'Ignorant Fanatick' (pp. v, 2–3). For accounts of Bunyan's controversies with Fowler see T.L. Underwood, '"It pleased me much to contend": John Bunyan as Controversialist', *Church History* 57 (1988), 456–69; Isabel Rivers, 'Grace, Holiness, and the Pursuit of Happiness: Bunyan and Restoration Latitudinarianism', in ed. N. H. Keeble *John Bunyan: Conventicle and Parnassus, Tercentenary Essays* (Oxford: Clarendon Press, 1988), pp. 45–69, and *Reason, Grace, and Sentiment: Studies in the Language of Religion and Ethics in England, 1660–1780* (Cambridge: CUP, 1991).

[21] Richard Garnett, *The Age of Dryden* (1895), in *Rochester: The Critical Heritage*, ed. David Farley-Hills (New York: Barnes and Noble, 1972), p. 255.

'lust denyed', and 'blasphemed my god and libelld Kings'.[22] After blasphemy, libelling monarchs is clearly presented as an ironic anticlimax to what is otherwise a lengthy catalogue of damnable vices. Restoration decadence does not come more comprehensively or more forcefully than this.

Not surprisingly, the canon of Rochester's poems stands as a testimony to a libertinism which, as James Turner has pointed out, operates on many planes simultaneously.[23] On one level, Rochester's seems to be a purely and often grossly sensual liberation, a luxurious immersion in both alcoholism and sexual transgression that, in his works if not in his life, apparently knows no bounds. His poems have become infamous for consecrating a debauchery characterized by misogyny, licentiousness, and sodomy all couched within a language often obscene if not pornographic: '*Cupid*, and *Bacchus*, my Saints are' is the poet Rochester's essential motto, 'With *Wine*, I wash away my cares, /And then to *Cunt* again.'[24] Poems like 'The Disabled Debauchee' and 'The Imperfect Enjoyment' thus dwell upon lewdness in both subject and terminology, presenting an indulgence in sexual 'pleasure' the debt for which must often be paid with dissatisfaction or, as in 'A Ramble in Saint James's Park', despair.[25] Counterpart to such a poetry of excess, moreover, Rochester's libertinism is also clearly intellectual and philosophical, as evidenced in the Hobbist materialism and Senecan mortalism often recognized by commentators as lying behind poems like 'Upon Nothing', a mock encomium to the 'Great Negative' which effortlessly

---

[22] Rochester, *Poems*, p. 103. See also the poem 'Regime d'viver' (*Poems*, p. 130). Walker cites the 'Downs' affair' (in which a fellow rioter died in a skirmish with the watch from which Rochester had fled) as evidence for the historical veracity of the Earl's cowardice in 'To the Post-boy' (*Poems*, pp. 292–3). Equally, there are many accounts which concur with this image of Rochester's violence, infidelity, craven behaviour, drunkenness and lechery, but many seem to remain factually 'hazy' with 'little reliable information' available (*The Letters of John Wilmot, Earl of Rochester*, ed. Jeremy Treglown (Oxford: Blackwell, 1980), pp. 18–20, 26–28, 55). Jeremy Lamb's biography revels in Rochester's reputation (explaining the Earl's behaviour in terms of alcoholism) but there is nevertheless a distinct absence of documentary evidence within it beyond what appears to be apocryphal: *So Idle a Rogue: The Life and Death of Lord Rochester* (London: Allison and Busby, 1993), pp. 116–22, 159–61, 164–5, 176–7, 193–5.

[23] James G. Turner, 'The Properties of Libertinism', *Eighteenth-Century Life* 9 (1985), special issue on 'Unauthorized Sexual Behaviour during the Enlightenment', ed. Robert P. Maccubbin, 75–87.

[24] Rochester, 'Upon his Drinking a Bowl' (lines 21–24), in *Poems*, p. 38.

[25] Rochester, *Poems*, pp. 97–9, 30–2, 64–8. For readings of Rochester's sexual libertinism and misogyny see Warren Chernaik, *Sexual Freedom in Restoration Literature* (Cambridge: CUP, 1995), pp. 1–115; Reba Wilcoxon, 'Rochester's Sexual Politics', *Studies in Eighteenth-Century Culture* 8 (1979), 137–49; Sarah Wintle, 'Libertinism and Sexual Politics', in *Spirit of Wit: Reconsiderations of Rochester*, ed. Jeremy Treglown (Oxford: Blackwell, 1982), pp. 133–65. For an extremely intelligent essay on Rochester's swearing and profanity see David Trotter, 'Wanton Expressions', in *Spirit of Wit*, pp. 111–32. On Rochester and alcohol see Lamb, *So Idle a Rogue*, pp. 20–25, 85–8, 109–10, 182–6, and J.D. Patterson, 'Rochester's Second Bottle', *Restoration*, 5 (1981), 6–15.

combines atheistic pessimism with bawdy innuendo and socio-political nihilism: in the empty universe of this poem, 'Brittish policy', 'Kings promises, and Whors vowes', all equally are 'nothing'.[26]

But just as Rochester's poems embody an apparently undeniable decadence, so too has his life been appropriated (fairly or unfairly) as a moral example of decay *par excellence*. Samuel Johnson's account of Rochester, for example, is so emphatic about the downward spiral into which such a degenerate lifestyle plunges that, in describing it, Johnson's prose is in itself obliged to helter-skelter towards the Earl's final and premature demise:

> Thus in a course of drunken gaiety and gross sensuality, with intervals of study perhaps yet more criminal, with an avowed contempt of all decency and order, a total disregard to every moral, and a resolute denial of every religious obligation, he lived worthless and useless, and blazed out his youth and his health in lavish voluptuousness, till, at the age of one and thirty, he had exhausted the fund of life, and reduced himself to a state of weakness and decay.[27]

As Gilbert Burnet's original biography *Some Passages of the Life and Death of Rochester* (1680) similarly concurs, Rochester's life (even so soon after his death) would prove useful as a warning to other decadents seeking a similar moral bankruptcy, especially those who may not get the opportunity, as Rochester did, of undergoing a death-bed repentance and last-minute conversion to something like a full-blooded Anglican moralism.[28]

John Wilmot's notorious life and decline could hardly be in starker contrast to that of John Bunyan: no such inverse example can be made of Bunyan's

---

26   Rochester, 'Upon Nothing' (lines 46–50), in *Poems*, pp. 62–4. For further evidence of Rochester's philosophical libertinism, see also Rochester's translation of a chorus from Seneca's *Troades* (in *Poems*, p. 51) and his evident interest in Charles Blount's theological scepticism (*Letters*, pp. 206–16, 234–41). On Rochester and Hobbesian philosophical thinking see Chernaik, *Sexual Freedom in Restoration Literature*, pp. 22–51; Marianne Thormälen, *Rochester: The Poems in Context* (Cambridge : CUP, 1993), pp. 141–6, 174–9; Vivian de Sola Pinto, *Enthusiast in Wit: A Portrait of John Wilmot, Earl of Rochester, 1647–1680* (London: Routledge and Kegan Paul, 1962), pp. 22–31; Dustin H. Griffin, *Satires Against Man: The Poems of Rochester* (Berkeley, Los Angeles and London: University of California Press, 1973), pp. 156–96, 260–88.

27   Samuel Johnson, *Lives of the English Poets* (1779), in *Rochester: The Critical Heritage*, p. 204.

28   Gilbert Burnet, *Some Passages of the Life and Death of Rochester* (1680), in *Rochester: The Critical Heritage*, pp. 47–92. For further evidence of Rochester's death-bed repentance see also *Letters*, pp. 35–7, 244–6. Christian dogma of any particular creed is, it seems, largely absent from Rochester's conversion and is, perhaps, less dramatic than Burnet's self-serving account purports. Bunyan would not have regarded it as a conversion at all, or an ineffectual one at best.

biography which is throughout, it would seem, wholly temperate, pious and faithful in all senses of the word. Despite the fact that Bunyan refers to himself autobiographically (along with many other Puritans and Nonconformists) as the 'Chief of Sinners', this self-nomination must be understood as more theological than anything else: there is little in Bunyan's life, even before grace abounded, that really justifies a title seemingly so extravagant and certainly more befitting of Rochester.[29] For this reason, a text like *Grace Abounding to the Chief of Sinners* (1666) is profoundly disappointing for any reader with prurient or spiritually spectacular interests in mind: the sins that the pre-converted Bunyan commits largely involve youthful bouts of swearing and cursing, playing at a game of 'Cat' on a Sunday, and bell-ringing, such crimes bearing a solemnity comprehensible only in the doctrinal terms of law and grace framing Bunyan's conversion narrative as whole.[30]

Because Bunyan's aim as a writer and preacher is solely evangelical, it is hardly surprising that, particularly from his 'Puritan' perspective, he is wholly condemnatory of the kind of licentious excesses that characterize the life and writings of Rochester. Throughout Bunyan's works he warns against the 'enormities' of 'Fornications, Adulteries, Lasciviousness, Murders, Deceit, &c.',

---

[29]   Robert Parson's *A Sermon preached at the Earl of Rochester's Funeral* (1680) refers to Rochester at one point as once being 'one of the greatest of Sinners', in *Rochester: The Critical Heritage*, p. 46. Vera Camden points out how delicate Bunyan's position is when it comes to being 'Chief of Sinners', as Bunyan must 'make the extent of his sin extreme enough to cover the worst sinner, while broad and indistinct enough to protect his reputation from the kind of character assault he will later experience in life': 'Blasphemy and the Problem of the Self', *Bunyan Studies: John Bunyan and his Times* 1 (1989), 5–21 (p. 14). While Macaulay understands the title 'Chief of Sinners' in its 'theological' rather than its 'popular sense' (Thomas Babington Macaulay, 'John Bunyan', in *Critical and Historical Essays*, 2 vols, ed. A.J. Grieve (London: J.M. Dent, 1907), II, pp. 399–410 (pp. 405–6), many other commentators find Bunyan's self-nomination simply an incredible exaggeration and an unoriginal one at that. See Margaret Bottrall, *Every Man a Phoenix: Studies in Seventeenth Century Autobiography* (London: John Murray, 1958), p. 85; Henri Talon, *John Bunyan: The Man and his Works*, trans. Barbara Wall (London: Rockliff Publishing, 1951; first pub. in French, 1948), p. 20; Barrett John Mandel, 'Bunyan and the Autobiographer's Artistic Purpose', *Criticism* 10 (1968), 225–43 (p. 237). Alternative self-confessed 'Chiefs of Sinners' include Oliver Cromwell, the Ranters Abiezer Coppe and Laurence Clarkson, Richard Norwood, Anna Trapnel, and Mris Sarah Wight. For others, see Mandel, 'Bunyan and the Autobiographer's Artistic Purpose', p. 237, fn. 34.

[30]   John Bunyan, *Grace Abounding to the Chief of Sinners*, ed. Roger Sharrock (Oxford: Clarendon Press, 1962), pp. 9–14. For a useful discussion of sin and legalism in *Grace Abounding*, see Dayton Haskin, 'Bunyan, Luther, and the Struggle with Belatedness in Grace Abounding', *University of Toronto Quarterly* 50 (1980–81), 300–313 (p. 306). On the theological significance of the title 'Chief of Sinners' see Margaret Olofson Thickstun, 'The Preface to Bunyan's Grace Abounding as Pauline Epistle', *Notes and Queries*, n.s. 32 (1985), 180–2; Rebecca S. Beal, 'Grace Abounding to the Chief of Sinners: John Bunyan's Pauline Epistle', *Studies in English Language* 21 (1981), 147–60.

The Pilgrim's Progress alone providing ample examples of the need for chastity, temperance and unworldly desires.[31] The danger in Faithful's encounter with Madam Wanton's 'flattering tongue' is, for instance, communicated by a sexual punning that is difficult to overlook: 'she lay at me hard to turn aside with her, promising me', he says, 'all carnal and fleshly content'.[32] In a similar way, Standfast of *The Pilgrim's Progress, Part II* is importuned by 'this vain World' appearing in the shape of the old hag Madam Bubble who offers him 'her *Body*, her *Purse*, and her *Bed*'.[33] Hence, the carnal matters that Rochester celebrates so darkly in his poetry can present for Bunyan only the most serious obstacles in the way of one's salvation. It is the duty of every Christian pastor, parent and employer to ensure order and godliness in households and communities, keeping children and servants especially 'temperate in all things, in Apparel, in Language' and away from 'ungodly, prophane, or heretical Books or Discourse', rebuking 'vice' in them 'that they be not Gluttons, nor Drunkards', nor 'carry themselves foolishly towards each other'.[34]

Bunyan's most sustained attack on Restoration decadence comes in *The Life and Death of Mr. Badman* (1680), a book-length diatribe against practically every form of sinfulness imaginable. Mr Badman himself is depicted as a womanizing whoremonger and adulterer, a shopkeeper who deals in false measures and weights, an outright drunkard, an inveterate swearer, and an atheist who regards the Scriptures as a catalogue of 'a thousand impossibilities' and 'the cause of all dissensions and discords that are in the Land'.[35] Badman's reprobate life thus provides a useful platform from which Bunyan's narrators, Attentive and Wiseman, can discuss a broad array of corruptions (social, moral, spiritual and physical) which are currently afflicting not only individual souls but, ultimately, the entire nation. While Bunyan can bewail the injustice of corrupt 'Hucksters', the kind of tradesmen who 'gripeth and grindeth in the face of the poor' and who 'destroy the poor because he is poor', the social critique of Badman as a whole is framed by an ominous feeling of impending judgement upon Restoration England in a broader sense.[36] The 'open way of Lying, Swearing, Drinking and Whoring' adopted by Badman and his multifarious 'Friends and Associates' is, Bunyan warns, 'like to drown our English world'. 'O Debauchery, Debauchery, what hast thou done in *England*!', Bunyan cries here, 'Thou hast corrupted our Young men, and hast made our Old men beasts; thou hast deflowered Virgins, and hast made

---

[31]   John Bunyan, *Christian Behaviour* (1663), in *The Miscellaneous Works of John Bunyan*, 13 vols, III, ed. J. Sears McGee (Oxford: Clarendon Press, 1987), p. 47.

[32]   John Bunyan, *The Pilgrim's Progress*, ed. with an intro. by N.H. Keeble (Oxford: OUP, 1984), pp. 56–7.

[33]   Bunyan, *The Pilgrim's Progress*, p. 252.

[34]   Bunyan, *Christian Behaviour*, pp. 23–6.

[35]   John Bunyan, *The Life and Death of Mr. Badman*, ed. James F. Forrest and Roger Sharrock (Oxford: Clarendon Press, 1988), pp. 127–8.

[36]   Bunyan, *Badman*, p. 109.

Matrons Bawds.' Such sin has lead to 'a swallowing up of a Nation, sinking of a Nation, and bringing its Inhabitants to temporal, spiritual, and eternal ruine'.[37] Hostility towards Restoration decadence does not come much more comprehensive or more forceful than this.

When it comes to decay, then, the works of Rochester and Bunyan are indisputably on different sides of a clearly divided literary and moral culture. In fact, one might even go as far to say that both Rochester and Bunyan's reprobate Mr Badman have come equally to exemplify the licentiousness of the Restoration, the latter being (in many respects, it seems) but a lower-class and far less glamorous version of the former. It is a curious coincidence, moreover, that 1680 should see the simultaneous publication of the lives and deaths of these two notorious libertines, both accounts illustrating the decay of their protagonists towards an all-important death-bed scene and both more broadly aiming to save the nation from ruin and corruption: 'by their Debaucheries', moralizes Gilbert Burnet in his *Life and Death of Rochester*, what 'Mischiefs' and 'Diseases' have 'our Libertines' 'brought on themselves and others by them'. Like Bunyan, Burnet too regards the effect of 'Intemperance and Lewdness' upon 'the whole Nation' as 'all too visible': 'how the Bonds of Nature, Wedlock, and all other Relations, are quite broken', he comments, 'Vertue is thought an Antick Piece of Formality, and Religion the effect of Cowardice or Knavery'. Like Badman's, the stinking names of such unrepentant decadents are 'the Scorn of the present Age' and they will 'rot in the next'.[38]

However, despite such obvious differences between Bunyan and Rochester, what they do have in common is fundamentally to do with decadence nonetheless and on a number of important levels. For example, Burnet's closing discourse against libertinism in his *Life and Death of Rochester*, though apparently directed only towards the likes of the Earl, could also be applied quite easily to religious sectarians and Independents in the Restoration. The word 'libertine' itself was used (like most terms of abuse in the period) in a very broad sense, one that could encompass intellectual and aristocratic libertinism on the one hand and radical religious libertinism on the other. Both types provide a useful vocabulary for Anglican polemicists to bewail, as Burnet does, the decay of the nation: rakes and Ranters share, it would seem, a propensity to blaspheme and indulge in antinomian and antisocial excesses, particularly in terms of sexual promiscuity. Hence, Anglican divines like Edward Stillingfleet, Joseph Glanvil, and Richard Allestree (among others) could denounce enthusiastic '*Sects, and Jovial Atheists*' in the same vitriolic sweep: rakes are but '*Zealots*' in wickedness' and '*Atheist*' libertines are but '*Fanaticks* [. . .] in Politicks; more traytorous than our mad

---

[37] Bunyan, *Badman*, pp. 1–2, 7–8.
[38] Burnet, in *Rochester: The Critical Heritage*, pp. 88–9. See also Bunyan, *Badman*, p. 149.

Enthusiasts, or the Canons of the Popish *Councils*'.[39] Equally, one of the most popular ways of denouncing Nonconformists and separatists like Bunyan was to accuse their churches of being little more than havens of all manner of vice and sexual licentiousness.[40] In this way, Nonconformists and Dissenters could be vilified as being no better than either radical Civil War sects (like the legendary Ranters) or infamous libertines like Rochester. Given such evident hostility and the ever-present threat of accusations about carnal hypocrisy, it is not surprising that Bunyan himself is so vehemently uncompromising about matters of lust and 'uncleanness'. As a matter of polity, it became imperative for Bunyan to protect the reputations of himself and his Church from any damaging sexual slanders.[41]

But it is precisely the marginalized, despised and persecuted status of Restoration Nonconformists that also links the likes of Bunyan and Rochester in a more broadly political sense. In fact, the kind of sexual decadence of which sectarians were often accused can be seen as but one aspect of the greater threat to social and civil order that Nonconformists like Bunyan were, both rhetorically and actually, often regarded as presenting to Restoration society. This fear is most

---

[39] Turner, 'Properties of Libertinism', pp. 78–80. Joseph Glanvil, *An Apology and Advice for some of the Clergy* (1674), p. 4, and Edward Stillingfleet, *Works* (1710), I, p. 245, both cited in Trotter, 'Wanton Expressions', pp. 127, 115–117. Richard Allestree, 'Sermon X', in *Eighteen Sermons* (1669), p. 179, cited in Gillian Manning, 'Rochester's Satyr Against Reason and Mankind and Contemporary Religious Debate', *Seventeenth Century*, 8 (1993), 99–121 (p. 109). See also J.G.A. Pocock, 'Within the margins: the definitions of orthodoxy', in *The Margins of Orthodoxy: Heterodox Writing and Cultural Response, 1660–1750*, ed. Roger D. Lund (Cambridge: Cambridge University Press, 1995), pp. 33–53. Christopher Hill characteristically finds 'Ranterish' parallels in both Rochester's and Mr Badman's libertinism: see, 'John Wilmot, Earl of Rochester (1647–1680)', *The Collected Essays of Christopher Hill*, 3 vols, I (Brighton: Harvester Press, 1985), pp. 298–316 (pp. 302–5), and Christopher Hill, *A Turbulent, Seditious, and Factious People* (Oxford: OUP, 1988; repr. 1989), pp. 232–3.

[40] See, for example, Thompson, *Unfit for Modest Ears*, Ch. 4 (on 'Anti-Puritanical' bawdy literature and attacks on dissent), pp. 40–56. Swift is, naturally, keen to promote such associations of enthusiasm with sexual libertinism: see *A Discourse Concerning the Mechanical Operation of the Spirit*, in *A Tale of a Tub*, pp. 184–5, 188–9. This is not a phenomenon limited to the Restoration, however. Radical sects during the Civil War period also had to defend themselves against sexual slanders as in Gerrard Winstanley's defence of the Diggers in his *Vindication* against accusations of the *Excessive Community of Women, Called Ranting* (1649).

[41] See, for example, Bunyan's vehement denials of adultery and fornication (presumably influenced by gossip about his supposedly illicit relationship with Agnes Beaumont, a member of the Bedford Church) appended to *Grace Abounding* from the fifth edition onwards (pp. 92–5, paragraphs 306–17). Agnes Beaumont's account of events leading to such rumours, *The Narrative of the Persecution of Agnes Beaumont* (first published in 1760) is usefully reprinted in *Grace Abounding with other Spiritual Autobiographies*, ed. with an intro. and notes by John Stachniewski with Anita Pacheco (Oxford: OUP, 1998), pp. 191–224. For an excellent reading of Bunyan's attitude to female sexuality within its political context see Tamsin Spargo, *The Writing of John Bunyan* (Aldershot: Ashgate, 1997), pp. 68–95.

evident, of course, in the writings of Anglican divines like Samuel Parker whose works articulate a loathing of Nonconformity and Dissent which (although extreme in Parker's case) exemplify an apparently widespread concern over the nation's safety where religious radicals, Independents and Presbyterians are concerned. According to Parker, the Nonconformist masses are 'a Wild and Fanatique Rabble' of 'Brain-Sick People' whose mindless zeal represents the foremost threat to civil peace in Restoration England: such members of the community are seditious and factious indeed ('the rudest and most barbarous people in the world'), whose aim is to 'blow up the very Foundations of Government' and bring the country into ruin and chaos.[42] Parker's mission is to rid the nation of such a corrupting infection, to 'lance' the 'Tumour' that such uncivil people constitute.[43]

In voicing such sentiments, Parker was not alone: John Tillotson, Joseph Glanvil, Thomas Sprat, Simon Patrick, Edward Stillingfleet, all are prominent Restoration Anglican divines who published treatises voicing concerns over the decay of society and civil order that Nonconformists, with their radical religious beliefs and their barbarous 'Cant' of spiritualized jargon, came to represent.[44] In fact, attacking Nonconformist language was a particularly popular way of presenting separatists like Bunyan as dangerous and extreme fanatics in the Restoration, with Samuel Parker calling for an Act of Parliament, no less, to put a stop to the 'slovenly Similitudes', 'wanton and lascivious Allegories', and 'phantastick Phrases' used by the 'ignorant Rabble' of Nonconformists in their 'Scripture-Expressions': such a measure would, Parker believes, 'be an effectual Cure of all our present Distempers' while putting a stop to a language which is but the verbal counterpart to affective face-pulling.[45] In the light of such a tradition, Swift's *Proposal for Correcting, Improving and Ascertaining the English Tongue* thus comes (though Swift does not acknowledge it) from the

---

[42]   Samuel Parker, *A Discourse of Ecclesiastical Politie* (London: 1670), pp. iv, xii–xiii.

[43]   Parker, *A Discourse of Ecclesiastical Politie*, p. x. For an account of Parker's life and writings see Gordon Schochet, 'Between Lambeth and Leviathan: Samuel Parker on the Church of England and political order', in *Political Discourse in Early Modern Britain*, eds Nicholas Phillipson and Quentin Skinner (Cambridge: Cambridge University Press, 1993), pp. 189–208, and 'Samuel Parker, Religious Diversity, and the Ideology of Persecution', in *Margins of Orthodoxy*, pp. 199–48.

[44]   For accounts of the polemical writings of these Church of England men see Richard Ashcraft, 'Latitudinarianism and Toleration: Historical Myth versus Political History', in *Philosophy, science, and religion in England, 1640–1700*, eds Richard Kroll, Richard Ashcraft and Perez Zagorin (Cambridge: Cambridge University Press, 1992), pp. 151–77; John Spurr, '"Rational Religion" in Restoration England', *Journal of the History of Ideas* 49 (1988), 563–85, and '"Latitudinarianism" and the Restoration Church', *Historical Journal* 31 (1988), 61–82.

[45]   Parker, *A Discourse of Ecclesiastical Politie*, pp. 71–7 (pp. 75–6).

soundest stock in Anglican polemics imaginable.[46] It is in the vein of such a condemnatory discourse, moreover, that Bunyan himself, despite an avowed and frequently stated political quietism and a conscious distancing of his beliefs from those of radical sects like Ranters and Quakers, became accused of enthusiastic fanaticism. As already noted, Bunyan's controversial skirmishes with the Anglican Edward Fowler left him slandered as 'a most Black-mouth'd Calumniator', 'as rank and Ranting an Antinomian as ever foul'd paper', 'a shameless abuser and perverter of holy Scriptures', and a promoter of 'filthy libertinism and mad licentious principles'.[47]

On one level, such extreme responses to heterodox religious practices in the Restoration can be understood in terms of a general reaction to what Swift refers to as the 'Usurpation'. The 'long eighteenth century' will never be comprehensible, one historian asserts, 'if we do not understand that it lived with the memory of the civil wars as the nightmare from which it was struggling to awake, or if you prefer, to go to sleep again.'[48] On a more specific level, however, the polemical diatribes against 'enthusiasm' and Nonconformity by divines like Parker are also, if not wholly, reactions to political crises and issues particular to the Restoration itself. The works of many Anglicans condemning Nonconformity appear, for instance, not arbitrarily but in response to an ongoing and quite specific debate on the matter of toleration and indulgence for Protestant Dissenters and separatists, one that has its troublesome roots in Charles II's Declaration of Breda (which, made just prior to his Restoration, involved a promise to ensure religious toleration) and which closes (though not entirely) with the Glorious Revolution of 1689. As a critical issue which dominated the Restoration from beginning to end, toleration for Nonconformists (being the freedom to worship separately from the Church of England) became, in fact, one of the central political questions of the whole period, claims for liberty of conscience being, as Gary S. De Krey has recently put it, 'the most important intellectual source of the long-term, continuing instability of the Restoration polity'.[49]

---

[46]   On the issue of Anglican 'plain style' and Nonconformist language in the Restoration see Vickers, 'The Royal Society and English Prose Style', pp. 5–7, 46–52; Roger Pooley, 'Language and Loyalty: Plain Style at the Restoration', *Literature and History* 6 (1980), 2–18; N.H. Keeble, *The Literary Culture of Nonconformity in Later Seventeenth-Century England* (Leicester: Leicester University Press, 1987), pp. 240–62; Harold Fisch, 'The Puritans and the Reform of Prose Style', *ELH* 19 (1952), 229–48.

[47]   *Dirt Wipt Off*, pp. 2–3, 17, 40, 71.

[48]   Pocock, 'Within the margins', p. 38

[49]   Gary S. De Krey, 'Reformation in the Restoration Crisis, 1679–1682', in *Religion, Literature, and Politics in Post-Reformation England, 1540–1688*, eds Donna B. Hamilton and Richard Strier (Cambridge: Cambridge University Press, 1996), pp. 231–52 (p. 247). Calling for toleration (the right for non-Anglicans to worship freely) was, it must be remembered, different from demanding political or civil rights. This is especially important to note in terms of the Restoration Test Acts which barred anyone refusing to

The reasons why indulgence of Dissenters became so crucial in the Restoration are, of course, obvious. From an Anglican perspective, Nonconformists and their conventicles are to be suspected as treasonous, a remainder and a reminder of the worst Civil War sectarianism, and hence a threat to the greater 'liberty' of a nation ruled through monarch and church. 'Indulgence and Toleration is the most absolute sort of Anarchy', Samuel Parker could claim, as 'Princes may with less hazard give Liberty to mens Vices and Debaucheries, than to their Consciences.'[50] The Anglican response to Nonconformity was thus to pursue a policy of coercion to persuade Dissenters forcibly to conform to the Church of England, the failure of which would justify a policy of persecution through which Nonconformists could be imprisoned (or even executed) and their goods and property seized.[51] It was through the harsh implementation of persecutory policies by the Cavalier Parliament (especially in terms of the Clarendon Code, a series of punitive Parliamentary Acts devised to limit Nonconformists' freedom to gather and worship) that Bunyan himself was imprisoned in Bedford gaol for twelve years.[52] In opposition to this, Protestant

take the oath of allegiance to the Established Church from holding political office, university positions, and so on. Dissenters sought freedom to worship but (as Protestants) could equally oppose policies which would grant Catholics as well as Protestant Nonconformists political rights. Indeed, many Protestant Nonconformists were ambivalent towards (if not opposed to) toleration that granted freedom of worship and political rights to Catholics too. The hysteria surrounding the Popish Plot suggests this amply. This paradoxical conflict of interests is especially prominent in the Exclusion Crisis towards the close of the 1670s, with the likelihood of a Catholic James II succeeding Charles, as well as in the Glorious Revolution of 1689. For further reflections on this situation, see Gordon J. Schochet, 'From Persecution to "Toleration"', in ed. J.R. Jones *Liberty Secured? Britain Before and After 1688* (Stanford: Stanford University Press, 1992), pp. 122–57; John Spurr, 'Religion in Restoration England', in ed. Lionel K.J. Glassey *The Reigns of Charles II and James VII & II* (London: Macmillan, 1997), pp. 90–124; Richard Greaves, 'Conventicles, Sedition, and the Toleration Act of 1689', *Eighteenth-Century Life* 12, n. s. (1988), 1–13, and reprinted in Richard Greaves, *John Bunyan and English Nonconformity* (London: Hambledon Press, 1992), pp. 207–22. I would like to thank Bill Myers for reminding me of such important distinctions.

   [50]   Parker, *A Discourse of Ecclesiastical Politie*, pp. liv–lv.
   [51]   On Anglican justifications for coercion and persecution of Nonconformists see especially Mark Goldie, 'The Theory of Religious Intolerance in Restoration England', in *From Persecution to Toleration: The Glorious Revolution and Religion in England*, eds Ole Peter Grell, Jonathan I. Israel, and Nicolas Tyacke (Oxford: Clarendon Press, 1991), pp. 331–68.
   [52]   The 'Clarendon Code' was introduced by Charles II's first minister, Edward Hyde, Earl of Clarendon, during the early 1660s comprising a number of Acts of Parliament clearly persecutory of Nonconformists and in direct opposition to the King's promises for liberty of conscience in the Declaration of Breda. For a basic account of persecution under Clarendon see Michael R. Watts, *The Dissenters: From the Reformation to the French Revolution* (Oxford: Clarendon Press, 1978; repr. 1985), pp. 221–43; Schochet, 'From Persecution to "Toleration"'. Bunyan remained in prison during the implementation of the 'Clarendon Code' having been arrested before its introduction in

Nonconformists like John Owen and their political spokespersons like Andrew Marvell (among many others) would argue in many different ways the case for a need to tolerate dissent.[53] Again, these arguments for indulgence often involved a call for 'liberty', albeit in a sense quite different from that defended by Anglicans like Parker and, ultimately, Swift.[54]

Although such groups adopt the same rhetoric of 'liberty' and 'reason' either to defend or denounce the persecution of Nonconformists, the divisions here are nevertheless quite clear: we have Protestant Nonconformists, often supported by those who were to become known as Whigs, on the one side and Anglicans, who were also to become known as Tories, on the other. This divisive situation over toleration becomes more complicated, however, when it comes to King Charles II and the Court. Despite the fact that the Restoration saw one of the most brutal regimes of religious persecution in English history, Charles II himself apparently (or perhaps ironically) pursued policies for promoting toleration for Nonconformists of all religious hues. It is for this reason that there is no unambiguous relationship between either Crown and Church or monarch and Parliament during the first fifteen years or so of Charles's restored reign: in opposition to the Cavalier Parliament and the arch-Tory first minister Clarendon, Charles deemed to dally with a long-term political interest in toleration. This interest is revealed in the king's publicly-stated intentions up to, at least, the mid-1670s: in the Declaration of Breda (1660), Charles promised liberty of conscience to all peaceful Christians upon his Restoration as monarch, a vow thwarted by the Cavalier Parliament and the Clarendon Code up to 1667, but renewed under the 'Cabal' ministry of 1667–73 through pro-tolerationist Ministers like Shaftesbury and Buckingham, culminating in a monarchical Declaration of Indulgence for all Nonconformists in 1672.[55] It was under this short-lived Indulgence (Charles being forced to renounce it the following year because it was unconstitutional, the king having declared it according to the

---

1660 under an old Elizabethan Act against Nonconformity (35 Eliz., c. i): *Grace Abounding*, ed. Sharrock, pp. xxii–xxvii, and *A Relation of My Imprisonment* (first published 1765), in *Grace Abounding*, pp. 104–31.

[53] For an excellent account of cases for liberty of conscience in the Restoration see Gary S. De Krey, 'Rethinking the Restoration: Dissenting cases for Conscience, 1667-1672', *Historical Journal* 38 (1995), 53–83.

[54] Swift, we should remember, presents himself emphatically as a defender of Protestant (Anglican) freedom: 'Fair LIBERTY was all his cry', he writes in 'Verses on the Death of Doctor Swift, D.S.P.D.', l. 351, in *The Complete Poems*, ed. Pat Rogers (Harmondsworth: Penguin, 1983; repr. 1989), pp. 485–98 (p. 494). For an excellent discussion of 'liberty' in the Restoration, see Tim Harris, '"Lives, Liberties, and Estates": Rhetorics of Liberty in the Reign of Charles II', in eds Tim Harris, Paul Seaward, and Mark Goldie *The Politics of Religion in Restoration England* (Oxford: Blackwell, 1990), pp. 217–41.

[55] See Watts, *Dissenters*, pp. 221–62; J.R. Jones, *Charles II: Royal Politician* (London: Allen and Unwin, 1987), pp. 43–50, 56–9, 79–107;

Royal Prerogative and without Parliament's consent) that Bunyan was finally released from prison.

This royal interest in toleration is not, of course, without complications. It can be argued that Charles II's commitment to indulgence was always uncertain, to say the least, not to mention motivated by far from libertarian concerns: it is often mooted that Charles pursued a policy of toleration only as a wartime necessity, or to establish an absolutism through the Royal Prerogative, to limit the Anglican Parliament's powers, or to provide political space for his own latent Roman Catholicism (he promised the French monarch Louis XIV that he would declare himself Roman Catholic in return for French war funds).[56] Ronald Hutton, one of Charles II's most recent biographers, can barely believe that the king was interested in toleration at all. Certainly after 1675, when Charles no longer had any political need for or interest in toleration, he advocated a regime of persecution more vigorous than ever, switching his allegiances to a pro-Anglican policy of intolerance (especially in the light of the so-called Popish Plot).[57] But despite all of these problems, what is nevertheless indisputable is that, for a time at least (particularly 1667–73, the period both of the Cabal ministry and of what De Krey refers to as the Restoration 'crisis over conscience'), something of an unholy alliance was indeed forged in Restoration culture and politics between Nonconformists and the Court.[58] It is thus upon the politics of the early to mid-1670s that this essay focuses because this is the time in which debates over toleration became most ferocious and politically onerous, marking in particular Charles II's most active participation in advocating toleration. It is important to note that this is also the period in which Rochester's most important satires were being circulated in manuscript and in which Bunyan's most famous work, *The Pilgrim's Progress*, ostensibly has its genesis.[59] It is, then, in the early 1670s that, as is implied in Swift's *Proposal*, the ambitions of 'enthusiasts' for a particular

[56] See, for example, Spurr, 'Religion in Restoration England', pp. 93–4; Watts, *Dissenters*, pp. 247–9; Ronald Hutton is particularly sceptical about Charles II's commitment to toleration in *Charles the Second: King of England, Scotland, and Ireland* (Oxford: Clarendon Press, 1989), pp. 201–2, 210–12, 266–7, 274, 284–5, 306, 455–7; John Miller is also cautious about such matters in *Charles II* (London: Weidenfield and Nicolson, 1991), pp. 55–7, 99–101, 135–41, 154–7, 165–6, 188–92, 203–5.

[57] See especially Hutton, *Charles the Second*, pp. 306, 334, 399–400, 424.

[58] For the idea of 1667–73 being a period of crisis over conscience, see De Krey, 'Rethinking the Restoration', and Richard L. Greaves, '"Let Truth be Free": John Bunyan and the Restoration Crisis of 1667–73', *Albion* 28 (1996), 587–605.

[59] On the dating of Rochester's poems see David M. Vieth, *Attribution in Restoration Poetry: A Study of Rochester's Poems of 1680* (New Haven: Yale University Press, 1963), and Walker's notes on the dates of 'Tunbridge Wells' and 'Satyr on Mankind and Reason' in Rochester, *Poems*. For an assertion that Bunyan's *The Pilgrim's Progress* was written long before publication in 1678 (and during the Restoration crisis over conscience), see Greaves, 'Let the Truth be Free', and 'Conscience, Liberty, and the Spirit: Bunyan and Nonconformity', in *John Bunyan and English Nonconformity*, pp. 51–70 (pp. 59–62).

kind of freedom are tied most closely with court politics over the distinctly anti-Anglican issue of toleration and liberty of conscience for Protestant Nonconformists, most of whom would be able, like Bunyan, to profess loyalty to a Protestant monarch while rejecting conformity to a state Church.

It was just this kind of liberty and indulgence, however, that Anglican polemicists would view as politically decadent and precipitous of the fall of the nation. That the King himself was interested in toleration in the 1660s and early 1670s could be viewed as but another sign of the inherent corruption of the Court: the 'liberty' and 'indulgence' promised to Nonconformists could easily be translated as counterpart to the king's more infamous preferences for a 'liberty' and an 'indulgence' both of more sexual and more Popish kinds, a connection which many of Charles II's detractors could exploit in one way or another.[60] This is a reaction quite understandable, moreover, given that the actual proponents of toleration within the Court party, especially during the Cabal ministry, were far from free of libertine notoriety. While Shaftesbury was famously a free-thinker, George Villiers, Second Duke of Buckingham (often regarded as Charles II's first Minister in the Cabal) has been more infamously vilified by many Restoration writers and wits as a grossly indulgent, irreligious decadent renowned for philandering and bankruptcy and whose free-thinking zeal was, unfortunately, far from matched by any political acumen. It is Buckingham who has been noted as 'the most spectacular casualty' of Court decadence in the Restoration: 'He had no principles of religion, virtue or friendship; no truth or honour, no steadiness of conduct in him', asserts Gilbert Burnet, 'Pleasure and frolic, and extravagant diversion' were 'all he minded' and through which he 'ruined one of the greatest estates in England, and perhaps one of the finest wits and finest personages that the world then knew'.[61]

Others, such as Butler and Dryden, could not be so generous about the aristocratically radical George Villiers.[62] But part of this contemporary hostility evident towards Buckingham is inevitably due to his position on toleration, especially during the Cabal years of 1667–73. As Richard Elias has recently posited, each 'member of the Cabal had a reputation for lechery fastened onto him by a contemporary satirist, whether this reputation deserved or not', this satirical trend reflecting most of all a 'public suspicion about the religious

---

    [60]   See, for example, 'The History of the Insipids' (1674) in *Poems on Affairs of State: Augustan Satirical Verse, 1660–1714*, ed. George de F. Lord, 7 vols (New Haven and London: Yale University Press, 1963–75), I, 243–51, in which Charles II is satirized both in terms of his numerous bastard children and for giving 'liberty to conscience tender' (lines 10–24, p. 244).

    [61]   Gilbert Burnet, *A History of his Own Times* (London: Dent, n.d.), p. 37, cited in Parry, *The Seventeenth Century*, p. 114.

    [62]   See Samuel Butler's *Characters*, ed. Daves, 'A Duke of Bucks', pp. 66–7, and Dryden's portrait of Zimri in *Absalom and Achitophel*, lines 543–62.

composition of the Court' being 'half-papist and half-fanatic'.[63] Unsurprisingly, it is Buckingham's libertine decadence which became lampooned most harshly (and against which he had to defend himself), largely because it was Buckingham who, along with Ashley (soon to be Earl of Shaftesbury), pushed for Charles II to make his Declaration of Indulgence for Nonconformists in 1672.[64] While this support for the royal Declaration can be seen as a boldly political matter of strengthening the king's autonomous or absolutist power, being motivated as much by an anti-Parliamentarianism as any desire to secure toleration, Buckingham was nevertheless a prime mover for and commentator upon the issue of toleration throughout Charles II's reign.[65] Even following the rescindment of the 1672 Declaration and his own subsequent political downfall, Buckingham pursued the issue of indulgence for Protestant Dissenters during the rest of his life and on a number of counts. Toleration, Buckingham could argue, is important for economics as a great majority of Nonconformists were perceived to be of the 'middling' sort, merchants and tradesmen.[66] Following Martin Clifford's *Treatise on Humane Reason* (1672), moreover, Buckingham states that it is simply against 'the Empire of Reason' to deny people liberty of conscience, while also defending 'an Indulgence to all Protestant dissenters' as an inherent part of the definition of an Englishman's 'Property'. Without toleration, Buckingham could only forewarn a familiar sounding kind of decay for Restoration England: 'A General Discontent; The Dispeopleing of our poor Country; And the Exposing us to the Conquest of a Foreign Nation.'[67]

---

[63]   Richard Elias, 'Political Satire in Sodom', *SEL* 18 (1978), 423–38 (pp. 430–2).

[64]   For a general account of Buckingham's reputation and of his refutation of it, see Allan Pritchard, 'A Defense of His Private Life by the Second Duke of Buckingham', *Huntington Library Quarterly* 44 (1981), 157–71. On Buckingham and the matter of toleration and the 1672 Declaration of Indulgence see Jones, *Charles II: Royal Politician*, pp. 79–107; Miller, *Charles II*, pp. 135–41, 154–7, 188–200; *Buckingham: Public and Private Man – The Prose, Poems and Commonplace Book of George Villiers, Second Duke of Buckingham (1628–1687)*, ed. Christine Phipps (New York and London: Garland, 1985), 'Biographical Introduction', pp. 3–54 (pp. 16–20, 41–2); Tim Harris, 'Revising the Restoration', in *The Politics of Religion in Restoration England*, pp. 1–28 (pp. 6–11, 13–14).

[65]   See also John H. O'Neill, *George Villiers, Second Duke of Buckingham* (Boston: Twayne, 1984), pp. 16–17, 44–51. Hutton is scathingly sceptical about the supposed prominence of Buckingham in the Cabal and his influence upon Charles II: *Charles the Second*, pp. 258–9. Bruce Yardley assesses Buckingham's commitment to toleration in particular in 'George Villiers, Second Duke of Buckingham and the Politics of Toleration', *Huntington Library Quarterly* 55 (1992), 317–37.

[66]   See 'A Letter to Sir Thomas Osborn . . . 1672' and 'The Duke of Buckingham's Speech in the House of Lords, November 1675', in *Buckingham: Public and Private Man*, pp. 90–7, 102–3. For a summary of economic and 'interest theory' arguments for toleration see De Krey, 'Rethinking the Restoration', pp. 60–3.

[67]   'To Mr. Martin Clifford on his Human Reason, 1672', 'The Duke of Buckingham's Speech in the House of Lords, November 1675', *A Short Discourse Upon*

It is in this context, one in which aristocratic libertines like Buckingham and free-thinking intellectuals like Martin Clifford and Sir Charles Wolseley side with the cause for the liberty of conscience of Nonconformists, that Rochester and Bunyan can finally be said to share something of a decadent political interest.[68] One need not look hard for evidence of this in the writings of these two authors either. As a persecuted Nonconformist, Bunyan has an innate interest in the liberty of conscience and his works resonate with the political fact of his own Church's continued persecution. Imprisoned, he writes from 'the Lions Den', advocating courage and passivity in the face of the ravages of Apollyon in *The Pilgrim's Progress* and the 'Bloodmen' in *The Holy War*: 'Stand-fast' and 'hold fast' are simultaneously spiritual and political encouragements from a Bunyan facing harassment by Restoration magistrates.[69] While recent Bunyan scholarship has emphasized the essentially pacifist nature of Bunyan's response to persecution under the Stuart regime such studies fail nevertheless to recognize his more militant responses to repression (persecution must be met with fighting, he seems to suggest in *An Exposition on the Ten First Chapters of Genesis*) and the place of his writings in the context of the Restoration 'crisis over conscience'.[70]

Equally, however, embedded within Rochester's satires are responses to Restoration politics which, though almost wholly ignored by critics, clearly align him with Buckingham's call for toleration (a fact which should hardly be

---

the *Reasonableness of Men's Having a Religion, or Worship of God* (1685), in *Buckingham: Public and Private Man*, pp. 87–9, 102–3, 113–20.

[68] John Spurr, 'Religion in Restoration England', pp. 123–4; De Krey, 'Rethinking the Restoration', p. 63.

[69] Bunyan, *Grace Abounding*, p. 1; *The Pilgrim's Progress*, pp. 46–50; *The Holy War*, ed. James F. Forrest and Roger Sharrock (Oxford: Clarendon Press, 1980), p. 232. For comments on the political role of the Bloodmen see Hill, *A Turbulent, Seditious, and Factious People*, p. 247, and Richard Greaves, 'Amid The Holy War: Bunyan and the Ethic of Suffering', in *John Bunyan and English Nonconformity*, pp. 169–83 (pp. 173–4).

[70] John Bunyan, *An Exposition on the Ten First Chapters of Genesis*, in *The Miscellaneous Works of John Bunyan XII*, ed. W.R. Owens (Oxford: Clarendon Press, 1994), pp. 179–80. On the political implications of Bunyan's posthumous works see Christopher Hill, *A Turbulent, Seditious, Factious People*, pp. 323–34, and Richard Greaves, 'The Spirit and the Sword: Bunyan and the Stuart State', in *John Bunyan and English Nonconformity*, pp. 101–26 (pp. 118–25) and 'Let Truth be Free', pp. 587–605. In the latter, Greaves suggests that 'Bunyan intended *The Pilgrim's Progress* in part to reiterate in dramatic fashion the basic case for Protestant freedom of conscience and the right of assembly that he had been espousing since 1660', concluding that '*The Pilgrim's Progress* may be more radical than *The Holy War*' in this respect (pp. 590, 604). For Greaves's discussions of Bunyan's politics and the persecution of Nonconformity in relation to *The Holy War*, see '*The Holy War* and London Nonconformity' and 'Amid *The Holy War*: Bunyan and the Ethic of Suffering', in *John Bunyan and English Nonconformity*, pp. 155–67 and 169–83. Of related interest see also Barrie White, 'John Bunyan and the Context of Persecution', in *John Bunyan and his England, 1628–1688*, eds Anne Laurence, W.R. Owens, and Stuart Sim (London: Hambledon, 1990), pp. 51–62.

surprising given that Villiers was 'one of Rochester's closest friends').[71] In 'Tunbridge Wells', for example, Rochester's satire against foppish society goes far beyond commenting merely upon the vanity of fashionable fools. At one point, Rochester shifts the focus of his attack significantly to join Andrew Marvell (whom he cites directly) in lampooning none other than that arch-Anglican intolerant, Samuel Parker, the 'Pert Bayes' who, Rochester claims, has been 'rais'd to an Arch-Deaconry,/ By trampling on Religion, Liberty'.[72] That Rochester aligns himself with Marvell (whose infamous attacks on Samuel Parker in *The Rehearsal Transpros'd*, Parts I and II (1672 and 1673) were much enjoyed by Charles II and which draw their title and the name 'Bayes' from Buckingham's play, *The Rehearsal* [1671]), is a clear sign of allegiance on the specific matter of toleration: here, Rochester is drawing upon a network of satirical referents all concerned specifically with liberty of conscience.[73] Hence, Rochester's attack upon the 'Tribe of Curates, Priests, [and] Canonicall Elves' in 'Tunbridge Wells' (lines 53–81) has its roots in something far more particular and political than the general philosophical or libertine anticlericalism which is often attributed to Rochester's attacks on churchmen.

In this context, moreover, the antagonism towards established religion in Rochester's most famous poem, the 'Satyr on Mankind and Reason', must be read in a clear and polemical light concerning Anglicanism and toleration. The poem's argument for 'right *Reason*' is clearly to be read as an attack upon the rational moralism of divines like Edward Stillingfleet (again cited directly by Rochester in the poem) which uses 'reason' to justify the persecution of

---

[71] Treglown, *Letters*, fn. p. 51. Rochester's and Buckingham's debaucheries together are legendary: see Lamb, *So Idle a Rogue*, pp. 161–65, and Hippolyte Taine, *History of English Literature*, trans. H. van Laun (1878), in *Rochester: The Critical Heritage*, pp. 241–3. On a more reliable note, Rochester and Buckingham evidently corresponded with one another and it was Rochester (along with Nell Gwynn and others) who procured Buckingham's release from the Tower in 1677: see *Letters*, pp. 51–2, 145–9, 151–5.

[72] Rochester, *Poems*, 'Tunbridge Wells: A Satyr' (lines 68–81), pp. 69–74 (p. 71).

[73] Marvell wrote *The Rehearsal Transpros'd* as a direct response to Parker's *A Preface shewing what grounds there are of Fears and Jealousies of Popery*, prefixing Bishop Bramhall's *Vindication of himself and the Episcopal Clergy from the Presbyterian Charge of Popery* (1672). In attacking Parker's general doctrine of intolerance about liberty of conscience, 'Marvell was able to adopt the role of defender of the king's own policy of toleration against the narrow fanaticism of the spokesman for the Anglican establishment' (Andrew Marvell, *Selected Poetry and Prose*, ed. Robert Wilcher (London and New York: Methuen, 1986), pp. 276–7). Charles II was a great fan of Marvell's *The Rehearsal Transpros'd* too, intervening to ensure its publication was approved by Sir Roger L'Estrange, Surveyor of the Press. For further comments on the political background to these texts see also the 'Introduction' to *The Rehearsal Transpros'd and The Rehearsal Transpros'd the Second Part*, ed. D.I.B. Smith (Oxford: Clarendon Press, 1971), pp. xi–xxv.

'irrational' enthusiasts.[74] The satire's dialogue with 'some formal Band, and Beard' (line 46) and the denigration of man as a rational animal thus go far beyond Hobbist materialism or libertine pessimism. Indeed, the echoes of Buckingham's and Clifford's arguments about reason and toleration in this poem are unmistakable, Rochester elaborating magnificently upon the latter's image of the *'Ignis fatuus'* to describe the fallacious rationalism of the Anglican and his 'Bladders of *Philosophy*' (lines 10–45). Unlike Butler's use of the same image for the false reason of enthusiasts like Ralpho in *Hudibras*, Rochester is again aligning himself explicitly, here, with a vocabulary not only of decadent scepticism but of a pro-tolerationist's hostility towards the persecutory *'Church-Man'* (line 191).[75]

What emerges, then, even from such a brief analysis of Rochester and Bunyan, is the ground for some important reconsiderations of Restoration politics, culture and literature in general. In returning to Swift's *Proposal for Correcting, Improving and Ascertaining the English Tongue*, for example, it is quite clear that Swift's focus on the Restoration as the locus of linguistic and social corruption has its source not simply in a discourse of reaction to the Civil War but, more specifically, in the issues of toleration and Dissent ever-present throughout the reign of Charles II. It is obvious that it is the likes of the Duke of Buckingham and the Earl of Rochester whom Swift is referring to as the kind of Courtier dangerously 'conversant in the Dialect' of *'Fanatick Times'*. Here, Swift again seems to be echoing other arch-Tories like Clarendon in complaining of the king's 'constant Conversation with Men of great prophaneness, whose Wit consisted in abusing Scripture . . . (a Faculty in which the Duke of *Buckingham* excelled)' and which lessened Charles II's 'natural Esteem and Reverence' for

---

[74]   Rochester, Poems, 'SATYR' (lines 99, 74), pp. 91–7 (pp. 94, 93). On the textual status of the phrase 'Stillingfleets replyes' in this poem see Thormälen, *Rochester: The Poems in Context*, pp. 163–7; Kristoffer F. Paulson, 'The Reverend Edward Stillingfleet and the "Epilogue" to Rochester's *A Satyr Against Mankind and Reason*', *Philological Quarterly* 50 (1971), 657–63.

[75]   Compare with Samuel Butler, *Hudibras, The First Part, Canto I*, lines 451–518 (esp. 499–508), in *Hudibras Parts I and II and Selected Other Writings*, eds John Wilders and Hugh de Quehen (Oxford: Clarendon Press, 1973), pp. 15–17 (p. 16). Compare the basic premises of Rochester's 'Satyr' also with Buckingham's 'To Mr. Martin Clifford on his Human Reason 1672', in *Buckingham: Public and Private Man*, pp. 87–9, in which Buckingham, writing of the 'true and perfect Liberty of Conscience' within the 'Empire of REASON', asserts that enemies to such 'Reformation' are 'Men that are so little Friends to God, and humane kind, that they are for destroying the very Distinction betwixt Man and Beast, that is Reason' (p. 88), which is precisely the point of Rochester's poem. Without reason and 'the interpretation of Scripture', Buckingham asserts, we must continually wander in the Dark after the Ignis fatuus of every opinion' (p. 89). For an understanding of reason and rationalism in the Restoration see Spurr, '"Rational Religion" in Restoration England'.

'the Clergy'.[76] Within this context, Swift's combining of Court decadence with the fanaticism of religious 'enthusiasts' is not only understandable but wholly traditional. As in so many of his other writings, Swift is drawing upon (if not rehearsing) a discourse of Anglicanism the roots of which lie directly in the writings of Restoration divines like Tillotson, Glanvil and Parker. The Restoration is, then, so important in Swift's view of the decay of language and society in the *Proposal* precisely because he intends to resuscitate its polemics for his own political purposes.

On a broader level, however, the issue of toleration for Nonconformists allows us to perceive connections within Restoration culture and its infamy for decadence which have, it would seem, largely gone unnoticed so far. Hence, while Bunyan cries '*let Truth be free*', to Rochester can be attributed an uncannily similar clarion call: 'set the nation free./ Let conscience have its force of liberty.'[77] Because poems like 'Tunbridge Wells' and the 'Satyr' are, like Bunyan's *The Pilgrim's Progress*, exactly contemporary with the most crucial Restoration debates over toleration in the early to mid-1670s, both Rochester and Bunyan can be placed together within a political context often ignored by critics and commentators. This aspect of Rochester's poetry certainly has not been investigated so far, his writings having been subjected to very little political analysis in these terms at all, and much the same can be said of Bunyan.[78] What this background enables us to recognize, therefore, is not only a large source for Swiftian political satire but how Restoration writers as morally and ethically and socially disparate as Rochester and Bunyan can actually be connected in terms of sharing a similar kind of political decadence, an ideology which, contrary to Anglicanism, promotes a desire for 'liberty' among all English Protestants.

---

[76] *The Life of Edward Earl of Clarendon* (Oxford: OUP, 1759), p. 360, cited in Manning, 'Rochester's Satyr Against Reason and Mankind', p. 109.

[77] Bunyan, *The Pilgrim's Progress*, 'Apology', p. 6; *The farce of Sodom, or The Quintessence of Debauchery* (first published in 1684), in *Rochester, Complete Poems and Plays*, ed. Paddy Lyons (London: Dent, 1993), pp. 125–54, Actus Prima, Scena Prima, lines 67–8 (p. 131). Although Lyons includes Sodom in his edition of Rochester's works, attribution still seems uncertain. However, understanding Rochester in relation to the toleration issue may offer a reading of the farce (if we accept that he wrote it) very different from Richard Elias's interpretation of it as a satire upon Charles's policy of indulgence ('Political Satire in *Sodom*', 423–38). Indeed, it could just as easily be read as an obscene lampooning of Charles II's failure to secure anything other than a sexual 'indulgence'.

[78] Some studies have placed Rochester's poems in the context of Latitudinarian writings and doctrines, but not specifically in relation to the matter of toleration: Trotter, 'Wanton Expressions'; Manning, 'Rochester's Satyr Against Reason and Mankind'; Thormälen, *Rochester: The Poems in Context*, pp. 162–239. For a theorized (but non-contextual) politicization of Rochester, see Kirk Combe, *A Martyr for Sin: Rochester's Critique of Polity, Sexuality, and Society* (Newark: University of Delaware Press, 1998).

Chapter 5

Dickensian Decadents

Vincent Newey

There are characters in Dickens that clearly predict the condition of *fin-de-siècle* decadence. I am thinking in particular of James Steerforth in *David Copperfield*, James Harthouse in *Hard Times* and Eugene Wrayburn in *Our Mutual Friend*, Dickens's last completed novel, though another obvious, if limited, example would be Jack Maldon, also in *David Copperfield*, a summary figure aptly described by John Lucas as signifying 'essential triviality and predatory sexual instinct'.[1] In his essay of 1893 on 'The Decadent Movement in Literature', Arthur Symons, one of its leading lights, termed the phenomenon an 'interesting disease' typical of an over-luxurious civilization, whose symptoms were 'an intense self-consciousness, a restless curiosity in research, an over-subtilizing refinement upon refinement, a spiritual and moral perversity'.[2] These qualities or these defects – the ambivalence of 'decadence' makes it impossible to say which – are all, up to a point and at some stage, manifest in Dickens's conceptions. Above all, we are aware of a 'perversity' that is at once inward and active in the fields of conduct and relationships.

I shall conclude with the most developed case, that of Eugene Wrayburn, after considering Steerforth alongside a significant variant of the type in the same novel, Uriah Heep. The relatively circumscribed and uncompromising portrayal of 'decadence' in Harthouse makes a good starting point.

* * *

Harthouse is physically self-indulgent (he smokes a lot, as Wrayburn does), and ostentatious in dress and appearance (on close encounter the novice decadent Tom Gradgrind perceives him admiringly through a cigar haze as all 'waistcoat' and 'whiskers').[3] He has abandoned a succession of career choices and travel plans as 'a bore', and at the time of the action of the novel is 'going in for' politics

---

[1]   John Lucas, *Charles Dickens: The Major Novels* (Harmondsworth: Penguin Books, 1992), p. 63.

[2]   Quoted in *The Concise Oxford Dictionary of Literary Terms*, ed. Chris Baldick (Oxford: OUP, 1990; paperback edn 1991), p. 51.

[3]   Charles Dickens, *Hard Times* (1854), ed. Kate Flint (Harmondsworth: Penguin Books, 1995), p. 137. Hereafter page references are cited in the text.

with the same lack of serious commitment. He tells Bounderby's young wife, Louisa,

> I assure you I attach not the least importance to any opinions. The result of the varieties of boredom I have undergone, is a conviction (unless conviction is too industrious a word for the lazy sentiment I entertain on the subject), that any set of ideas will do just as much good as any other set, and just as much harm as any other set [. . .] What will be, will be. It's the only truth going (133).

His guiding principle lies in having none, his sole creed in taking things as they come.

The picture is not an entirely negative one. Dandyism always has its attractions (as in real nineteenth-century life Byron and Disraeli famously saw when making names for themselves).[4] Harthouse is appealing not only in his wit, colour and ease of manner but in a sensitivity – or, to recall Symons, 'restless curiosity' – indicative of the artistic temperament. There is something of the poet in his early response to the mystery of Louisa, whose complex bearing 'baffled all penetration' (132); something of the novelist's powers of analysis in his reflections on the Bounderbys' 'cheerless' house and Louisa's singular reliance on her ungracious brother as an object of her love, which reveals to him how 'much the greater must have been the solitude of her heart, and her need of someone on whom to bestow it' (135). His indifference, which is linked to his upper-class origins, brings him an insouciant freedom that surfaces both as active mobility – as the narrator puts it, one who finds 'everything to be worth nothing' is 'equally ready for everything (128) – and a capacity, like that of the satirist, for exposing hypocrisy, as when he frankly admits to the Utilitarians' ability to 'prove anything' by statistics, and to his own motive in joining them because on their political wing they form 'the largest party' and give him 'the best chance' (134).

Yet ambiguity is one thing, endorsement quite another. We are not, of course, meant to approve of James Harthouse. Within the network of evaluative metaphor that Dickens constructs in this novel, he is described as a 'demon' and as the 'tempter' (138, 139). He visits Louisa on horseback and speaks to her like a knight in a romance, saying, for example, 'There never was a slave at once so devoted and ill-used by his mistress' (211); but this is the ploy of the schemer and seducer, not the obeisance of the genuine errant adventurer; and the more circumspect rhetoric of persuasion with which he regularly addresses Louisa, expertly distinguished by Roger Fowler as an 'elaborated code' dominated by complicated syntax and verbal device, 'a literary, educated form',[5] marks him not

---

4   See Andrew Elfenbein, *Byron and the Victorians* (Cambridge: Cambridge University Press, 1995), pp. 213–18 especially.

5   Roger Fowler, 'Polyphony and Problematic in Hard Times', in ed. Robert Gittings, *The Changing World of Charles Dickens* (London: Vision Press, 1983), pp. 100–1.

only as upper-class, a 'fine gentlem[a]n' (128), but as an agile exponent of
fiendish *legerdemain*. He is in a line of descent from Milton's Satan through the
Lovelace of Richardson's *Clarissa*. When, later on, in his exchanges with Sissy
Jupe, Harthouse himself calls the progress of his steps with Louisa 'perfectly
diabolical' (234), it is as part of an attempted self-justification: something was
happening beyond his control. With Sissy, however, no amount of special
pleading will even begin to work; his devilish nature is simply, and literally, put
to flight by her innocence – her 'child-like ingenuousness', her 'modest
fearlessness', her 'truthfulness' (233) – rather as Comus is by the Lady in
Milton's masque. This scene is followed by a wonderfully pointed exposure of
Harthouse's corruptness, his shallow egotism, in one of those moments of social
and moral illumination that are Dickens's outward-looking, liberal humanist
counterpart to the self-sufficient Romantic epiphany, and are crucial to the
operation and status of his texts as a secular scripture. We would, the narrator tells
us, expect Harthouse to have valued his prompt retreat from Coketown as a way
of making some amends for the 'very bad business' arising from his previous
actions; in fact, 'A secret sense of having failed and been ridiculous [. . .] so
oppressed him, that what was about the very best passage in his life was the one
of all others he would not have owned to on any account, and the only one that
made him ashamed of himself' (238). This is the last we hear of him. For this lost
soul there is no call to redemption.

* * *

In Eugene Wrayburn Harthouse is reincarnated and reclaimed. Before that, and
indeed rather earlier than *Hard Times*, comes Steerforth. He has basic traits in
common with Harthouse, showing, for instance, an inclination to get so 'bored to
death'[6] that he goes in for nothing, except, that is, the seduction of Little Emily,
in which he energetically succeeds – only to get bored and try to abandon her to
his servant, the hideous Littimer. The marks of class do not show well in
Steerforth. The hauteur with which he automatically talks of the Peggotys as 'that
sort of people' immediately takes a sinister turn when he comments that 'they are
not to be expected to be as sensitive as we are [. . .] and they may be thankful that,
like their coarse rough skins, they are not easily wounded' (352). This sense of
others as almost a separate species, such casual denial of their feelings, threatens
tragic repercussions; and the attitude is repeated just afterwards in Steerforth's
review of the evening David and he have passed at the Peggotys' home, where
Little Emily has made an immediate impression:

---

    6   Charles Dickens, *David Copperfield* (1849–50), ed. Trevor Blount
(Harmondsworth: Penguin Books, 1966; repr. 1985), p. 346. Hereafter cited in the text.

'A most engaging little Beauty!' said Steerforth, taking my arm. 'Well! It's a quaint place, and they are quaint company, and it's quite a new sensation to mix with them.'

'How fortunate we are, too,' I returned, 'to have arrived to witness their happiness in that intended marriage! I never saw people so happy. How delightful to see it, and to be made the sharers in their honest joy, as we have been!'

'That's rather a chuckle-headed fellow for the girl; isn't he?' said Steerforth.

He had been so hearty with him, and with them all, that I felt a shock at this cold reply. But turning quickly upon him, and seeing a laugh in his eyes, I answered, much relieved:

'Ah, Steerforth! It's well for you to joke about the poor! [. . .] When I see how perfectly you understand them, how exquisitely you can enter into happiness like this plain fisherman's, [. . .] I know that there is not a joy or sorrow, not an emotion, of such people, that can be indifferent to you. And I admire and love you for it, Steerforth, twenty times the more!'

He stopped, and, looking in my face, said, 'Daisy, I believe you are in earnest, and are good. I wish we all were!' (376–77)

If Steerforth treats Emily and the rest as (to use John Lucas's word)[7] a 'connoisseur' would a set of picturesque objects (apparent in the phrase 'little Beauty', which might be used of an animal, as well as in the relatively new coinage 'quaint' meaning 'old-fashioned'), David's own response is in its way hardly less formulaic and detached. Enthusiastically naive where his friend is nonchalantly experienced, David, in his stilted language ('How delightful [. . .] to be made the sharers in their honest joy', 'this plain fisherman'), seems to be imagining a conventional literary pastoral. We certainly respect the earnestness and sympathy in David which Steerforth's closing statement highlights, and see these qualities as proper to the emergent novelist (his phrase 'enter into' suggests the famous Keatsian gift of 'negative capability'), but we also realize that there is another level of knowing and reporting the world, going deeper, working harder as revelation and comment.

This other order is amply displayed in the great Chapter 7, the scene of the public humiliation of the poor schoolmaster, Mr Mell, at Creakle's Academy (148–55). Not only does Steerforth the snob contemptuously and contemptibly mock the master's low origins – 'You are always a beggar, you know' – he is ready to use the confidence David had let slip about his pauperized mother to turn the knife – 'If he's not a beggar himself, his near relation's one'. This is a strong example of Steerforth's ruthless disregard for the feelings of those socially beneath him, but even more frightening is his perfunctory refusal of Mell's very existence – 'I don't give myself the trouble of thinking at all about you'. This searing exposé of aggressive self-centredness, which introduces the important

---

7   Lucas, *Charles Dickens: The Major Novels*, p. 57.

theme of class antagonism, is immediately enforced and modified by Dickens's
focus upon the reactions of other participants in the drama: David's discomfort
and regret at having, if inadvertently, supplied Steerforth with his cruellest
weapon; Mell's gentle, reassuring touch upon the boy's shoulder, twice; Traddles'
insistence, at the cost of isolation from his classmates and a sound beating at the
hands of Creakle, that Mell has been 'ill-used', an insight born of the desolation
within Traddles himself that is expressed habitually in his drawing of skeletons;
Steerforth's quick announcement that he intends of course to write home for some
money to be sent to Mell (who has been sacked), an act suspended between
troubled defensiveness, self-justification, and a strategic reasserting of authority;
the fact that the whole company were 'glad' to see Traddles so put down, where
the apparently simple word implies all the pressure of relief from an uneasy
conscience, no less than the group's exultant participation in the triumph of its
(ironically) 'noble' and 'unselfish' leader and better. There is in all of this a
profound lesson, for David and for the reader, in the best, the worst, and the
undecidable in human nature. It is the Dickensian secular scripture at its subtlest
and most powerful.

Why, then, does David go on loving Steerforth, in spite of his 'pollution of a
honest home' (516) and his other transgressions? Why is 'decadence' not merely
repellent? There is a clue in what happens at Salem House school, where, David
recalls, 'I thought of him very much after I went to bed, and raised myself, I
recollect, to look at him in the moonlight, with his handsome face turned up, and
his head reclining easily on his arm. He was a person of great power in my eyes:
that was, of course, the reason of my mind running on him' (140). The
homoerotic content of adolescence, declared here all the more plainly for being
displaced as hero-worship, persists, still an open secret, as a bonding that
transcends issues of morality. At their last meeting Steerforth, as ever, calls David
'Daisy'; and to his ominous wish always to be thought of 'at my best' David
replies, 'You have no best to me, Steerforth, [. . .] and no worst. You are always
equally loved, and cherished in my heart' (497). The chain of attachment is
vividly reinscribed when, years later, the body of Steerforth, washed up on the
beach, appears to David in the same symbolic attitude as in their schooldays:

> But, he led me to the shore. And on that part of it where she and I had
> looked for shells, two children – on that part of it where some lighter
> fragments of the old boat, blown down last night, had been scattered by the
> wind – among the ruins of the home he had wronged – I saw him lying
> with his head upon his arm, as I had often seen him lie at school (866).

David's memory of Emily, with whom he was once infatuated, is flat, void of
enchantment; not so that of the sleeping Steerforth. We see in the syntax of this
passage that the violation of the Peggoty home exists in David's recollections as
a parenthesis while the image of his friend is their unspoken first term and their

end point. When, at the opening of the next chapter, he talks of being unable to condemn Steerforth 'now [. . .] looking on this sight' he not only refers to the body in the landscape but also confesses, and celebrates, the lure of the picture within. The dead Steerforth is alive to David still and has power to fascinate and to move him.[8]

Yet love and imaginative fixation provide only one of the explanations for David having feelings of 'sorrow' towards his friend but no 'angry thoughts' or 'reproaches' (517). There is also an ideological factor at work. *David Copperfield* undoubtedly endorses a hierarchical and fundamentally conservative view of society. Goodness matters, but so does blood: Steerforth may be seen to err but cannot be scorned. Conversely, Ham Peggoty can, as in Steerforth's own reference of this 'chuckle-headed fellow', a remark about which John Lucas entertains the telling speculation that 'Dickens displaces on to Steerforth doubts [about Ham's limitations] he can't allow his hero to entertain'.[9]

It is the presentation of Uriah Heep, however, that most strikingly inscribes Dickens's commitment to a fixed order of subordination. As Steerforth stands above the taints of decadence, so in Uriah Heep, the low-born charity boy, they are relentlessly reinforced.

Surely, no character in literature rivals Uriah as an article of disgust. He is described as everything from 'frog' and 'vulture' to 'devil'. There is obsessive denigration of his face, which is said to be 'cadaverous' and set in a 'carved grin' like that of a gargoyle, of his hand, which is 'long, lank' and 'cold damp', of his whole body, contorted in 'snaky twistings' (275, 292, 437–8, 443–4). We cannot

---

[8]   The erotic charge of the David-Steerforth relationship is brought into sharp focus by D.A. Miller, *The Novel and the Police* (Berkeley: University of California Press, 1988), pp. 198–9. For an extended discussion, see Martha C. Nussbaum's brilliant exploration of this and related matters in 'Steerforth's Arm: Love and the Moral Point of View', *Love's Knowledge: Essays on Philosophy and Literature* (New York: OUP, 1990), pp. 335–63. Nussbaum (p. 349) notes a third crucial materialization of the sensuous figure of Steerforth in the circuit of David's emotion-infused memory – when, on the last occasion David sees his friend before the seduction of Emily, 'He was fast asleep, lying, easily, with his head upon his arm, as I had often seen him lie at school' (497–8).

    Linda M. Shires, 'Literary Careers, Death, and the Body Politics of David Copperfield', in ed. John Schad, *Dickens Refigured: Bodies, Desires and Other Histories* (Manchester: Manchester University Press, 1996), pp. 117–35 comments briefly on the way both Steerforth and Uriah Heep are 'implicated with David in homoeroticism' (p. 132). Eve Kosofsky Sedgwick, though she can be no less stimulating than Nussbaum, sacrifices the depth of this particular Dickens text to her schematic interest in the narrative of male socialization when stating that 'David's infatuation with his friend [. . .] is *simply* part of David's education': 'Homophobia, Misogyny, and Capital: The Example of Our Mutual Friend', in ed. Steven Connor, *Charles Dickens* (London: Longman, 1996), pp. 178–96 (p. 192: italics mine); repr. from Eve Kosofsky Sedgwick, *Between Men: English Literature and Male Homosocial Desire* (New York: Columbia University Press, 1985), pp. 163–79.

[9]   John Lucas, *Charles Dickens: The Major Novels*, p. 57.

but read this on one level psychologically, seeing in the gross physicality, which is focused upon deathliness and deformity, and upon orifices and limp or sinewy parts, the reverse of David's love for Steerforth, with Uriah as the locus of homophobic energies in the narrator-hero; or we may detect, more precisely, the notation of an intense ambivalence involving compulsion towards and fearful recoil from the male body as object of desire – self-expression inextricably bound up with self-aversion. From the beginning, indeed, it is a concern to David whether he 'liked Uriah or detested him' (311); and the mixture of attraction and revulsion reaches its eerie climax when, with Uriah asleep in the next room, David dreams of running him through the body with a 'red hot' poker, and cannot help going to look at him over and over again 'lying on his back, with his legs extending to I don't know where, gurglings taking place in his throat, stoppages in his nose, and his mouth open like a post-office' (443). In the same sequence, moreover, Uriah translates into the distorted reflection of David's repressed longing for Agnes Wickfield, as, for instance, David grows 'giddy' with imagining Agnes 'outraged by [. . .] this red-headed animal'; when David becomes strangely aware of 'what [Uriah] is going to say next' (441) it is because his rival is the exteriorization of his own buried instincts, his primitive double. Even here, however, in the midst of the most extreme psychodrama, a socio-political position is being promulgated. David's sublimation of base impulse, which at its deftest transforms Agnes into the celestial beauty of a 'stained glass window' (280, 570), is a part of his being a true gentleman, middling compared with Steerforth but impeccably upright. Uriah's pursuit of Agnes and his offensiveness in sexual matters – he refers to her, for instance, as an unripe pear to be 'plucked' in due course of time, for 'it'll ripen yet! It only wants attending to' (645) – is one with his 'whole scheme' for, as he puts it, 'emerging from my lowly station' (441).

Uriah, with his strategic ''umbleness', is a grotesque demonization – indeed criminalization – of the ethic of upwards mobility. He is given a language of self-help and success in order to discredit them. To David he says, for example, referring to his partnership in Wickfield's law firm, 'I am very umble to the present moment, Master Copperfield, but I've got a little power!' (639): rising in the world is, by implication, really about power and about exercising it. At other times, the arraignment is made explicitly:

> The reversal of the two natures, in their relative positions, Uriah's of power and Mr Wickfield's of dependence, was a sight more painful to me than I can express. If I had seen an Ape taking command of a Man, I should hardly have thought it a more degrading spectacle (578).

Wickfield the well-to-do solicitor, a weak and helpless alcoholic, is the 'Man', Uriah the industrious clerk, good at the job, is the 'Ape' – genetically inferior. Uriah is stamped with a decadence that is not excess, or fecklessness, or a fall from grace, as in his superiors, but the fixed result of origins. And the impression is driven ever deeper. Much later in the process of Wickfield's decline and Uriah's rise to dominance the narrative designates the former 'the broken gentleman' and the latter a 'baboon' (640, 637). Uriah has often been associated with rudimentary forms of life – a 'fish' (293) as well as a frog and a snake – but he now becomes something pointedly less than human, recognisably inferior on the evolutionary scale.

But the question of Uriah's status in the novel and of his rivalry with David is in fact never quite resolved. The quotation about having 'got a little power' rounds off a passage of autobiography, a sort of apologia, which throws a surprising light on Uriah, giving access to reasons for his behaviour:

> 'Father and me was both brought up at a public, sort of charitable establishment. They taught us a deal of umbleness – not much else that I know of, from morning to night. We was to be umble to this person, and umble to that; and to pull off our caps here, and to make bows there; and always to know our place, and abase ourselves before our betters. And we had such a lot of betters! Father got the monitor-medal by being umble. So did I. Father got made a sexton by being umble. He had the character, among the gentlefolks, of being such a well-behaved man, that they were determined to bring him in. "Be umble, Uriah," says father to me, "and you'll get on. It was what was always being dinned into you and me at school; it's what goes down best."'
>
> It was the first time it had ever occurred to me, that this detestable cant of false humility might have originated out of the Heep family. I had seen the harvest, but had never thought of the seed [. . .] I had never doubted his meanness, his craft and malice; but I fully comprehended now, for the first time, what a base, unrelenting, and revengeful spirit, must have been engendered by this early, and this long, suppression (639).

At least David sees that Uriah's actions were not without reason, a motiveless malignity. But his claims to full comprehension are hardly justified when his language – 'detestable cant [. . .] meanness [. . .] revengeful spirit' – is everywhere that of indignant condemnation, rather than of understanding. Moreover, when he does achieve an insight into causes he uses terms – 'originated out of', 'seed', 'engendered' – that suggest some *natural* process, an unavoidable source of baseness. He sees that behaviour arises from conditioning, a 'long suppression' as well as family circumstance, but nowhere does he impugn the system that produced Heep father and son, nor contemplate grounds either for reforming it or for forgiving Uriah.

This passage discloses serious limitations in David's viewpoint and personality and further questions are asked by Uriah's own resistance in the face of attack. *He* forgives David when he strikes him; *he* refuses to quarrel at all in this seething encounter where the blow to Uriah's cheek serves only to bind

David more intimately to his adversary, the physical marks which leave the skin 'a deeper red' being mirrored in the more searing wound of David's 'slow fire' of torment for having somehow made a false move and come off second best (686–7). Amazingly, when he is finally exposed as a swindler Uriah accuses David of the very misdeeds for which we are supposed to reject Uriah: he calls him an 'upstart' and one who has always been 'against' him (828); he charges him with being 'proud' and being driven by 'envy' of another's 'rise' (816); most disturbingly, he alleges hypocrisy, asking David, 'You think it justifiable [. . .] you who pride yourself so much on your honour and all the rest of it, to sneak about my place, eaves-dropping with my clerk? If it had been me, I shouldn't have wondered; for I don't make myself out a gentleman [. . .] but being you!' (817). Is there not something in what Uriah says? Is not decadence lifting the veil, however slightly, from self-proclaimed rectitude?

David's progress is the novel's official 'plot' (itself an ambiguous word, which Uriah applies (816) to the elaborate moves to defeat him), a model of personal development and social adjustment defined as virtuous application and selfless fulfilment, with nothing in it of strategy, worldliness or competitive achievement. When, at the beginning of Chapter 42, he reflects at length upon the advances he has made, he attributes them to the 'golden rules' of 'punctuality, order and diligence', 'sincere earnestness', and sees struggle and misdoing, not as involving others, but as solitary conflict, 'a war within his breast' where the neglect of talents or the waste of opportunities are continually checked by 'steady, plain, hard-working qualities'. This ethos, which is a version of Protestant conversion experience and ideals of living,[10] is then augmented by Agnes's letter to David after he has left England following the deaths of Dora, Steerforth and Ham, which upvalues adversity, and the ability to surmount it, in specifically non-material terms, as a source of inner strength: 'As endurance of my childish days had done its part to make what I was, so greater calamities would nerve me on, to be yet better than I was' (888). We hear later that his writing is a 'vocation', not a profession. The success of his novels prompts him to the virtue of 'modesty'; self-interest, the market, money, do not feature at all: 'They [his fictions] express themselves, and I leave them to themselves' (758), in splendid isolation. Uriah's 'counterplot' (816) does nothing to decentre the philosophy of being that is thus communicated through David, and is, on the contrary, the aberration by which the privileged norm is legitimized; but it does unsettle its grip by querying its impartiality and by implying concealment, a mask to be lifted.

---

[10]   The same ideals are set out in Cowper's *The Task* (1785), the popular voice of the Evangelical tradition and a poem very widely read in the nineteenth century. The manifesto of the contemplative man whose 'warfare is within' at the end of Book VI (ll. 906–1024) is especially relevant to David's emphasis upon the 'war within his breast' (672), though even Cowper the recluse is keen, like David, to claim that he has a useful place in the world, if no 'public praise', because he sets a 'fair example'.

The strange episode of Uriah Heep's much later appearance in gaol for forgery and conspiracy, where David improbably comes across him again, may be explained by a desire to shut him up and put him in his place once and for all. Dickens does not analyse the prevailing system here either. He is apparently in favour of prisons, though, judging by some brusque satire, not of an experimental regime that consults inmates about the standards of food they are getting and thinks it can make 'sincere and lasting converts and penitents' (921) out of convicted criminals. In a sense, Uriah's imprisonment is his true destiny. The house of correction continues the charity school in which he and his parents were brought up to be 'umble' and well-behaved. It is important to note, moreover, that the magistrate in charge of the new reforming code is none other than Creakle, once headmaster, not of Uriah's humble place of instruction, but of David's and Steerforth's higher, if itself dubious, establishment for the middle classes. School and prison are society's interconnected mechanisms for structuring and managing its human components: for making them fit and fitting, and, if necessary, keeping the misfits out of circulation.[11]

Yet even in prison Uriah is a source of discomfiture. Not that he is a direct threat to the system; far from challenging the rules, he plays the game to perfection, an exemplary inmate 'changed' and safe from 'sin', proclaiming to those who come to view him that 'It would be better for everybody, if they got took up, and was brought here' (928). (The terminology implicates religion too in the structures of categorization and control.) In any case the warders who routinely patrol the place are always alert to possible deceit – they 'knew pretty well what all this stir was worth' (929) – and thus provide a fail-safe device should reluctant co-operation go beyond the required mark and become troublesome. Uriah's situation raises uncomfortable questions precisely because it makes evident to the reader the network and agencies of social engineering and enforcement that normally avoid inspection, or are taken for granted.

At the same time, David is provoked into declaring hidden motivation and suppositions in himself when Uriah dredges up the memories most calculated to throw him off balance – the blow David had long ago landed on his face and the answering offer of forgiveness, which is now renewed (928). The point is not only that Uriah still refuses to be kept down or to let David off the hook of his own violent inclinations but that he draws from him at this very point a revealing condemnation, shared only with Traddles and addressed privily to the reader, of the two 'hypocritical knaves' (Steerforth's old servant, Littimer, is also in gaol for stealing from an employer) who 'knew [the] market-value' of their professed contrition 'in the immediate service it would do them when they were expatriated', and of their 'rotten hollow, painfully-suggestive piece of business' (930). The language here denounces both David's enemies and the whole

---

[11] For the seminal account of this theme in *David Copperfield*, see Miller, *The Novel and the Police*, pp. 217–20 especially.

capitalist order of 'market-value' and 'business', which is linked to an assumption of corrupt and corrupting practices; but it also again betrays an underlying partisan stance on David's part, and on Dickens'. It is tempting to define their position straightforwardly as, to adapt Raymond Williams's formulation, the separation of virtue from the practical world that is a feature of the later phases of Puritanism and still later of Romanticism.[12] But there is more to it than that. Through the hero of *David Copperfield* Dickens channels an ideology that does negotiate effectively, and aggressively, with and within the world but cloaks the realities of social and economic stationing in an idealism of goodness and patient privacy.

In the last chapters of the novel that ideology is extended in terms of the values of domesticity and the family, with Agnes famously 'pointing upward', support and moral guide, as she accompanies David and their children along the road of life (946–8). This theme, however, I wish to reserve for consideration in relation to *Our Mutual Friend* and the history of Eugene Wrayburn, the most complicated of Dickens' 'decadents'.

* * *

Wrayburn replicates Harthouse, but in a finer tone. As late as Chapter 10 of the third book of *Our Mutual Friend* he appears in the stereotypical pose of the 'decadent' gentleman, standing 'half amused and half vexed, and all idle and shiftless' beside the bench of Jenny Wren, the dolls' dressmaker.[13] Although such elementary traits are there for almost all the novel, however, they are rarely so isolated or so superficially paraded. When we first encounter Wrayburn it is as 'the gloomy Eugene', 'indolent', 'languidly upper-class and public school', repelled by the word 'energy' and lacking all commitment to his profession; but this lassitude is interestingly linked to positive neglect (he uses the word 'hate' of his attitude to his job) and the denial of familial expectations: 'It was forced upon me', he says, 'because it was understood that we wanted a barrister in the family. We have got a precious one' (57, 61–2). Later the rejection is more specifically of the filial duty and paternal authority in which the stability and very continuance of the dynasty are vested; for Eugene's mockery of his calling to 'legal eminence' is one with the conscious irreverence he shows towards his father's wishes in being, as he puts it, 'the married man I am not' (193). Marriage and the family resurface in due course as major themes of the novel.

Eugene is also cast in the familiar moulds of snob and seducer. The former trait comes out in two notable episodes. In one he literally fumigates Jenny Wren's wretched alcoholic father, whom he has named 'Mr Dolls', with a shovel of live ashes (600–3). His treatment of Bradley Headstone, star product of the

---

[12]   Raymond Williams, *The Country and the City* (London: Paladin Books, 1973), p. 84.

[13]   Charles Dickens, *Our Mutual Friend* (1864–65), ed. Stephen Gill (Harmondsworth: Penguin Books, 1971; repr. 1985), p. 595. Hereafter cited in the text.

pauper schools, is more viciously contemptuous and amounts to uncompromising class antagonism. In a scene reminiscent of Steerforth's humiliation of Mr Mell but more harrowing, he turns into a sharp-edged weapon the stratagem he playfully practises on 'Dolls' and relentlessly taunts Headstone with the name of 'schoolmaster', simultaneously denying him an individual identity, fixing him on a relatively lowly rung of the social ladder, and transforming his only badge of respect into a mark of ridicule. Headstone, unlike Mell, has the fight in him to assert his claims as an upward achiever – 'You reproach me with my origin [. . .] But, I tell you, sir, I have worked my way onward [. . .] and have a right to be considered better than you' (346). Yet, as with Uriah Heep, this ultimately does him no good. In Dickens' world, and with Dickens' blessing, the ability to 'get on', to rise from obscurity, is itself no match for high breeding, however insolent and overbearing the latter may be. Headstone knows his own helplessness in this: 'That lad who has just gone out could put you to shame in half-a-dozen branches of knowledge in half an hour, but you can throw him aside like an inferior. You can do as much by me, I have no doubt' (344). To situate others at the level of a social function, 'schoolmaster', or an object of amusement, 'Mr Dolls', or a racial type, for Eugene says of the good Mr Riah '*I* give him the name of Aaron' (598), is to exercise real and automatic power.

The immediate bone of contention between Wrayburn and Headstone is Lizzie Hexam, whose possible fate is memorably implied in the *double entendre* of Eugene's remark to Jenny Wren, 'I think of setting up a doll, Miss Jenny', and in her pointed retort, 'You are sure to break it. All you children do' (288–9). Eugene's plan to arrange an education for Lizzie, daughter of a Thames body-scavenger, is not born of philanthropic altruism or any levelling instinct. But it is in his relation to her that we are most immediately struck by an ambiguity in his character. When he first sees her, through the window of her waterside hovel, it is with the voyeuristic gaze of the sensual aesthete:

> It showed him the room, and the bills upon the wall respecting the drowned people starting out and receding by turns. But he glanced slightly at them, though he looked long and steadily at her. A deep rich piece of colour, with the brown flush of her cheek and the shining lustre of her hair, though sad and solitary, weeping by the rising and the falling of the fire (211).

The poetic sensibility that elsewhere negligently indulges in 'contemplation of the sky' (340) warms into a lingering caress of beauty in living cipher. This scene is reminiscent of Satan's rapt attention to Eve caught unawares in paradise in Milton's epic.[14] It is not only predacious threat we are reminded of, however, but also the fact that Satan is, if only fleetingly, disarmed of his malice by the sight of 'graceful innocence' (9.459). The mixture of delinquency and worthier disposition that exists for only a moment in Satan is a definite thread in

---

[14] Milton, *Paradise Lost*, 9.444–72.

Wrayburn's personality. Lizzie Hexam comes to him as something between potential prey and a promise of renovation in the midst of death – the pictures of the drowned people literally forming a background and contrast to her lustrous vitality, while the rising and falling of the fire casts an undecided pattern of darkness and light, tragic and regenerative possibilities, simultaneously with the evocation of erotic aura and energies, themselves redolent with both peril and hope. Her appealing image represents the creative, if dangerous, side of an imaginative temperament in Eugene of which the solipsistic reverse is his obsessive authoring of Headstone as a quarry to be viciously destroyed:

> I goad the schoolmaster to madness [. . .] Having made sure of his watching me, I tempt him on, all over London. One night I go east, another night north, in a few nights I go all round the compass [. . .] I seek those No Thoroughfares at night, glide into them by means of dark courts, tempt the schoolmaster to follow, turn suddenly, and catch him before he can retreat. Then we face one another, and I pass him as unaware of his existence, and he undergoes grinding torments (606).

These are the 'pleasures of the chase' (606). The story of Eugene and Lizzie is different, as we shall see; linear rather than moving in ever-decreasing about-turns. As soon as he stops spying on her a better self emerges, pointing forwards. He experiences remorse: 'If the real man feels as guilty as I do [. . .] he is remarkably uncomfortable' (212).

Eugene is always a two-sided, enigmatic character; in his own words, 'an embodied conundrum' (339). Harthouse is entirely amoral, while Steerforth has only flashes of incipient compunction, as when, in the exchange about the Peggotys that we have already considered, he says to David, 'Daisy, I believe you are in earnest, and are good. I wish we all were!' (377). In Eugene, on the other hand, the insouciance of the 'decadent', and the freedom it brings, are under constant pressure from the constraints of conscience: he can feel 'a little ashamed' even of his treatment of 'Mr Dolls' (604). It is above all in a capacity for self-scrutiny and for reflecting upon his own situation and behaviour that he differs from his Dickensian precursors. His development is by and large the history of the enhancement of this faculty under the influence of Lizzie herself (whereas Harthouse, we recall, was altogether impervious to the goodness of Sissy Jupe); until, when the two meet secretly in the countryside to which Lizzie has retreated, he receives such 'a deep impression' from the 'purity' with which she expresses her own love and her own suffering that he falls suddenly into an assessment of their relationship and respective natures. In himself he recognizes the deficiencies, the carelessness and self-regard, inclined to exact 'pains and penalties all round'; but there is a voice within that at the same time speaks what we already know, that he is at bottom a serious young man capable of genuine commitment, who dares anyone to tell him that his feeling for Lizzie is 'not a real sentiment on my part, won out of me by her beauty and her worth, in spite of myself, and that I would not be true to her' (765). Set against his earlier flippant conceit on the value of his unused kitchen as a constellation of 'moral influences expressly meant to promote the formation of domestic virtues' (349), this riverside monologue gives the measure of Eugene's progress in sensitivity and psychological health.

Inward advance, however, is no point of resolution. There remains in Eugene a current of what the narrator calls outright 'wickedness', which surfaces to prompt a dilemma: '"Out of the question to marry her," said Eugene, "and out of the question to leave her. The crisis!"' (766). The impasse is so emphatic and summary as to suggest a deliberate contrivance by Dickens, a coil from which to launch a definitive movement in the text, which thereafter drives towards patent affirmation of 'domestic virtues', or, that is, of middle-class 'domestic ideology'.[15] This ideology functions throughout the novel, as in the conception of Lizzie in terms of ideals of selfless devotion (towards her father and brother), purity (she loves Wrayburn but flees his unsolicited approaches), and, most tellingly of all in view of her technical working-class status, genteel speech and manners.[16] In the later reaches of *Our Mutual Friend*, however, we are much more aware of a programmatic discourse. The conventional happy ending and the cleansing of 'decadence' become contexts for framing a code of best social practice and regulation.

This is most obvious, perhaps, in the marriage of the novel's other central couple, John Harmon and Bella Wilfer, which aligns mutuality and romantic love with wealth, lineage, and inheritance; for, in Chapter 12 of the fourth book, conjugal bliss is rendered complete only when John, to soothe his lurking 'uneasiness' (826), lays public claim to the considerable patrimony of which he has already secretly taken possession; and a bouncing baby duly appears to consolidate the present and secure the future. The ivory casket full of jewels for Bella and the nursery for his child on which John splashes out are immediate tokens of affection but also disguised long-term investments in family bonding and forwards prosperity.

The union of Eugene and Lizzie is suffused with comparable values, though the 'normalization' that it represents is more densely textured. Lying at death's door following Headstone's murderous assault, Eugene is presented by his companion Mortimer Lightwood, after a great deal of fuss and searching for a healing spell, with 'a word' – 'Wife' (811). That the real name of Jenny Wren the Dolls' Dressmaker, who actually comes up with the magic word and slips it to Lightwood, is Fanny Cleaver suggests a regulation of sexual energies, their

---

[15] This is the phrase recurrently used in Catherine Waters, *Dickens and the Politics of the Family* (Cambridge: CUP, 1997), which includes an excellent chapter on *Our Mutual Friend*.

[16] See Waters, p. 199.

translation from wayward appetite to sanctioned disposition; an effect enforced
by the way her delicately sensuous ministration as sickroom nurse – a 'touch
upon his breast or face', an easing of the pressure of the bedclothes, a kiss upon
his cheek or 'poor maimed hand' (809–11) – subsumes the libidinal in the chaste
and intercedes to defer, while also predicting, bodily intimacy between the
intended couple.[17] At the same time, the homoerotic dimension in Eugene's
history is conclusively dissolved at the very instant of its strongest expression,
when Lightwood, the friend with whom he had shared a home, goes off to
summon Lizzie for the bedside ceremony: 'Touch my face with yours, in case I
should not hold out till you come back. I love you, Mortimer' (812). (That
Eugene is bludgeoned from behind by Bradley Headstone in the near-fatal attack
on the riverbank may also symbolize an emptying of homoerotic potency.)
Matrimony itself gives solid effect to the repentance Eugene has come to feel –
'I have wronged her enough in fact [. . .] still more in intention' (808) – and puts
his whole life on a new course, steadying the coming and going, the 'wandering
away I don't know where' (807), which in the aftermath of his illness has replaced
yet still echoes his former aimlessness. Lest we miss the fact of his redemption
as it is expressed in these motifs of journeying and orientation, delirium and
recovery, there is a clear-sighted exchange at the end of the next chapter in which
he regrets his 'trifling wasted youth' and 'humbly hope[s]' to do better henceforth
(825). The regularization of his relations with Lizzie is then carefully extended
outwards to embrace the approval of his father, which is reported in language that
implies the sanctity of the larger, collective interest. Eugene talks of his marriage
receiving 'paternal benediction' and 'being thus solemnly recognised at the
family altar' when it is suggested that Lizzie should have her portrait painted
(884) – presumably for the ancestral gallery, which would draw her formally into
line. The beauty that Eugene had once threatened to plunder as he viewed it
through the frame of the hovel window has now become a propitiatory offering
and legitimate family possession. The rejection of dynastic authority with which
his story commenced has been comprehensively reversed.

A commentator on the uses of popular literature wrote in 1849 that

> The province of the literary philanthropist is clear – to circulate widely,
> under every shape, elements of truth; to strengthen the bands of society by
> instruction, and to cement national union by social and domestic recre-
> ation. The love of families engendered by this potent, but quiet influence,
> extends and evolves itself into patriotism, and a correct sense of social and
> political freedom, grounded on the only safe basis – discipline of mind.[18]

---

[17]   See Miriam Bailin, *The Sickroom in Victorian Fiction: The Art of Being Ill*
(Cambridge: CUP, 1994), pp. 103–4.
[18]   'Cheap Reading', *Eliza Cook's Journal* 1 (1849), 2. A vigorous brief account
of 'love of families' as a keystone in the edifice of the bourgeois hegemony is given in E.J.
Hobsbawm, *The Age of Capital 1848–1875* (1975; London: Abacus, 1995), pp. 278–83.

This focuses specifically on cheap magazines, but there can be no doubt of its application to the hegemonic function of an up-market serial like *Our Mutual Friend*.[19] All the standard components of middle-class ideology are there. Even the virtue of honest work gets in as Eugene, announcing a change of attitude in his professional life, creates a motto: 'in turning to at last, we turn to in earnest' (885). Yet there are, nonetheless, some distinctive manoeuvres on Dickens' part that merit attention. For one thing, he goes out his way to insist upon a redefinition of the concept of the gentleman, when, of all people, the hitherto timorous Twemlow is given the honour, in almost the last words of the novel, of publicly putting down high 'Society', which disapproves of Eugene marrying beneath his station:

> 'Pardon me, sir,' says Twemlow, rather less mildly than usual, 'I don't agree with you. If this gentleman's feelings of gratitude, of respect, of admiration, and affection, induced him (as I presume they did) to marry this lady [. . .] I think he is the greater gentleman for the action, and makes her the greater lady. I beg to say, that when I use the word, gentleman, I use it in the sense in which the degree may be attained by any man'. (892).

Worth goes with sound sentiment and conduct, rather than with title, money or connections. The gentleman as unaccountable upper-class adventurer, like Harthouse or Steerforth, or Eugene in an earlier guise, gives way to the gentleman as man of feeling, good husband and responsible scion. Another, more striking redrawing of social boundaries lies in the very fact of the union of Eugene and Lizzie, who is at this stage a factory girl. It is as if Harthouse had learned his lesson and married Sissy Jupe, or Steerforth had done the decent thing by Little Emily – though, again, it must be remembered that Lizzie's attributes and disposition, so improbable by standards of verisimilitude, already qualify her for her upwards relocation.

The ideological preferences of *Our Mutual Friend* continue those of *David Copperfield* but with some loosening and reordering of class relations. Pure meritocrats like Headstone and his star pupil Charley Hexam make no more headway in Dickens' approbation than Uriah Heep had done; but, while David had unproblematically married a solicitor's daughter of straight middle-class pedigree, Eugene does have to adjust his lifestyle and thinking to the solid ground around and, in taking Lizzie, beneath him. It seems on close analysis impossible to designate Dickens either a reactionary or a radical. He is both. When our student of mass periodicals applauds their effect in 'strengthen[ing] the bands of society' the phrasing suggests a commitment to the principles both of hierarchical

---

[19] For discussion of the importance of Dickens and *Our Mutual Friend* in the history of the mobilization of mass audience engagement with serial fiction, see Jennifer Hayward, *Consuming Pleasures: Active Audiences and Serial Fictions from Dickens to Soap Opera* (Lexington: University Press of Kentucky, 1997), pp. 21–83.

structure, 'banding', and of promoting cohesion, 'bonding'; and in *Our Mutual Friend* Dickens extends his own pursuit of these twin objectives by prioritizing nobility of *character* and by crossing dividing lines.

Dickens was not alone in doing this. The most dedicated of all propagators of Victorian values, Samuel Smiles, did not publish the volume actually entitled *On Character* until 1871, but Dickens may well have been influenced by the earlier *Self-Help*, which proclaims this theme alongside the gospel of work and had already gone into four editions and eight reprints between 1859, the year of publication, and 1864 when the first part of *Our Mutual Friend* came out. There is, for instance, a close parallel between Dickens' definition of the true gentleman and that formulated at length in the final chapter of Smiles' guidebook to national standards in conduct and achievement: 'Riches and rank have no necessary connexion with genuine gentlemanly qualities. The poor man may be a true gentleman – in spirit and in daily life. He may be honest, truthful, upright, polite, temperate, courageous, self-respecting, and self-helping.'[20] It is high-mindedness and behaviour that matter in life, not birth or material possessions. Smiles' specific reference to 'the poor man' renders transparent his, and Dickens', outflanking of the problem of inequality and possible conflict between the classes.

Smiles was also instrumental in circulating that other great prescription for social stability, the doctrine of 'home' and 'separate spheres', which associated men with the realm of business and charged women with maintenance of what Ruskin famously, or notoriously, called the 'temple of the hearth'.[21] Smiles' highest term of praise is 'manly', and among his most important measures of worth are the discretion and forbearance with which a man '*exercise[s] power* over those subordinate to him', of which 'women and children' head the list (477). The records of heroes and their exploits that pack the pages of *Self-Help* are ghosted by the wives and mothers whose special duty was moral guardianship and service in the home as, in the words of one contemporary journalist, a 'place of happiness [. . .] which alone can make compensation for all the troubles [. . .] with which men of all classes must meet in public life, and business, and occupation of any description'.[22] And such is the impression we get in the penultimate chapter of *Our Mutual Friend*, where, on a visit to the Harmons, 'Mr Eugene Wrayburn' imparts to 'Mrs John Harmon' the confidence that 'please God, she should see how his wife had changed him', and Lizzie duly appears to

---

[20]	Samuel Smiles, *Self-Help, With Illustrations of Conduct and Perseverance* (1859; London: John Murray, 1908), p. 470. Hereafter cited in the text.

[21]	John Ruskin, 'Of Queens' Gardens', *Sesame and Lilies* (1865; London: Cassell, 1909), p. 73.

[22]	'Woman in Domestic Life', *Magazine of Domestic Economy* 1 (1836), 66. Smiles outlines the duties of women directly in Chapter 2 of *On Character*, entitled 'Home Power', where, for example, command of the useful art of preparing healthy food is contrasted with the pointless aspiration of having the vote.

fill out the image of regenerative sway and constant support: '"But would you believe, Bella," interposed his wife, coming to resume her nurse's place at his side, for he never got on well without her: "that on our wedding day he told me he almost thought the best thing he could do, was to die?"' (883–4).

Some critics have taken a very dim view of the ending of *Our Mutual Friend*. Eve Kosofsky Sedgwick, for example, an influential analyst of culture formation, talks of 'this homophobic reinscription of the bourgeois family' that is particularly 'crippling' to Lizzie Hexam, who is 'unrelentingly [. . .] diminished by her increasingly distinct gender assignment'.[23] There is a point here of course: the 'wife' (the term becomes so ubiquitous as to be an identity tag) who assumes 'her nurse's place' at her husband's side and has to be persuaded by her friend Bella to go out for ride (884) certainly lacks the appealing robustness and mystery of the veiled figure rowing a scavenger boat on the Thames. To accommodate Lizzie to the presiding ideology requires her diminution, her sanitization.

But are things ever that simple? In its afterlife, the text as we read it now, the conclusion of *Our Mutual Friend* is on several levels a self-subverting artefact. Core affirmations are undermined and called in question. The continual foregrounding of 'wife' as a word – Chapter 10 of the fourth book is actually entitled 'The Dolls' Dressmaker Discovers a Word' – exposes marriage as a constituent in a symbolic order, rather than a necessary or organic state; even, in human terms, it becomes a choice that can be accepted or refused. Similarly, the idea of gentlemanliness with which the book ends is so isolated and bracketed off as the unlikely utterance of a minor character that it inevitably declares its part as a tactic in a design that, as we have seen, at once supports and hides a system of inequality. Most notable in the light of Sedgwick's misgivings, however, is the fact that whatever the falling-off in Lizzie's independence and vitality, Eugene is a great deal more depleted and put down. Determined to argue that Eugene is privileged over Lizzie, Sedgwick writes that he 'already, by the end of the novel, looks almost "as though he had never been mutilated"';[24] but this is unfaithful to the text, which really says that the glow on his face as he talked of defending Lizzie to the last against her detractors 'so irradiated his features that he looked, *for the time*, as though he had never been mutilated' (886: italics mine). The recovery of viripotence is provisional and uncertain – especially when we recall the previous information that 'it was declared by the medical attendants that he *might not be much disfigured by-and-by*' (883: italics mine). Far from Eugene's position being, as Sedgwick claims, 'awash with patriarchal authority',[25] the overwhelming impression is of his dependency, as he walks 'resting on his wife's arm, and leaning heavily upon a stick' (883). She may be the womanly 'nurse',

---

[23] Sedgwick, 'Homophobia, Misogyny, and Capital', *Charles Dickens*, ed. Connor, pp. 193–4.
[24] Ibid., p. 193.
[25] Ibid.

but he is the patient; and, what is more, his physical incapacity is matched by a psychological one, for all he can do when Lizzie is away – *she* retains some degree of mobility – is 'look [. . .] forward to [her] coming back' (886), like a child missing its mother. Whereas he had once led Headstone a merry dance all over London, he can now only sit waiting for his wife to return from an outing. The figuring of middle-class domestic ideology in this novel is achieved at the price of Eugene's abiding disfigurement and unmanning. The whole edifice of that ideology is destabilized, even as it is being built, by a quirkiness in the design and distortions in the relation of parts. We can turn Sedgwick around and say that in the misalignment of gender positions, which is all the more apparent in comparison with the normative Harmon household, we detect the distinct outline of a female empowerment.

Yet, when all is said, the tensions we have just identified in *Our Mutual Friend* can also be viewed in another light. The subordination of Eugene and Lizzie to the purposes of ideology is, in a sense, the sacrifice of Dickens' imaginative art. It repeats that long-standing conflict that had emerged early in his career in *Oliver Twist* with the upvaluing of the world of Mr Brownlow and the Maylies at the expense of that of Fagin, Sikes and their associates. The issue is that of order against energy, or of narrative – that is, the teleology of middle-class values – against the life of fiction. Recalcitrance, the grotesque, violence, the most piquant ingredients of Dickensian fictionality, resurface of course, among the characters we have considered, in Uriah Heep and Bradley Headstone; and they are present too, in a lower key, in the unreclaimed Eugene Wrayburn, not least in his 'goad[ing] the schoolmaster to madness' (where the syntax attaches the madness equally to the hunted and the hunter). But there is something else in this side of Eugene: as we have noted, it is a doubling of the darker authorial temperament itself, just as in his steady contemplation of the solitary Lizzie he enacts a sensuous aestheticism that is both creative and predatory. The reactions of generations of readers (including Sedgwick) have indicated, however, that, though ideology overrules imagination in *Oliver Twist* or *Our Mutual Friend,* it does not subjugate or erase its appeal. This is a characteristic irresolution – another way in which Dickens' text questions itself. His last finished novel technically cleans up 'decadence' yet actually remains its host.

Chapter 6

Defining Decadence in Nineteenth-century French and British Criticism

Julian North

British critical interest in literary decadence has usually been seen as having started with Pater in the 1870s and become more widespread only in the 1880s and 1890s, with the emergence of a self-consciously decadent movement in literature and the arts. The word 'decadence' had, of course, existed in English long before this period, denoting the decline of civilizations and thus encompassing cultural degeneration in a general sense. It was, however, only rarely applied by earlier nineteenth-century British critics to specific aesthetic effects and was not fully naturalized until later in the century.[1] When, in 1823, De Quincey came across the term he felt it pointed 'to another language than English', and it was still considered a 'barbarous Gallicism' by one writer in 1871.[2] We must, indeed, look to France if we are to find explicit discussions of literary decadence from the early to mid-nineteenth century. The first major anatomization of a decadent aesthetic was by Désiré Nisard, whose study of the late Latin poets, published in 1834, compared modern French poetry to the degenerate works of Lucan and his contemporaries.[3] Nisard's understanding of decadence was largely, although not exclusively, hostile, but in 1857 Baudelaire

---

[1]   The *Oxford English Dictionary* cites the earliest occurrence as *The Complaynt of Scotland* (1549), Chapter 7, 'My tiumphant stait is succumbit in decadens'. A characteristic mid-nineteenth-century usage is in Lord Lindsay's *Sketches of the History of Christian Art*, 3 vols (London: John Murray, 1847), I, p. 114, where he describes the eleventh century as 'marking the lowest decadence of Byzantine art'.

[2]   Thomas De Quincey, 'Anecdotage: Miss Hawkins's Anecdotes' (1823), in ed. David Masson, *The Collected Writings of Thomas De Quincey*, 14 vols (London: A. and C. Black, 1896–7), V, pp. 146–64, see especially p. 161. See also L.M. Hawkins, *Anecdotes, Biographical Sketches, and Memoirs* (London: F.C. and J. Rivington, 1822), vol. 1, p. 123, where the word 'decadent' is used to describe a social come-down. J.B. Mayor, 'Decadence', *Journal of Philology* vol. 3 (1871), pp. 347–8, see especially p. 347.

[3]   Désiré Nisard, *Etudes de moeurs et de critique sur les poètes latins de la décadence* [*Moral and Critical Investigations into the Latin Decadent Poets*], 3 vols (Brussels: Louis Hauman, 1834).

responded by making the term an honorific.[4] Baudelaire's poetic practice as well as his critical pronouncements stimulated further influential discussions of decadence in France, including Théophile Gautier's preface to the 1868 edition of *Les Fleurs du mal* and Paul Bourget's essay on the poet published in 1881.[5] It was only in the wake of this tradition within French criticism, and especially following on from Henry Havelock Ellis's exposition of Bourget's theory in 1887, that the term began to be used more widely in Britain to describe certain features of content and form in French and British writing.[6] The French example, whether in theory or practice, remained a central influence on definitions of decadence in critical essays by Lionel Johnson, Richard Le Gallienne, Arthur Symons and others in the 1890s.[7]

However, as R.K.R. Thornton argues, the speed with which the term gained currency in Britain during the *fin-de-siècle* period 'suggests that the phenomenon it describes was well-known before the word was found to name it'.[8] This essay will explore the ways in which some of the major documents of British criticism from the Romantic and early to mid-Victorian periods, while not necessarily employing the word itself, were nevertheless deeply engaged with the idea of a decadent literary language. In so doing I will be developing and qualifying the important work done by Linda Dowling who has extended the standard history of nineteenth-century British decadence.[9] I aim, thereby, to come to a closer

---

[4]   Charles Baudelaire, 'Notes nouvelles sur Edgar Poe', *Nouvelles histoires extraordinaires* (1857) ['New notes on Edgar Poe', *New Strange Stories*], in ed. Claude Pichois, *Baudelaire, Oeuvres complètes, Bibliothèque de la Pléiade*, 2 vols (Paris: Editions Gallimard, 1975-6), II, pp. 319-37, see 319-20. For moments when Nisard softens towards decadence, see e.g. Nisard, vol. 3, pp. 15 and 226-8, where he acknowledges that there is a 'plaisir inquiet, hésitant' ['an anxious, hesitant pleasure'] to be found in Lucan's style, that the classical and the decadent Latin poets complement, rather than eclipse each other, and that there is a kind of beauty, albeit quickly satiating, in the stylistic brilliance of Lucan and his fellow poets.

[5]   Théophile Gautier, 'Charles Baudelaire', in *Baudelaire, Oeuvres complètes*, 4 vols (Paris: Michel Lévy frères, 1868-9), I, *Les Fleurs du mal [Flowers of Evil]*, pp. 1-75; Paul Bourget, 'Charles Baudelaire' (1881), in Paul Bourget, *Oeuvres complètes de Paul Bourget*, 9 vols (Paris: Plon and Nourrit, 1899-1911), I, pp. 3-25.

[6]   Henry Havelock Ellis, 'A Note on Paul Bourget' (1887), in Ellis, *Views and Reviews, First Series: 1884-1919* (London: Harmsworth, 1932), pp. 48-60, see pp. 51-3. Note this reprint mistakenly claims that Ellis's article originally appeared in 1889.

[7]   See Lionel Johnson, 'A Note Upon the Practice and Theory of Verse at the Present Time Obtaining in France', *Century Guild Hobby Horse* 6, 22 (April, 1891), 61-6; Richard Le Gallienne, 'Considerations Suggested by Mr. Churton Collins' "Illustrations of Tennyson"', 7, 27 (July, 1892), 77-82; and Arthur Symons, 'The Decadent Movement in Literature', *Harper's New Monthly Magazine* 87, 522 (November, 1893), 858-67.

[8]   R.K.R. Thornton, *The Decadent Dilemma* (London: Edward Arnold, 1983), p. 35.

[9]   Linda Dowling, *Language and Decadence in the Victorian Fin de Siècle* (Princeton: Princeton University Press, 1986).

understanding of what literary decadence meant for nineteenth-century writers and of the process by which the definition of this cultural phenomenon took place.

Instead of focusing on the French tradition, Dowling argues that literary decadence in Britain had its origins in late eighteenth-century, and early nineteenth-century, German philology. Even on a broader, cultural level, she claims, decadence stemmed from

> a linguistic crisis [. . . created by] a spectre of autonomous language – language as a system blindly obeying impersonal phonological rules in isolation from any world of human values and experience . . .[10]

Dowling's contention is that this vision, or 'spectre', of autonomous language, was raised by the new comparative philology, originating with Herder in the late eighteenth century and introduced decisively into Britain, from Germany, by Max Müller, in his *Lectures on the Science of Language*, delivered in 1861.[11] These lectures emphasized 'that language was organized on purely linguistic principles, independent of both men and representation', and that it was 'essentially constituted by sound'.[12] The first of these claims, she argues, undermined the Victorian ideal of the English language as an expression of the nation, and so threatened the ideal of civilization itself.[13] The second claim threatened to subvert the status of literature, since written language was now portrayed as a petrified falsification of speech: 'In the linguistic order ushered in by the new comparative philology, the only instance of decay in language was writing.'[14] Dowling represents Pater as the initiator of literary decadence in Britain by means of his erudite style, based on a scholarly exhumation of English, considered as a dead language.[15]

This book is suggestive in many respects, but especially so in the author's insistence upon the centrality of a concept of autonomous language to the theory and practice of literary decadence, and her willingness to talk of the 'spectre' of such a language, thereby broadening the scope of inquiry into the history of decadence beyond the use of the term itself. Her focus on German philology as the origin of British decadence has some unfortunate side effects, however, most particularly in leading to a comparative neglect of French criticism – notably of Nisard, who is, oddly, hardly mentioned. This, I believe, creates a somewhat distorted picture of the history of nineteenth-century decadence generally and of British decadence in particular. As we shall see, Nisard's work may have exerted

---

10   Ibid., pp. xi–xii.
11   Ibid., pp. 46–103.
12   Ibid., pp. 61–2.
13   Ibid., p. 62 ff.
14   Ibid., p. 84.
15   Ibid., pp. 104–40.

a direct influence on some British critics in the 1840s and 1850s and there are certainly significant parallels between some early to mid-nineteenth-century British criticism and the French theorization of decadence. By broadening out the discussion from a specific focus on the history of Romantic philology, and by comparing French and British critical texts from this earlier period, it is possible to see, at the heart of both, an anxious vision of a destructive linguistic autonomy.

Désiré Nisard's *Etudes de moeurs et de critique sur les poètes latins de la décadence* (1834) is commonly cited as a useful starting-point in assessing what decadence meant for nineteenth-century writers and critics, but it deserves closer attention than it is usually given if we are to understand the meanings that decadence held for French critics and to recognize the parallels with earlier nineteenth-century British visions of a decadent literary language. Nisard's work must be seen in the context of a revival of classicism in the 1830s in France. Along with the critics Gustave Planche and Saint-Marc Girardin, Nisard was part of a conservative reaction against the Romantic tendencies within contemporary French literature.[16] The bulk of Nisard's *Etudes* is taken up with an account of the writings of the late Latin poets as a debased aftermath of the classical ideals of Homer and Virgil. From this basis he goes on to argue that modern French poetry has reached a comparable stage of decadence.[17] Nisard thus uses the term both to denote a broad cultural degeneracy within the two societies he discusses, and to describe specific features of content and form in the writing they have produced. Above all he defines decadent poetry by the nature of its language and style.

Both the Latin and the French decadent poets, according to Nisard, are obsessed with descriptive detail. Lucan and his contemporaries anatomize the material world, smothering all philosophical thought or moral feeling in a '*luxe de détails*' ['profusion of details'], with a penchant for those which are unpleasant or ugly.[18] The French poets, although concentrating on their inner lives, show a similar love of description: '*même intempérance de détails, même recherche des nuances*' ['the same intemperance of details, the same quest for nuances'], and the same preference for the horrible.[19] The Latin and the French decadents are both backward-looking, imitating the curious detail of former ages – pagan or medieval – in a spirit of sterile erudition.[20] The descriptive and the erudite tendencies of the decadents both display their vitiated passions and lack of inventive power.[21] The result is that both late Latin and modern French poetry have become pure style – all the effects of Lucan's verse are '*dans le style*' ['in

---

[16] René Wellek, *A History of Modern Criticism, 1750–1950*, 5 vols (1965; London: Jonathan Cape, 1970), III, *The Age of Transition*, pp. 17–22.
[17] Nisard, *Etudes*, vol. 3, pp. 52–9, 245–66.
[18] Ibid., p. 6, also see pp. 1–59.
[19] Ibid., pp. 257–8.
[20] Ibid., pp. 60–94, 256–7.
[21] Ibid., pp. 37, 49–50, 61, 90, 257.

the style'] – determined by form, rather than by content.[22] All is sacrificed to '*le trait*' ['flashes of beauty'].[23] Modern French poetry is consumed by a '*luxe de mots et de tornures*' ['an abundance of words and phrases'].[24] In short, literary decadence is, for Nisard, a falling off from things to words:

> *La question est tombée des choses aux mots* [. . . the decadent poets] *vont du mot à la chose, et non de la chose au mot.*[25]

> [The matter has descended from things to words [. . . the decadent poets] go from the word to the thing, and not from the thing to the word.]

But there is more to it than this. Words have not only become dislocated from thought and feeling in decadent poetry, they have, in so doing, taken on a malign life of their own and are actively engaged in destroying these things: '*la forme a étouffé le fond*' ['form has stifled content'].[26] Decadence for Nisard is first and foremost an issue of literary style, but style is not a trivial matter for him. Decadence is not merely about a number of poems being over-written, incoherent, perhaps even immoral. The decline in modern French poetry promises to destroy the very culture of which it is part, for the cultivation of obscure idiolects by these poets threatens the '*langue nationale*' – '*je crois que rien n'est plus propre à détruire une langue que cette espèce de poésie*' ['I believe that nothing is more suited to destroying a language than this kind of poetry'].[27] At such moments Nisard's tract voices precisely the fears that Dowling has identified as the product of Romantic philology. He sees the destructive power of the word, unloosed from meaning and imperilling the national language, as a vital part of a wider social and cultural decline.

Although, on the whole, more favourably disposed towards the idea than Nisard, the other well-known nineteenth-century French theorists of decadence are in fundamental agreement with his account of what constitutes a decadent literature. As for Nisard, so for Baudelaire the '*Littérature de décadence*' is anti-classical, typified by a magnificently ornamented style and based on a cult of artifice, as opposed to the classical ideal of '*la simple nature*'.[28] This time, however, the language of the late Latin poets, full of barbarisms and solecisms, is welcomed as a model for modern poetry.[29] Gautier, similarly, argues that the

---

[22] Ibid., p. 15.

[23] Ibid., pp. 226–8, 258.

[24] Ibid., p. 258.

[25] Ibid., pp. 91, 166–7.

[26] Ibid., p. 93.

[27] Ibid., pp. 259–61.

[28] Baudelaire, 'Notes nouvelles' (1857) in ed. Pichois, *Baudelaire, Oeuvres*, vol. 2, p. 319.

[29] Baudelaire, note to 'Franciscae meae laudes' (1857), in ibid., vol. 1, p. 940.

decadent style is anti-classical, a late style, after the example of the Latin Decadents. It is the final effort of the word in the last hours of civilization: '*le dernier mot du Verbe sommé de tout exprimer et poussé à l'extrême outrance*' ['the last saying of the Word called upon to express everything and pushed to the extreme limit'].[30] Nisard's sense of the quite literal decadence, or decomposition, of the text which is based on descriptive detail, a dying language and a style asserting an autonomous power, is developed by Bourget in his famous analogy between literary decadence and the decomposing organism. Just as an organism or a whole society decays if the cells or individuals rebel against the whole, so a decadent style is

> *celui où l'unité du livre se décompose pour laisser la place à l'indépendance de la page, où la page se décompose pour laisser la place à l'indépendance de la phrase, et la phrase pour laisser la place à l'indépendance du mot.*[31]

> [that in which the unity of the book decomposes to make way for the independence of the page, in which the page decomposes to make way for the independence of the sentence, and the sentence to make way for the independence of the word.]

For all of these critics, then, decadent literature represents a dissolution of classical ideals. It is a literature concerned with the nuance of individual feeling. It is based on a language which has reached a late stage of its development and begun to show signs of petrifaction or decomposition, and it cultivates the autonomous powers of that language in a cult of style working apart from content.

What evidence can we find in early to mid-nineteenth-century British criticism of a similar interest in literary decadence, defined in this way? We might begin by looking at a well-known passage from Wordsworth's *Essays Upon Epitaphs* (1810), where he considers the relation of form and content in poetry and imagines the consequences of a language which is not the incarnation of thought, but a power in its own right:

> Words are too awful an instrument for good and evil to be trifled with: they hold above all other external powers a dominion over thoughts. If words be not [. . .] an incarnation of the thought but only a clothing for it, then surely will they prove an ill gift; such a one as those poisoned vestments, read of in the stories of superstitious times, which had power to consume and to alienate from his right mind the victim who put them on. Language,

---

[30]   Gautier, 'Charles Baudelaire', in *Baudelaire, Oeuvres complètes* (1868–9), vol. 1, p. 35.

[31]   Bourget, *Oeuvres complètes*, vol. 1, pp. 15–16. For Bourget's debts to Nisard see J. Kamerbeek, 'Style de Décadence', *Revue de littérature comparée* 39 (1965), 268–86.

if it do not uphold, and feed, and leave in quiet, like the power of gravitation or the air we breathe, is a counter-spirit, unremittingly and noiselessly at work to derange, to subvert, to lay waste, to vitiate, and to dissolve.[32]

The consequences of words when they do not fuse with thought and feeling are not, according to Wordsworth, to be underestimated. The result as he sees it is decadence not merely on the level of textual incoherence – bad poetry – but also a mental dissolution and what seems at the end of this passage to be universal destruction. Dowling reads this vision of an autonomous literary language, consuming the text, in the context of Romantic philology: 'The *Essays on Epitaphs* [sic] strike just that note of demoralization about the Romantic logos that, in a more urgently apocalyptic key, Victorians were to hear in literary Decadence.'[33] She argues that Wordsworth's ideal of poetic language as a purified, rural speech and his emphasis on pre-verbal feeling, are both part of a reaction against his distrust of the dangerously independent power of words. He 'did not seek so much to collapse the Enlightenment polarity of word and thing into a new "incarnational" unity of word and thing as to reverse the axis of that polarity *from* words *to* things or feelings'.[34] As this suggests, Dowling sees his poetic theory as demonstrating an underlying lack of faith in the strength of the relationship between language and culture.[35]

We might broaden Dowling's context for Wordsworth's vision of the 'spectre' of decadence by comparing it to the explicit discussions of decadence in French criticism, and especially to Nisard's *Etudes*. The fact that Wordsworth clearly differs from Nisard in the romantic aspects of his theory should not distract attention from the common ground of conservative, neo-classical values held by the two critics. Despite Nisard's anti-Romanticism, there is much in his argument that is reminiscent of Wordsworth's pronouncements in the 'Prefaces' and 'Appendix' to *Lyrical Ballads* (1800, 1802) and the *Essays Upon Epitaphs*. Both critics adhere to a version of literary history as a decline from a primitive poetry of feeling to a learnt literary language, or what Wordsworth calls 'poetic diction'.[36] Both share a nostalgia for the primitive as pure and natural, and a distrust of modern literature (albeit differently defined) as artificial and corrupt. Wordsworth does not, like Nisard, employ the term decadence, yet his anxieties concerning a destructive linguistic autonomy invading modern literature are identical to those expressed more directly by Nisard in his polemic on decadence.

---

[32]   William Wordsworth, 'Essays Upon Epitaphs' (1810), in eds W.J.B. Owen and J.W. Smyser, *The Prose Works of William Wordsworth*, 3 vols (Oxford: Clarendon Press, 1974), II, pp. 84–5.

[33]   Dowling, *Language and Decadence*, p. 20.

[34]   Ibid., p. 21.

[35]   Ibid., p. 22.

[36]   See Wordsworth, 'Appendix' to the Preface to *Lyrical Ballads* (1802), in *The Prose Works of William Wordsworth*, vol. 1, p. 162.

This becomes clear in the language employed by both critics. The passage from *Essays Upon Epitaphs* quoted above, may be compared to subsequent nineteenth-century evocations of decadence – by Gautier and Wilde, for instance – in using a metaphor of poisoning to describe the effects of autonomous language.[37] Its closest parallel, however, is with a passage from the *Etudes* where Nisard describes the decadent style by ironically reworking the neo-classical commonplace that language is the dress of thought. Instead it becomes a grotesquely ill-fitting garment:

> *un style décousu, tantôt trop étriqué pour une pensée qui voulait du développement, tantôt trop ample pour une pensée maigre qui s'y perd, comme un corps fluet dans un vaste manteau antique.*[38]

> [a disjointed [literally unstitched/unpicked] style, sometimes too skimpy for a thought which needs some growing-room, sometimes too full for a slight thought which is lost in it, like a slender body in a huge old-fashioned cloak.]

Just as, in Wordsworth's simile, the word liberated from thought and feeling is like the shirt of Nessus, poisoning and consuming the body, and alienating the mind, so, in Nisard's, decadent style is like a coat which either constricts or swamps its contents. Both passages describe the central concern of these critics that language, once divorced from thought and feeling, will turn upon and destroy these things. Both critics, despite their differences, share a rooted conservatism that leads to a distrust of the modern and the artificial. It is this distrust which surfaces in visions of a literary decadence which must both be seen as part of the fabric of the history of nineteenth-century decadence.

As already acknowledged, Wordsworth's view of exactly where decadent literary practice was to be located in the history of poetry was not the same as Nisard's. Wordsworth was not always clear about the specific instances of corruption he had in mind, but he looked back, at least in part, to the artificial 'poetic diction' visible in eighteenth-century, neo-classical poetry – including works by Pope.[39] Nisard, on the other hand, although equally unwilling to point the finger at specific modern French poets in the *Etudes*, clearly had the Romantic tradition in mind. He focuses on the decadent subjectivity of modern French poetry and, in a later essay, he targeted Victor Hugo for the same misdemeanours

---

[37] Compare for example Gautier, 'Charles Baudelaire', in *Baudelaire, Oeuvres complètes* (1868–9), vol. 1, p. 17, on the *'verts empoisonés'* ['poisonous greens'] of decadent poetry; and ed. Isobel Murray, *Oscar Wilde, The Picture of Dorian Gray* (1890; London: Oxford University Press, 1974), p. 125, for the 'poisonous book'.

[38] Nisard, *Etudes*, vol. 3, p. 226.

[39] See e.g. Wordsworth, 'Appendix' to the Preface to *Lyrical Ballads* (1802), in *The Prose Works of William Wordsworth*, vol. 1, p. 162, where he states that Pope's 'Messiah' is a perfect example of 'poetic diction'.

described as decadent in the *Etudes*: excessive description without feeling, *'Langue, qui pour vouloir tout peindre, substitue des images aux réalités, des couleurs aux pensées'* ['Language which, wishing to depict everything, substitutes images for reality, colours for thoughts'].[40] In this respect Wordsworth's visions of decadence are less akin to Nisard's than some later British criticism, which does not merely raise the 'spectre' of a decadent literary language, but also lays the crime of decadence at the feet of the Romantic poets.

In British criticism from around the 1830s to the 1850s there was a strong vein of hostility to Romantic poetry and a resurgence of conservative, neo-classical values, comparable to that occurring in French criticism at the same period. This has not, I think, previously been seen as relevant to the history of decadence. However, one of the effects of this anti-Romantic backlash was that, in repeated instances, Romantic poetry was described as a decadence – not merely in a generalized sense, but in a way that quite specifically parallels the definitions of Nisard and later French and British theorists of decadence. I will focus on just three essays, by Henry Taylor, William Edmondstoune Aytoun and Matthew Arnold, to exemplify what was a widespread phenomenon.

Henry Taylor's preface to his play *Philip van Artevelde*, published in the same year as Nisard's *Etudes*, takes a similar line of argument to that of the French critic. Like Nisard, Taylor discusses contemporary Romantic poetry as a literature in decline, spoilt by its unremitting subjectivity and the obliteration of content by form. The English Romantics were guilty, argues Taylor, of 'unbounded indulgence in the mere luxuries of poetry', substituting feeling for reflection, and form for subject-matter – 'an image was always at hand when a thought was not forthcoming'.[41] Echoing Wordsworth's phrase, although in the context of a disgust with Romantic sensibilities, Taylor writes that modern poetry has degenerated into 'little more than a poetical diction, an arrangement of words implying a sensitive state of mind'. With the example of Shelley in mind, he warns 'Let no man sit down to write with the purpose of making every line and word beautiful and peculiar'.[42] Taylor's characterization of Romantic writing as a degenerate art, a luxurious self-indulgence in feeling and in the *recherché* aesthetic appeal of style for style's sake is not presented explicitly within the framework of decadence, but defines a literary decadence, nevertheless, in a negative image.

In the 1840s and 1850s the anti-Romantic reaction was focused particularly on the so-called 'Spasmodic' school – a group of poets including P.J. Bailey, Sidney Dobell, J.W. Marston and Alexander Smith, who created epics modelled

---

[40]   Nisard, *Essais sur l'école romantique* [*Essays on the Romantic School*] (1836–7), quoted in Wellek, vol. 3, p.275.

[41]   Henry Taylor, Preface to *Philip van Artevelde: A Dramatic Romance* (London: Edward Moxon, 1834), pp. x–xi.

[42]   Ibid., pp. xx, xxii, xii.

on the works of Byron and Goethe but written in an extravagantly metaphorical style. Again we find a decadent literary language defined in reaction to what was regarded by the critical establishment as Romantic excess. William Edmondstoune Aytoun, the major scourge of the Spasmodic poets, and the inventor of their nickname, described them as 'blazing away whole rounds of metaphor, to mask their absolute poverty of thought'.[43] Aytoun's verse drama *Firmilian* (1854) parodied this aspect of their work with a profusion of images, which might, indeed, bear comparison with the self-consciously decadent catalogues of Wilde's *Salomé* (1894): 'O my beautiful!/ My seraph love – my panther of the wild – / My moon-eyed leopard – my voluptuous lord!'.[44] In a review of 1857 Aytoun described 'Spasmodic' linguistic excess explicitly in terms of a literary decadence:

> the whole attention of the artist is lavished upon expression. This, if we are to judge from antecedents, is a symptom of literary decadence [. . .] sound and pretension are becoming more esteemed than sense and deliberate purpose [. . .] brilliant writing, or writing which seems brilliant, is esteemed as of the highest kind, without regard to congruity or design.[45]

A literary decadence is, for Aytoun, as for the better-known commentators on decadence, a matter of style – a late-Romantic ascendancy of form over substance so that 'expression', 'sound', 'brilliant writing' become all in all, with a resulting structural decomposition. The similarities between Aytoun's definition and Nisard's suggest that he may have been familiar with the *Etudes*.

The best-known critical essay relating to the Spasmodic controversy is Arnold's Preface to his *Poems* (1853).[46] Here, too, we find Romantic poetry portrayed as in a state of decadence, defined in large part by its tendency to allow words a disruptive autonomy. Like Nisard before him, Arnold upholds the classical ideal as a standard from which modern poetry has, sadly, fallen away, and like Nisard he protests against poetry which puts expression before content, individual beauties before the coherent structure of the whole.

> [the ancient Greek poets . . .] regarded the whole; we regard the parts. With them, the action predominated over the expression of it; with us, the

---

[43] W. E. Aytoun, review of his own play, *Firmilian: A Tragedy*, first published *Blackwood's Magazine* (May, 1854). See ed. F. Page, *Poems of William Edmondstoune Aytoun* (Oxford: Humphrey Milford/OUP, 1921), p. 504.

[44] W. E. Aytoun, *Firmilian: or the Student of Badajoz. A Spasmodic Tragedy* (Edinburgh: William Blackwood and Sons, 1854), p. 139.

[45] Aytoun, 'Mrs. Barrett Browning – *Aurora Leigh*', *Blackwood's* 81, 495 (January, 1857), 23–41, p. 40.

[46] For the Spasmodic controversy as a context for Arnold's preface, see M.A. Weinstein, *William Edmondstoune Aytoun and the Spasmodic Controversy* (New Haven: Yale University Press, 1968), pp. 99–107.

expression predominates over the action [. . .] We have poems which seem to exist merely for the sake of single lines and passages; not for the sake of producing any total impression. We have critics who seem to direct their attention merely to the detached expressions, to the language about the action, not to the action itself [. . . the great artist] subordinates expression to that which it is designed to express.[47]

Arnold laments the fact that contemporary poetry sacrifices coherence to 'occasional bursts of fine writing' and 'a shower of isolated thoughts and images'.[48] He regrets that Keats favoured 'happy single expressions' over the action of the whole, and that even Shakespeare's language can become similarly 'artificial', his poetic gift 'degenerating sometimes into a fondness for curiosity of expression.'[49] He also protests against 'morbid' situations in poetry, in which 'suffering finds no vent in action'.[50] Thus, without using the word 'decadence' Arnold conjures up a decadent literature in which a moribund language has gained the upper hand, in which stasis has replaced action and in which the text, consequently, has begun to decompose structurally and morally. In all this Arnold's proximity to Nisard and subsequent theorists of literary decadence is apparent. It is made clearer still if we look at a letter to Clough, written a few years previously, but nevertheless an important gloss on the 1853 Preface. Arnold writes that

> one of the signs of the Decadence of a literature, one of the factors of its decadent condition indeed, is this – that new authors attach themselves to the poetic expression the founders of a literature have flowered into, which may be *learned* by a sensitive person, to the neglect of an inward poetic life.[51]

This is an unusually early use of the word 'decadence' in English, and may show knowledge of Nisard's *Etudes*. Certainly Arnold's understanding of the term is consistent with the views of both Nisard and Wordsworth. For Arnold in this letter and later in the preface of 1853, a literary language operating as an autonomous, artificial system, independent of and threatening to the shared human experience which formed the foundations of a cultural heritage, is a decadent language.

---

[47] Matthew Arnold, *Preface to Poems* (1853) in ed. R.H. Super, *The Complete Prose Works of Matthew Arnold*, 11 vols (Ann Arbor: University of Michigan Press, 1960-77), I, pp. 5, 7, 10.

[48] Ibid., p. 7.

[49] Ibid., pp. 10–11.

[50] Ibid., pp. 3, 2.

[51] Letter from Arnold to Clough, dated late 1847 or early 1848, in ed. H.F. Lowry, *The Letters of Matthew Arnold to Arthur Hugh Clough* (1932; Oxford: Clarendon Press, 1968), p. 64.

For Wordsworth, Taylor, Aytoun and Arnold, decadence is defined by way of naming everything that they believe a literature and a culture ought *not* to be. This would seem to distinguish this earlier phase of thinking about decadence in British criticism quite clearly from the more positive definitions of a decadent aesthetic in the last decades of the century. In practice it is difficult to draw such a distinction. Inevitably in these earlier essays the negative image defines the positive and decadence thus becomes perversely necessary to what these critics deem a literature and a culture *should* be. Indeed, the failure to repress decadence generates an audible anxiety particularly in the essays by Wordsworth and Arnold. Conversely even once the 'spectre' of decadence was made flesh in the work of Baudelaire, Gautier, Huysmans, Symons, Wilde and others, anxieties remained, so much so that having trumpeted a decadent *avant garde*, both Baudelaire and Symons decisively rejected the term.[52] Decadence must, perhaps necessarily, receive an equivocal welcome and the definition of decadence in nineteenth-century British criticism cannot be seen simply as the belated imitation of a French embrace of the concept. As becomes clear when we look both at direct European influences on British discussions of literary decadence and at parallel developments, the process of defining decadence has a subtler and a longer history than has usually been granted – a history deeply embedded within Romantic and Victorian criticism.

---

[52]   See Baudelaire 'Lettre à Jules Janin' (c. 1865), *Baudelaire, Oeuvres complètes*, vol. 2, p. 237: '*Décadence. C'est un mot bien commode à l'usage des pédagogues ignorants*' ['Decadence. It is a very handy word for the use of ignorant pedagogues']. Symons retitled the revised version of his essay 'The Decadent Movement in Literature' (1893), *The Symbolist Movement in Literature* (1899).

Chapter 7

Somewhere there's Music: John Meade Falkner's *The Lost Stradivarius*

Nicholas Daly

The discourse of aestheticism, as it develops in the late nineteenth century, comes to offer, inter alia, a language for the articulation of subjugated sexualities. In fact it is probably not overstating it to say that the first modern gay male subculture is that of the aesthete. There is more at stake here of course than some cliché of the gay man as a connoisseur of pretty things, or as a creator of the house or apartment beautiful: aestheticism's cult of art and artifice, and its deconstruction of the 'natural,' offer a means of understanding identity, and within that sexual identity, as something constructed, as a formal rather than a moral entity. Linda Dowling, in her study, *Hellenism and Homosexuality in Victorian Oxford*, has traced the prehistory of the gender politics of aestheticism, locating its proximal origins in the attempts by Benjamin Jowett and others to reform the programme of undergraduate study at Oxford, with a view to training a cadre of men able to lead Victorian England through a disorienting period of modernization (cf. Matthew Arnold's advocacy of Hellenic culture as a cure for the ills of modern England). To put it crudely, this involved a shift from the study of Latin grammar to Greek culture, as well as a new emphasis on the personal tutorial and self-development. But as Dowling points out, this celebration of Greek culture and *Bildung* also provided writers like J.A. Symonds and Walter Pater with the basis for a Hellenistic counter-discourse in which they could appeal to the authority of the classics to defend the 'spiritual procreancy' of male love.[1] The 'wider intensification of sensuous culture', and the emphasis on individual development that Dowling shows as linking the different liberal projects of such figures as Arnold, Jowett and J.S. Mill, thus also came to underwrite Pater's *Studies in the History of the Renaissance*, which places male love at the very heart of the tradition of European art. Pater's cult of experience in the famous 'Conclusion', with its injunction 'to be forever curiously testing new opinions and courting new

---

[1]   Linda Dowling, *Hellenism and Homosexuality in Victorian Oxford* (Ithaca and London: Cornell University Press, 1994), pp. 67–103.

impressions'[2] (and read at the time in the light of the rumours circulating about Pater's private life) would in turn come to underwrite both a more strident variety of aestheticism – that we might identify with 'decadence' – and, less evidently, a new variety of male homoerotic culture.[3] Oscar Wilde has come to act as a sort of shorthand symbol for both of these tendencies.

With aestheticism came the aesthetic (or perhaps more accurately, anti-aesthetic) novel, beginning with W.H. Mallock's satirical portrait of Oxford Hellenic culture, *The New Republic* (1877), and even the aesthetic operetta, Gilbert and Sullivan's *Patience* (1881), which pokes fun at those 'anxious for to shine in the high aesthetic line'.[4] However, the two *fin-de-siècle* novels which most explicitly deal with the links between aestheticism and love between men are written not in the mode of social satire, but in what I will call, with some reservations, late Victorian gothic, this convergence of gothicism and aestheticism providing one possible gloss on the term decadence.[5] Both Wilde's *The Picture of Dorian Gray* (1890) and John Meade Falkner's novel, *The Lost Stradivarius* (1895) explore the perils and pleasures of following Pater's aesthetic injunction in *The Renaissance* to 'grasp at any exquisite passion' in a world where 'all melts under out feet', and both use a distinctly gothic register to trace

---

    [2]   Walter Pater, *The Renaissance: Studies in Art and Poetry* (London: Macmillan, 1873. This edition: New York and Oxford: OUP, 1986), p. 152.

    [3]   Lawrence Birken in *Consuming Desire: Sexual Science and the Emergence of a Culture of Abundance, 1871–1914* (Ithaca, N.Y.: Cornell University Press, 1988) suggests another way of tracing the gender politics of aestheticism, by exploring the family resemblance among aestheticism, late Victorian neo-classical economics, and a new understanding of the polymorphous nature of desire. Birken illustrates how in the late nineteenth century the shift from a productivist to a consumerist tendency in economic theory parallels the rise of late Victorian sexology. The latter, he suggests, is drawn in two directions: toward a productivist, Foucauldian policing of sexuality, but also toward a more 'democratic' or consumerist deregulation of desire. Thus just as the economists were beginning to argue that idiosyncratic desire, not need, drove the economy – sometimes tulips might be more valuable than diamonds – the sexologists were, at least some of the time, beginning to theorize human desire as genderless and 'play-oriented' (Birken, *Consuming Desire*, p. 14). Aestheticism seems to form the bridge between the worlds of economics and sexual economy. The cult of beauty, of the unique hand-made object, is the flip side of the industrial mass market and the proliferation of indistinguishable factory-produced consumer goods. But the cult of beauty also becomes a sexual discourse: Oscar Wilde, the man who was anxious to 'live up to [his] blue china', was also an enormously influential advocate and practitioner of self and sexual self-fashioning.

    [4]   The best-known of the anti-aesthetic novels is probably Robert Hichens's *The Green Carnation* (1894), which represents a somewhat later satirical effort directly targeting Wilde.

    [5]   For a more nuanced account of the term see R.K.R. Thornton, *The Decadent Dilemma* (London: Edward Arnold, 1983). Nicholas Zurbrugg's account of decadence in this volume – that it simultaneously rejects realism and retreats before technomodernism – suggests one way of understanding these gothic elements.

the connections between aestheticism and male–male relationships.[6] In this essay I will read Falkner's novel – with frequent cross-references to Wilde's – as a way of exploring the sexual politics of the decadent novel. In particular I want to stress the ways in which the representation of sexuality in Falkner's novel is routed through two rather different entities: music, and national identity.

John Meade Falkner is scarcely a forgotten figure – his novels are, after all, available in paperback from Oxford University Press – but a brief introduction to the man and a short summary of *The Lost Stradivarius* may be useful at this point.[7] The son of an Anglican clergyman, Falkner obtained a mediocre degree at Oxford before becoming a tutor in the household of Andrew Noble, an important figure in the armaments firm of W.G. Armstrong and Company. Falkner's duties changed from those of tutor to John and Philip Noble to secretary to Andrew Noble himself, and later to secretary of the firm. He rose steadily in the company, becoming Chairman (of what was by then Armstrong Whitworth) in 1915. Between his assumption of the role of secretary and that of Chairman he also wrote three novels: *The Lost Stradivarius* (1895), *Moonfleet* (1898) and *The Nebuly Coat* (1903). He married Evelyn Adye in his forties, and while he worked in the arms industry at Tyneside all his life, he and his wife lived in the quiet cathedral town of Durham, where Falkner was actively involved in the affairs of the Cathedral.[8] He became a well-known collector of, and expert in, incunabula, and was later in life made Reader in Paleography at the University of Durham. It would scarcely be an exaggeration, then, to say that Falkner led a peculiarly modern double life that looks forward in some ways to that of T.S. Eliot, or of Wallace Stevens.

The success of *Moonfleet* has meant that Falkner is often remembered as a children's author, but his two other novels are very different to that tale of smugglers and lost treasure. *The Nebuly Coat* is to my mind an interesting and indeed haunting work, but it is Falkner's first novel that concerns us here. Published in 1895 (the year, of course, of Oscar Wilde's three trials), *The Lost Stradivarius* tells the story of Sir John Maltravers, an Oxford undergraduate and keen amateur musician, whose life is altered irrevocably when his college friend, William Gaskell, gives him a piece of seventeenth-century Italian sheet music. The novel is in the form of two first-person narratives, written in the 1860s, some twenty years after the principal events of the story. The first narrative is that of the late Maltravers's sister, Sophia, and is addressed to her nephew, Sir Edward

---

6   Pater, *The Renaissance*, p. 152.

7   For the biographical details that follow I have drawn on Kenneth Warren's *John Meade Falkner, 1858–1932: A Paradoxical Life* (Lewiston, Queenston and Lampeter: Edwin Mellen Press, 1995).

8   His late, childless (and, by some accounts, loveless) marriage, together with some other factors, have fuelled speculation that Falkner may have been primarily attracted to men. See Warren, *John Meade Falkner*, op. cit., pp. 135–46.

Maltravers, now in his turn an Oxford student.[9] In accordance with his late father's wishes she is giving Sir Edward this account of his father's life upon his coming of age. Painful though it has been to write she feels that he should hear the truth from her rather than 'garbled stories from others'.[10] The second narrative is a note by Mr Gaskell, giving his version of the events leading up to the early death of Sir John.

Like *Dorian Gray*, *The Lost Stradivarius* is a tale of a handsome youth led astray by an older man, but in this case the older man is quite some years older than Lord Henry Wotton. The spirit of Adrian Temple, an eighteenth-century libertine who had once lived in Maltravers' Oxford rooms, comes to haunt Maltravers (at least in Sophia's version of events – Gaskell's is more circumspect), eventually causing his early death following a period of dissolution in Italy. Temple's spirit is set free by the playing of a seventeenth-century Italian dance tune, a *Gagliarda*, but it is when Maltravers finds Temple's old violin, a genuine Stradivarius, hidden in a secret cupboard, that the evil spirit's power really develops. Maltravers' marriage seems to offer an escape from his obsession with Temple, but the woman he marries is in fact a descendant of Adrian Temple, and a portrait of him hangs in her family home. His efforts to follow in Temple's footsteps take Maltravers to Italy, first on his honeymoon, and then alone. There he becomes increasingly attached to a young Italian, Raffaelle Carotenuto, and more and more estranged from his sister, and his young wife and child. He restores Temple's old house, the Villa de Angelis, at Naples, and his efforts to perform Temple's neo-Platonic rituals apparently leave him with a permanently whitened visage (like Temple before him) and destroy his already attenuated health. Raffaelle Carotenuto, who sings to him, becomes his constant companion. He returns to something of his old self for a time, and is taken back to England by his sister, where he is nursed by her and by his long-estranged friend, Mr Gaskell. Despite signs of improvement he dies that Christmas, shortly after the old violin breaks under the strain of its modern strings, while he plays it in his sleep, watched by Mr Gaskell.

A number of details suggest why the novel should be read as a companion text to *Dorian Gray* rather than as simply another late-Victorian ghost story. Most circumstantially, the date of Sophia's narrative, 1867, was also the year in which Pater published the first part of *The Renaissance*, his essay on the eighteenth-century devotee of classical art, Winckelmann. Other details are, perhaps, more telling. As in Wilde's novel, a key component in John Maltravers' ruin is the gift of a book from another man. If Dorian's sensuous adventures begin in earnest with the gift of 'a book bound in yellow paper, the cover slightly torn and the

---

[9]   The term 'student' in this context may mean either undergraduate or fellow. See *The Lost Stradivarius* (London and Edinburgh: Blackwood, 1895. This edition: Oxford and New York: OUP, 1991, ed. Edward Wilson), p. 167.

[10]   Falkner, *Lost Stradivarius*, p. 2.

edges soiled',[11] (generally identified with Joris-Karl Huysmans' *A Rebours*), Maltravers' spiritual decline begins when he finds along with the lost Stradivarius 'two manuscript books containing an elaborate diary of some years of [Adrian Temple's] life'.[12] Linda Dowling notes that the gift of a book is a 'central literary trope for imaginative initiation among late-Victorian Decadent writers'.[13] The proximal source may be Pater's own novel, *Marius the Epicurean* (1885), where in Chapter 5, 'The Golden Book,' Marius and Flavian together read a book (Apuleius' *Metamorphoses*) that 'awaken[s] the poetic or romantic capacity [. . .] but was peculiar in giving it a direction emphatically sensuous'.[14] The perusal of Temple's diaries leads Maltravers into dabbling with 'Neo-Platonism', and the unspeakable 'pagan mysteries' that Temple attempted to revive at his villa in Naples. If we are slow to take the hint that Temple's unspeakable practices somehow represent the ultimate fruit of Pater's Hellenism, Gaskell's narrative makes the connection clearer by mentioning a 'tolerance for aesthetic impressions' as a key component of neo-Platonism.[15] Edward Wilson has noted this and other echoes of the discourse of aestheticism in the novel, pointing out that the whitened faces of Temple and Maltravers also link them to the 'Aesthetic Men of the 1880s and '90s' for whom the lily came to be an emblem.[16]

But how exactly does Falkner's novel thematicize male love, and how do aestheticism and homoeroticism intersect in the novel? Wilde's *Dorian Gray* again provides a sort of yardstick. At the centre of *The Picture of Dorian Gray* is the picture of Dorian Gray, and Dorian's relation to his own portrait, but this cannot be read purely as an allegory of the relations between life and art. Eve Sedgwick puts it clearly: 'The novel takes a plot that is distinctively one of male–male desire, the competition between Basil Hallward and Lord Henry Wotton for Dorian Gray's love, and condenses it into the plot of the mysterious bond of figural likeness and figural expiation between Dorian Gray and his own portrait.'[17] Love between men is reworked, in other words, as a relationship between different facets of the one man, and thus the novel's aesthetic thematics

---

[11] Oscar Wilde, *The Picture of Dorian Gray* (London: Ward Lock and Bowden, 1890. This edition: New York: Airmont, 1964), p. 126.

[12] Falkner, *Lost Stradivarius*, p. 139.

[13] Dowling, *Hellenism and Homosexuality*, p. 86. Her work suggests that this may be because the Oxford tutorial system – where the gift or recommendation of a book by an older man to a younger would scarcely be unusual – contributed in no small degree to the contours of late Victorian homoerotic culture.

[14] *Marius the Epicurean: His Sensations and Ideas* (London: Macmillan, 1885. This edition: Oxford and New York: OUP, 1986, ed. Ian Small), p. 32. Like Dorian's, Flavian's book comes in a 'handsome yellow wrapper' (*Marius*, p. 33).

[15] Falkner, *Lost Stradivarius*, p. 147.

[16] Edward Wilson, 'Introduction' to the OUP edition of *The Lost Stradivarius*, p. xxii.

[17] Eve Kosofsky Sedgwick, *Epistemology of the Closet* (Berkeley and Los Angeles: University of California Press, 1990), p. 160.

mesh with a thematics of the divided self, which in turn comes to provide both an expression of, and alibi for, male–male love. Dorian Gray also has recourse, though, to an older homoerotic persecution plot, in which the desire to kill another man takes the place of more 'unspeakable' desires, and this too eventually connects to the aesthetic plot. In such plots, by what Sedgwick terms an 'eroto-grammatical transformation', the sentence 'I (a man) love him (a man)' becomes 'I do not *love* him – I *hate* him' and this substitution provides the persecutive dynamics of such novels as *Caleb Williams*, *Frankenstein* and *Our Mutual Friend*.[18] Thus there is a whole series of violent male–male tableaux in *Dorian Gray*: Dorian is grabbed from behind and threatened with death by James Vane, the brother of the actress, Sybil Vane, whom Dorian drives to suicide; Dorian stabs to death (from behind) the painter, Basil Hallward; and indeed, the 'consummation' of the narration takes place when Dorian stabs his own portrait, and thus 'himself', with that same knife.

The Lost Stradivarius certainly uses the murderous male–male 'persecution plot' that I have just described. Standing as a sort of 'primal scene' in the narrative is the eighteenth-century Neapolitan episode in which Adrian Temple is stabbed to death by his Italian friend, Palamede, after the latter discovers that Temple has seduced his wife, Olimpia. While Temple and Olimpia dance the Gagliarda, 'Palamede from behind [drives] a stiletto into his friend's heart'.[19] Temple's body is then thrown into the cellar, where Maltravers, now apparently 'possessed' by Temple, finds the unburied remains some hundred years later. This tableau, combining as it does a phobic image of male love, becomes murderous violence, and a love triangle in which Temple and Palamede's affection is routed through Olimpia is important for the subsequent events (subsequent, that is, at the level of *fabula*, though earlier at the level of *sjuzhet*). Gaskell imagines a version of this scene (the dancing couples 'using free and licentious gestures')[20] when the two friends play the Gagliarda in John Maltravers' Oxford rooms, and Temple's violent death appears to be one reason why his spirit lingers on the earth to trouble Maltravers a century later.

Additionally, the model of displaced love that this 'primal scene' offers helps us to read a series of other triangulated relations in the novel. Thus the close 'musical' (already a coded term by this period within late Victorian homosexual or 'Uranian' culture)[21] friendship of John Maltravers and Mr Gaskell shades into the (frustrated) heterosexual romance between Gaskell and Maltravers' sister, Sophia. A less ghostly version of the relationship between Maltravers and Adrian Temple is evoked when we are told that the woman with whom Maltravers falls

---

18   Ibid., p. 161.
19   Falkner, *Lost Stradivarius*, p. 150.
20   Ibid., p. 14.
21   See Dowling, *Hellenism and Homosexuality in Victorian Oxford*, p. 125, n. 25.

in love, and marries, Constance Temple, resembles her dead ancestor.[22] Just as
Sophia is able to give expression to feelings that her brother cannot about
Gaskell, she can also express an attraction to Temple that her brother cannot:
'More than once I had been discovered by Mrs. Temple or Constance sitting
looking at the picture [i.e. of Adrian Temple], and they had gently laughed at me,
saying that I had fallen in love with Adrian Temple'.[23] As we shall see, there is a
further set of substitutions in which Italy comes to stand in for England and
Raffaelle Carotenuto for Gaskell (a singer taking the place of a player).

But this, one might say, is only half the story. There is also the specifically
aesthetic component of Falkner's novel. If Basil Hallward's picture of Dorian
Gray somehow stands as the narrative and thematic cynosure of *The Picture of
Dorian Gray*, the Stradivarius, hidden by Temple, found by Maltravers,
ultimately burnt by Gaskell, occupies an analogous position in *The Lost
Stradivarius*. The love of men, in Falkner's novel as in Wilde's, appears as the
love of an *object of connoisseurship*. In both novels a certain transfer of qualities
between subjects and objects is manifest.[24] Dorian becomes increasingly a
'thing', an unchanging automaton whose defining trait is an appetite for
sensation, as his portrait becomes increasingly lifelike. Not realizing the extent of
his own reified secondariness, Dorian attempts to destroy the painting, but only
succeeds in killing himself. In Falkner's novel it is the violin that appears to
become more of a living thing as John Maltravers himself grows to be more of an
instrument. When the violin breaks ('its last sound [is] not a musical note, but
rather a horrible scream [. . .] a sound such as a wounded beast might utter')[25], we
know that Maltravers cannot long outlive it.

How do we read these instances of what we might term an unusual variety of
commodity fetishism in light of these novels' homoerotic thematics? What is at
issue, I think, is less the ascendancy of objects as a certain waning of the subject.
As Eve Sedgwick points out, it is possible to read the sequestered portrait of
Dorian Gray in terms of an emerging concept of the closeted gay man.
Maltravers's discovery at his Oxford rooms of the Stradivarius in its hidden
cupboard certainly lends itself to a similar reading. The opening of this cupboard
is one of the most highly charged scenes in the novel. Maltravers finds the
cupboard when he goes to straighten 'a picture hung askew'.[26] Behind this picture
he finds the lost cupboard. 'Curiosity' is quickly replaced by the 'feverish anxiety
to re-open this cupboard door [which] took possession of him'.[27] The lock of the
cupboard is painted over, but he is able to 'loosen the paint in the cracks with a

---

[22]   Falkner, *Lost Stradivarius*, p. 66.
[23]   Ibid., p. 69.
[24]   Not unlike that reversal of the positions of people and things that Marx
identifies in commodity fetishism.
[25]   Falkner, *Lost Stradivarius*, p. 132.
[26]   Ibid., p. 38.
[27]   Ibid., p. 39.

penknife'.[28] 'His excitement had now reached an overmastering pitch; for he anticipated, though he knew not why, some strange discovery to be made in this sealed cupboard.'[29] He searches the room for a suitable 'weapon with which to force the door' and eventually he cuts away enough wood to 'enable him to insert the end of the poker in the hole'.[30] Read aloud with a certain emphasis, this scene almost suggests parody: not to put too fine a point on it, the 'musical' Maltravers recovery of his closeted self seems to involve a sort of rape of the closet.

Most interesting, though, is the way in which the involuntariness that comes increasingly to define John Maltravers already echoes in its language. If he is violating the cupboard/closet, there is a sense in which he himself is operating under some compulsion. Something has taken 'possession' of him; he is 'overmaster[ed]'. With occasional interruptions this same involuntariness will shape his life through to its premature end. His behaviour will come to seem more and more like a rehearsal of the life of the dead Adrian Temple; his musicality will end in the violin's playing *him*: like Dorian Gray, John Maltravers may appear to be engaged in a search for the limits of experience, but he also appears to have minimal choice in the matter.

A more figurative loss of self-control, then, yields to the actual loss of Maltravers's self to Temple and to the violin; the resources of Gothic (haunting, possession, instrumentality) provide a flexible vocabulary to represent such a loss. While *Dorian Gray* also has its Gothic moments, this same waning of the will appears there in a different register, that of addiction. As Eve Sedgwick describes, 'new developments in homo/heterosexual definition' were enmeshed in the developing medical discourse of addiction 'and the corresponding new social entity of drug subcultures'.[31] Thus we are shown Dorian under the spell of 'a mad craving' staring at 'a large Florentine cabinet' in his library. He unlocks it, opens a hidden drawer in it, and takes out 'a small Chinese box' containing 'a green paste, waxy in lustre, the odour curiously heavy and persistent'.[32] In the next chapter he leaves the house and travels across the city to a dockside opium den. As he travels, the craving intensifies: 'The hideous hunger for opium began to gnaw at him. His throat burned and his delicate hands twitched nervously together.'[33] At the den itself, the narrator embarks upon a disquisition on free will: 'There are moments, psychologists tell us, when the passion for sin, or for what the world calls sin, so dominates a nature that every fibre of the body, as every cell of the brain, seems to be instinct with fearful impulses. Men and women at such moments lose the freedom of their will. They move to their terrible end as

28   Ibid.
29   Ibid.
30   Ibid.
31   Sedgwick, *Epistemology of the Closet*, p. 171.
32   Falkner, *Lost Stradivarius*, p. 182.
33   Ibid., p. 184.

automatons move.'[34] While Wilde uses aestheticism and its rhetoric of conscious self-fashioning to outflank an older conception of sexual identity as a 'given', he also has resort, then, to a language of compulsion to describe the workings of desire.

There is an interesting shift in emphasis between the registers that *The Picture of Dorian Gray* and *The Lost Stradivarius* use to figure the loss of individual will, between the language of addiction and that of instrumentality, both of which I am reading as at some level figurative of male love. This shift suggests a reading of *The Lost Stradivarius* that does not simply see it as an anti-Paterian, and by extension, homophobic narrative. This reading depends on the role that music and national identity play in the novel. As indicated, the main device through which automatism manifests itself in the case of John Maltravers is music. Thus one of the first signs of Maltravers' self-estrangement is that he gives up his duets with Gaskell to play by himself, and that he obsessively plays the Gagliarda on the violin once owned (and still in some sense possessed by) Temple. His musicianship improves dramatically, so much so that listeners sometimes think that he sounds like two violinists. Gaskell in his Note muses on the influence that music can have for good or evil, given its ability to lift one above ordinary levels of consciousness.[35] From Gaskell and Sophia's accounts, though, we get the very clear impression that there is something demonic in the character of Maltravers' playing – the violin, and or Temple, appear to have taken him over: he has himself become something of an instrument. 'He never for a moment ceased playing. It was always one dreadful melody, the Gagliarda of the 'Areopagitica', and he repeated it time after time with the perseverance and apparent aimlessness of an automaton.'[36]

Maltravers' automatism also touches on issues of nationality. It is by no means adventitious that the violin, and the music that Maltravers plays on it, are of foreign origin. They are both Italian, and so too is Raffaelle Carotenuto, the young Italian who sings to Maltravers at the Villa d'Angelis, and who appears to be rather more than a servant to him. We sense that Maltravers is losing not only his self-control but also his *national* identity. Gaskell talks of neo-Platonism as being 'dangerous to the English character'.[37] If Dorian Gray's slide into unspeakable, or at least in 1890, unprintable vice is somehow over-determined by his exposure to continental literature, not to say oriental drugs, Sir John Maltravers' forsaking of marriage for the companionship of Raffaelle Carotenuto seems to be due in no small part to the influence of Italy.

To understand the issue of national identity in the novel, we have to return to Pater, since Falkner's use of Italy can be traced to the novel's coded engagement

---

34   Ibid., p. 188.
35   Ibid., pp. 26–7, n. 146.
36   Ibid., p. 98.
37   Ibid., p. 147.

with Pater's *The Renaissance*. In this, Italy looms large, and in the chapter on Winckelmann, a visit to Italy involves more than a 'merely intellectual' journey.[38] Winckelmann escapes the 'crabbed Protestantism' and 'repression' of his youth in Germany and eventually, in the middle of the eighteenth century, he travels to Rome, where he has full scope to develop his love of classical art, but also of the modern Italians.[39] As Pater is careful to tell us '[t]hat his affinity with Hellenism was not merely intellectual, that the subtler threads of temperament were inwoven in it, is proved by his romantic, fervent friendships with young men'.[40] Like Adrian Temple, Winckelmann is murdered in Italy by one Arcangeli, a 'fellow-traveller'.[41] Despite this grim ending to his trip to the south, there is no intimation in Pater, as there is in Falkner, that Italy is a *dangerous* place; rather it is the locus of self-culture. In the sunny south, and following 'in morals, as in criticism' 'the clue of instinct', Winckelmann is able to penetrate 'into the antique world by his passion', 'perfecting himself and developing his genius' in directions barred to him in his native Germany.[42]

Pater's association of Winckelmann and 'instinct' relates at some level, surely, both to Dorian's addiction and, more directly, Maltravers' possession. If Winckelmann's self-development depends on his relationship with Hellenism, his openness to the Hellenic spirit in turn depends on something *innate*: 'This key to an understanding of the Greek spirit, Winckelmann possessed in his own nature, itself like a relic of classical antiquity, laid open by accident to our alien modern atmosphere.'[43] Winckelmann's own nature, that is, resembles a lost relic found by accident. It does not seem too fanciful to see in this a foreshadowing of Maltravers' discovery of the violin, another relic of antiquity exposed to an alien atmosphere. We might further speculate that Maltravers finds the violin because something in his nature responds to it. Even before the discovery of the violin and Temple's notebooks, Gaskell describes him as 'highly strung'.[44]

It is possible to assume, then, that Maltravers' nature, like Winckelmann's is able to expand in the air of the sunny south, that things become possible for him in Italy that were not in England. As in the case of Pater's *Renaissance*, there is a complicated relation in Falkner's novel between the past as another country, and Italy as a country. Winckelmann's trip to Italy is also very much a journey into antiquity; both journeys appear to involve an escape from the limits of 'one's Fatherland'.[45] In both Pater and Falkner, Italy is as much a symbolic landscape as a place one finds on the map: it is the land of sensuousness. For Sophia this is

---

[38]   Pater, *Renaissance*, p. 122.
[39]   Ibid., pp. 120, 122.
[40]   Ibid., p. 123.
[41]   Ibid., p. 126.
[42]   Ibid.
[43]   Ibid.
[44]   Falkner, *Lost Stradivarius*, p. 138.
[45]   Pater, *Renaissance*, p. 115.

threatening. Contemplating the 'perfection' of the Villa de Angelis she 'experience[s] a curious mental sensation, which I can only compare to the physical oppression produced on some persons by the heavy and cloying perfume of a bouquet of gardenias or other too highly-scented bosoms.'[46] Here one is reminded of the effects of Italy upon two other very different heroines, Dorothea Casaubon and Lucy Honeychurch, who are both challenged by their experience of the place. Italy is in effect a heterotopia,[47] where Victorian fantasies are given a local habitation, if not always a name.

We do not have to assume, though, that Sophia's claustrophobic vision of Italy is that of Sir John, or for that matter, of Falkner. Like other heterotopias, Italy in *The Lost Stradivarius* is not completely different from the land that it displaces. Falkner's Italy in effect provides a sort of extension of the novel's Oxford. It is Oz to Oxford's Kansas: relationships and tendencies that are hinted at in the latter are rather more obvious in the former;[48] in a species of double displacement, some events are placed in Italy and in the past as well. The most obvious example of this is of course the way in which the eighteenth-century episode involving Temple's murder provides a sort of template for subsequent events in England. But there are more straightforward continuities between home and away. Maltravers' musical friendship with Gaskell dies in England, but is reborn in Italy as the more obvious *affaire de coeur* between him and the Italian singer, Raffaelle Carotenuto. In the accounts of events presented by Sophia Maltravers and Mr Gaskell, Italy may appear as a danger to the English character; indeed, as a veritably infernal region. But it is not merely playful to suggest that England and Italy are connected not as Heaven and Hell, but rather as sepia-coloured Kansas and technicolor Oz. For John Maltravers, as for Winckelmann, leaving behind the 'Fatherland' may mean an escape into possibilities of self-expansion. The loss of his 'English character' may be a prerequisite of self-discovery.

Such a reading of the novel is more plausible when we bear in mind that we don't actually have Sir John Maltravers' version of events, nor do we have a 'neutral' third-person narrator; we hear Maltravers' story only as mediated by his sister and his old college friend. Where *Dorian Gray*'s third-person narration makes us read somewhat against the grain to see Dorian's journey into experience as anything but a rather gloomy moral tale, we may decide to treat Sophia Maltravers and William Gaskell as unreliable narrators (indeed the differences between their accounts mean we *have* to assume this to some extent). Nor is theirs an account written just for the record: it is aimed at another generation of the

---

46   Falkner, *Lost Stradivarius*, p. 112.
47   On heterotopias see Michel Foucault, 'Of Other Spaces,' translated by Jay Miskowiev, *Diacritics* 16.1 (1986), pp. 22–7.
48   The exotic heterotopia seems to have become an important topos in film representations of same-sex desire. One thinks of such recent films as *Heavenly Creatures* and *Ma Vie en Rose*.

Maltravers family, Sir Edward, 'who has been brought up to think more of a cricket-bat than of a violin-bow'.[49] While we are given little or no basis to speculate on how he might receive this highly mediated message from the past, we might choose to think that as an Oxford student in 1867 he might very well read it against the grain, and discern in it voices other than those of his aunt and guardian.

To conclude, while it is possible to read *The Lost Stradivarius* as a deeply phobic text that turns Paterian aestheticism into a sort of Hammer Horror Satanism, it is also possible, indeed more tempting, to see Falkner's novel as a veiled but affirmative account of male love. The man at the centre of this account is dead, and all we have are the interpretations of his life that other characters supply. If they choose to read that life as a horror story, that does not mean that we are obliged to do so.

---

[49]   Falkner, *Lost Stradivarius*, p. 165.

Chapter 8

'Squalid Arguments': Decadence, Reform, and the Colonial Vision in Kipling's *The Five Nations*

Andrew St John

In the aftermath of the South African war, social degeneration became an issue uppermost in the minds of British politicians and political commentators. The war, which had begun for the British with a series of embarrassing military reversals, dealt a severe blow to confidence in the traditional imperial values, political mechanisms, and social structures of the nation. To explain the poor showing of the troops in South Africa, social reformers pointed to the cities, and the physical deterioration, mental inactivity, and indifference to the empire associated with urban life. Such an acknowledgement of the impact of social conditions upon Britain's imperial standing united a range of political parties in the quest for national efficiency and the establishment of an 'imperial race' that would safeguard the future of the empire. As I shall illustrate, in the hands of the reformers the relation of England – the 'mother country' – to the colonies was typically defined in functional and economic terms, with progress, productivity, and wealth explicitly determining the course of political developments.

My purpose in this essay is to suggest that, although he shared some of their concerns, Kipling's views on the social decline of England differed from those of the major political parties and reformers, not least in his refusal to put England before the empire in imperial affairs and in his resistance to the conventional economic and social interpretation of the empire. In my reading of poems from *The Five Nations* (1903), the word 'decadence' refers more directly to social and political concerns than to aesthetic or literary movements, which is consonant with the use of the word by the reformers I shall discuss. The period described in this essay constitutes a significant moment of European cultural transition, in which the British empire finally lost the air of invincibility – the 'illusion of permanence' – that it had carried over from the nineteenth century, signalling a period of restructuring, upheaval and insecurity that, as Kipling and others had already begun to predict, would contribute to the political uncertainties and international conflicts of the early twentieth century. Hence the idea or the theme of 'decadence' (a term, incidentally, he never employed) serves, in *The Five Nations*, to connect his Boer War writings with British social and political developments that were integral to their meaning but are nowadays easily overlooked. Before turning to the poems, it is important to understand the extent and the nature of support for the empire among the major parties and in less likely political movements during the early years of the century.

Reformist politics were frequently inspired by a fear of, and, paradoxically, admiration for Germany, whose programme of state socialism under Bismarck in the 1880s served as a model for British campaigns for national efficiency.[1] Bernard Semmel argues that the South African war gave the impetus, in British politics, to a populist ideology known as social-imperialism,[2] which allied the twin aims of expansionism and national reform, aiming, with the promise of jobs and improved living conditions, to win a broad base of support for the empire. In what has come to be known as the 'squalid argument', Joseph Chamberlain made a blunt connection between the prosperity of the nation and the possession of the colonies, reminding the working classes that peace and plenty depended upon the securing of foreign markets.[3] It was this direct equation of colonialism with prosperity that gave rise to the deprecatory term 'squalid argument', which was a criticism of the narrowly economic focus of Chamberlain's policy, and was coined, ironically, by Chamberlain himself, who feared that it would be a phrase likely to be used against him by the Opposition.[4] His call for the formation of a National Party that would 'put the country before the interests of any faction' reflects the growing trend towards insularity and protectionism in wider international affairs.[5] The 'squalid argument' can be viewed, ultimately, as a distillation of the social-imperialist message, placing the efficiency of the nation above other competing interests – whether internal or external to the state. From around 1903 onwards, Chamberlain and the Tariff Reform League were busy putting their argument to the British working classes. The chief organs in the campaign were *The Daily Express* and the *Daily Mail*, which, though they met with resistance to taxes on foreign food imports, set about converting the masses to protectionism and imperial preference with the famous slogan: 'Tariff Reform

---

[1]   G. R. Searle, *The Quest for National Efficiency: A Study in British Politics and Political Thought, 1899–1914* (Oxford: Basil Blackwell, 1971), p. 54. For an example of the use of Germany as a model of municipal government, see Chiozza Money, *Riches and Poverty* (London: Methuen and Co., 1905), pp. 206–7.

[2]   Bernard Semmel, *Imperialism and Social Reform: English Social and Imperial Thought 1895–1914* (London: George Allen and Unwin, 1960), p. 13.

[3]   Ibid., p. 93.

[4]   Ibid.

[5]   *National Review* XXIII (1894), 7–9; quoted in Semmel, *Imperialism and Social Reform*, p. 92.

Means Work for All'.[6] The press campaign was accompanied by a spate of music-hall tunes and a leaflet campaign involving cartoons, diagrams and sheets of statistics aimed at arousing instincts of self-preservation and patriotism in the working classes. As Semmel explains, in the leaflets of the Tariff Reform League the foreigner is usually a 'bloated "Herr Dumper"' who speaks in unhelpful phrases such as '"hullo mein freindt"'.[7] Alternatively, he adopts the corporate shape of the American Beef Trust, the Chicago Meat Trust, or the American Hop Trust.[8] Leaflet headlines such as 'Your Wages in Danger', and rabble-rousing challenges to the pride of workers: 'We are being unfairly beaten by the foreigner. Shall we take it lying down?',[9] were calculated to drive home the 'squalid argument' with a minimum of attention to complicated issues of federation or concepts of 'civilizing' responsibilities.

Usually associated with Chamberlain and the tariff reformers, social-imperialist values appealed, as I have suggested, to a wide range of political parties. In the British Fabian Society, the South African war led the party to publicly support the empire and recognize the importance of colonial policy to the reform process – an imperial focus reflected in their 1900 election manifesto, *Fabianism and The Empire*. During the war, the leaders of the Fabians, Sidney Webb and George Bernard Shaw supported the action against the Boers and led a campaign for the formation of a party of 'National Efficiency' to address the pressing issues of urbanization, overcrowding, and physical deterioration. Webb established a 'brains trust' for such a party, named the Coefficients, which included a number of eminent socialists, liberals and conservatives committed to social reform and the 'rearing of an Imperial race'.[10]

If the 'squalid argument' was compelling to many reformers, there were other, more squalid developments in store for the social and imperial debate. As with Fabians including Webb, Shaw and H.G. Wells, a number of radical reformers were drawn towards social-Darwinism and eugenic theory in the pursuit of greater efficiency. In *Anticipations* (1902), Wells argued that 'the nation that most resolutely picks over, educates, sterilizes, exports, or poisons its People of the Abyss [the unemployed]' and 'turns the greatest portion of its irresponsible adiposity into social muscle [. . .] will certainly be the ascendant or dominant nation before the year 2000'.[11] For Wells, the South African war confirmed the need for a eugenic programme aimed at increasing the 'muscle' of the nation – a programme similar in effect to the right-wing policy of Arnold White, who urged

---

6 Ibid., p. 112.
7 Tariff Reform League Leaflet No. 212; quoted in Semmel, *Imperialism and Social Reform*, p. 117.
8 Ibid.
9 Ibid.
10 Sidney Webb, 'Lord Rosebury's Escape From Houndsditch', *Nineteenth Century and After* CCXCV (1901), 385–6.
11 H.G. Wells, *Anticipations* (London: Chapman and Hall, 1902), p. 212.

the sterilization of the unfit and the discouragement of breeding among the lower classes.[12] In another example of this flirtation of radical politics with eugenics, Sally Ledger has recently outlined the attractions of imperialism and eugenic theory to the women's movement in the early part of the century, acknowledging the disquieting possibility that 'both feminism and socialism in some respects share the same intellectual subsoil as fascism in the twentieth century'.[13]

While Kipling also believed that the South African war had exposed the 'decadence' of the English and had provided a much-needed 'lesson' in the preparedness and efficiency of the nation, he avoided the racial, economic and eugenic response that proved irresistible to so many imperialists and reformers at the time. His poems are not only indictments of English 'decadence', but also, indirectly, of the conventional nationalistic and patriotic dimension of reformist thinking. In many respects, his writings of these years can be considered an attempt to distinguish his own imperialist values from those of political parties and factions asserting measures of social and state intervention of which he was deeply suspicious. Emphasizing the role of the colonies in the war, and playing down the centrality of the 'mother country', he questioned the importance of the English and celebrated the role of the emergent nations of the empire – dissociating his work from the popular strain of social-imperialism inspired by the South African conflict. As Ledger argues: 'the political emphasis of eugenic discourses was primarily on the preservation and continuation of the English middle classes'.[14] In almost every respect – whether in terms of race or class – Kipling's response to the war produced an entirely different 'political emphasis'. Many of the poems in *The Five Nations* (1903) suggest that the lower classes, and more directly their counterparts in the colonies, had not only saved the empire but were essential to its future.

Throughout the war, his views on the English middle and upper classes, whom he pejoratively termed the people of 'the Island', were, to say the least, unsympathetic. He believed that the Islanders were 'bung-full of beastly unjustified spiritual pride [. . .] material luxury and overmuch ease'.[15] They 'went about despising things and people', and had become, collectively, a 'fatted snob'.[16] In the early months of the fighting, he matched his remonstrances against the decadent English with a typically eccentric contribution to military

---

    [12] Arnold White, *Efficiency and Empire* (1901; Brighton: Harvester Press Ltd, 1973), p. 117.
    [13] Sally Ledger, 'In Darkest England: The Terror of Degeneration in fin de siècle Britain', *Literature and History*, 4, 2 (1995), 75.
    [14] Ibid., p. 73.
    [15] To Charles Eliot Norton, 19 May 1901; in ed. Thomas Pinney, *The Letters of Rudyard Kipling* [hereafter referred to as *Letters*], 5 vols (Basingstoke: Macmillan, 1996), III, p. 53.
    [16] Ledger, 'In Darkest England: The Terror of Degeneration in *fin de siècle* Britain', *Literature and History* 4, 2 (1995), 53.

preparedness, importing a machine-gun and establishing a rifle-range in the village of Rottingdean, East Sussex, where he oversaw the drilling of the hapless locals in preparation for the coming 'Armageddon'.[17] Kipling's actions during the war have, over the years, had a detrimental effect on the reception of his writings, which have been frequently considered the literary counterparts of his reactionary behaviour. Even during frequent spells in South Africa, which he visited with his family each winter, he kept a strict eye on the running of the club, issuing military-style instructions and regulations that were despatched to Sergeant Johnstone, the Instructor at Rottingdean preparatory school.[18] During his African visits, he adopted a high-profile, propagandist role: giving speeches, touring cantonments and visiting wounded soldiers in hospitals. Between April and March of 1900 he served on *The Friend of the Free State* in Bloemfontein, a newspaper established by Lord Roberts after the military takeover of the town, providing morale-boosting articles for the troops and offering a hand of reconciliation to defeated Boers.

When, in March of 1900, he arrived in Bloemfontein to work on the newspaper, he was assured in an editorial welcome that, amongst the soldiers, drawn 'from every quarter of the globe', he would find 'the actual physical fulfilment of what must be one of his dearest hopes – the close union of the greatest parts of the greatest empire in the world'.[19] Joseph Chamberlain's view of the troops in South Africa as 'trustees of a federation',[20] finds an echo in many of Kipling's Boer War poems. But more importantly, the colonials offer the pure vision, untroubled by the decadence of the Mother Country. For example, in 'The Parting of the Columns', an English serviceman sings the praises of his Canadian fellow-soldiers:

'Twas how you talked an' looked at things which
made us like you so.
All independent, queer an' odd, but most amazin' new,
My word! You shook us up to rights. Good-bye –
good luck to you![21]

The serviceman's acknowledgement of kinship with the Canadians – 'Our blood 'as truly mixed with yours – all down the Red Cross train' – is a dramatic

17 See *Letters*, pp. 41 and 45. Birkenhead explains how '[w]ith an eye all ready on the next war, he regarded his club with deadly seriousness. He always shot in the competitions, adequately, in spite of his eyesight, coming over at three or four in the afternoon in his wide-brimmed hat and leather-patched clothes' (Lord Birkenhead, *Rudyard Kipling* (1978; London, W.H. Allen and Co., 1980), pp. 233–4).

18 Birkenhead, *Rudyard Kipling*, p. 234.

19 Julian Ralph, *War's Brighter Side* (London: C. Arthur Pearson, 1901), p. 51.

20 Speech to the House of Commons, 5 February 1900; in ed. Charles W. Boyd, *Mr Chamberlain's Speeches*, 2 vols. (London: Constable, 1914), II, p. 67.

21 Rudyard Kipling, *The Five Nations* (London: Methuen, 1903), p. 177.

reminder of the affinities between the colonial contingents. The passage also implies a growing internationalism and an interest in the wider colonial picture – all 'independent, queer an' odd' – that jarred with the patriotic and protectionist jargon of the penny-press, which, as Semmel argues, encouraged the suspicion among the working classes of foreigners and foreign competition, fomenting a strongly pro-English attitude to the empire. There was little in the 'squalid argument' to arouse interest in what might be 'independent' or 'amazin' new' either in the colonials or the minds of the working classes. Kipling's soldiers, erstwhile residents of the 'man-stifling towns',[22] had, by contrast, become citizens of the empire – harbingers of a 'five-nationism' that disputed Britain's dominant position over the colonies, and thereby challenged the isolationism of the social-imperialists and radical reformers.

In 'The Sin of Witchcraft', a newspaper article attacking disloyal citizens in the Cape, Kipling argues that judgement on the rebels should be exacted by the colonies rather than the 'island-English': 'for they too [the colonials] have known the life that is lived out between a horse and a verandah under hot blue skies'.[23] Such a comment was a thinly veiled attack on the inability of the 'island-English' to run their own imperial affairs. They were, he suggests, neither as clear-sighted nor as pragmatic as their colonial counterparts – a view that finds its way into poems such as 'The Return', where a former serviceman recalls the excitement of South Africa and the educating experience of life among 'Men from both two 'emispheres / Discussin' things of every kind'.[24] Similarly, in 'Chant Pagan', an ex-serviceman finds it impossible to 'take on / with awful old England again', vowing, instead, to 'trek South' and work for 'a Dutchman I've fought 'oo might give/ Me a job were I ever inclined'.[25] The important point is that Kipling's soldiers freely voice their discontent at the decline of their native society, and look, instead, to a widening colonial vision for guidance and renewal. Even more significantly, he allowed the colonial soldiers not only to offer the 'clear vision', but to voice a commitment to *their* homelands that was generous and freely given, where the English soldier was merely disillusioned. If, then, the eagerness of Kipling's soldiers to leave England coincided with their new-found enthusiasm for the colonies – for news of 'Calgary, an' Wellin'ton, an Sydney and Quebec; / Of mine an' farm, an' ranch an' run, an' moose an' cariboo'[26] – it offered a telling contrast with this loyalty of the colonial soldier to his homeland. In other words, Kipling, like his soldiers, responded to the social decline of England by

---

[22] Kipling, 'The Song of the Dead', *The Seven Seas* (London: Methuen, 1896), p. 6.

[23] 'The Sin of Witchcraft', *The Times*, 15 March 1900; reprinted in ed. R.E. Harbord, *The Reader's Guide to Rudyard Kipling's Works*, 8 vols (Canterbury: privately printed, 1970), V, p. 2551.

[24] *The Five Nations*, p. 212.

[25] Ibid., 159–62.

[26] Ibid., p. 177.

embracing the emerging identities of the other nations of the empire. For example, in 'Lichtenberg', an Australian soldier sees in the South African landscape an almost perfect picture of home:

> And I saw Sydney the same as ever,
> The picnics and brass-bands;
> And the little homestead on Hunter River
> And my new vines joining hands.
> It all came over me in one act
> Quick as a shot through the brain –
> With the smell of wattle round Lichtenburg,
> Riding in, in the rain.[27]

It is no accident that the realization comes to him '[q]uick as a shot through the brain': in many respects the national claims of Australia were no different to the claims of the Boer Republics, and the conflict might easily have been between Englishman and Australian. Hence, beneath the association of Sydney with Lichtenburg there is the faintest suggestion of an understanding between Australian and Boer, to the potential exclusion of the British. As Van Wyk Smith comments, many Australians questioned the British cause, and were drawn to the Boers for their mutual 'love for and identification with the veld and wild places'.[28] These sympathies exposed the fragility of the claims of the mother country upon either the lands or the military support of the colonies. Given the superior political judgement and military powers attributed to the colonials in *The Five Nations*, it was a support that the island-English could ill-afford to lose, and one which appeared far more precarious than supporters of the 'squalid argument', with its pragmatic approach to the economy of the empire, might suggest. Even in 'Our Lady of the Snows', written to mark the Canadian preferential tariff of 1897, Kipling ends the poem with an assertion of Canadian autonomy in the petulant words of the 'Lady' (Canada) to her Mother: 'Daughter am I in my mother's house, / But mistress in my own!'[29] Similarly, in 'The Young Queen', written to mark the inauguration of the commonwealth of Australia in 1901, the 'Old Queen' describes the nation as 'Daughter no more but Sister', pledging the Young Queen 'her people's love'.[30] These were poems that, while celebrating the unity, also reflected the loosening of political relationships between the five nations: England, Canada, Australia, New Zealand and South Africa.

It is worth noting Kipling's influence on the Australian Republican poet, A.B. (Banjo) Paterson, whose criticism of 'the narrow ways of English folk' has much

---

[27] Ibid., p. 192.
[28] M. Van Wyk Smith, *Drummer Hodge: The Poetry of the Anglo Boer War (1899–1902)* (Oxford: Clarendon Press, 1978), p. 86.
[29] *The Five Nations*, p. 87.
[30] Ibid., p. 102–3.

in common with Kipling's suspicion of the 'Island-English'. Kipling's demotic and often disillusioned response to the English was, perhaps ironically, attractive to writers asserting the distinct literary and political voice of the colonies. Paterson writes, in 'Old Australian Ways' (1902):

> The narrow ways of English folk
> Are not for such as we;
> They bear the long-accustomed yoke
> Of staid conservancy:
> But all our roads are new and strange,
> And through our blood their runs
> The vagabonding love of change
> That drove us westward of the range
> And westward of the suns.[31]

In terms of its style, metre, rhythm and themes, 'Old Australian Ways' directly echoes poems such as 'Chant Pagan' and 'The Return'. Paterson's debt to Kipling clearly owes something to the latter's shared concern for the 'new and strange' in both the landscape and the political views of the five nations. It should also be recognized that Kipling's attention to the colonies – to their perspective, culture, landscape and 'poetic' value – occurred at a time of indifference, even hostility, to emergent colonial nationalisms and literary traditions. Poems such as 'Lichtenburg' were a corrective to what A.G. Stephens described, in the *Bulletin Story Book* (1901), as 'the grotesque English prejudice against things Australian, founded on no better reason than that they are unlike English things'.[32] Again, the interest of Kipling's servicemen in their colonial counterparts – 'Think o' the stories round the fire, the tales along the trek',[33] intimates the beginnings not only of a political, but also of a narrative tradition independent of the mother country. The Canadian writer, Sara Jeanette Duncan, had urged the development of such an independent literary voice in her essay, 'Colonials and Literature' (1886).[34]

Let us return to the relationship between Kipling's views on the South African war, and those, for example, of the right-wing imperialist and social reformer, Arnold White. There was, it appears, at least some similarity in their viewpoints: both advocated compulsory national service, the abandonment of aristocratic privilege,[35] the increase of naval power, and, later on, strident political measures

---

[31]   Elleke Boehmer, ed., *Empire Writing: An Anthology of Colonial Literature 1870–1918* (Oxford: OUP, 1998), p. 175.

[32]   Ibid., p. 189.

[33]   *The Five Nations*, p. 177.

[34]   Boehmer, ed., *Empire Writing: An Anthology of Colonial Literature 1870–1918*, p. 95.

[35]   Although he bemoaned 'bad smart society' (*Efficiency and Empire*, p. 74), White ultimately remained committed to an aristocratic principle of government, arguing that there existed a species of 'true' or proper aristocrat, who would rise to the top of the

to halt the progress of imperial Germany (White advocated a pre-emptive strike to destroy the German fleet).[36] But there were also crucial differences, which illustrate Kipling's more general disagreement with the eugenicists and social-imperialists. In the immediate aftermath of the war, White campaigned for the total dominance of the Anglo-Saxon race in South Africa through a programme of colonization that would be, in his own words, 'not altruistic, but selfish, not benevolent, but prudential'.[37] Such an unscrupulous programme for the colonies was the natural counterpart of White's eugenic approach to social problems at home. It was a short step from the view that the 'philoprogenitiveness of an unsound proletariat is sheer decadence',[38] to the belief that by segregating the unfit – which included the street-bred soldiery, the unemployed, and recipients of charitable aid[39] – the nation would purify its racial stock and extend its right to dominion over other less vigorous nations of the world. White's views illustrate how, in responding to the decadence of Edwardian social and political life, Edwardian political reformers adopted measures of social intervention and segregation that, when extended to the colonies, prompted an aggressive approach that bore little resemblance to the 'paternalistic' traditions that Kipling had absorbed during his years in British India. Not surprisingly, the British domination urged by White was frankly and consistently discouraged in poems such as 'Chant Pagan', where it is the English serviceman who works for the Dutchman, and again in 'The Settler', where the serviceman imagines an equal union of Boer and British interests in South Africa:

> Here, in a large and a sunlit land,
> Where no wrong bites to the bone,
> I will lay my hand in my neighbour's hand,
> And together we will atone
> For the set folly and the red breach
> And the black waste of it all,
> Giving and taking counsel each
> Over the cattle-Kraal.[40]

As I suggested earlier, in literary circles Kipling was to pay a heavy price for his unremitting support of the war. A number of critics have echoed the opinion of

---

social hierarchy according to their superior efficiency: 'The gentle folk will always win in a crowd whenever they take the trouble – for aristocracy is nothing more than the most efficient people in the nation, whose efficiency has been graded up by generations of training' (ibid., p. 23).

[36] G.R. Searle, introduction, *Empire and Efficiency*, pp. ix–x.

[37] Arnold White, *Efficiency and Empire* (1901; Brighton: Harvester Press Ltd, 1973), p. 253.

[38] Ibid., p. 111.

[39] Ibid., pp. 113, 117, and 258.

[40] *The Five Nations*, p. 153.

his biographer, Lord Birkenhead, who suggested that the war revealed '[t]he rigidity of [his] thinking and the unyielding nature of his prejudice'.[41] A poem such as 'The Settler', with its plea for reconciliation with South Africa, resistance to aggressive programmes of colonization, and admission of the 'folly' and 'waste' of the war, suggests a far more complex response. By acknowledging degeneration and decadence as important concerns for imperialists at the time, it is possible read the poems in *The Five Nations* as both conscious and critical of the reactionary, patriotic and often racist agenda evident in discussions of the war and its social impact upon Britain. Such a reading brings to light important and neglected elements in Kipling's poems, revealing that they were, by comparison, far more critical of the pro-war campaign than either his public role or the adverse critical reaction implies.

Edward Shanks makes the important point that none of Kipling's poems celebrate British victories during the fighting.[42] In this respect, they have little in common with the aggressively patriotic verse of, for example, Algernon Charles Swinburne or William Ernest Henley. The day after war was declared, Swinburne urged the English, in 'The Transvaal', to 'scourge these dogs, agape with jaws afoam, / Down out of life. Strike England, and strike home'.[43] In his celebration of the unconditional surrender of the Boers, 'The First of June, 1902', he rejoiced in the prospect of the nation's enemies 'shamed and stricken blind and dumb as worms that die'.[44] Similarly, in his collection, *For England's Sake* (1900), W.E. Henley portrayed the war as a step towards the establishment of English racial supremacy in South Africa: 'That, stung by the lust and pain of battle, / The One Race ever might starkly spread, / And the One Flag eagle it overhead!'[45] The war would prove, as he announced in the final poem of the volume, that England was 'Mother of mothering girls and governing men'.[46]

In *The People of the Abyss* (1903), Jack London quoted Kipling's 'The Sea Wife' as an example of former imperial hubris and an illustration of the depths to which the nation had sunk – a judgement he formed after spending two months

---

[41]   Lord Birkenhead, *Rudyard Kipling*, p. 215. More recently, Ann Parry argues that Kipling's Boer War writings assert the ideology of the radical right (*The Poetry of Rudyard Kipling: Rousing the Nation* (Buckingham: Open University Press, 1992), p. 106). See also Van Wyk Smith, *Drummer Hodge: The Poetry of the Anglo Boer War (1899–1902)* for the view that, during the war, Kipling succumbed to 'the worship of a vast and ultimately nebulous panorama of imperial ideology' (ibid., p. 98).

[42]   Edward Shanks, *Rudyard Kipling: A Study in Literature and Political Ideas* (London: Macmillan, 1940), p. 189.

[43]   Chris Brooks and Peter Faulkner, eds., *The White Man's Burdens: An Anthology of British Poetry of the Empire* (Exeter: University of Exeter Press, 1996), p. 320.

[44]   Ibid., p. 333.

[45]   'Last Post', *For England's Sake: Verses and Songs in Time of War, The Works of W. E. Henley*, 8 vols (London: David Nutt, 1908), II, p. 157.

[46]   'Envoy', ibid., p. 162.

in the squalor of the East End.[47] Ironically, Kipling's Boer War poems illustrate that, for the most part, he shared London's view of the mismanagement of the empire and the declining position of England in international affairs. Incompatible with the narrow remit of imperial debate in the early years of the century, his time in the colonies and in America lent his work an international perspective at odds with the dominant political parties. The union of the Five Nations contained within it the seeds of the undoing rather than the enforcement of British nationalism, locating the prospects for wider colonial relations in the working classes – the returning soldiers of the Boer War, whose experience of the world, like his own, would unsettle the easy conviction of imperial power and force the little-Englanders to acknowledge the dependence of the nation upon the empire. Such a view allowed him to broach the least acceptable dimensions of British society within an imperialistic remit – redirecting the forces of social change onto a wider colonial identification and work. In so doing, despite its many detractors, the Boer War poetry opposed the insularity of the reformist agenda, and contributed to a widening of horizons and concerns – however skewed in the service of imperialism – that was both necessary and valuable in the face of 'squalid arguments' for the pre-eminence of the national interest.

Kipling was, as I have suggested, outraged by the 'fatted' contentment of the English, and began to discern in the Boers many of the qualities of courage, resilience and resourcefulness he thought lacking in the people of 'the Island'. For example, he placed the poem 'General Joubert', written to commemorate the leader of the Boer forces, who died on 17 March 1900, alongside his epigraph on Cecil Rhodes, 'The Burial' – illustrating the measure of his respect for the South African commandant-general. Joubert, whose 'hands were clear of gain', persisted 'subtle, strong, and stubborn, gave his life / To a lost cause, and knew the gift was vain'.[48] It was an act of self-sacrifice that contrasted directly with the leaders of the British forces in 'Stellenbosh', whose attempts to safeguard their own reputations (Stellenbosh being the town to which British officers who displeased their superiors were sent) ultimately put the lives of their men in danger:

> An' it all went into the laundry,
> But it never came out in the wash.
> We were sugared about by the old men
> (panicky, perishin' old men)
> That 'amper an' 'inder an' scold men
> For fear o' Stellenbosh![49]

---

[47] Jack London, *The People of the Abyss* (London: Isbister and Company Limited, 1903), p. 185.

[48] *The Five Nations*, p. 65.

[49] Ibid., p. 196.

Chapter 9

The Metamorphoses of a Fairy-Tale: Quillard, D'Annunzio and *The Girl With Cut-Off Hands*[1]

Julie Dashwood

In Gabriele D'Annunzio's second full-length play, *La Gioconda* (1898), Silvia Settala's hands have to be amputated when they are crushed as she tries to prevent her husband's mistress, and model, Gioconda Dianti, from destroying one of his statues.[2] Writing of this play, Mario Praz says:

> *Gioverà qui ricordare che nel 1886 era apparso pei tipi della Pléiade un poema drammatico di Pierre Quillard,* La Fille aux mains coupées, *ove la protagonista si fa tagliare le mani contaminate dalle "caresses incestueuses et brutales" del proprio padre? Codesto poema del Quillard non fa che riprendere un'antichissima leggenda [. . .] di cui si trovano versioni nel* Cunto de li Cunti *di Basile* (La Penta manomozza) *e nelle favole del Grimm* (Das Mädchen ohne Hände).[3]

> [Is it perhaps useful at this point to recall that in 1886 the Pléiade Press had published a dramatic poem by Pierre Quillard, *The Girl with Cut-Off Hands*, in which the heroine has her hands cut off because they were

---

[1]   On the issue of the spelling of D'Annunzio's surname see John Woodhouse's *Gabriele D'Annunzio: Defiant Archangel* (Oxford: Clarendon, 1998), pp. 12–13. Woodhouse writes 'the question of the spelling of the name, d'Annunzio or D'Annunzio, is still debated. D'Annunzio always signed himself "Gabriele d'Annunzio", the form which implied a noble origin [which he did not have]. More down-to-earth compilers of library indexes incline to D'Annunzio in all circumstances.' I have come down on one side for reasons of factual correctness.

[2]   Gabriele D'Annunzio, *La Gioconda* in *Tutto il Teatro di Gabriele D'Annunzio*, vol. 1, *Tragedie Sogni e Misteri* (Milan: Mondadori, 1939), pp. 231–339. All references are to this edition, and are given henceforth in the text. Originally published Milan: Fratelli Treves, 1898.

[3]   Mario Praz, *La carne, la morte e il diavolo nella letteratura romantica* (Milan, Rome: La Cultra, 1930; this edition: Florence: Sansoni, 1966), p. 244, n. 106. Translated by Angus Davidson as *The Romantic Agony* (Oxford: OUP, 1933).

contaminated by the "brutal and incestuous caresses" of her father. Quillard's poem merely recounts a very ancient legend [. . .] versions of which can also be found in Basile's *Story of Stories* (*The Girl with Maimed Hands*) and in Grimm's fables (*The Girl without Hands*)].[4]

The tale Praz refers to is one whose traditional 'happy ending', throughout the centuries, concludes a story of attempted incest, female mutilation, duplicity, banishment and miraculous regeneration. Following on from Praz's note, what interested me in my work on modern Italian theatre was the treatment of this 'very ancient legend' by two symbolist-decadent writers within a relatively short time-span at the end of the nineteenth century.

My approach to the two plays by Quillard and D'Annunzio respectively has in part been shaped by twentieth-century theories of the folk-tale. Theorists working earlier in the century analysed the tale in the light of their own universalizing tendencies. So in 1910 Antti Aarne began the work of the Scandinavian School by publishing the first systematic catalogue of the tale. In 1928 Stith Thompson added to this catalogue and subsequently new variants were included until its publication in the 1960s in greatly enlarged form. Their work was based on the notions of 'story type', 'version' and 'variant' and 'motif', and they grouped together those tales whose similarities were considered to be more notable than their differences. They further argued that for each story type there is an archetype, an original form of the tale, from which all other versions derive.[5] Aarne's seminal work was acknowledged by Vladimir Propp in his fundamental *Morphology of the Folktale* where he sets out to provide 'a description of the tale according to its component parts and the relationship of these components to each other and to the whole'.[6] Propp's structural analysis of some hundred Russian folktales according to a syntagmatic series of thirty-one functions describes the formal organization of the text. His analysis is linear and sequential, and he argues that it is the invariable order of the functions in the tale as it develops that constitutes the canonical structure of the folktale. Finally, and however briefly, we should mention the use of the fairy-tale in psychoanalysis, noting that Freud sees the tale as an attenuated form of myth, and draws on folklore, as on dream and art, to illustrate his theories. So, in *The Theme of the Three Caskets* (1913) for example, he draws on *Cupid and Psyche* and *Cinderella* to argue that in *King*

---

[4]   The translations throughout are mine.

[5]   Antti Aarne, *The Types of the Folktale. A Classification and Bibliography*, translated and enlarged by Stith Thompson (1928; Helsinki, Suomalainen Tiedeakatemia: Academia Scientiarum Fennica, 1964). *The Maiden Without Hands* is classified under the story-type of 'The Banished Wife or Maiden', No. 706, pp. 240–1.

[6]   Vladimir Propp, *The Morphology of the Folktale*, 1st edn translated by Laurence Scott, 2nd edn revised and edited by Louis A. Wagner, new introduction by Alan Dundes (Austin and London: University of Texas Press, 1968), p. 19. Propp's book was first published in 1928 (Leningrad: Academia) but was scarcely known in the West until 1958.

Lear Shakespeare has represented the 'inevitable relations that a man has with a woman'.[7] This approach allows Freud to use psychoanalytical concepts in his interpretation of the phantasms which haunt humanity, and also of the work of the text, which is analogous to the dream-work. Finally, Jung and his followers find archetypal phenomena in the tales, as in dream and myth, proposing that certain symbols in these forms were the residues of ancestral memory preserved in the collective unconscious.[8]

It is not my intention to attempt to invalidate any of these approaches to the fairy-tale; indeed, I shall draw heavily on the work of Antti Aarne and Stith Thompson in particular. Recent theorists, however, have argued convincingly that we should also, as Catherine Velay-Vallantin puts it in her fascinating study *L'histoire des contes*,[9] '*traiter le conte come un objet historique*' [treat fairy-tales as historical objects] and, following the work of Jack Zipes,[10] should see them in relation to the society which produces, transmits and receives them. By this analysis, '*Le conte, inscrit dans la longue durée, n'est pas pour autant un objet immobile*' [fairy-tales are inscribed throughout the centuries, but this does not mean they never change].[11] Even more recently, Marina Warner has pointed to the continual process of metamorphosis which takes place within and around a fairy-tale, arguing that :

> However universally distributed, stories spring up in different places dressed in different moods, with different twists and regional details and contexts which give the satisfaction of particular recognition to their audience.[12]

In relation to the present volume, therefore, fairy-tales can be seen as an ideal subject for a study of transition.

The fairy-tale I want to consider certainly had 'universal distribution', in both time and space. Velay-Vallentin says that it goes back to at least the thirteenth century, and that versions of *The Girl With Cut-Off Hands* have been found throughout Europe, in the Middle East, in Japan, and in some regions of Africa and of North and South America.[13] Throughout its long history it traditionally contained four main episodes which, based on the work of Aarne-Thompson and Velay-Vallentin and on my own reading were as follows:

---

    [7]   Sigmund Freud, *Art and Literature*, ed. Albert Dickson, *The Penguin Freud Library*, gen. ed. James Strachey, 15 vols (London: Penguin, 1956), XIV, p. 247.
    [8]   C.J. Jung, *Dreams*, trans. R.F.C. Hull (1900; London: Ark Paperbacks, 1985).
    [9]   Catherine Velay-Vallentin, *L'histoire des contes* (Paris: Fayard, 1992), p. 38.
    [10]   Jack Zipes, *Fairy Tales and Fables from Weimar Days* (Hanover and London: University Press of New England, 1989).
    [11]   Velay-Vallentin, *L'histoire des contes*, p. 39.
    [12]   Marina Warner, *From the Beast to the Blonde* (London: Vintage, 1995), p. xxviii.
    [13]   Velay-Vallentin, *L'histoire des contes*, p. 99.

1. The heroine cuts off her hands, or has her hands cut off, in order to resist the incestuous advances of her father, or because she does not want to marry her father, or because her father has sold her to the devil, or her mother is jealous of her.
2. She escapes into the woods, or is taken into the woods or is sent over the sea and is found by a king.
3. The king marries her, but is absent when their child/children are born. The heroine's mother-in law (or another antagonist such as the devil or a jealous sister-in-law) gains possession of the letter sent to the king to announce the birth of their child and substitutes another in which the heroine is said to have given birth to a monster (or an animal). The king replies saying that his wife and child must be kept safe, but this letter is also intercepted and replaced by one ordering the death of the heroine and her child. The heroine again manages to escape.
4. By a miracle the heroine's hands grow again. The king searches for her, and eventually they are reunited.[14]

As well as setting out the main episodes of the story, and their accompanying motifs, this summary will also enable us to establish how far Quillard and D'Annunzio, while making extensive use of the traditional tale, also depart from it and transform it for their own artistic purposes. The key to these transformations can be found in what was happening in *avant-garde* theatre, in particular in France. To summarize briefly, the Théâtre Libre, founded by André Antoine (1858–1943), became between 1887 and 1894 the 'most successful and most important group in the first *avant-garde*'.[15] Antoine and his company, following the precepts of the great novelist, failed playwright, theatre critic and political journalist Emile Zola (1840–1902) quickly became the major exponents of the naturalist drama, and their influence in bringing naturalism to the theatre and in altering conceptions of the roles and relationships of director, actors and stage-designers was enormous. Antoine was concerned with representing reality on the stage, and so with creating the illusion on stage of a three-dimensional scene where 'real' characters could play their parts surrounded by 'real' objects. But as even Antoine himself saw, the faithful and honest representation of reality, however artistically created, could be limiting. A reaction against it came when Paul Fort (1872–1960), then a poet of seventeen, founded the Théâtre d'Art in 1890, originally to stage the works of young symbolists.

The major theorist of symbolist drama was the poet Stéphane Mallarmé (1842–98), many of whose theories were published during the 1880s, and who

---

[14] Aarne-Thompson, *The Types of the Folktale*, pp. 240–1 (story 706); Velay-Vallantin, *L'histoire*, p. 99.

[15] John A. Henderson, *The First Avant-Garde 1887–1894. Sources of the Modern French Theatre* (London: Harrap, 1971), p. 44.

advocated what came to be known as a 'poet's theatre', where movement, colour and sound would combine to express the poetry of the universe. For Mallarmé the poet's existence in the material world could only be tragic, and he wanted theatre to aspire to dream and mystery and to use movement, particularly ballet, and music in order to penetrate, and convey, the inner self and the life of the spirit.16 It was ideas such as these which influenced Pierre Quillard when he wrote *La Fille aux Mains coupées* (first published in 1886),[17] and which led Paul Fort to choose the play for the programme performed at the Théâtre d'Art on 20 March 1891. Fort himself was the director, the set was by the symbolist painter Paul Sérusier and if, when it was written, the play appears to have been (largely) an illustration of Mallarmé's theories it became, at this its first performance, the first example of symbolist *mise en scène*.[18]

Pierre Quillard (1864–1912) was a minor poet, philologist, translator and critic, and the author of two plays (*L'Errante* as well as *La Fille aux Mains coupées*).[19] He was an admirer of Mallarmé and a friend of Proust and of some of the best-known symbolists of his generation. He contributed to a number of literary reviews, and was frequently to be seen at literary meetings (including Mallarmé's famous 'Mardis'). After his one brief moment of fame as a playwright, he travelled as a teacher to Turkey in the 1890s, and when he returned to France in 1896 he took up the campaign in favour of the Armenians. A supporter of Dreyfus, he spoke out against persecution in different parts of the world.

His essay *De l'inutilité absolue de la mise en scène exacte* [On the utter pointlessness of accurate staging] can be read as a defence of the first production of his play, and also shows how much he had absorbed of Mallarmé's theories. He says, for example, that theatre should be a pretext for dreaming, and that décor should be a pure ornamental fiction which completes the illusion through analogies of colour and line with the play.[20] *La Fille aux Mains coupées* lasts only about an hour in performance but, as John Henderson observes: 'Coming at a time when naturalist drama was showing signs of fatigue, Quillard's work struck an entirely new note, and this slight play is in a sense a turning-point.'[21]

---

16   Mallarmé's reviews and essays can be found in the volume of his *Oeuvres complètes*, eds H. Mondor and G. Jean-Aubry (Paris: Gallimard, 1945). The collected articles were published as *Divagations* (Paris: Bibliotheque Charpentier, 1897).

17   I have used the text of the play established and edited by Jeremy Whistle in his *Deux Pièces symbolistes* (Exeter: University of Exeter 'textes littéraires', 1976). All references are to this edition, and are given in the text. A translation (to be used advisedly) by Jacques F. Hovis can be found in *The Drama Review* 20, 3 (September 1976) pp. 123–8.

18   This aspect of the play has been analysed by Frantisek Deak in his fundamental book *Symbolist Theatre. The Formation of an Avant-Garde* (Baltimore and London: The Johns Hopkins University Press, 1993), pp. 142–8.

19   P. Quillard, *La Fille aux Mains coupées*, in *La Pléiade, Revue littéraire, musicale et dramatique* (April 1886), pp. 33–41.

20   Henderson, *The First Avant-Garde*, p. 79.

21   Ibid., p. 94.

Many episodes of the fairy-tale remain: the attempted incest by the father of the Girl, the cutting off of her hands, her wanderings (in Quillard's version, she approaches Paradise), the miracle by which her hands grow again and her acceptance (here reluctantly) of the love of the king. The text consists of prose, for the stage-directions, and verse, when the characters speak, and when the play was performed the prose sections, which indicate character and events and mark changes in place and time were read by a 'narrator' (played by Suzanne Bernard). Poetry, then, as Marcel Collière put it in the Théâtre d'Art programme for *La Fille aux Mains coupées*, retains its *'fonction essentielle et exclusive: exprimer lyriquement l'âme des personnages'* [essential and exclusive function: to express lyrically the soul of the characters].[22] In some respects the text of the play marks a shift from Hellenizing (or Parnassian) tendencies towards the 'subtlety, mystery, morbidity, and paradox' that we associate with the decadent style.[23] If the poets of the Parnasse used whiteness to indicate 'an art beyond life',[24] and wanted to exclude disordered feeling from the creation of ideal beauty and order, the reverse seems to be happening in Quillard's play. So at the beginning of the play the Young Girl is kneeling and praying to Christ *'en sa blancheur adorable de lys'* [in her adorable lily whiteness] (p. 3) to be saved from *'le malin'* [the devil], but she is told by a Chorus of Angels that the gates of heaven are closed to her, that the Earth has been given over to Eros and that her *'froides fleurs des soirs polaires'* [cold flowers of polar evenings] (p. 4) will melt. Then the Young Girl prays to the Virgin to safeguard her purity and chastity, but her prayer is interrupted by the sound of fighting offstage, and her father enters to cover her hands with *'caresses incestueuses at brutales'* (the caresses mentioned by Praz) (p. 5). Horrified, she commands her servant to cut off her hands and to take them to her father. At the beginning of the second part of the play her father places her in a boat and sends her off on a stormy sea, but she is saved by invisible archangels and has a series of ecstatic visions, experiencing a mystic rapture in which she believes she is dead. At this point her hands regenerate, and she is symbolically prepared not for a mystic union with Christ but for sensual-sexual initiation into adulthood by the Poet-King. At this point Quillard's text brings to mind what Velay-Vallantin says about the use of the tale of the Girl With Cut-Off Hands in theatre, and more specifically in the Basque pastoral. Velay-Vallantin argues that acting in a pastoral was a kind of apprenticeship for the girls who took part, and that the stories of the cycle of the banished woman *'sont pour ces filles, futures épouses et mères, l'ultime répétition de leur conduite à venir'* [are for these girls, future wives and mothers, the last rehearsal for their future conduct].[25]

---

22 Published as an appendix to the Whistle edition of the play, op. cit., p. 31.

23 I am indebted in this part of my paper to Philip Knight, *Flower Poetics in Nineteenth-Century France* (Oxford: Clarendon Press, 1986). For this definition of the decadent style, see his p. 232.

24 Ibid., p. 162.

25 Velay-Vallentin, *L'histoire*, p. 119.

The plays, that is, were used as a kind of preparation for adulthood, and a rite of passage through the necessary stages on the way to the roles assigned to them in adulthood.

Quillard's play, by contrast, both as text and in performance, is a preparation for and a celebration of 'poet's theatre'. The Young Girl submits to her destiny, and goes, torn between love and fear, towards the king (who, as already indicated, is not, as in traditional versions of the tale, just a king but a poet as well) '*comme résignée aux flammes d'une imminente géhenne*' [as though resigned to the flames of an imminent gehenna] (p. 9). The Girl's story is, in a sense, sacrificed as in the performances of the play the requirements of the new aesthetics were paramount. Deak says that the company played behind a transparent gauze scrim; that there were no objects of any kind on stage; that on the backdrop of shining gold framed with red draperies Paul Sérusier had painted multicoloured angels kneeling in prayer; and that the spectators cheered as the set 'brought symbolist painting into the theatre for the first time and also marked the invention of symbolist stage design'.[26] As we have seen, Quillard argued in *De l'inutilité absolue de la mise en scène exacte* that the set should be a pure ornamental fiction, used to create an impression of infinity of time and space. The spectators would no longer be distracted by the set or, in this most static of theatres, by action on stage, but would give themselves fully to the poet, whose words would lead them into their own private dream-world. But, as Deak points out, if the production of *La Fille aux Mains coupées* was conceived as that of a 'theatre of voice', where language is used to create images in the mind and imagination of the audience, the decor was also important.[27] It was the coming together of text, symbolist poetics and symbolist stage-design which made *La Fille aux Mains coupées* into a landmark in modern theatre, and which transformed the fairy-tale, and its heroine, into a vehicle for 'poet's theatre'.

It is virtually impossible to synthesize the colourful, turbulent life and vast and varied output of Gabriele D'Annunzio (1863–1938).[28] He began to write poetry at the end of the 1870s and early on turned also to narrative. He started to write for the theatre because of his meeting, and affair, with Eleonora Duse, and between 1897 and 1903 he wrote a number of plays for her, and in 1900 published a novel, *Il Fuoco* [*The Fire*], in which he describes their affair. D'Annunzio is a dominant figure on the Italian literary (and political) scene for much of the twentieth century, and his influence was felt by many writers, including Eugenio Montale, up to the Second World War. He was one of the major channels through which new ideas flowed into Italy, to the extent that, writing of him as a reviewer and journalist in the 1880s and 1890s, Ezio Raimondi says:

---

[26] Deak, *Symbolist Theatre*, pp. 142–3.
[27] Ibid., p. 144.
[28] I refer readers to John Woodhouse's excellent new biography of D'Annunzio: *Gabriele D'Annunzio. Defiant Archangel* (Oxford: Clarendon Press, 1998).

Si sa che nelle sue avventurose esplorazioni critiche di recensore e
cronista il D'Annunzio non esita a combinare gli elementi piú diversi ed
eterocliti con la disinvoltura eclettica di un collezionista che si appropria
di tutto quanto gli fa comodo, purché sia alla moda e francese.[29]

[We know that in his adventurous critical explorations as a reviewer and
journalist D'Annunzio does not hesitate to bring together the most diverse
and unusual elements with the eclectic nonchalance of a collector who
appropriates all that suits him, provided it is fashionable and French.]

The detailed and finely argued work of Guy Tosi shows clearly that in the early
1890s D'Annunzio learnt much from French symbolism,[30] and this, together with
D'Annunzio's passion for the *dernier cri*, makes it unlikely that D'Annunzio was
ignorant of what was happening in the Parisian *avant-garde*.

The play into which he incorporates his version of *The Girl With Cut-Off
Hands* is *La Gioconda* (1898; the title is obviously from that of Leonardo's
painting). He dedicated it, with a phrase that can be read as sinister given what
happens in the play, to Eleonora Duse *'dalle belle mani'* [with the beautiful
hands] (p. 231). The plot revolves around the relationships between a sculptor,
Lucio Settala, who is recovering from a suicide attempt, his devoted and virtuous
wife, Silvia, and his mistress, who is also his artistic inspiration and model, the
femme fatale Gioconda Dianti. Lucio and Silvia have a daughter, Beata, who
becomes particularly important in the final act, and Lucio himself is torn between
his love for his wife and daughter and an overwhelming sense of powerlessness
when faced by the attractions of Gioconda. The struggle, as embodied in the two
women, seems to be one between virtuous family life and the claims of art. In Act
III the two women, and what they represent, confront each other in a kind of clay-
wrestling match over Lucio and his art. To try to put an end to this Silvia,
presented up to this point as the pure and virtuous woman, lies when she says she
has read the contents of a letter which Gioconda sent to Lucio that morning, and
tells Gioconda that Lucio wants her to leave. Gioconda is furious, and attempts
to destroy the statue Lucio has made of her. Then, as I said at the beginning of
this paper, Silvia's hands are crushed when she tries to save it. In the final Act
Lucio has returned to Gioconda, and Silvia and a strange, almost sea-creature, La
Sirenetta, are left to play out the consequences of Silvia's actions. Female
mutilation is, therefore, one of the motifs which D'Annunzio takes from the fairy-
tale on which he drew. But there are also reversals in D'Annunzio's text when
compared to the tale. Silvia is already married and has a child before her hands
are amputated; she 'appropriates' the letter which Gioconda sends to Lucio, and

---

[29]   Ezio Raimondi, *Il D'Annunzio e il simbolismo* in *D'Annunzio e il simbolismo
europeo*, ed. Emilio Mariano (Milan: Il Saggiatore, 1976), p. 32.
[30]   Guy Tosi, 'D'Annunzio et le symbolisme français', in Raimondi, *Il
D'Annunzio*, pp. 223–82.

tries to use it to rid herself of her rival, so becoming aligned with the malignant characters of the fairy-tale; there is no miraculous regeneration except in the 'fairy-tale' sequence in Act IV when Silvia tells La Sirenetta that sometimes she has the hallucination that her blood is flowing into her fingertips. Clearly, on placing the tale in a bourgeois setting, D'Annunzio has made it naturalist: miracles are no longer possible, only the well-known illusion of feeling in an amputated limb. Finally the virtuous, submissive and devoted Silvia becomes the transgressor and loses her roles as wife and mother.

There is an excellent analysis of this play, and its place as the culmination of the decadent texts she discusses, in Barbara Spackman's book *Decadent Genealogies*,[31] Spackman argues that:

> of all the 'parts' that litter D'Annunzio's texts, none is more pervasive and eroticized (or more subject to description as fetish in common parlance) than the hand. Whiter than white, smoother than marble, the hand seems to stand for the woman.[32]

La Gioconda is, indeed, as Spackman says, a play about fragments, about the relationship between part and whole, and she discusses extensively the function of synecdoche and the 'logic of fetishism' in the play. When Silvia's hands have been amputated, which Silvia herself sees as a punishment for the lie she has told, the absence, which for Freud is the 'mother's penis', is, for D'Annunzio, the 'mother's hands', and as Spackman comments that absence is 'hidden' on stage and therefore cannot be seen, "*La mutilata*" is also "*la castrata*".[33]

I want to argue that there is another way in which Silvia is mutilated. As I have said, she loses her role as wife, and because she has no hands she no longer able to respond and reach out to her daughter. What this inability signifies is indicated by La Sirenetta when she extols the attributes of Silvia's (former) hands:

> *Com'erano belle, com'erano belle! Credi tu che io non me ne ricordi? Te le ho baciate; tante tante volte te le ho baciate con questa bocca. Mi davano il pane, una melagrana, una tazza di latte [. . .] erano belle come se te le avesse fatte l'Alba con un fiato, bianche come il fiore della maretta, più fini di quei ricami che fa il vento nell'arena; si muovevano come il sole nell'acqua, favellavano meglio della e delle pupille, quello che dicevano era come una parola benigna, quello che prendevano per donare diventava tutt'oro . . .* (p. 325)

---

[31]   Barbara Spackman, *Decadent Genealogies* (Ithaca and London: Cornell University Press, 1989), esp. pp. 191–210.
[32]   Ibid., pp. 193–4.
[33]   Ibid., pp. 201–2.

[How beautiful, how beautiful they were! Do you think I don't remember them? I've kissed them; I've kissed them so very many times with this mouth of mine. They gave me bread, a pomegranate, a cup of milk . . . they were as beautiful as if the Dawn, in a breath, had made them for you, white as the foam on the waves, finer than the patterns the wind makes in the sand; they moved like the sun in the water, they spoke better than the tongue and the eyes, what they said were like a kind word, what they picked up to give became pure gold . . .]

In this speech, when she says that Silvia's hands 'spoke', La Sirenetta creates a link between speech and gesture, between the tongue and the hands, and this link has a famous precedent in relation to women. In *Titus Andronicus*, a play where rape, mutilation, revenge and cannibalism all have a part, Lavinia's tongue is cut out and her hands are cut off to prevent her from revealing the names of her rapists. Her situation is, therefore, even worse than that of Philomela, in the passage from Ovid's *Metamorphoses*, which Shakespeare draws on, whose tongue is cut out but whose hands are left to her. Philomela cannot name her rapist, but she is able to use her hands to weave the story of what happened to her and so reveal it to her sister. Lavinia cannot do this, but even though she is a 'map of woe' her father claims to be able to 'read' the signs she makes. Lavinia, however, is able to help herself a little when she finds a copy of the story of Philomela; as a result of which Marcus, her uncle, shows her how to write the names of her rapists on the sand. Silvia, though, is apparently rendered completely helpless by the loss of her hands, becoming isolated and, in everything important to her, 'speechless'.[34] Her role as creator of life has been appropriated by her husband, but then he is enervated and becomes an automaton, (over)-producing statues under the watchful gaze of Gioconda.

I have argued that in Quillard's play the story of Young Girl is appropriated and transformed into a vehicle for 'poet's theatre'. There is a similar 'filching' in *La Gioconda*, where mutilation becomes a denial of access to language. The 'very ancient legend' with which we began has become, at the end of the nineteenth century, a means not for telling a woman's story but of appropriating that story for symbolist and decadent poetics.

---

[34] On the use of the figure of *geminatio* in *La Gioconda* see Spackman, *Decadent Genealogies*, p. 206.

Chapter 10

A Passion for Dismemberment: Gabriele d'Annunzio's Portrayals of Women[1]

Susan Bassnett

In his private notebook, never intended for publication, Gabriele d'Annunzio wrote:

> With the passing of the years, my *awareness* becomes increasingly merged with my *instinct*, and my intentions *ever more closely with my powers*.[2]

In this sentence, d'Annunzio reflects on his own interior processes, using several of the keywords that he endowed with special meaning: instinct, awareness, power. Self-obsessed to an extreme, d'Annunzio constantly reflected on his own creativity and his own development, though always with insistence on a series of factors upon which he based both his public and private lives. Those factors include a belief in his own strength, physical, sexual and psychological, a belief in the superiority of his lineage and his mind and a belief in his special role both as artist and as Italian patriot. D'Annunzio developed his own particular version of the Superman, modelled upon himself, and no study of any of his works can fail to take into account the deliberate process of self-dramatization that went on throughout his life. His last home, the Vittoriale on the shores of Lake Garda, is an extraordinary monument to that life. There is not a single room that is not crowded with objects, all endowed with a particular symbolic significance, from the dead tortoise on the dining room table, a reminder to guests of the consequences of over-indulgence, to the coffin on rockers in which he sometimes slept, a simultaneous symbol of life as an interlude between infanthood and death.

D'Annunzio created the Vittoriale in 1921, when he was fifty-eight years old. He was then one of Italy's most famous writers and a notorious public figure, following the Fiume episode of a few months earlier, when he had occupied the

---

[1]   Throughout this essay 'd' is used in 'd'Annunzio', which the author himself used to indicate his supposed noble origins. See Julie Dashwood's essay, fn. 1.
[2]   Gabriele d'Annunzio, *Di me a me stesso* (*From Me To Myself*), ed. Annamaria Andreoli (Milan: Mondadori, 1990), p. 7.

Dalmatian city in an attempt to convince the world that it was part of Italy's Adriatic empire, a perspective ignored by the League of Nations when drawing up the settlement at the end of the First World War. Photographs of the small, bald, moustachioed figure in military uniform or at the controls of an aeroplane circulated in the media, but after what he saw as a betrayal, d'Annunzio retreated to Lake Garda and spent the rest of his life creating a kind of shrine to himself. Besides the house he created an open air theatre, a war museum and a great park, in which he placed the battleship, 'La Fida', which was dismantled and carried up the mountainside where it was reassembled as a gigantic monument.

D'Annunzio was born in far more humble circumstances, in Pescara, in 1863, to a respectable middle-class family. He studied at the Reale Collegio Cicognini in Prato, one of Italy's best schools of the day, where he distinguished himself as a promising poet, publishing his first collection, *Primo vere*, in 1879. It is important to note that d'Annunzio began his literary career as a lyrical poet of considerable talent, and his ability to write beautiful descriptive accounts of landscape and natural phenomena shows the early training and interest in poetry. His life and literary career changed once he went to university in Rome, where the talented boy from the provinces set out to reinvent himself. Through his early marriage to Maria Harduin dei Duchi di Gallese he obtained an entry into aristocratic Roman society, where he quickly established a reputation as a society wit and *bon viveur*. Gradually, he reconstructed his childhood, hinting at a noble bloodline in the Abruzzi territories of his origins, and writing lyrically about the wild beauty of his birthplace. Time and again, his protagonists move between the elegance of urban Roman society and the savage, passionate mountains, where peasant life is still quintessentially pagan, and Christianity only a veneer over that primitive existence.

D'Annunzio's literary career falls into several phases: the early period, when he was primarily a poet, followed by his decadentist phase, marked by the publication of his highly successful novels such as *Il Piacere* (*Pleasure*) in 1889, *Il Trionfo della morte* (*The Triumph of Death*) in 1894, *Le vergini delle Rocce* (*The Virgins of the Rocks*) in 1896. In 1895 he had begun a relationship with Eleonora Duse, one of Italy's leading actresses, and turned his attention to the theatre. The years following the staging of his first play, *Sogno di un mattino di primavera* (*Dream of a Spring Morning*), in 1897 can be seen as his apprenticeship in the art of writing for the theatre. Some of his plays, such as the vastly expensive, elaborately staged *Francesca da Rimini* (1901), were not commercially successful but *La figlia di Iorio* (1904), a tragedy set in the Abruzzi countryside, was a hit. Widely regarded as Italy's greatest writer, pre-eminent as poet, novelist, and playwright, d'Annunzio moved to Paris in 1910, where he worked with Debussy and Ida Rubinstein and tried his hand at writing for the cinema.

D'Annunzio's lavish language and controversial subject matter, coupled with his extravagant private life made him a centre of public attention, often of

ridicule. His pomposity and overblown posturing failed to convince even those
who admired his lyricism. But there was another side to d'Annunzio, that came
to the fore when war broke out in 1915. D'Annunzio, like his contemporary
Pirandello, was disillusioned with the new Italy, with the way the country had
been governed since the long-sought-for unification in 1870. Also like Pirandello,
he saw the way forward as linked to the fortunes of Benito Mussolini, the man he
believed was capable of restoring the pride of a nation that felt grievously under-
rewarded in the settlement that followed the end of the war. Once he began his
Vittoriale project, with help from Mussolini and the Italian government,
d'Annunzio's fortunes became increasingly tied up with fascism. D'Annunzio,
the intellectual from the Adriatic coast who wanted to believe in his own unique
destiny as a great Italian, had much in common with Mussolini, also a child from
the Adriatic, who fought his way out of the village and into radical socialist
movements, before founding his own lethal brand of national socialism.

Parallels have often been made between the physical appearance of these two
men, and between their legendary pursuit of women, the one tangible sign of the
virility they continually proclaimed in all aspects of their lives. But d'Annunzio
saw himself principally as an aesthete, a man of taste and discernment, and
sought relationships with some of the most beautiful and talented women of his
age. Tom Antongini, d'Annunzio's secretary and sometime biographer, describes
his peculiar habit of giving his lovers a nickname:

> For d'Annunzio the woman who was worthy of receiving a truly special
> name from him entered automatically into his kingdom, into his sphere.
> From that moment she could boast that she belonged to a very select order
> of which, of course, d'Annunzio was the sole male member. It was most
> unusual for him to give a name in jest, and I recall no case where he
> rebaptized a woman who failed at all to interest him.[3]

This curious practice illustrates an important aspect of d'Annunzio's life: the
deliberate naming of people, places and things that he saw as a necessary part of
his desire for control. The conferral of a name seems to have carried some quasi-
mystical significance, and within the Vittoriale, rooms are carefully named as
well. But while his names for women generally refer to their physical
characteristics or to an aspect of their personality, in his house the naming process
seems to have had some other meaning. Two in particular stand out: the 'Stanza
del lebbroso' (the Room of the Leper) and the 'Stanza del Monco' (the Room of
the Stump). Both testify to d'Annunzio's variety of black humour: the Room of
the Leper is full of references to the special position in medieval society held by
lepers, held to be somehow holy, touched by God and outside society.
D'Annunzio drew a conscious parallel between himself and the figure of the

---

        3   Tom Antongini, *D'Annunzio* (London: Heinemann, 1938), p. 68.

leper, at once special and shunned. The Room of the Stump ostensibly refers to d'Annunzio's habit of telling people he was unable to answer the thousands of letters he received from his admiring fans because he had lost his right hand in an accident.

His right hand was, of course, intact, but he did lose an eye in 1916 and was painted by Ercole Sibellato in the same year, in a strange portrait that shows the writer sitting in a chair, one eye heavily bandaged, looking down at a cockerel that is pecking a lizard to death. The painting is entitled *Orbo veggente (The Watchful Orb)*. This painting is one of the most striking examples of d'Annunzio's fascination for the body in decay or dismemberment, a fascination that can best be described as fetishistic. The Vittoriale is full of death masks and sculpted body parts, and the fact that he chose to have his portrait painted right after his accident is further indication of his obsessive interest in imperfections of the body. Given that the theme of mutilation and dismemberment recurs so often in his writing, it is perhaps not improbable to speculate that this obsession may be linked with the gap between his origins and his self-created persona. D'Annunzio may have tried to live like a Renaissance prince, just as Mussolini tried to live like an imperial Roman leader, but both were authors of their own fortunes, however they might aspire to distinguished forebears.

D'Annunzio's best-known novels all appear to be, in different ways, autobiographical. Read chronologically, they give an insight into the way he was developing artistically and ideologically. His themes are those that he would also develop in his plays: incest, adultery, rape and martyrdom, combined with studies of frustrated sexual desire and suicidal depression. The narrative voice is very much that of the male, and women are objectified, either as emblems of idealized perfection or destructive figures of obscure desires. What is also striking is the extent to which d'Annunzio punishes women in his writing. For a man who claimed to adore women, he subjects his female characters to all kinds of torments, to violent deaths, rapes, miscarriages and abortions, torture and dismemberment. The reader's relationship to such events as these is mediated by the narrator, and the detachment with which some of the more barbaric episodes are narrated reinforces the ambiguity of these works. For although he learned a great deal from naturalism, from the verismo school of writers such as Verga, d'Annunzio went beyond naturalism, working towards a more introspective style of narration. When it suits him, he employs the technique of harrowing naturalistic depiction of real life, particularly peasant life, but juxtaposes this with a completely different narrative tone. The naturalistic descriptions serve to disturb the reader, for in this way the reader is led into the narrative, only to be abruptly held at bay. D'Annunzio is not concerned with psychological realism, his interest is in the depiction of evanescent states of mind. Perhaps this is why he is so good at writing about characters who are disturbed, whose thought processes are not linear and who suffer, in some way, from forms of mental illness.

One of his early stories, *La vergine Orsola* (*Orsola, the Virgin*), published in his *Le novelle di Pescara* (*Tales from Pescara*) (1884–86), is a striking example of how he employs and then transcends naturalism. The story opens with an account of Orsola dying of typhus, and then moves, through her recovery, to become a study of how her sexuality begins to force its way into her consciousness, leading to the moment when she is raped by the revolting Lindoro, the man who delivers wine to the house and acts as a go-between for her with her admirer, Marcello. The account of the rape, though inviting sympathy for Orsola, is presented in strong visual terms, almost photographically:

> But at a certain point, involuntarily, because of that blind instinct which warns a woman that she is faced by an aroused man, she swiftly moved her hand to fasten the hooks over her throat, her breasts. That movement by which Orsola acknowledged the man in the go-between, that unexpected gesture provoked in Lindoro's abjectness an uprush of masculine pride. Ah, he had made a woman respond to him! – And he came closer; and then, since the wine gave him courage, this time no cowardly restraint held the brute in check.[4]

The narrative seems already to be hinting at the woman's collusion with her rapist, and by shifting to Lindoro's interior monologue, the objectification of Orsola becomes complete. This passage ends Chapter XIV, and Chapter XV opens with a sentence describing Orsola lying inert on the floor, 'her entire body expressing the dishevelment of An outraged woman'. But we are given no chance of identifying with her plight, for immediately the narrator records that as she hears her sister's step on the stairs, she jumps to her feet and invents an excuse about an attack of sudden weakness. A few pages later, the ambiguity of Orsola's reaction is made explicit. She goes back over the rape in her mind, reflecting that she had not resisted in any way

> she had surrendered, all her strength drained, no longer able to distinguish anything, feeling only an immense joy mingled with the pain flooding through her body.[5]

Here the sadism of the narrative becomes apparent. Orsola has been raped because she wanted to be raped, her physical desires, stimulated by the after-effects of the fever, have led her to her doom. The story charts her descent into degradation, as she becomes pregnant, tries to procure an abortion and bleeds to death on the floor.

The attribution of blame to women for everything from their own rape to unhappy love affairs runs through d'Annunzio's writing. Women are always

---

[4]   Gabriele d'Annunzio, 'The Virgin Orsola', trans. Raymond Rosenthal, in *Nocturne and Five Tales of Love and Death* (London: Quartet, 1993), p. 41.
[5]   Ibid., p. 45.

punished. If they are cruel, they are made to suffer, but if they are noble and self-sacrificing, they are made to suffer more. *Il Piacere*, d'Annunzio's first major prose success, focuses on the young count Andrea Sperelli, d'Annunzio's alter ego, who falls in love with two women. One, the beautiful and mysterious Elena, leaves Andrea at the height of their passion, and goes off to make an advantageous marriage, returning later to Rome prepared to betray her husband and Andrea as well. The other, the gentle, loving Maria, gradually steels herself to leave her husband for Andrea, as this latter tries to decide which of the women he really loves. Gradually, the narrative depicts Elena as less and less worthy and desirable, but at the same time hints about Maria's tragic fate increase. The lovers go to visit the tomb of Keats and Shelley. Evening falls in the cemetery, Andrea goes down on his knees to offer Maria a handful of rose petals and declare his adoration for her. She is described in terms of the classic *fin-de-siècle* heroine:

> She then drew back the veil from before her face and looked at Andrea with eyes that were a little dazed. She looked very beautiful. The shadows round her eyes were darker and deeper, but the eyes themselves burned with a more intense light. Her hair clung to her temples in heavy hyacinthine curls tinged with violet. The middle of her forehead, which was left free, gleamed by contrast, in moonlike purity. Her features had fined down and lost something of their materiality through stress of love and sorrow.[6]

The veil, the roses, the hyacinthine hair, the face refined by suffering as well as her name all serve as signifiers of the link between Maria and the Virgin Mary. Maria is, of course, also a mother, and d'Annunzio's treatment of motherhood would merit a study in its own right. But despite this idealization, it is significant that once again the portrait of the beloved woman is stripped down to its component parts. Time and again in his descriptions, d'Annunzio takes the female body to pieces, focusing on hands or feet or eyes or mouths, reducing the woman to a collage of essential elements. Women are not whole creatures in d'Annunzio's universe, they are composites that come into existence only when they are the object of a man's desire.

Maria's destruction comes swiftly. Andrea is still drawn to Elena, though recognizes that his love for Maria is worth far more. He has lied about his feelings for Elena to Maria, but the time has come for him to make a decision. Maria's husband has been ruined and the family will have to leave Rome. She is distraught, but comes to spend her first, and possibly last night with him. He knows and believes that she truly loves him, and for the first time in his life he has the chance of being with someone who trusts him completely. The lovers embrace and he buries his face in her hair:

---

6   Gabriele d'Annunzio, *The Child of Pleasure*, trans. Georgina Harding (Sawtry, Cambs: Dedalus, 1991), p. 302.

> All at once, she struggled free of his embrace, her whole form convulsed
> with horror, her face ghastly and distraught as if she had at that moment
> torn herself from the arms of Death. That name! That name! – She had
> heard that name![7]

Andrea Sperelli loses the woman he loves because he is unable to separate her
from the other object of his desire, and speaks the wrong name. With one word
he destroys his own happiness and Maria's, but the novel charts the inexorability
of this conclusion, given Andrea's inability to take decisions and to act. He is a
dandified figure, presented without a trace of irony, and carries within his
heritage the seeds of his own destruction. Coming from a noble family, he is
nevertheless guilty from the outset of sophistry. Insincerity, towards himself
rather than to others, the narrator reminds us early in the novel, is a habit of mind
so engrained that he cannot ever be sincere or fully in control of himself.

Giorgio, the protagonist of d'Annunzio's next novel, *The Triumph of Death*,
is plagued by different demons. He too is torn between two kinds of love, but the
situation is much more complex. He is passionately in love with Ippolita, whom
he seeks to possess completely, but he is also driven by love for his mother and
sister in the Abruzzi, who have to cope with his brutal father. He is unable to stand
up to his father, and is terrified that he may in some way have inherited the old
man's vulgarity and cruelty. Unable to cope with the forces that drive him close
to madness, Giorgio increasingly contemplates suicide. The violence of his manic
depressive moods is pictured in the novel by lurid accounts of the hideousness of
peasant life in the mountains. The physical ugliness of the peasants, with their
deformed bodies, swollen goiterous necks, missing limbs, sour breath, pustulated
skin and rotting teeth is contrasted by the beauty of the mountain landscape, over
which the Majella presides in majesty.

In this novel d'Annunzio takes up an almost Swinburnian repudiation of
Christianity. The religious festival that inspires the peasants is presented as a
pagan 'baccanalia'. The god of the peasants, the Madonna who receives their
prayers have nothing to offer Giorgio. He brings Ippolita to live with him in a
rural retreat, but their intimacy produces increasing disillusionment. Giorgio
perceives himself as a being set apart, isolated from the rest of the human race by
his innate superiority. In one episode, when he takes Ippolita swimming, he looks
at her feet and notes that 'the toes were misshapen, plebeian, wholly without
refinement, and bore unmistakable signs of low origin'.[8] In another scene, we
learn that she suffers from epilepsy and lives in fear of an attack. Giorgio
struggles with the jealousy that comes from his imaginings about Ippolita, about
the life she has lived, her dreams and her fantasies. That he has cause to worry is
made explicit in an extraordinary scene where she stabs a moth with a hairpin and

---

[7]   Ibid., p. 306.
[8]   Gabriele d'Annunzio, *The Triumph of Death*, trans. Georgina Harding (Sawtry,
Cambs: Dedalus, 1990), p. 235.

fixes it, still struggling, in her hair as an ornament. Giorgio is appalled by what he perceives as cruelty, but equally fascinated by it. He begins to harbour murderous thoughts about Ippolita and, as the moth episode indicates, it is clear that the narrative invites the reader to share Giorgio's perspective, written as it is from his point of view. Towards the end of the novel Ippolita is commenting on how brown she has become living in the countryside, and holds out her hands to him , so that he can see the difference between the whiteness of her hands and the brown of her arms:

> Ippolita held out her two hands to him. 'Kiss!' she said.
> He caught one of them, and made a pass with his knife as if to cut it off at the wrist.
> 'Cut away,' she said fearlessly; 'I shall not move.'
> As he made the pass he gazed earnestly at the delicate blue lines under the skin, which was so white it seemed as if it might belong to another body, to a fair woman.[9]

As he considers Ippolita's hands, Giorgio jokes that they are her vulnerable point, a sign that she will die of loss of blood. This is the crucial moment, because at this point the narrative suggests that he will indeed kill her. The suggestion comes from the vision that he experiences as he holds her hands, a vision in which she appears like Philomel, with her limbs severed:

> On the marble threshold of a doorway, dark with shadow, appeared the woman who was about to die, her arms extended, and from her wrists, where the pulse arteries had been severed, two crimson jets sprang up and throbbed.[10]

Dismemberment is here a symbolic prelude to murder. Shortly after this experience, Giorgio takes Ippolita with him up the mountainside, to the edge of the precipice that she has always been afraid of. In the last few lines of the novel, written almost entirely as dialogue, Giorgio drags Ippolita to the edge, and she resists as she realizes what he is about to do. The end is inevitable:

> There was a brief but savage struggle, as between two mortal foes who had nourished a secret and implacable hatred in their souls up till that hour [. . .] Then they crashed down headlong into death, locked in that fierce embrace.[11]

The protagonists of both *The Child of Pleasure* and *The Triumph of Death* engage with the object of their passion as though with a deadly enemy. Giorgio destroys

---

[9]   Ibid., p. 303.
[10]   Ibid., p. 304.
[11]   Ibid., p. 315.

Ippolita and himself in a single lethal act, while Andrea, who has failed to defeat Elena, takes his unconscious revenge on the innocent Maria. The male protagonists in both these novels are similarly driven by internal anguish, that derives from their sense of being men set apart in some special way. On the one hand, they have to deal with the problems of living in the world from day to day, but on the other they aspire to some state that places them above the world. The abyss between their actuality and their aspirations is the source of their internal crisis. The women they love are opponents; d'Annunzio implies that woman can never be a companion, and the relationship between men and women is inherently conflictual.

The influence of Nietzsche is clearly present in *The Triumph of Death*, and even more present in *The Virgins of the Rocks*, published in 1895, the first in the sequence of Romances of the Lily.[12] In this novel, written in the first person, the protagonist, Claudio, is an archetypal superman, who finds himself in the position of having to choose between three sisters, all equally beautiful in different ways and all secretly besotted with him. Characterization is minimal, and the three women are constantly objectified through physical description. In his first meeting with Violante, for example, the narrator describes the mechanics of her body climbing a flight of stairs, and comments that her power was so strong

> that I could not take my eyes off her movements: and I lingered behind so that my entire gaze should encircle her. She seemed to drive my spirit back into the marvellous epoch when artists drew from dormant matter those perfect forms which men regarded as the only truths worthy of worship on earth. And I thought as I looked at her and ascended behind her: 'It is right she should remain untouched. Only by a god could she be possessed without shame.'[13]

The narrator focuses upon Violante's head and feet, and then, when Anatolia appears, he describes her through an account of her beautiful hand, 'ready to clasp and give support'.[14] The third sister, Massimilla, is described in terms of her silvery voice. All three women are thus reduced to body parts, and although Claudio reflects on how their trinity is a symbol of the perfection of human love, his behaviour through the novel leads to a betrayal of all of them. Unable to choose between the more overtly sensual Violante, the deeply caring Anatolia holding her family together by caring for her mother, who has gone mad and whose presence blights all their lives, and the gentle Massimilla who aspires to

---

[12]   D'Annunzio planned to divide his novels into three groups: Romances of the Rose, Romances of the Lily and Romances of the Pomegranate. The concluding novel of the series of nine, beginning with *The Child of Pleasure* was to be called *The Triumph of Life*. The only Romance of the Lily to be completed, however, was *Il fuoco*.

[13]   Gabriele d'Annunzio, *The Virgins of the Rocks*, trans. Agatha Hughes (London: Heinemann, 1899), pp. 82–3.

[14]   Ibid., p. 84.

enter a convent, Claudio finally declares himself to Anatolia. But she understands that he is deceiving both of them:

> Then she turned upon me, and fixing her eyes on mine with a kind of impetuous force, she asked – 'Is it true your heart has chosen me? Have you examined your heart to the depths? Or does some illusion hang over you like a veil?' I was so much disturbed by her look, and these sudden doubts of hers, that I felt myself turn pale as if she had accused me of falsehood.[15]

With *The Virgins of the Rocks* d'Annunzio moved into another stage of his representation of the male protagonist, the alter-ego figure who shared his own taste for high society and passion for the wild beauty of the Abruzzi. The shift into the first-person narrative is significant, for we are invited to see solely through his eyes. Throughout the novel, which contains long lyrical passages of great beauty, d'Annunzio does not depict character, but rather locates the women in a landscape, suggesting that they are actually part of that landscape, creatures adrift in time, rather than flesh and blood human beings. Their feelings are described only in terms of what the narrator sees – glittering eyes, veiled faces, flowing hair, moving hands or feet, curved backs. Claudio as a character appears to be beyond human feelings; he tells us all the time that he is extraordinarily sensitive, that he is aware of the great sense of sadness that hangs over the once-proud Montaga family, but his actions offer a different story. He appears completely uncaring and devoid of all responsibility for the pain that he causes the three sisters. Even at the end, when Anatolia has refused him and it is clear that by making his declaration he has destroyed the happiness of all three of them, he accepts no responsibility and the novel concludes with another lyrically descriptive passage redolent with symbolism:

> Over our heads the sky bore no traces of clouds, save a slight shadow like the ashes of a burnt-out funeral pyre. The sun was scorching the peaks all around, outlining their solemn features on the blue sky. A great sadness and a great sweetness fell from above into the lonely circle, like a magic draught into a rough goblet. There the three sisters rested, and there I caught their final harmony.[16]

What distinguishes Claudio from other protagonists of d'Annunzio's novels is the fact that he sees himself principally as a creative artist. In the Prologue, the narrator looks back through the filter of his imaginative memory at the three sisters, each waiting to see who will be 'the elect'. Again, d'Annunzio uses his favourite image of blood flowing through hands:

---

[15] Ibid., p. 239.
[16] Ibid., p. 247.

> Bending and breaking as they were beneath the weight of their own
> maturity, like autumn trees overladen with bounteous fruit, they were
> unable either to sound the depth of their misery or to give voice to it. Their
> anguished lips revealed to me only a small portion of their secrets. But I
> could understand the ineffable things spoken by the blood flowing in the
> veins of their beautiful bare hands.[17]

After the prologue, we do not encounter the sisters again for another forty-five
pages, during which d'Annunzio sketches out his view that the world represents
the sensibility and ideas of the few superior men who created it. These superior
beings exist on a different plane from the rest of struggling humanity. Declaring
himself to be one of these beings, linked by a mysterious bond to past blood-
brothers such as Leonardo da Vinci, the narrator lays out his philosophical
position before returning to the narrative of the three sisters. In this novel, we see
the objectification of woman take a new twist, for these women exist only insofar
as the narrator creates them and transforms them into his muses. The
wretchedness of their lives, three good-looking women of marriageable age
wasting away in a castle in the mountains caring for a family racked by disease
and grief, is turned into material for the narrator's own purposes.

Of all d'Annunzio's novels, the one that blurs the lines between
autobiography and fantasy most obviously is *Il fuoco* (*The Flame*), which
appeared in 1900.[18] This novel depicts the relationship between a brilliant young
writer, Stelio Effrena, and his lover, the ageing actress known as La Foscarina.
Set in Venice, the novel charts the gradual disintegration of their once passionate
relationship, and ends with an account of the young man's witnessing the funeral
of Richard Wagner.

D'Annunzio had begun an affair with Eleonora Duse, the leading actress of
her time, in 1894, but by the time *The Flame* appeared the relationship was on the
wane, and Duse was deeply hurt by the way in which d'Annunzio used intimate
details of her private life in his novel. Typically with d'Annunzio, everything is
exaggerated: the young Stelio is depicted as brimming over with spring-like
virility in contrast with the ageing, autumnal Foscarina, whereas in actuality Duse
was only four years older than d'Annunzio. In the novel, the exaggerated age
difference is used to justify Stelio's desire for another, younger woman. Once
again, the novel depicts a male protagonist who is a kind of superman, the man
upon whom the mantle of the great Wagner comes to rest. In the first part, there
is a lengthy speech about the relationship between sensuality and art, based on
d'Annunzio's own speech on the same theme given in 1895. The play that Stelio
is working on is d'Annunzio's own *La citta morta*, the long speech in which La
Foscarina recalls her debut playing Juliet as a young girl is based on Duse's own

---

personal account of the same event. D'Annunzio has effectively created himself as a character in a novel that is little more than a collage of autobiographical materials from different sources.

It is also a novel in which d'Annunzio daringly makes explicit his own ambiguous sexual desires. His passion for La Foscarina is actually intensified by his fantasies about her being possessed by other men. We encounter this same motif in *The Child of Pleasure* and in *The Triumph of Death*. D'Annunzio goes beyond describing jealousy to the point where the fantasies enhance sexual desire, though there is also a latent desire for revenge. Stelio's deliberate torture of La Foscarina is explicit in the scene where they go into a maze together, and he hides from her. Hidden behind a hedge, he hears her becoming increasingly panic-stricken:

> 'You're not going, are you? Don't be afraid, please don't. There is absolutely no danger.' And while he was talking like that to reassure her, he could feel the inanity of what he was saying, the disparity between his entertaining adventure and her dark disturbance that was due to an entirely different cause. Now he too could feel the strange ambiguity within himself that made such a slight incident seem to be two different things, for beneath his solicitude he was holding back an urge to laugh, and her suffering was as new to him as those disturbances that are born from extravagant dreams.[19]

As her panic rises he runs away, then, realizing that she is becoming hysterical, the joke comes to an end and he faces instead the reality of the gulf that separates them, 'and the fading light gave him the impression of blood dripping away'.[20]

D'Annunzio's fascination with dismemberment is closely linked to his depiction of women, which in turn is connected to another of his recurrent obsessions, the death-bed. It was, therefore, a logical conclusion that he should build the image of the death-bed and the image of the amputated hand into the home he chose to create for himself at the height of his notoriety. His life is inextricably interwoven into his writing, especially his fiction, and the novel seems to have been the place above all where he could chart the stages of his self-invention and cathartically expunge from the personae of his supermen the ambiguities about origins that always troubled him. How the talented poet from the provinces turned himself into the quasi-mythical d'Annunzio was due, in large part, by the opportunities offered to him through his relationships with women. From his long-suffering wife, who introduced him into the *beau monde*, to Eleonora Duse who risked her career to perform in some of his less successful plays, to the countless women who made the pilgrimage to the Vittoriale in the

---

[19] Ibid., p. 223.
[20] Ibid., p. 224.

latter part of his life, he was always helped by women. That very fact may explain the hatred with which he repaid them, in art as in life, and his constant dismembering of women, both in his descriptions of their bodies as component parts and in his ever-present fantasies of female mutilation.

Chapter 11

The Escape from Decadence: British Travel Literature on the Balkans 1900–45

Andrew Hammond

'I feel that we Westerners should come here to learn how to live.'
Rebecca West, *Black Lamb and Grey Falcon* (1942)

Evelyn Waugh's *Scoop* (1933), a satire on modern journalism, contains a curious tale of escape from Western decadence. William Boot, the novel's simple and long-suffering hero, is a young man for whom the decline of English society has particular poignancy. As country squire and columnist for a major London newspaper, William's life is ensnared in both the decaying world of the country classes and the corrupt values of a new urban modernity, an existence, in other words, which absorbs the dual consequences of Victorian social transition. It is a predicament for which his newspaper, through a series of fortuitous blunders, presents a surprising means of release. He is sent to report on a civil war in Ishmaelia, a primitive African state whose medieval structures of power, and primordial stretches of countryside, suggest all the beauty, romance and adventure that had been absent from the drab society of the West. Yet the exotic potential of the country fails to materialize. After a month of general tribulation, and the unexpected 'scoop' of the title, William returns to the tedium and impoverishment of his former lifestyle as if nothing had been learnt from the journey, and no alternative to the malaise of Western society had presented itself.

While typifying the enduring despair that decadence aroused in the English novelist, Waugh's doubts about the possibilities of the journey are unusual. Since ancient times, human consciousness has eluded the crises and concerns of civilization through an idealized vision of pre-modern reality. With the sense of decline current in antiquity, for example, a belief in the temporal existence of an earthly paradise, the so-called 'life under Kronos',[1] was gradually invested with the attributes of spatial location. As Neil Rennie relates in *Far-Fetched Facts*

---

[1]   See R.K.R. Thornton, *The Decadent Dilemma* (London: Edward Arnold, 1983), p. 2.

(1995), such a myth 'sought to locate in a geographical present what was lost in a historical past',[2] sustaining the hope that the questing Hero could emerge from a state of moral and spiritual malaise and set out towards a locale of pre-lapsarian splendour. Naturally, such mythological 'travel' not only produced the etymological 'travail' of William's passage but also the synonymous 'progress' of quest, growth and realization. So great was the potential of the primitive destination, in fact, that reports of discovering a lost Golden Age of folk and religious custom recurred in the imaginative accounts of medieval and Renaissance voyaging. Moreover, after the unprecedented social transitions of the nineteenth century, and the tangible menace of civilized modernity in the early decades of the twentieth, the pursuit and discovery of an earthly paradise began to assume even greater prevalence in the literature of a more contemporary age.

It was in the autobiographical journeys of the travelogue, rather than the fictional travels of the novel, that the yearning for pre-modern society can be found. Eschewing the scientific empiricism of Victorian exploration, the early twentieth-century traveller returned to the primitive places of the globe in a purely sentimental quest for lost traditions. Popular destinations like the Americas, the African Equator and the South Sea isles, regions that had once been denigrated in Victorian colonial discourse, were now portrayed with an uncompromising mixture of romance, esteem and exoticism. At the same time, a sense of having entered realms of sacred custom inspired the travel writer to lavish accounts of spiritual and emotional renewal. It was a remnant of the old mythological notion of journeying which, with the sense of arrival in a temporal, as much as spatial, location, had clear implications for a degenerate West. In *Loneliness and Time* (1992), Mark Cocker went so far as to term the travel writer 'a prophet-like figure: [. . .] someone with a deeply unpopular message to communicate, which is yet of vital importance to society.'[3] The modern-day pilgrimage also retained an optimism contrary to the general trend within English literature. From the lowest form of publicity guide-book, to the 'high' prose of a writer like D. H. Lawrence, travel writing produced revelations which disclaimed both the dreary speculations of early twentieth-century fiction and the escape into aestheticism and artifice by the Decadent movement of the 1890s.

One region that inspired exemplary enthusiasm from the British traveller had been the south-east European peninsula known as the Balkans. Despite lacking the far-flung exoticism of Waugh's Africa, Albania, Romania, Bulgaria and the ex-Yugoslavia formed the closest appropriate destination for what has been

---

    [2]   Neil Rennie, *Far-Fetched Facts: The Literature of Travel and the Idea of the South Seas* (Oxford: Clarendon Press, 1995), p. 5.
    [3]   Mark Cocker, *Loneliness and Time: British Travel Writing in the Twentieth Century* (London: Secker and Warburg, 1994), p. 158.

termed the 'Westerner's quest for origins'.[4] The region had been severed from the social and political transition of Western Europe ever since the Ottoman conquests of the Middle Ages, enduring an isolation into which the intellectual currents of the Renaissance had barely penetrated. It was a period from which many of the contemporary preconceptions about the region derived. By the terms of English colonialism, the Balkans typified the backwardness, savagery and division of pre-Enlightenment society, a paradigmatic 'otherness' compounded by the accounts of early travellers who, as Brian Hall put it, 'took their last meals and night's lodging in Austrian Zemun and in the morning crossed the Sava as though it were the Styx'.[5] For the modern generation of travellers, however, a palpable mistrust in the products of the Enlightenment led to a stark renunciation of the colonial perspective. The history of isolation had created a swathe of pre-decadent culture within the very borders of Europe, and, with its suggestion of an embryonic version of the West's own cultural mores, the traveller's response was ecstatic. The travel records of Mary Edith Durham, Rose Wilder Lane and George Sava in Albania and Bulgaria, for example, or E.O. Hoppé, Walter Starkie, Patrick Leigh Fermor and Rebecca West in Romania and Yugoslavia, all depicted the Balkans in a style suffused with helpless admiration. Moreover, in a manner that would typify the travel writing of the period, their experience of Europe's more uncivilized backwaters held revelatory implications for a modern civilization in decline.

The primitive climate of the region, firstly, compared favourably to what Matthew Arnold termed the 'depression and *ennui*' of decadent society.[6] Mary Edith Durham's experience in *High Albania* (1909), a remote tribal region still governed by the code of the blood feud, represents a fine example in kind. As with many female travellers of the period, Durham had emerged from the rigours of Victorian domesticity, a background of such dismal and limited convention that the journey would act as a profound personal liberation. Accompanied only by guide and muleteer, and in defiance of Ottoman regulation, Durham set off on a series of mountain hikes and cross-country treks that offered the almost constant thrills of peril and mayhem. Moreover, despite striving for the empirical tone of ethnology, the narrative barely contains her rollicking, infectious delight at this chaotic 'land of the Living Past'.[7] The crude beauty of its customs, songs

4   Heather Henderson, 'The Travel Writer and the Text: "My Giant Goes With Me Wherever I Go"', in ed. Michael Kowalewski, *Temperamental Journeys: Essays on the Modern Literature of Travel* (Athens, Georgia and London: The University of Georgia Press, 1992), p. 233.
5   Brian Hall, *The Impossible Country: A Journey Through the Last Days of Yugoslavia* (London: Minerva, 1996), p. 86.
6   Matthew Arnold, 'From "On the Modern Element in Literature"', in ed. Miriam Allott, *Selected Poems and Prose* (London: J.M. Dent, 1978), p. 151.
7   Mary Edith Durham, *High Albania* (London: Edward Arnold, 1909; this edition: Virago Travellers, London: Virago Press Ltd, 1985), p. 296.

and superstitions, the 'majestic and primeval'[8] frugality of its homes, and the inexorable vigour of the tribal warriors all lead her to 'wonder [. . .] why people ever think they would like to be civilised'.[9] In the case of the warriors, her portrait of a gathering before a village feast reveals a taste for primitive masculinity that foreshadows Lawrence's 'noble savagery' of the 1930s:

> Etiquette demanded that the Skreli people, being the hosts, should not wear their best clothes, it is for the guests to do the peacocking. And peacock they did. Many carried splendid silver mounted weapons, and even though wearing revolvers, thrust great silver ramrods in their belts, for 'swagger.' Snow-white headwraps dazzled in the sun [. . .] and the splendidly decorative black braiding of the tight-fitting *chakshir* [. . .] set off the lean supple figures to the greatest advantage.[10]

While illustrating Durham's love of the picturesque, the passage's evident fondness for weaponry forms a motif that runs throughout the narrative. The custom of firing a salvo upon greeting acquaintances, for example, which the English gentlewoman joined in with abandon, certainly brings out the best in her writing. 'As each batch came in sight of the church they yelled for the priest', she writes on the Skreli gathering; then 'bang, bang went fifty rifles at once; swish-ish-ish flew the bullets; pop, pop, pop, pop, pop, pop replied the priest's old six-shooter.'[11] It was the wild vitality of pre-modern Albania that determines much of Durham's narrative engagement, with even the riotous gun-culture of the feud receiving such lengthy and lively attention that one timid reviewer bewailed that her 'book literally reeks of blood'.[12]

Yet the Westerner's sympathy for primitive culture far from reflected the 'spiritual and moral perversity' of nineteenth-century decadence.[13] Alongside the malaise of British society, the Western processes of transition and decay also found wretched contrast to the structures of Balkan society, and aroused a good deal of ethical reflection from the Balkan traveller. Much of Durham's revelation in Albania, for example, derives from her perception of a living continuum of European tradition utterly unsullied by the rot of European modernity. In the more anthropological sections of the book particular significance is drawn from the 'Canon of Lek', a body of archaic Illyrian codes that still dictated such village mores as marriage, property and the protocol of blood vengeance. For Durham, the Canon not only forms the kind of primitive communal structure from which

---

    [8]   Ibid., p. 60.
    [9]   Ibid., p. 175.
    [10]   Ibid., pp. 49–50.
    [11]   Ibid., p. 49.
    [12]   Unnamed reviewer quoted in John Hodgson, 'Introduction' to Durham, *High Albania*, p. xiii.
    [13]   Arthur Symons, 'The Decadent Movement in Literature', quoted in R.K.R. Thornton, *The Decadent Dilemma*, op. cit., p. 52.

Western history has diverged,[14] but creates a humane and simple virtue that has somehow been lost during the course of the Western Enlightenment. While accepting the shortcomings of the feud, for instance, the rigid order, sacrifice and personal honour that derive from adherence to its tenets are a continual object of Durham's veneration. At the same time, the kindliness and hospitality encoded within primitive law are pointedly distinguished from 'the meannesses of what is called civilisation'.[15] In order to emphasize its spiritual and cultural value, Durham depicts the Canon through a host of biblical and classical allusions which, despite the notion of 'fall' innate within Greek and Hebraic thought, imbue her Albania with a sense of stasis, coherence and continuity. With the reckless acceleration of public and private time within Britain, and the threats such transition held for individual existence, it is an impression that brings a distinct spiritual relief to the author:

> I looked at them with awe; for I saw them through a vista of thousands of years. The river of evolution had left them stranded – waifs of a day when men had not yet learnt to form a nation, and had whirled me and mine through all the ages – though tribes, principalities, kingdoms – washing, as it went, the Divine right off kings, and hurrying us none knows whither . . .[16]

Only five years after those words were written Britain found itself on the brink of the First World War. Although inaugurated by an upsurge in Balkan nationalism, the catastrophe had thrust Durham's misgivings about the value of Western transition into sharper focus. The brutal nature of the fighting across Western Europe, combined with the machinations of Great Power interests that lay at its source, not only undermined the creeds of civilized European society but exposed the very idea of civilization as little more than a hollow sham. 'All that we call civilisation', Rose Wilder Lane claimed in 1922, 'is like a tune heard yesterday, a little thing floating on the surface of our minds'.[17] Amongst the Western intelligentsia at least, the notions of progress, modernity and empire, would never again find the widespread patronage they had achieved during the Victorian era.

In terms of the Balkan travelogue, the Great War also produced a distinct yet subtle shift in the style of regional portraiture. The post-war settlement had finally

---

[14] 'The wanderer from the West stands awestruck' she enthuses, 'filled with vague memories of the cradle of his race, saying, "This did I do some thousands of years ago; thus did I lie in wait for mine enemy; so thought I and so acted I in the beginning of Time."' Durham, *High Albania*, p. 1.

[15] Ibid., p. 255.

[16] Ibid., p. 205.

[17] Rose Wilder Lane, *The Peaks of Shala: Being a Record of Certain Wanderings Among the Hill-Tribes of Albania* (London and Sydney: Chapman and Dodd Ltd, 1922), p. 53.

brought national sovereignty to all the Balkan countries and, within the consequent flurry of travelogues that appeared in the 1920s, Durham's primitivist idealism was rarely repeated. It was as though the realities of the recent conflict, with its reports of primordial conditions and front-line savagery, had finally attuned the Balkan traveller to the threat of society's more rudimental urges. Certainly, a new craving for warmth, colour and comfort – all those pleasures that stand in contrast to the experience of war – came to hold more importance for writer and reader than Durham's encounters with hardship and danger.[18] Lane's *Peaks of Shala* (1922), one of the first Albanian journals of the 1920s, demonstrates the kind of modification of the Balkan landscape that resulted. Despite following Durham's route around the harsh terrain of the north, the account finds the region 'a fragment of this great [. . .] romantic world', with 'fairy-tale' towns and a 'magic country' of flowers, fruit-trees, waterfalls, gentle woodlands, and mountain scenery the colour of 'an American Beauty rose'.[19] It was a particular reconstruction of the landscape which continued to suggest an alternative to spiritual confusion and industrial malaise, yet rejected the ideals of primitivism in favour of pastoralism. A primitivism, that is, with the rough and uncomfortable edges removed.

The new method of representing the Balkans was perhaps best illustrated by British travel writing on Romania. In contrast to Albania's tribal fastnesses, the Romanian countryside formed a softer, more sympathetic landscape of agrarian and folk tradition which, at least in the eyes of the passing traveller, seemed to fit the latest desire for rustic idyllicism. That the style could also evoke simpler, happier ages by which to contrast the West was demonstrated by E.O. Hoppé's *In Gipsy Camp and Royal Palace* (1924). Although travelling by train and car, the author's sense of moving into a bygone era of Chaucerian cottages, dashing landlords and fairy-tale castles conjures up both the pre-industrial charm of eighteenth-century England and the harmonious social structure of the middle ages. It was a new form of temporal journeying that actually improved upon Durham's portrait of pre-decadent Europe. In his dealings with the peasantry, for example, Hoppé evokes a world of unblemished pastoral innocence, in which harvesters stand 'like lilies of the field', homesteads 'are dotted with flowering shrubs', 'maidens sang [. . .] with wholehearted happiness' and, to complete the Arcadian picture, humanity is characterized by a marked 'feudal humility'.[20] Similarly, the rural governing classes all combine a certain picturesque vitality with such 'Lord of the Manner'[21] courtesy that Hoppé discerns an elementary

---

[18]   Fussell considers the search for placid and exotic climes a major impulse of the inter-war travelogue as a whole; see Paul Fussell, *Abroad: British Literary Traveling Between the Wars* (New York, Oxford: OUP, 1980), pp. 3–23.

[19]   Lane, *Peaks of Shala*, pp. 9, 12, 54 and 35.

[20]   E.O. Hoppé, *In Gipsy Camp and Royal Palace: Wanderings in Rumania* (London: Methuen and Co. Ltd, 1924), pp. 80, p. 81 and 127.

[21]   Ibid., p. 115.

version of the English aristocracy. The impression of a venerable social order is heightened during his engagements with Queen Marie of Romania, 'a modern fairy queen' with whom Hoppé has several encounters.[22] Her strength of character, captivating beauty, and, most of all, her sympathetic regard for the peasantry, inspire the most overt passages of medieval pastoralism of the book. 'It is not surprising that she is beloved by her people', the author writes on a drive they take together.

> and I witnessed many proofs of their affection and regard for her on the journey. We stopped several times on the way, and she conversed freely with the peasants, on one occasion begging for a beautiful rose which grew in a cottager's little garden. The people along the route cheered her lustily, and she acknowledged their warm greetings by waving her hand.[23]

Hoppé's discovery of feudal harmony, with its social unity and rustic pleasures, was a common feature of the Romanian travelogue of the period. Walter Starkie's *Raggle-Taggle* (1933), for instance, and Patrick Leigh Fermor's remembered landscape of *Between the Woods and the Water* (1986), both summon up that merry hierarchy of peasant, aristocrat and monarch central to romantic feudalism. Although reformulating the nature of the region's pre-modernity, the revelations that such works drew from the medieval format were not dissimilar to those of the primitivist. The vibrancy of the region continued to arouse the travel writer's appreciation, with Fermor calling Romania a place 'of comedy, adventure and delight', and Starkie contrasting Balkan life to the 'self-conscious mediocrity' of Western urban existence.[24] Nor were the structures of medieval faith and simplicity lacking ethical resonance for a British readership. As Evelyn Waugh illustrated in *Scoop*, British society of the 1920s and 1930s had acquired a religious doubt and social aimlessness of stark disparity to the knowable universe that the travelogues evoked. For the humblest peasant up to the crowned monarch, the medieval design was one of duty, belief, regulation and an assurance in cosmic order which, as Hoppé's rustics demonstrate, endowed the individual with a spiritedness remote in time and place from 'the *langueurs* of a tired civilisation'.[25]

Such discoveries, of course, had little to with Balkan reality. Throughout the period the whole of south-east Europe was fraught with both the political afflictions common to post-colonial nations, and the economic effects of a slump

---

[22] Ibid., p. 69.

[23] Ibid., p. 66.

[24] Respective references are Patrick Leigh Fermor, *Between the Woods and the Water* (Harmondsworth: Penguin, 1988), p. 146; Walter Starkie, *Raggle-Taggle: Adventures with a Fiddle in Hungary and Roumania* (London: John Murray, 1933; this edition: London: Edward Arnold, 1935), p. 6.

[25] Hoppé, *In Gipsy Camp*, p. 43.

in agricultural prices. To discern a living golden age within the resultant poverty, discontent and corruption clearly involved a wholesale rearrangement of the contemporary landscape. Ironically, the traveller's invention of a natural paradise, while remaining moral in intent, duplicated two of the main literary techniques by which the Decadents had created their fictional worlds of artifice. The first is what Richard Le Gallienne termed the 'expression of isolated observations',[26] the couching of a subject in a particularly selective form of commentary. In the case of Hoppé, Starkie and Fermor, this involved briefly admitting peasant hardship, or rural injustice, before going on to obliterate the allusion through a sustained accumulation of Arcadian imagery. The second technique was the unremitting literary elegance with which inter-war Balkan travel writers adorned their subject. The scrupulous formality of Hoppé's prose, for instance, combined with the precocity of much of the diction – 'beloved', 'cottager', 'maiden' (either 'pretty' or 'little') – imbued his Romania with the same mixture of charm and wistful regret as Huysmans and Wilde invested in artificial beauty. An even greater example was Patrick Leigh Fermor's 'decorative confection of brilliant language',[27] as *The Spectator* phrased it. The following depiction of female attire in Transylvania offers a brief flavour of his prose:

> Each village and valley enjoined a different assembly of colours and styles: braids, tunics, lace, ribands, goffering, ruffs, sashes, caps, kerchiefs, coifs and plaits free or coiled [. . .] There were bodices, flowing or panelled sleeves, embroidery, gold coins at brow or throat or both, aprons front and back, a varying number of petticoats and skirts jutting at the hips like farthingales . . .[28]

The emphasis on quaint terminology builds up throughout his book to form a level of textual beauty by which Romania is coloured rather than revealed. The foregrounding of style that such emphasis produced, compounded by his frequent listing of archaic coinages, implied that his subject was not so much a genuine living entity, tainted with recognizable faults and failings, but an impeccable achievement of words.

The two techniques are useful for indicating the sheer resolve with which travel writers pursued their goal. The processes of literary refinement, along with the quite outlandish idealization of pre-decadent society, made up for a lack of social realism by forging an unshakeable world of escape for writer and readership. In fact, with the increasing threat of a new European crisis during the

---

[26] Richard Le Gallienne, 'Considerations Suggested by Mr. Churton Collins' "Illustrations of Tennyson"', quoted in Thorton, *Decadent Dilemma*, p. 46.

[27] Unsigned, 'An Extravagance of Curiosity', in eds Marsden-Smedley and Jeffrey Klinke, *Views from Abroad: The Spectator Book of Travel Writing* (London: Paladin Grafton Books, 1989), p. 28.

[28] Fermor, *Between the Woods*, p. 148.

1930s, the determination to wrestle a romantic refuge from the Balkans became more compelling than ever. Whereas travel books like Waugh's *Robbery Under Law* (1939), or Graham Greene's *The Lawless Roads* (1939), may have absorbed the pessimism of the times, the Balkan travelogue continued its discourse of refinement, romanticism and revelation. George Sava's *Donkey Serenade* (1940) offers a significant example in kind. Set only a year before the outbreak of the Second World War, the narrative recounts a trek around the Bulgarian countryside with scant reference to the prospect of hostilities that would soon devastate the region. Instead, inspired by the tales of R.L. Stevenson, and armed with the Scotsman's *Travels with a Donkey*, Sava details a quixotic, and highly literary, world of comic brigands, medieval pilgrims, wandering story-tellers, and exquisite village traditions. When set against his charmingly evoked rustic backdrop, the author's 'Stevensonian Odyssey'[29] does much to suggest the continuing pathos that pre-modernism held for a Europe descending into war.

The issue was epitomized, naturally, by Rebecca West's *Black Lamb and Grey Falcon* (1942), arguably the greatest journal of literary travel in the English language. West's notorious thousand-page aggregation of apocalyptic musing, dramatized historical vignettes and sustained stylistic flourishes managed to both capture the menacing climate of pre-war Europe and exaggerate the idealism that her forebears had drawn from the Balkan locale. On a basic narrative level, the book records a Yugoslavian excursion taken with her husband, Henry Maxwell Andrews, in 1937. Within the passages dealing with the journey, and the environment of the journey, West's account displays a straightforward similarity to those of her predecessors. Her motive for departure, firstly, reveals the normal antagonism to the society of her background, with modern Britain depicted as a realm of unnatural complexity, soulless monotony, and such a passionless and decadent political life that the author wonders whether the rising tide of Nazism will ever be arrested. Similarly, her decision to travel to the Balkans is the same quest for the value and meaning that the West has so evidently lost. A previous sojourn in the region has taught her that Yugoslavia is 'a land where everything is comprehensible, where the mode of life was so honest that it put an end to perplexity',[30] and where a crucial proximity to spiritual truth has been somehow retained. So typical is her motive for departure that it is no surprise to find the depiction of the country slipping into the usual discourse. The journey is, significantly, taken during springtime, and West portrays a remarkable nation of glorious medieval order and ancient pagan belief whose revelatory possibilities are again exhibited to the reader through that familiar mixture of stylistic elegance and bewitched respect.

---

[29] George Sava, *Donkey Serenade: Travels in Bulgaria* (London: Faber and Faber, 1940; this edition: London: The Travel Book Club, 1941), p. 16.
[30] Rebecca West, *Black Lamb and Grey Falcon: The Record of a Journey Through Yugoslavia in 1937*, 2 vols (London: Macmillan, 1942), I, p. 1.

Where West differed from previous travel writers, however, was in the final extremity of that revelation. The most pronounced philosophical aim of her journey is to understand the inertia of the Western democracies in the face of a mounting call to arms, an inertia to which pre-modern Yugoslavia, on the one hand, brings shocking clarification. The defining moments of the narrative occur during West's experiences with the eponymous lamb and falcon. The first is sacrificed in an archaic fertility rite witnessed by the author in Macedonia, while the second is part of a Serbian myth she hears at Kosovo, in which a prince's choice of an 'earthly' over a 'heavenly kingdom' on the eve of battle in 1389 ushers in five hundred years of Ottoman subjection.[31] At both points in the book, the author is struck by the terrible notion that '[a]ll our Western thought is founded on this repulsive pretence that pain is the proper price of any good thing.'[32] With her very soul rising in revolt, West recounts how the images of Western art, Christ's crucifixion, even the submissive flavour of the English liberal movement, all presume that defeat, sacrifice and death form the only true path to righteousness and innocence. It is a pattern through which the wider crisis within Western politics is finally understood. The apparent decline of British democracy into indolence and frailty is no longer viewed as the lassitude of an empire in its autumn years, but as an actual urge towards death; 'the belief in sacrifice,' as West puts it, 'and a willingness to serve as the butchered victim acceptable to God.'[33] With the nature of the Western malaise clarified, the apocalyptic tone of much of her writing gains powerful, and emotive, legitimacy.

On the other hand, what she terms the 'comprehensibility' of pre-modern culture also assists West in her search for a solution. The main disclosure comes during her attendance at an Easter gathering in Macedonia. As the feast draws to a close, West observes an Orthodox bishop distributing painted eggs to the guests with such magical intensity that the whole table resonates with faith, hope and unity. In clear contrast to morbid symbolism of lamb and falcon, the moment is viewed as an emblem of life, a joyous act of creation and integration which induces the comforting feeling 'that defeat is not defeat and that love is serviceable.'[34] Although she also mentions that 'its victories cannot be won on the material battlefield',[35] West offers the process of creation and unity as a counter to the Western urge towards self-destruction. Among the various examples of its efficacy presented in the book, perhaps the finest is the political structure of Yugoslavia itself. After the final rout of the Ottomans, the south Slav peoples had been allied under the Serb royal dynasty, an experiment in ethnic unification whose increasingly rancorous nature was only checked by the centralism and

---

31   West, *Black Lamb and Grey Falcon*, II, p. 293.
32   Ibid., p. 205.
33   Ibid., p. 519.
34   Ibid., p. 92.
35   Ibid.

autocracy of the Serbian monarchy. Rejecting the very genuine grievances of its detractors, West lauds the monarchical project both for its maintenance of the life and unity of the region, and its display of exemplary strength and resolve. It is a point driven home through a series of fanciful romanticisms, as illustrated by her portrait of a Serbian friend, Constantine, who accompanies West and her husband during much of their tour. For the author, Constantine's ebullience as poet and raconteur, and, crucially, his status as a Belgrade government official, both indicate a similar knowledge of the magical 'integrating process' of life to that of the Orthodox Bishop.[36] Not only the stories and poems he summons up in conversation but the structures of the nation he creates in his work at the Ministry assume the profound and harmonious beauty of 'figures in a poet's dream'.[37] At a time when Britain was succumbing to the divisive power of Nazism, the unitary aims of a basically medieval autocracy emerge as a powerful symbol of creation, a 'poem', as West sees it, fragile and doomed, yet beautifully crafted.

On an aesthetic level alone such methods of representing a Balkan nation marked a significant advance on the techniques of previous travel writers. Although deploying the same stylistic elegance as Hoppé and Fermor, one realizes that West has created not merely an attractive world of escape for the reader, but a vast and highly unique figurative landscape. Along with the major emblems of lamb, falcon, Orthodox faith and Serbian dynasty, the minor threads of the perceived Yugoslavia – the baking of bread, German tourists, folk embroidery – are all incorporated into the life/death fabric of her symbolism. With the rigid, albeit unnatural, textual harmony that results, West's book itself becomes a kind of magical act of creation, emphasizing the attainment of life over death by the Yugoslav Church and State, and aiming to inspire their qualities of strength, faith and unity in an apparently fatalistic Western Europe. And it is on this polemical level that the real extremity of the work is disclosed. The colourful proposal that attributes of the Balkan region could actually assuage the problems of the civilized states was utterly absent from the work of her predecessors. For Durham, Hoppé and their contemporaries, the lauding of a pre-modern destination may have evolved from a genuine disaffection with decadent society, and entailed harsh condemnations of its religious and political culture, but the idea that Western Europe should regress into the archaism or medievalism with which they sympathized was never advanced. For West, at a time when chaos and division were spreading throughout the continent, the simplicity of primitive faith, and the homogeneity created by a centralized monarchy, represented ideals that she held and advocated with evangelical fervour. 'I feel that we Westerners', she concludes at Kosovo, 'should come here to learn how to live.'[38]

---

[36] Ibid., II, p. 212.
[37] Ibid., II, p. 383.
[38] Ibid., II, p. 301.

The true interest of West's book, however, was one it held in common with those of her predecessors. Throughout the records of early twentieth-century Balkan travel, a significant feature of the writing was the travellers' belief in having achieved profound psychological distance from the decadent ideology of their background. West's experiences with the lamb and falcon, for example, as with Durham's discovery of the Canon of Lek or Hoppé's encounters with Queen Maria, were moments in which a gulf was felt to emerge between the established patterns of Western existence and life in a more vital or authentic form. It was a sensation that Lane had termed the 'soft landslide' of the mind,[39] a sudden awareness of having had the mental conceits and conventions of civilization driven out through one's exposure to primitive reality. In this way, the autobiographical retreat into pre-modernity seemed to reiterate the belief in epiphany current in the modernist writings of the period, merely exchanging Joyce's faith in literature for a faith in the liberating properties of ancient custom and tradition. In fact, so associated did pre-modernity become with the attainment of personal autonomy that an environment like West's Yugoslavia was deemed to hold revelatory potential before the journey had even begun. 'It was only two or three days distant,' as West wrote with the oncoming war in mind, 'yet I had never troubled to go that short journey which might explain to me how I shall die, and why.'[40]

This impression of psychological distance was also central in the production of what was, in essence, a remarkably original perspective on the vagaries of Western society. The narrative of Balkan travel, like those of the modernist and Decadent movements, was one in which the infirmity of Western assumptions were judged, not from the narrow bias of party or national politics, but from an extraordinary attempt at totality. Despite the textual chaos of *High Albania*, for example, or the rather free-wheeling focus of *Black Lamb and Grey Falcon*, the disclosures that the books presented all revolve around a few basic notions, of which the supposed otherness of a region is perhaps the most significant. The social and cultural division between civilization and pre-modernity had been the dominant assumption of colonial theory, constructing the pre-modern locale as a wholly negative 'other' by which 'enlightened' Europe could perceive and promote its own collective sense of progressive virtue. While claiming that the region was in no way separate from the currents of European history as a whole, the traveller's sense of stumbling upon a more ancient form of that history actually produced a fascinating inversion of conventional Balkan otherness. The accusations of division, chaos, savagery, perplexity and religious backwardness levelled at the region, qualities that would recur in Cold War and contemporary discourse, were now reconstituted as peculiarities of modern decadence. In turn, the unity, order, clarity, and moral and spiritual righteousness central to the group-

---

[39]   Lane, *Peaks of Shala*, p. 59.
[40]   West, *Black Lamb*, I, p. 24.

image of the enlightened states, were now considered unique to the pre-decadent society. If the Balkans were indeed the 'other' of the grand colonial West, then it was otherness that rebounded to the eternal credit of the tiny, and supposedly insignificant, states of south-east Europe.

Yet the ability to attain psychological distance, and the all-encompassing critique which it had inspired, were both soon to vanish. By the time West had published her compendium of Yugoslav wisdom, the Second World War was already underway, inaugurating the sweeping social transitions that would characterize the latter half of the century. In the Balkans, the rapid development of industry, tourism and urbanism meant that the landscape would lose that certain shock of difference through which the decadence of the West had once been gauged. In the West, although British democracy never did sacrifice itself on the altar of fascist ideology, the Victorian constraints of Durham's day, and the intricacies of the 1930s, finally passed to the harrowing crisis of postmodernity. With the massive forces of corporation and state penetrating Western society, and the increasingly cynical nature of individual existence, the extravagant romanticism of writers like Durham, Hoppé and West was seldom seen again. The literary traveller, like a character from a contemporary novel, would gradually assume the situatedness already typified in that prototype of the postmodern traveller, the long-suffering William Boot. Within the series of revelations offered by Balkan travel writers, it was the continuing ability to establish distance between themselves and the wiles of decadent civilization that represents perhaps the greatest revelation of them all.

Chapter 12

Books and Ruins: Abject Decadence in Gide and Mann

Martin Halliwell

In a 1951 *New York Times* review of the American critic Albert Guerard's psycho-biographical study André Gide, the German novelist Thomas Mann discusses what he calls Gide's 'unending sense for harmony'.[1] Mann is more complementary about Gide as a novelist than about Guerard as critic; he applauds Gide's 'prankishness', his 'tendency to hoax', his 'demonic unfaithfulness' and his 'delight in teasing' readers, whereas he is critical of Guerard for making unsubstantiated judgements about the relative qualities of Gide's novels.[2] Of course, in commending Gide's major novel *Les Faux-Monnayeurs* (*The Counterfeiters*, 1925) over his earlier decadent novella *L'immoraliste* (*The Immoralist*, 1902), Mann reflects his own tendency to favour the high modernist novel of narrative experiment and stylistic trickery, most notably evident in his modernist picaresque *Bekenntnisse des Hochstaplers Felix Krull* (*Confessions of Felix Krull, Confidence Man*), which he began in 1909 but did not publish in incomplete form until two years after the review. The mixture of realism, experimentation and 'new classicism' in Gide's work stimulates Guerard to call him 'a cautious radical and a daring conservative' and motivates Mann to confess his 'brotherly feelings' toward the French writer.[3] Despite their different cultural and linguistic backgrounds, Mann's brotherly feelings toward Gide – a brotherhood combining a mixture of friendship, respect, inspiration, rivalry, and misunderstanding – makes for fruitful comparison of their respective work.[4]

---

[1]   *New York Times Book Review*, 19 August 1951; reprinted in Albert J. Guerard, *André Gide*, 2nd edn (Cambridge, Mass.: Harvard University Press, 1969), pp. xxi–xxix.

[2]   Ibid., xxvi. Even Gide wrote to Guerard to express his surprise that the critic rated *The Immoralist* so highly; ed. David Walker, *André Gide* (London: Longman, 1996), p. 125. Guerard's book remains one of the most insightful critical studies of *The Immoralist*, even though at times his treatment over-simplifies the psychological continuum between Gide's life 'as a man of letters' and his fictional work; Guerard, *André Gide*, p. 183.

[3]   Guerard, *André Gide*, p. xxvii.

[4]   The two writers began correspondence in early 1922, but did not meet until May 1931; Pollard, *André Gide: Homosexual Moralist* (New Haven: Yale University Press, 1991), p. 459). Mann was six years younger than Gide and displays the typical anxiety symptoms of a troubled younger brother, especially in his early period as a writer.

In the *New York Times* review Mann goes on to lionize Gide's 'hobgoblinism' and 'intellectual restlessness' as manifestations of his 'unending search for truth, and a readiness to suffer the solitude of freedom which could be called heroic', whereas he deems *The Immoralist* to be a work of 'faded originality, whose capacity to shock has largely been lost through the decades, and whose title, inspired by Nietzsche, smothers the content by sheer philosophical dead weight'.[5] Mann's stated aversion to both Nietzsche (one of his early philosophical influences) and *The Immoralist* (which bears striking resemblance to his 1912 novella *Der Tod in Venedig*; *Death in Venice*), may represent an intertwined anxiety of influence of which he was eager to rid himself.[6] Both novelists deploy dialectic models to render what Mann calls the tricky task of cultivating 'extremes' in order to hold them in 'precarious harmony'.[7] For example, Michel in *The Immoralist* swings between the poles of hedonism and asceticism without being able to fully harness them and in a 1920 letter Mann claims that *Death in Venice* was an attempt to find an aesthetic 'equilibrium of sensuality and morality' which he finds 'perfected' in Goethe's *Wahlverwandtschaften* (*Elective Affinities*, 1809).[8] As Guerard notes, although Gide was attracted to Goethe's 'comprehensiveness and equilibrium', he was also critical of the German's 'hatred of darkness'.[9] It is this narrative 'darkness' which makes *The Immoralist* a much more disturbing tale of decadence than Mann acknowledges.

Anthony Heilbut even comments that Gide taught Mann 'how to live' as well as write; Anthony Heilbut, *Thomas Mann* (London: Macmillan, 1996), p. 472.

[5]   Guerard, *André Gide*, pp. xxvi, xxiv.

[6]   As Heilbut comments, Nietzsche, Wagner and Schopenhauer were the three chief intellectual influences on Mann in his early years as a writer; Heilbut, *Thomas Mann*, p. 32. Nietzsche's presence can be discerned throughout Mann's writing and his influence on Gide's early work is evident in Michel's exploration of moral boundaries and limits in *The Immoralist*. In *Götzen-Dämmerung* (*Twilight of the Idols*, 1889) Nietzsche discusses the need to differentiate between higher morality and socially-sanctioned morality, with the former often being considered immoral from the perspective of the latter. He also argues that the split between appearance and reality is itself symptomatic of a declining or decadent society and discusses the difficulty which the *fin-de-siècle* artist faces in attempting to distance himself from decaying values, which, for Nietzsche, would only reconstitute another kind of decadence; Friedrich Nietzsche, *Twilight of the Idols*, trans. R.J. Hollingdale (London, Penguin, 1990), pp. 43–9.

[7]   Guerard, *André Gide*, p. xxv.

[8]   From a letter sent to the critic Carl Maria Weber on 4 July 1920 in Richard and Clara Winston, eds and trans., *The Letters of Thomas Mann, 1889–1955* (Harmondsworth: Penguin, 1975), p. 94. Mann's original stimulus for *Death in Venice* derived from the story of the ageing Goethe's desire for a girl he met at Marienbad baths and to whom he proposed; see Walter Stewart, '*Der Tod in Venedig*: The Path to Insight', *Germanic Review* 53 (1978), pp. 50–4.

[9]   Guerard, *André Gide*, p. 234. *The Immoralist* and its companion tale *Le Porte étroite* (*Strait is the Gate*, 1909) offer a series of philosophical counterpoints, but without neutralizing the dark elements of each other.

In this essay I argue that, contrary to Mann's stated aims, even if 'precarious harmony' is achieved at the end of *Death in Venice*, Mann's comment overlooks one of the major issues of *The Immoralist*, in which Gide's dark and reckless 'hobgoblinism' undermines the veneer of narrative order and artistic control. In other words, Mann's preoccupation with harmony and balance is really a diversion, or a manner of sublimating, a darker undercurrent, which in part derives from the surrendering of aesthetic control and in part from the homoerotic content of Gide's tale. Although the French writer's sexual impulses were caught uncomfortably between what Mann calls 'unfettered puritanism' and his cultivation of an individual ethic ('the self-preservation of a natural drive that deviates from the so-called "natural"'), Gide's homosexuality is more apparent than in the work of his German counterpart.[10] For example, Mann famously pronounced that 'homoeroticism' is only incidental in *Death In Venice*; instead he claimed 'passion as confusion and a stripping of dignity was really the subject of my tale'.[11] In this essay, I argue that Mann's emphasis on balance and order is an attempt to preserve or, rather, to resurrect heroism and heroic freedom from the decadence and chaos of modernity. This would correspond to what the French theorist Julia Kristeva in *Pouvoirs de l'horreur* (*Powers of Horror*, 1980) calls the attempt to preserve the 'clean and proper' body: that is, a moral and virtuous form from which the messy aspects of corporeality have been cleansed or purged.[12] This essay outlines Kristeva's theory of abjection and applies it constructively to the decadent concerns of the two novellas, in order to discuss Mann's misreading of *The Immoralist* based on his narrow understanding of decadence: whilst both novellas are concerned with what Michel describes as his obsession with 'books and ruins', only *The Immoralist* explores the ruins of modernity in a life-affirming way.[13] As such, the essay locates abjection at the point in the two tales where decadent sensibilities and moral concerns meet, intersect and are thrown into conflict, in order to contest the modernist myth that aesthetic harmony is recoupable from those very qualities that Mann most admires in Gide's work: his prodigality, 'demonic unfaithfulness' and 'hobgoblinism'.

Death in Venice can be interpreted as a strong misreading of *The Immoralist* in the way in which it works through a similar kaleidoscope of impulses, but with

---

10   Ibid., p. xxv.
11   Richard and Clara Winston, eds, *The Letters of Thomas Mann*, p. 94.
12   Julia Kristeva, 'Approaching Abjection', *Powers of Horror*, trans. Leon S. Roudiez (New York: Columbia University Press, 1982), pp. 1–31. Abjection is an appropriate term for dealing with self-obsessed and, at times, self-repressed characters like Michel and Aschenbach. Kristeva claims that abjection 'is a precondition of narcissism': in other words, 'the more or less beautiful image in which I behold or recognize myself rests upon an abjection that sunders it as soon as repression, the constant watchman, is relaxed'; ibid., p. 13.
13   André Gide, *The Immoralist*, trans. Dorothy Bussy (London: Penguin, 1960), p. 15.

a different set of consequences.[14] Mann develops and exaggerates certain
decadent aspects in *The Immoralist* at the expense of others: particularly, the
sense of place and a fascination with the trappings of a decadent lifestyle over and
above Gide's exploration of textual and psychic limits, borders and transitions.
Gide cultivates an open narrative in *The Immoralist*: the narrative is structured
through a series of framing devices (the authorial preface, the letter to the Prime
Minister and the scene of Michel's tale); the story is told as a fragment of
Michel's life after an absence of three years; there are gaps and omissions in his
story; and the reader quickly realizes he is an untrustworthy narrator. These
techniques appear as signs of authorial control, but the contradictory impulses of
potency and uncertainty embedded in Michel's tale eventually overwhelm and
destabilize the narrative frame which ostensibly contains it.[15] These techniques
can be contrasted to the narrative closure of *Death in Venice* when Aschenbach
dies of cholera on a Venice beach. Indeed, despite the narrator's ironic tone and
critical distance from the protagonist, the story follows a downward spiral in
which the reader is forewarned (even in the title) of Aschenbach's heroic death.
The issue of heroism, what Charles Baudelaire called the dandy's 'last flicker of
heroism in decadent ages', serves to divide the two writers: Michel's heroism is
burlesqued and undermined by his own actions, whereas Aschenbach's dignity is
preserved despite his moral and corporeal demise.[16] By the end of *The Immoralist*
(after his wife Marceline's death) Michel is able to acknowledge his own

---

[14]   Harold Bloom describes the notion that 'strong poets' and writers creatively
misread their primary literary and intellectual influences and display a 'persistence to
wrestle with their strong precursors, even to the death'; Harold Bloom, *Anxiety of
Influence: A Theory of Poetry* (London: OUP, 1973), p. 5. This quotation is particularly
relevant for considering Mann's relationship to Gide, his misreading of Gidean decadence
and the denouement of *Death in Venice*.
[15]   This argument is substantiated by Gide's prefatorial comments that the book is
neither 'an indictment' nor 'an apology', but rather an exploration of the European
decadent sensibility. He claims the 'problem' of decadence is 'of very urgent import': a
problem which 'existed before my book' and 'will continue to exist' in the European mind,
even though readers may view Michel as 'a special case'; *The Immoralist*, pp. 7–8. G.
Norman Laidlaw characterizes Gide as an 'openminded' writer who is able to see 'several
sides of the question at once – the dédoublement (dissociation or double perspective) that
can be expressed . . . in paradox, ambiguity, or the open question'; G. Norman Laidlaw,
Elysian Encounter: Diderot and Gide (New York: Syracuse University Press, 1963), p. 16.
[16]   Charles Baudelaire, 'The Painter of Modern Life', *Baudelaire: Selected
Writings on Art and Literature*, trans. P.E. Charvet (London: Penguin, 1992), p. 421. The
dandy figure is important in both novellas: although Michel and Aschenbach are much
more passionate than the 'blasé' and 'elegant' *flâneur* whom Baudelaire describes.
Michel's double life in which he embraces the 'grave and the gay' and Aschenbach's
fanatical dedication to work, together with his eventual transformation into the parodic
dandy figure whom he encounters on his arrival in Venice, both suggest a fusion of
extreme character traits which Baudelaire associates with the nineteenth-century Parisian
dandy; ibid., pp. 419 and 420.

abjection, whereas Aschenbach continues to deny himself even to the last.[17] Because Aschenbach does not, or cannot, face his own abjection, his death vision of Tadzio walking Eros-like into the Adriatic sea, with 'floating hair out there in the sea, in the wind, in front of the nebulous vastness', represents what Kristeva calls an 'eroticization of abjection', or 'an attempt at stopping the hemorrhage' of modernity, rather than developing the role of the 'borderlander' on the threshold of change as adopted by Michel at the end of The Immoralist.[18]

In other words, if Death in Venice is a tale about death, then The Immoralist is a story about dying in which the protagonist continues to dwell in the crevice between life and death as a kind of Foucauldian limit experience, but (as I will argue) not an heroic limit experience. In the second volume of The History of Sexuality (L'Usage des plaisirs; The Uses of Pleasure, 1984) Foucault discusses the idea of 'thinking the limit': both an intellectual engagement with the liminal, and an experience of living up to and transgressing the limit. In this vein, Foucault writes that 'philosophical activity [. . .] does not exist, in place of legitimating what one already knows, [but] in undertaking to know how, and up to what limit, it would be possible to think differently'.[19] Michel pays a heavy price for thinking and living the limit (the death of his wife) but he continues to do so at the close of the novel, whereas Aschenbach is debilitated and eventually consumed by his desire. This is not to valorize Michel and denigrate Aschenbach as moral protagonists (in many ways Michel is the more despicable of the two), but to indicate that, although on the surface Death in Venice is explicitly about abjection – one of Aschenbach's best known books is entitled Ein Elender (A Study in Abjection) and he repeatedly hovers between misery and ecstatic spasms until his final decline – it is The Immoralist which explores the indeterminate and unassimilable aspects of abjection as a central feature of the European decadent sensibility. In short, Death in Venice only deals with abjection as a surface issue, whereas Michel in The Immoralist embodies and enacts an abject life.

[17]   The narrative modes of the two novellas are crucial for creating these effects: the first-person narrative of Michel is presented as a confession (with the framing sections acting as critical commentaries on it), whereas the third-person narrative in Death in Venice (together with the ironic tone of the narrator) distances the reader from a sympathetic engagement with Aschenbach. However, as Heilbut notes, although Mann declared his novella 'a partial parody' – a 'caricature' of decadence rather than a decadent confession – his biographical identification with his protagonist is obvious, from Aschenbach's foreign blood of his mother to the titles of his novels which Mann himself had intended to write; Heilbut, Thomas Mann, pp. 250 and 262.

[18]   Thomas Mann, Death in Venice and Other Stories, trans. David Luke (London: Minerva, 1996), p. 267; Kristeva, Powers of Horror, p. 55.

[19]   Michel Foucault, The Use of Pleasure, trans. Robert Hurley (London: Penguin, 1985), pp. 8–9.

Comparative decadence

The two novellas reveal a series of remarkable comparisons, but here I will offer four examples which bear explicitly on the theme of abjection: namely, travel, doublings, homosexuality and illness. The next section discusses Kristeva's theory of abjection to indicate that all these themes involve the contemplation, and potential transgression, of borders and limits: some of them spatial, some psychic and some corporeal. As I have already stressed, Mann's misreading of Gide generates many of the textual disparities in the two tales, especially their respective visions of decadence. This is evident in each of the endings: *The Immoralist* offers an alternative to heroic decadence as Michel finally acknowledges abjection in himself after Marceline's death, whereas Aschenbach is 'attacked by waves of dizziness' and overwhelmed by an 'increasing sense of dread' which renders him lifeless, with only the diminishing vision of Tadzio as consolation.[20] However, the complex interplay of similarities and contrasts in the two novellas makes a comparative study of them fascinating and suggests Mann's brotherly feelings toward Gide are not entirely imaginary.

Firstly, both tales involve travel to and beyond the outer limits of Europe. Aschenbach travels to an Adriatic island before being drawn to Venice where he falls in love with Tadzio (a Polish boy whose name Aschenbach is forced to guess from a number of exotic-sounding alternatives) and where he contracts Asiatic cholera. Michel and Marceline go on honeymoon to North Africa (where Michel discovers a passion for Arab boys); they travel outside Europe, return to France and then travel again via Italy (noticeably Michel·'gives up' Venice) to Algeria.[21] Both journeys produce profoundly destabilizing effects on the protagonists: Venice physically paralyses Aschenbach even as it frees his desire and Michel contracts tuberculosis on his first trip to Africa and then suffers from a kind of psychotic restlessness later in the narrative. Travel not only symbolizes the fragility of early twentieth-century European identity when it is propelled to the edges of the Continent, but also symbolizes the fascination with, and threat of, the cultural Other: for Michel the Arabic and for Aschenbach the East European and Asian. Just as Aschenbach imagines 'the glinting eyes of a crouching tiger' in his vision of exotic travel, so too is Michel's sensibility refined 'at the touch of new sensations' on his arrival in Tunis.[22] The twin themes of the 'foreign' and the 'estranged' suggest what Kristeva calls 'the hidden face' of identity which 'lives within' and threatens to 'wreck' the individual. Aschenbach's and Michel's heightened awareness of their new environments and their own physical changes are both an acknowledgement of Otherness (the foreign within themselves, as well as the cultural Other) and symptoms of the illnesses which threaten their

---

20 *Death in Venice*, p. 265.
21 *The Immoralist*, p. 65.
22 *Death in Venice*, p. 200; *The Immoralist*, p. 19.

existence.[23] However, Aschenbach is eventually overwhelmed by his disease, whereas Michel discovers therapeutic understanding and resilience from within his illness: what Kristeva calls a new 'path' which emerges only if one has 'the strength not to give in'.[24]

Secondly, both novellas reveal a decadent fascination with literal and psychic doublings: Aschenbach meets a demonic stranger who inspires him to travel; he watches with a 'spasm of distaste' the dandified young-old man when he arrives in Venice, whom he later literally becomes when he is 'made over' with cosmetics; and he encounters a surly gondolier and a grotesque street musician, all of whom are projections, distortions, debasements of, and therefore threats to, Aschenbach's identity.[25] In *The Immoralist* Michel and Marceline have a relationship of reversals: Michel contracts tuberculosis on honeymoon and is nursed by Marceline, and when she develops the illness later in the narrative he is forced to nurse her (although he does this rather badly). In addition, Michel and his friend Ménalque (modelled on Oscar Wilde, whom Gide first met in Paris in 1891 and then on a trip to Algeria in 1895) have a dialectic relationship, offering a series of counterpoints without reconciliation: whereas Ménalque preaches an heroic and courageous existence ('I maintain the sensation of a state of precariousness, by which means I aggravate, or at any rate intensify, my life'), Michel toys with his philosophy but later embodies 'precariousness' as an unheroic or banal mode of existence.[26] In this way, both tales can be read as critiques of Nietzschean individualism: Aschenbach embraces the Dionysian principle toward the end of his demise in an orgiastic dream, but at the expense of himself and his art, and Michel adopts Ménalque's heroic decadence at the expense of his wife, only later to realize the possible alternative of banal decadence.[27]

---

[23]   Julia Kristeva, *Strangers to Ourselves* (*Etrangers à nous-mêmes*, 1988), trans. Leon S. Roudiez (New York: Columbia University Press, 1991), p. 1. In *Strangers to Ourselves*, Kristeva develops her discussion of abjection in *Powers of Horror* by introducing the notion of living on the border between familiarity and strangeness as a positive mode of existence which co-affirms both similarity and difference.

[24]   Ibid., p. 5. Kristeva's notion of 'strength' does not correspond to the kind of religious or military discipline which Aschenbach displays in his writing, discussed by Harvey Goldman in *Max Weber and Thomas Mann: Calling and Shaping the Self* (Berkeley: University of California Press, 1988), but an acknowledgement of the foreign, unruly and unassimilable elements within the self.

[25]   *Death in Venice*, p. 211.

[26]   *The Immoralist*, p. 95.

[27]   Nietzsche's 'transvaluation of values', in which the true moralist becomes the immoralist or, conversely, the immoralist becomes the true moralist in an age of suspect morality, is an important thread weaving through both tales. However, the heroic action which Nietzsche would have identified is contested at the end of *The Immoralist* in favour of Michel's more immanent moral existence. Although Guerard reads *The Immoralist* as a critique of 'Nietzschean individualism', my position regarding the ending of tale differs from his reading of Michel's final 'futile anarchy'; Guerard, *André Gide*, pp. 102 and 99.

Thirdly, both tales deal with homosexuality as a shock and challenge to the psychic worlds of the two protagonists. Aschenbach's discipline as artist is carried out with fanatical effort: he writes in solitude with an almost religious fervour and with an altar-like pair of 'tall wax candles in silver candlesticks placed at the head of his manuscript'.[28] At first, his appreciation of Tadzio is described in purely aesthetic terms, but underlying this is an unrequited carnal desire for the boy, corresponding to the corporeality which Aschenbach denies in himself. By way of contrast, Michel emphasizes his naïveté at the beginning of his narrative: he is twenty-four when he marries Marceline and claims to have 'barely cast a glance at anything but books and ruins'.[29] When Michel falls ill Marceline innocently brings the 'dark-complexioned' Arab boy Bachir with 'large silent eyes' to tend to him; however, Michel immediately feels 'embarrassed' when he notices the boy's nakedness under his thin garments.[30] Although Michel's homosexual impulses are far less repressed than Aschenbach's (he is fascinated by many of the boys – Ashour, Lassif, Lachmi and especially Moktir), the two novellas offer a number of comparisons: the protagonists both fall for adolescent boys despite themselves; they are both narcissistic in their self-obsession; and the mother figure is significantly absent in both tales: she is a distant retrospective figure in *The Immoralist* (she dies when Michel is fifteen in comparison to the narrative presence of Michel's dying father) and Aschenbach's mother is long absent: she is the daughter of 'a director of music from Bohemia' and is described as possessing 'darker, more fiery impulses' than his German clergyman father.[31] The oscillation between the similarity of same-sex love and the differences between the protagonists and their paramours in terms of physicality, nationality and age makes homosexuality an important symbolic site in the two novellas.

Lastly, both tales deal with the symbolic intersection of corporeality and illness, evident both in the descriptions of decadent sensuality of North Africa and Venice and the preoccupation with the physical body. The type of illness contracted by the two protagonists is crucial for an understanding of their respective characters: Michel's tuberculosis is figured as a spiritual disease (one that Mann later mines for its symbolic riches in his modernist novel *Der Zauberberg*; *The Magic Mountain*, 1924), whereas cholera destroys Aschenbach from the base upwards. This opposition between a wasting illness that attacks the lungs and a disease which infects the bowels and intestine is characteristic of the relative ages of the two protagonists (Michel in his mid-twenties and Aschenbach his mid-fifties) and their respective sensibilities. Crucially, the stage in the narrative when the illnesses become manifest determines the fate of the individuals: Michel's

---

[28]   *Death in Venice*, p. 204.
[29]   *The Immoralist*, p. 15.
[30]   Ibid., p. 26.
[31]   *Death in Venice*, pp. 202–3.

tuberculosis manifests itself while on his honeymoon early in the novella and he is nursed back to health by Marceline, whereas Aschenbach seems compelled to stay in Venice even after he suspects a cholera outbreak and detects the 'mouldy smell of sea and swamp'.[32] Had Aschenbach left Venice and had Michel been left to fend for himself their outcomes may have been very different.

The symbolic implications of tuberculosis and cholera are analogous to the oppositions between tuberculosis and cancer which Susan Sontag discusses in her essay on *Illness as Metaphor* (1978): 'TB takes on qualities assigned to the lungs, which are part of the upper, spiritualized body, cancer is notorious for attacking parts of the body (colon, bladder, rectum . . .) which are embarrassing to acknowledge.'[33] Although tuberculosis is often figured as a romantic disease which prioritizes the spiritual over the corporeal (dissolving 'the gross body' and rendering 'the personality' ethereal), the illness does not prevent Michel from acknowledging the importance of his physical existence: 'I am going to speak at length of my body. I shall speak of it so much you will think I have forgotten my soul.'[34] In contrast, Aschenbach spends the first half of his Venetian trip sublimating carnal desire in an aesthetic appreciation of Tadzio: 'there, like a flower in bloom, his head was gracefully resting. It was the head of Eros, with the creamy lustre of Parian marble'.[35] Even though, slightly later in the narrative, he detects Tadzio's 'jagged and pale' teeth with their 'brittle transparency', he does not acknowledge this morbid decadent fascination until cholera has reduced him to nightmarish visions of carnal excess.[36] Aschenbach's cholera, which would be fascinating to decadents such as Joris-Karl Huysmans' alter-ego Des Esseintes in *A Rebours* (*Against Nature*, 1884), does not usher in a sustainable decadent lifestyle, in contrast to Michel's more conventional romantic illness. In this way, Aschenbach's denial of corporeality and Michel's acknowledgement of his body, at least partially, determine their ability to confront abjection.

Abject decadence

In *Powers of Horror*, Julia Kristeva begins from the position (reworked from Mary Douglas's sociological work *Purity and Danger*, 1967) that the formation of binary oppositions in the symbolic order – a social as well as a linguistic order – is also indicative of the conflict between, and the impossible separation of, the socially acceptable (the morally edifying) and the abject (filth). Kristeva argues that any conviction (whether aesthetic, moral or spiritual) contains within it a

---

[32]   *Death in Venice*, p. 231.
[33]   Susan Sontag, *Illness as Metaphor/AIDS and its Metaphors* (London: Penguin, 1991), p. 18.
[34]   Ibid., p. 20; *The Immoralist*, p. 33.
[35]   *Death in Venice*, p. 223.
[36]   Ibid., p. 228.

trace of its own subversion. However, in order to act in the world it is necessary to erect borders and boundaries to ward against contradictions and socially unacceptable desires. In Kristeva's psychoanalytic language, these desires belong to the unruly and chaotic world of pre-oedipal corporeality which the socially constructed self attempts to transcend. Noticeably, Michel and Aschenbach both attempt to develop two techniques for staving off such unruly elements: firstly, they attempt to control their personal environments by relying on rituals and ritualistic action (Aschenbach's discipline as a writer, his candlesticks and his daily walks and Michel's meticulous care of his body) and, secondly, they try (yet fail) to transcend the banality of their situations, Aschenbach with monumental vision and Marcel (until the end of the tale) with an affirmation of hedonistic sensuality.[37]

Kristeva argues that if social identity is formulated by the construction of a 'clean and proper' body (corresponding to the expectations of the symbolic order and the structuring of a personal self) then the abject – the filth of bodily processes like ingestion, egestion and putrefaction – becomes 'the jettisoned object, is radically excluded and draws me towards the place where meaning collapses'.[38] The acquisition of language in which one can place and describe oneself in the symbolic order also represents a throwing, or casting away, of the bodily functions which are ontologically prior to, and which enable one to adopt, this place. Paradoxically, then, in constructing the clean and proper body one denies the very dimension which makes identity possible. The feeling of abjection which emerges at times of anxiety or emotional crisis is an ambivalent awareness of the limits of sanity or health as a double-experience of horror and fascination, in which the individual is drawn to the limit beyond which social identity collapses and at the same time repelled by the terrifying abyss of non-identity.[39] This sense of wavering is evident as each protagonist attempts to impose his heroic existence on the flux and chaos of psychic life. Michel wishes to throw off the restraints of his social identity 'whom education had painted on the surface' and discover the 'very flesh of the authentic creature that had lain hidden beneath it': he investigates his naked body for the first time and

---

[37] *The Immoralist*, p. 54. Kristeva considers such rituals as attempting to maintain the borders between cleanliness and filth, or between health and illness, but they are 'flimsy protections against disintegration'; Kelly Oliver, *Reading Kristeva: Unravelling the Double-Bind* (Bloomington: Indiana University Press, 1993), p. 58.

[38] Kristeva, *Powers of Horror*, pp. 8 and 2.

[39] Such ambivalent feelings are analogous to Freud's notion of the uncanny (*unheimlich*) in which the foreign and the strange are found in, and implicated by, the everyday and the familiar. Thus, the uncanny represents a region within, or inside, the homely which disturbs: 'the uncanny is that class of the frightening which leads back to what is known of old and long familiar'; James Strachey and Anna Freud, eds, *The Standard Edition of the Complete Psychological Works of Sigmund Freud*, vol. 17 (London: Hogarth, 1964), p. 220.

[40] *The Immoralist*, pp. 51 and 65.

'experiences a delicious burning' in his search for 'a wilder, more natural state'.[40] However, his attempt to transform himself from the 'bookworm' into the heroic and self-styled hedonist results not in 'pleasure' but the 'fear' that his 'mind had been stripped of all disguise, and it suddenly appeared redoubtable'.[41] Aschenbach styles himself as a morally virtuous and heroic writer but continues to suffers bouts of wretchedness: his book *A Study in Abjection* is a moral treatise condemning 'an age indecently undermined by psychology', but his life is 'haunted by an impulse that had no clear direction' and 'a fleeting sense of dread, a secret shudder of uneasiness'.[42]

In Lacanian thought, the polymorphous whole of early childhood is a fragmentary unification of what the adult views as divided and distinct; the boundary of the body does not exist in the manner in which one articulates me-you, subject-object, or inside-outside, but the jettisoning of this pre-oedipal unity is necessary if the child is to take its place within the symbolic order. At such time, the disorderly, unclean and anti-social elements must be, to a greater or lesser extent, renounced, sublimated or overcome. The degree of such renunciation is dependent on specific cultural conditions and social expectations (for instance, the widespread attitude to homosexuality in Western Europe at the *fin de siècle*), but most often leads to psychic conflict, as the individual attempts to purify him or herself of the very baseness which forms identity. However, because a renunciation of the abject does not mean its annihilation, Kristeva explains that:

> there looms, within abjection, one of those violent, dark revolts of being, directed against a threat that seems to emanate from an exorbitant outside or inside, ejected beyond the scope of the possible, the tolerable, the thinkable. It lies there quite close, but it cannot be assimilated.[43]

Both Michel and Aschenbach fail to locate the source of their impulses, but anxiety continues to loom within their psychic world and disturbs their self-constructed identity. Kristeva argues that the abject has no object which can be identified with the self or a desired Other, but nevertheless has a tangible presence which usually manifests itself as a 'sudden emergence of uncanniness which . . . now harries me as radically separate, loathsome. Not me. Not that. But not nothing, either. A "something" that I do not recognize as a thing.'[44] In other words, the abject is a point of disruption in the self which cannot be wholly elided with, or redirected into, a desire to travel to a particular place (Biskra or Venice) or the desire for another (Moktir or Tadzio).

---

[41] Ibid., pp. 57 and 58.
[42] *Death in Venice*, pp. 206, 207, 209 and 214.
[43] Kristeva, *Powers of Horror*, p. 1.
[44] Ibid., p. 2.

By applying Kristeva's insights to the two novellas it becomes clear why Aschenbach is overwhelmed by his vision of Tadzio, whereas Michel emerges from Marceline's death with an new orientation toward life. Kristeva argues that the aesthetic of the sublime (associated with the European Romantic preoccupation with immensity and magnitude) is an attempt at controlling or dissipating the abject: 'the abject is edged with the sublime. It is not the same moment on the journey, but the same subject and speech bring them into being'.[45] Aschenbach cannot contend with the looming feeling of abjection because he invests all his emotion in the resplendent vision of Tadzio:

> And to behold this living figure, lovely and austere in its early masculinity, with dripping locks and beautiful as a young god, approaching out of the depths of the sky and the sea, rising and escaping from the elements – this sight filled the mind with mythical images, it was like a poet's tale from a primitive age, a tale of the origins of form and of the birth of the gods.[46]

Aschenbach's vision of the classical body of the Polish boy releases his mind 'from the elements' as he attempts to transcend the bodily world for the mythological Platonic realm of ideas. However, such a vision only temporarily satisfies Aschenbach's 'longing for the unarticulated and immeasurable, for eternity, for nothingness'.[47] Aschenbach's fantasy is increasingly troubled by his unacknowledged physical desire for Tadzio; his spiritual vision is undermined by the corporeality (symbolized in the cholera epidemic) which he denies in himself and which is eventually to consume him. In this way, he is rendered impotent by his inability to either consummate his desire or release himself from his fixation on Tadzio. Abjection creeps up on him unawares and manifests itself too late in the narrative for him to contend with.

Although Michel's early commitment to heroic decadence hinders a full acknowledgement of abjection until the end of the tale, his obsessions are mercurial and many-faceted: he is narcissistic in his self-love; he swings between tenderness for Marceline and feelings of superiority over her; he is surprised by his desire for Arab boys but he does not become fixated on any particular paramour; and his relationship with Ménalque fuses sexual game-playing with intellectual skirmishing. This is not to assert that Michel does not suffer from abjection, but he manages to diffuse desire across a libidinal continuum rather than invest all his feelings in a sublime fascination for an unattainable love. In line with Gide's 'hobgoblinism', Michel lives an existence of dissimulation, contradiction and paradox without trying to fold conflicting elements into a consistent lifestyle. Rather than assimilating the 'glimmerings of a thousand lost

---

45   Ibid., p. 11.
46   *Death in Venice*, pp. 226–7.
47   Ibid., p. 224.

sensations' that arise from the depths into monumental vision, he acknowledges 'that even during those early studious years they had been living their own latent, cunning life'.[48] Unlike Aschenbach, Michel does not attempt to stop 'the hemorrhage' of the abject (although he experiences haemorrhages during his tuberculosis), but, by the end of the tale, he manages to keep 'open the wound' in a therapeutic mode of existence: in Kristeva's words, a 'heterogeneous, corporeal, and verbal ordeal of fundamental incompleteness'.[49]

Books and ruins

Both *The Immoralist* and *Death in Venice* explore the manner in which the protagonists' ruined lives – Michel's abject nihilism emerging after Marceline's death and Aschenbach's abject demise into the 'inert, deep-sunken' figure on the beach – are symbolized by ruined language.[50] It is important that both protagonists are literary men – Aschenbach is a respected writer and Michel lectures on ancient history and archaeology – because Kristeva claims that the sublimated forms of literature, art and music explore the manner in which the abject returns to haunt those processes which try to purify it. She is particularly interested in modernist literature (she lists Dostoyevsky, Proust, Artaud, Kafka and Céline, but Gide is a notable exception) and claims that certain types of 'literature may also involve not an ultimate resistance to but an unveiling of the abject'.[51] Abjection, then, is the attitude of the subject who recognizes the impossibility of purification, an attitude which Kristeva claims is most productively explored in modernist aesthetics. As such, both novellas are ultimately concerned with 'books and ruins'. This is particularly relevant for considering the role of abjection in the two texts as inscribing a process of ruination: the ruination of lives of the protagonists and the ruination of language in which their individuality and desires are structured.[52] As Kristeva asserts, modernist writing in particular concerns itself with 'an elaboration, a discharge, and a hollowing out of abjection through the Crisis of the Word'.[53]

---

48   *The Immoralist*, p. 39.
49   Kristeva, *Powers of Horror*, pp. 55 and 27.
50   *The Immoralist*, pp. 155–9 and *Death in Venice*, p. 267.
51   Kristeva, *Powers of Horror*, p. 208.
52   The way in which modernist literature reflects what Sontag calls 'the nihilistic energies of the modern era' and makes 'everything a ruin or fragment' makes a study of these writers pertinent for dealing with theories of abjection; cited in Liam Kennedy, Susan *Sontag: Mind as Passion* (Manchester: Manchester University Press, 1995), p. 11. As a point of comparison, Maud Ellman applies Kristeva's theory of abjection to T.S. Eliot's modernist lament *The Wasteland* (1922) in *The Poetics of Impersonality: T.S. Eliot and Ezra Pound* (Brighton: Harvester, 1987), pp. 91–113.
53   Kristeva, *Powers of Horror*, p. 208.

Early on in *The Immoralist* Michel claims that 'nothing attracted me [to Tunis] except Catharge and a few Roman ruins'.[54] After his first disappointing visit to the amphitheatre of El Djem he returns to the ruins and searches 'in vain for inscriptions on the stones'.[55] That night his illness worsens as he begins to spit blood, almost as if his body has taken on the character of the ruined amphitheatre. Further on in the narrative, during a visit to Syracuse, Michel attempts to avoid the ruins because 'every thought of the festivals of antiquity made be grieve over the death of the ruin that was left standing in their place; and I had a horror of death'.[56] This abject recoiling from ancient culture informs Michel's lectures, in which he describes late Latin culture as:

> welling up in a whole people, like a secretion, which is at first a sign of plethora, of a superabundance of health, but which afterwards stiffens, hardens, forbids the perfect contact of the mind with nature, hides under the persistent appearance of life a diminution of life, turns into an outside sheath, in which the cramped mind languishes and pines, in which at last it dies. Finally, pushing my thought to its logical conclusion, I showed Culture, born of life, as the destroyer of life.[57]

Michel's realization that most forms of 'culture' serve only to secure the 'sheath' of life, instead of life itself, stimulates him to devote less and less attention to both ruins and books: on their later journey through Italy Michel and Marceline travel with eight trunks, but there was one Michel 'never opened in the whole journey, entirely filled with books'.[58] By the end of the narrative Michel has entirely renounced books and archaeological research in favour of a minimalist lifestyle of ruination which has its own kind of simplistic beauty.[59] This enactment of an abject decadence not only prefigures the French Surrealists' interest in the 'poeticisation of the banal' twenty years later but offers an aesthetic counterpoint to the kind of heroic stance espoused by Ménalque in *The Immoralist*.[60]

---

[54] *The Immoralist*, p. 19.

[55] Ibid., p. 20.

[56] Ibid., p. 50.

[57] Ibid., p. 90.

[58] Ibid., pp. 137 and 140.

[59] Michel looks forward to 'a land free from works of art; I despise those who cannot recognise beauty until it has been transcribed and interpreted'; ibid., p. 148. This position is a development from the earlier decadent aesthetic espoused by Walter Pater in *The Renaissance* (1873). For Pater, 'to burn with this hard, gem-like flame' is to live an authentic and intense life within the world of art and culture, whereas Michel attempts to discover such authenticity outside the cultural realm; Pater, *The Renaissance* (Oxford: OUP, 1986), p. 152.

[60] See Liam Kennedy's discussion of Sontag's view that the French Surrealists linked 'satirical and therapeutic' functions in their art – both a 'social corrective' and a 're-education of the senses' – which in part derives from Gide; Kennedy, *Susan Sontag*, pp. 31–3.

By way of contrast, in the ruins of one of the most glorious Renaissance cities, *Death in Venice* plays out a number of issues which Aschenbach fails to confront. In his book *A Study of Abjection*, Aschenbach proclaims his 'renunciation of all moral scepticism, of every kind of sympathy with the abyss'. However, the stylistic 'purity, simplicity and symmetry' which characterizes his 'moral resoluteness' stimulates the narrator to question the 'two-faced' nature of writing which often hides the 'resurgence of energies that are evil, forbidden, or morally impossible' beneath the surface of moral intention.[61] This understanding is very similar to Michel's realization that the trappings of culture often shroud real life with the illusion of it, but crucially it is only the narrator who understands this point in *Death in Venice*. Aschenbach is drawn to Venice as 'a city irresistibly attractive to the man of culture, by its history no less than its present charms', but the narrator warns the readers that we should be suspicious of this 'glib empty talk'.[62] Indeed, the Venice in which Aschenbach finds himself is overrun by commercialism and ridden by pestilence: a city fallen from aesthetic grace to its ruinous state as a commercial tourist trap. It is not that Aschenbach does not detect these signs (they come to him in his half-memories of Plato's *Phaedrus* as part of the 'tissue of strange dream-logic'), but, rather, he fails to act on his decision to leave the city.[63] Instead he resurrects the sublime vision of Tadzio from the ruins of Venice and bolsters up his decaying body by 'cosmetically brightened lips' and by acquiring a straw hat and a scarlet necktie. Ironically, in this cosmetic transformation into a parody of the late-nineteenth-century dandy, Aschenbach gives himself over the abyss which he had earlier renounced. His last experience of cholera-induced feelings are 'waves of dizziness, only half physical, and with them an increasing sense of dread, a feeling of hopelessness and pointlessness'.[64] However, although Aschenbach's symptoms resemble Michel's state of mind at the end of *The Immoralist*, Aschenbach is too sick to cultivate an existence which can contend with such emotions and he collapses under the weight of his ruination.

Both *Death in Venice* and *The Immoralist* are both preoccupied with the possibilities as well as the impossibilities of enacting the border between the moral and the abject which Kristeva discusses in *Powers of Horror*. This symbolic border takes on various forms in the two tales as the protagonists hover uncertainly between two conditions: between the paralysis of the abject caught between horror and fascination and the desire to be mobile and to travel; between the need to retain identity and the blurring of borders between self and Other, especially in terms of sexual proclivity; and between the unruly aspects of corporeality and the quasi-spiritual visions of the protagonists. This symbolic line is most powerfully symbolized by Michel's fascination with, and fear of, shadows

---

61 *Death in Venice*, p. 207.
62 Ibid., p. 210.
63 Ibid., p. 265.
64 Ibid.

throughout the book and Aschenbach's vacillation between conscience and desire during his aborted attempt to leave Venice.

Because the abject is a point of disruption (according to Kristeva neither subject, object, nor non-object) it erodes distinctions between structural oppositions – intellect and passion, conviction and inclination, the moral and immoral – rather than reconciling them. Although these dichotomies are discernible in both novellas, the respective ways in which Gide and Mann explore abject decadence diverge significantly. Aschenbach's inability to deal with the contradictory impulses of responsibility and inclination (or Apollonian control and Dionysian desire) leads inexorably to his death, whereas Michel (after Marceline's death) continues to lead a kind of 'shadow' life, or what Kristeva calls a 'forfeited existence':

> It is simply a frontier, a repulsive gift that the Other, having become alter ego, drops so that 'I' does not disappear in it but finds, in that sublime alienation, a forfeited existence. Hence a jouissance in which the subject is swallowed up but in which the Other, in return, keeps the subject from foundering by making it repugnant. One thus understands why so many victims of the abject are its fascinated victims – if not its submissive and willing ones.[65]

Even though Michel is often blind to his own motives, the first-person mode of narration reveals much more about his psyche than the detached third-person narrative voice discloses about Aschenbach. The standard reading of the conclusion of *The Immoralist* is that Michel justifies his story and actions to his friends who are themselves readers of his story: 'We felt, alas, that by telling his story, Michel had made his action more legitimate.'[66] However, the ending can be read alternatively as Michel's attempt to accept his abject life in a ruined world by embracing the shadow-line which so fascinated him earlier in the tale.

Michel continues to live an abject life as a 'forfeited existence', whereas Aschenbach is invaded and finally totally overcome by his desire and illness. In other words, Michel finds the courage to live dangerously, but not heroically, at the limit, whereas Aschenbach (apart from his dream of a Bacchanalian orgy) is rendered aimless after his self-disciplined life has been eroded by his confrontation with a decadent Venice. In *Sexual Dissidence* (1992), Jonathan Dollimore discusses this idea of courage not as continuous with the morally virtuous and disciplined Victorian hero, but as an act of 'demoralization': the courage to 'liberate' the self 'from moral constraint rather than dispirit'.[67] But,

---

65   Kristeva, *Powers of Horror*, p. 9.

66   *The Immoralist*, p. 157.

67   Jonathan Dollimore, *Sexual Dissidence: Augustine to Wilde, Freud to Foucault* (Oxford: Clarendon Press, 1992), p. 4. Dollimore notes that Gide learnt this sense of 'demoralization' from Oscar Wilde; but 'whereas for Wilde transgressive desire

crucially, after Marceline's death, it is not heroic transgression which Michel embodies but a banal negotiation of borders between memories and action, intellect and passion and homo- and heterosexuality in what Kristeva calls the life of the borderlander.[68]

Despite his trials and losses Michel manages to improvise a 'demoralized' code of ethics which engages with the abject, whereas Aschenbach is totally debilitated by excessive bodily drives. The 'forfeited existence' which Michel lives is a ruined life in which he confronts the provisonality and impermanence of the modern world, a life which has its own existential authenticity but which is still in the process of becoming:

> What frightens me, I admit, is that I am still very young. It seems to me sometimes that my real life has not begun. Take me away from here and give me some reason for living. I have none left. I have freed myself. That may be. But what does that signify?[69]

He claims earlier in the narrative that 'the miscellaneous mass of acquired knowledge of every kind gets peeled off in places like a mask of paint, exposing the bare skin', but at the end he is reduced to a series of sexual encounters and the almost Beckettian practice of repeatedly cooling pebbles in the shade and then warming them in his hand, not as a protective ritual, but as a way of comprehending the limits of his fragile and 'broken' life constantly under threat from the hedonistic forces that consumed him earlier in the story.[70] Even though he claims to live 'for next to nothing in this place', it is the 'next to nothing' which gives his life some meaning as he finally abandons his books for life to cultivate a ruined or forfeited decadence.[71] For this reason, the elements in Gide's writing which most appeal to Mann in his *New York Times* review do not actually conform to the German writer's desired pattern of 'precarious harmony': they are finally irreconcilable by means of aesthetic wizardry or the Joycean paring of fingernails. Instead, the fragmentary elements of Michel's life represent an embodiment of banal and abject decadence, enabling him to embrace a liminal and prodigal mode of existence and to confront the abjection of modernity even though he cannot fully overcome it.

---

leads to a relinquishing of the essential self, for Gide it leads to its discovery, to the real self, a new self created from liberated desire'; ibid., p. 13. However, although the language of authenticity permeates the early sections of *The Immoralist*, Michel's new-found ability to embrace a 'forfeited existence' suggests a different kind of ontology to essentialism and a wary attitude to the kind of heroic limit experience discussed in Foucault's later work.

[68] This exploration of psychic borders is prevalent throughout French modernism, especially in the work of Artaud, Bataille, Genet and Foucault, and helps to account for the different cultural emphases which Gide and Mann place on decadence.

[69] *The Immoralist*, p. 158.

[70] Ibid., p. 51.

[71] Ibid., p. 158.

Chapter 13

Resisting Decadence: Literary Criticism as a Corrective to Low Culture and High Science in the Work of I. A. Richards

Daniel Cordle

The notion of decadence lurks within all three of I.A. Richards' early extended formulations of literary criticism: *Principles of Literary Criticism* (1924), *Science and Poetry* (1926), and *Practical Criticism* (1929).[1] It hovers most obviously around his representations of early twentieth-century Western society and culture. These are seen to be decadent because they are dominated by popular, rather than high, culture, and by the sciences rather than the arts. This primacy of the popular and the scientific is associated with the threat posed to civilization by the forces of chaos, and Richards' views on the role and the methodology of literary criticism will be shown, in this essay, to be a direct response to that threat.

It will, therefore, be argued that the objectivity which Richards strives for in his literary criticism can be shown actually to rest upon views of culture which are very clearly rooted within a specific, subjective perspective. Because he sees the world around him as decadent, and because he sees literary criticism as a corrective to that decadence, the 'New Critical' methodology which he formulates, and which was so powerful in the shaping of English as an academic subject, actually rests on some highly localized assumptions. Marina Spunta argues elsewhere in this volume that established categories are challenged 'at every decline of the century' (see below, p. 200). Written less than thirty years into the new century, Richards' work comes after, and is in many ways a response to, this process of destabilization, for in it he aims to re-establish categories and mitigate the Angst which Spunta suggests arises when certainties are threatened.

The assumptions Richards makes are about the nature of order and chaos, and the nature of great and poor literature. He stresses these strongly in his work so

---

[1]   I.A. Richards, *Principles of Literary Criticism* (1924; London: Routledge, 1989), *Poetries and Sciences: A Reissue of Science and Poetry* (1926, 1935) with Commentary (London: Routledge, 1970), *Practical Criticism: A Study of Literary Judgement* (1929; London: Routledge, 1964).

as to draw out the influence of debased culture upon the individual and thence upon society, and the role a vigorous literary criticism can play in reasserting order by both defining high culture and refining its influence upon us. Less clearly asserted, but as crucial to the methodology of literary criticism that he proposes, are definitions of the sciences and the arts. These definitions, by no means original to Richards, resurface later in the century in the acrimonious 'two cultures' dispute between F.R. Leavis and C.P. Snow, and continue to this day to determine the nature of the debate about how we divide up our knowledge into different academic disciplines.[2]

In order to demonstrate the truth of these assertions about Richards' criticism, and the importance of his view of early twentieth-century society as decadent, I am going to do three things. I will begin by exploring exactly how Richards uses key concepts, defining terms like *individual* (*reader*), *literature* and *science*. These are important terms because literature is defined in terms of its opposition to science, and the definition of the individual which Richards uses dictates the effect that he sees literature having upon individuals in a collective sense; its effect, in other words, upon society. I will then, secondly, establish in greater detail how these different elements relate to one another, and draw out the importance of decadence to Richards' vision of early twentieth-century society. It will then be possible to see how the model of reading and of criticism which Richards advocates, grows out of these concerns.

Key terms for an understanding of Richards' work

Richards implicitly, and sometimes explicitly, proposes a two-fold model of the human mind, comprising intellect and emotion. This picture of the human mind is at the core of his presentation of the individual, and is important because the roles of literature and science in Western culture follow on from it.

The representation of the first element, the intellect, is very similar to that which we find in René Descartes' influential *Discourse on Method*, where the human mind is portrayed as something which is essentially ordered and able to make rational, objective judgements about the world with which it is faced.[3] In

---

    2   C.P. Snow coined the phrase 'the two cultures' in his 1959 Rede lecture, in which he argued that a gulf of mutual misunderstanding had arisen between the Arts and the Sciences, and which led to a furious debate, principally between Snow and F.R. Leavis. For the main texts in the debate, see C.P. Snow, *The Two Cultures and the Scientific Revolution* (Cambridge: Cambridge Univeristy Press, 1959), and F.R. Leavis and Michael Yudkin, *Two Cultures? The Significance of C. P. Snow with an Essay on Sir Charles Snow's Rede Lectures* (London: Chatto and Windus, 1962). This debate, and its contemporary incarnation in the form of the 'science wars,' are discussed in my book, *Postmodern Postures: Literature, Science and the Two Cultures Debate* (London: Scholar, 1999).
    3   René Descartes, *Discourse on Method and Other Writings*, trans. F.E. Sutcliffe (1637; Harmondsworth: Penguin, 1968).

this sense Richards is drawing on an understanding of the mind which is strongly rooted in Western culture's preoccupation with rationalism – a preoccupation which stems back at least as far as the Enlightenment.

However, although he draws on this tradition of rationalism, Richards is also influenced by contemporary psychology. Whereas Descartes struggled with the problem of the mechanism by which the mind could affect the body (which he eventually solved, rather unsatisfactorily, by suggesting that the pineal gland offered the medium by which thoughts had material consequences), Richards acknowledges the roots of the mind in physical reality. As a result he produces a less static view than that proposed by Descartes; indeed, in his formulation the mind is fairly dynamic, and demonstrates a tendency to change, to become more ordered, and to improve. For instance, human development is charted by Richards as a process of the progressive systematization of the mind itself: 'At every stage in this astonishing metamorphosis [from child to adult], the impulses, desires, and propensities of the individual take on a new form, or, it may be, a further degree of systematization.'[4]

This insistence upon the tendency towards increased order, as a positive, natural development, is extremely important, as will become apparent. Elsewhere, this emphasis is even more obvious: 'we should picture the mind as a system of very delicately poised balances, a system which so long as we are in health is constantly *growing*'.[5]

Order – as a value – underpins much of Richards' work. Not only is it essential to his vision of a healthy mind, and hence to his definition of the individual, but it is also seen as a vital component in the artist's work, and crucial to a healthy society. Recent criticism analysing the cultural values given to chaos and order suggests that this is a viewpoint which is specific to a certain historical period, being particularly prevalent from the Enlightenment through to at least the middle of this century.[6] Indeed, if we read Richards' work with the revised cultural associations of chaos and order in our minds – where order is seen as restrictive and limiting instead of valuable, and chaos becomes a fruitful source of new meanings instead of a straightforward threat to order – the meaning of his work is rendered problematic.

Richards assumes a second element in his model of the individual mind, in addition to the rational Cartesian intellect. This is his proposal that, though having rational, logical faculties, the human mind is primarily a 'system of interests': 'It may seem odd that we do not make the thoughts the rulers and causes of the response. [. . .] [But] though his intellect is what is distinctive in man, he is

---

4   Richards, *Principles of Literary Criticism*, p. 34.
5   Richards, *Poetries and Sciences*, p. 25.
6   See, for example, N. Katherine Hayles, *Chaos Bound: Orderly Disorder in Contemporary Literature and Science* (Ithaca: Cornell University Press, 1990). Hayles argues that 'chaos' has been redefined in the second half of this century to mean that which lies between order and disorder.

not primarily an intelligence, he is a system of interests. Intelligence helps man but does not run him'.[7] This aspect of the mind, which is prioritized over the intellect, can be thought of as broadly equivalent to the emotional, 'feeling' side of the mind, and it is this sharp division of the mind into rational and emotional elements that lends literary theory its defining characteristics at this time.

Science, associated with the Cartesian 'intellect', had been tremendously successful in providing explanations of the world since the Enlightenment, particularly in the nineteenth and twentieth centuries. For literary study to survive, as a serious academic discipline, it would need to carve out its own territory, and find a purpose, away from the influence of science. This is where the distinction between the intellect and the 'system of interests' becomes so important and begins to take us towards particular definitions of *literature* and *science*. If science is configured as the province of the intellect, but the mind is redefined not as pure intellect, but as a 'system of interests', then the effect is to imply that there is a territory which is clearly not associated with science and which is beyond the reach of science – at least for the time being: 'If we knew enough it might be possible that all necessary attitudes [of the mind] could be obtained through scientific references alone. Since we do not know very much yet, we can leave this remote possibility, once recognized, alone.'[8]

Once the mind is perceived to be beyond scientific description (as the rather haughty phrases, 'it might be possible' and 'this remote possibility,' suggest), literature takes on the role of both organizing the individual's mind (which I will return to later), and expressing all that science cannot describe. If the rational side of the mind was to deal with the verifiable truths with which science was concerned, so the rest of the mind was to be concerned with other territories composed of value (an important term for Richards), art and so forth.

We therefore get a split between two cultures, one scientific and one literary (or, more broadly, artistic) which mirrors the split between the two sides of the mind which Richards assumed to exist. Literature and science were seen to operate in separate territories (rather like the 'two cultures' that were later to be debated by Leavis and Snow), and interactions between them could only be of the most banal sort. Because this cultural split is seen to mirror a 'natural' split in the mind between the intellectual and emotional sides of human character, the sharp division between the sciences and the arts itself becomes naturalized in Richards' work.

It is worth pointing out that this science/literature split draws on very traditional, perhaps even stereotyped, cultural assumptions about the natures of science and literature. Science is associated with logic, truth and objectivity, while literature is associated (perhaps because of the lasting influence of the Romantics) with more emotional and intuitive responses to the world.

---

7   Richards, *Poetries and Sciences*, p. 30.
8   Richards, *Principles of Literary Criticism*, p. 211.

However, although science is separated from literature, and the two are placed in autonomous cultural territories, it must be stressed that they are seen as part of the same grand cultural enterprise: the ongoing refinement and development of the human response to the world. It is in their very failure to work in parallel that Richards' perception of early twentieth-century culture as decadent has its roots. Co-extensive developments in the two territories of literature and science were not taking place because advances in science were rapidly outstripping all other concerns, leaving a dangerously unbalanced culture in which the body of objective, scientific knowledge was not matched by an equivalent system of values and emotional understanding. As a rigorous application to that other, emotional culture, literary criticism becomes, in this view, a corrective to the decadence created by this state of affairs:

> As the finer parts of our emotional tradition relax in the expansion and dissolution of our communities, and as we discover how far out of our intellectual depth the flood-tide of science is carrying us [. . .] we shall increasingly need every strengthening discipline that can be devised. [. . .] The critical reading of poetry is an arduous discipline; few exercises reveal to us more clearly the limitations under which, from moment to moment, we suffer. But, equally, the immense extension of our capacities that follows a summoning of our resources is made plain.[9]

This sense of literature and science being separate, and yet at the same time part of a complementary project, leads directly to the two-cultures debate between F.R. Leavis and C.P. Snow thirty years later. What Richards effectively does, in statements like these, is to set science against literature by implying that literary studies should become a central pillar in both the education system and in the wider life of civilization.

This broad literature/science divide, which is so crucial to Richards' general observations about the individual and the culture, also permeates other aspects of his work. Two examples will suffice to illustrate this.

First, in *Science and Poetry*, Richards describes two streams of experience, 'intellectual' and 'emotional,' that arise when we read poetry. The former is a minor stream which accords roughly with the verifiable truths and certainties about what the words in a poem mean – a sort of logical, scientific truth. The latter is described as being more active because from it 'all the energy of the whole agitation [in the mind] comes'.[10] By making this distinction Richards both establishes an opposition between literature and science, and asserts the dominance of the former over the latter.

Second, in *Practical Criticism*, Richards writes about two categories of belief. The first, 'intellectual' belief, is scientific in character: 'The whole use of

---

9   Richards, *Practical Criticism*, pp. 350–51.
10   Richards, *Poetries and Sciences*, p. 25.

intellectual belief is to bring *all* our ideas into as perfect an ordered system as possible.'[11] 'Emotional' belief, on the other hand, underwrites literature and the reading experience, and is about satisfying our demands as human beings: 'an emotional belief is not justified through any logical relations between its ideas and other ideas. Its only justification is its success in meeting our needs'.[12] The existence of these two categories of belief is again legitimized by an assertion that they are 'natural' expressions of the division between the rational (scientific) and emotional (artistic) sides of our nature: 'Behind the intellectual assumption stands the desire for logical consistency and order in the receptive side of the mind. But behind the emotional assumption stands the desire or need for order of the whole outgoing emotional side of the personality, the side that is turned toward action.'[13]

So it appears that there is a binary opposition between the literary (artistic) and the scientific underpinning much of Richards' work, and this is manifested in a desire for a subversion of the contemporary status quo so that the literary would replace, or at least equal, the dominance of the scientific side. This is not, it should be stressed, wholly straightforward. There is, indeed, something rather paradoxical about the way in which this is articulated because the scientific resurfaces in Richards' representations of the literary. This occurs, firstly, in his references to contemporary pscyhology, which invoke scientific 'truths' in order to lend legitimacy to his work; and, secondly, in his insistence that there is a stable object of study (the words on the page that are the exclusive object of New Criticism's focus) which permits the critic to adopt an investigative role which is similar, in its objectivity, to that popularly associated with the scientist.

Nevertheless, we should note that the primary justification for literary study is the ability it gives us to bring back to equilibrium a culture which has lost its balance. Exactly how Richards envisaged that this should be achieved can be seen if we now turn to a more detailed consideration of the effect that he saw literature to have on the individual, and thence upon society.

The effect of literature on the individual and on society

We have seen that Richards views the individual mind as being split between emotional and scientific sides, and that this split corresponds to a general split in the culture between the sciences and the arts (with both configured in conventional terms, science being associated with truth and objectivity, and literature with value and subjectivity). We can now go on to ask what effect he sees literature having on the individual, and thence on society. In other words, how does he bring his notions of *literature*, *science* and the *individual* together?

---

[11] Richards, *Practical Criticism*, p. 274.
[12] Ibid., p. 276.
[13] Ibid., p. 274.

Crucially, the impact of the arts upon people is described as profound: 'The raising of the standard of response is as immediate a problem as any, and the arts are the chief instrument by which it may be raised or lowered.'[14] There are two things that are interesting about this statement. Firstly, literature and the arts in general are the most important instruments by which 'the standard of response' is affected, and so it is implied that the study of literature is going to be extremely important. Secondly, the arts can have either a beneficial or a malign effect and so a distinction between good and bad art becomes necessary (because a separation between that which has a positive, and that which has a negative, effect is needed). This necessitates some sort of theory of literature and of how it affects society.

Importantly, the emphasis in this theory is again on order. We have already seen that Richards charts human development as a process of increasing systematization and order, with the result that 'the fine conduct of life springs only from fine ordering of responses far too subtle to be touched by any general ethical maxims'.[15] This is taken further in Richards' assessment of what constitutes a good artist or poet – they enable 'further developments of organizations' which our minds (those of readers) have, and therefore are able to 'give order and coherence, and so freedom, to a body of experience'.[16] In other words they are 'better organized' individuals than the rest of us. As a result the literature which they produce disseminates their superior principles of mental organization among those who read it: 'We pass as a rule from a chaotic to a better organized state by ways which we know nothing about. Typically through the influence of other minds. Literature and the arts are the chief means by which those influences are diffused. It should be unnecessary to insist upon the degree to which civilization, in other words, free, varied and unwasteful life, depends upon them in a numerous society.'[17] Notice that freedom is assumed to follow on from order here, instead of being perceived to be restricted by it. Crucially, in view of Richards' desire to systematize and promote the study of literature, it is only art, not science, that can produce this better ordering of experience: 'It is never what a poem says which matters, but what it is. The poet is not writing as a scientist. He uses these words because the interests whose movement is the growth of the poem combine to bring them, just in this form, into his consciousness as a means of ordering, controlling and consolidating the uttered experience of which they are themselves a main part.'[18]

Conversely bad art – and this is the moment at which the need to distinguish great from poor literature in an objective sense enters Richards' work – is perceived as having a negative effect by increasing chaos. In the following

14 Richards, *Principles of Literary Criticism*, p. 184.
15 Ibid., p. 47.
16 Ibid., pp. 53 and 57.
17 Ibid., p. 43.
18 Richards, *Poetries and Sciences*, p. 33.

example bad art is popular art, with cinema used (as Richards often uses it) as the most notorious example of the dangers posed by popular culture: 'No one can intensely and wholeheartedly enjoy and enter into experiences whose fabric is as crude as that of the average super-film without a disorganization which has its effects in everyday life. The extent to which second-hand experience of a crass and inchoate type is replacing ordinary life offers a threat which has not yet been realized.'[19] So, while 'good' art helps us to become more organized as individuals and societies, 'bad' art is dangerous because it introduces 'disorganization' and 'inchoate' experiences into our minds. It is this perception of an encroaching chaos – spread by the mass art forms of the twentieth century – that is at the heart of the decadence that Richards sees within early twentieth-century culture. This sense of threat serves to legitimize attempts to define a canon of English literature, an elite constellation of literary stars by which society can navigate as it seeks to edge forwards.

This explains the fear, which Richards expresses elsewhere, that contemporary culture is composed of too many facets, and is becoming too broad, and too disorganized, to be beneficial to us. Commenting on what he perceives to be a decline in the quality of literature, he writes that,

> The most probable reasons for this [decline] are the increased size of our 'communities' (if they can be so called, when there remains so little in common), and the mixtures of culture that the printed word has caused. Our everyday reading and speech now handles scraps from a score of different cultures [. . . I am referring] to the fashion in which we are forced to pass from ideas and feelings that took their form in Shakespeare's time or Dr Johnson's time to ideas and feeling of Edison's time or Freud's time and back again.[20]

Richards' fear of a dilution of cultures echoes the suggestion (at least in its contemporary, popularized forms) by the Second Law of Thermodynamics that the universe is itself threatened by disorder. In contrast to popular narratives of evolutionary change (that suggest that change over time equates with progress, with the production of better, more organized and sophisticated life forms), this suggests that in the long run the universe is threatened by entropy, and that it is gradually 'winding down' towards a condition of less and less order and, eventually, heat death. Richards seems to suggest that culture must itself be closed off, sealed and preserved against the influence of other cultures much as literary territory must be protected against the encroachment of scientific culture. Indeed, it is interesting that, in this quotation, the culture of the past is associated with the literary (Shakespeare and Dr Johnson), and the culture of the present is associated with the scientific (Freud, who may not conform to everyone's

---

19   Richards, *Principles of Literary Criticism*, p. 182.
20   Richards, *Practical Criticism*, p. 339.

definition of scientific, but almost certainly did to Richards', and Edison). The 'order' of culture is threatened by dilution or 'disorder' if it is not rigidly protected against outside influences. This is in stark contrast to some of the notions of order and disorder which are currently popular, where 'chaos' is often presented as a fruitful source of new meanings in popular versions of chaos theory, and where postmodernist literature mixes discourses from different cultures (particularly from high and low cultures) quite explicitly.[21] For Richards, however, disorder is threatening – a signal of decadence – and the artist stands against it, championing order: 'The artist is concerned with the record and perpetuation of the experiences which seem to him most worth having. [. . .] [W]hen he succeeds, the value of what he has accomplished is found in a more perfect organization which makes more of the possibilities of response and activity available.'[22]

Because the study of literature is a process of learning to distinguish good from bad literature for Richards, and because by successfully making this distinction we can raise 'the standard of response' by promoting a greater degree of order, it is possible to see how his work constitutes a rhetorically powerful case for an accepted body of 'good' literature – a 'canon' of the sort proposed perhaps most blatantly by F.R. Leavis in *The Great Tradition*[23] – to stand at the centre of the culture. Science has to be subservient to literary study because, it is implied, without the development in our minds that good literature can produce, we lack the control to utilize our scientific knowledge correctly. Literature, of a certain kind, is 'good' for you because it manifests an exceptional organization of experience by the artist, and disseminates this amongst the readers of the literary work. It is not difficult to see how this is associated with the perception that the value of high culture lies in its beneficial influence upon society, the possibilities it makes available for a progressive ordering of human experiences and responses to the world.

The role of literary criticism

Having seen how society is perceived to be affected by literature, we can now go one step further and ask a final set of questions of Richards' work: how should the individual read, and what is the role of the literary critic? In other words, what lessons does Richards draw from the definitions of *science*, *literature* and the

---

21   Contrast Richards' conception of literature with, for instance, that apparent in a novel like Kurt Vonnegut's *Breakfast of Champions* (London: Jonathan Cape, 1973) which contains childlike drawings, and in which the narrator (who is called Kurt Vonnegut and claims to be synonymous with the author) is happy to proclaim that 'I would bring chaos to order [. . .] which I think I have done', p. 210.

22   Richards, *Principles of Literary Criticism*, p. 46.

23   F.R. Leavis, *The Great Tradition* (1948; London: Chatto and Windus, 1962).

individual that he formulates, and the interaction that he perceives to take place between the three?

A good reader, according to Richards' formulation, is one who recreates the experience of the writer in his or her mind when reading literature. By doing this the reader will gain access to the writer's superior ability to organize experience: 'the reader who approaches it [poetry] in the proper manner [will get] a response which is as passionate, noble and serene as the experience of the poet, the master of speech, because in the creative moment he is the master of experience itself'.[24]

In order to become good readers, however, we should not adopt a biographical approach, focusing directly on the author's mind, which is 'far too happy a hunting-ground for uncontrollable conjecture',[25] but must focus instead on the text itself, which manifests the writer's ordering of experience. We should do this, Richards argues, in order to see which features of the writing produce which effects in our minds: 'often the critic [. . .] affirms that the effect in his mind is due to special particular features of the object. In this case he is pointing out something in addition to its effect upon him, and this fuller kind of criticism is what we desire'.[26] To become this better sort of reader we need to be 'sensitive',[27] and the habit of good reading is a matter of developing this sensitivity. This will allow one to distinguish good from bad literature in an objective sense, overriding one's personal feelings as one comes to a detached literary judgement about the work in question.

Therefore, by implication, the role of the literary critic is twofold: to act as a guide for those unable to judge which literature is and is not of value; and to impart the secrets of making such judgements. This is certainly the role of the implied author in *Practical Criticism*, where Richards comments at length on his own students' inadequate responses to unannotated pieces of literature, setting himself up as someone who knows the difference between good and bad literature, and offering to guide the rest of us as we strive to reach a similar status as adept readers. Indeed, there is something mystical about Richards' presentation of the skill of the literary critic. While realist literature, which makes similar assumptions to Richards about knowledge,[28] implies the author as omnipotent god, practical criticism emphasizes the literary critic as priest/vicar to the god's word. The essential role of the critic is, in this view, that of a mediator between the Word and those for whom the Word is intended.

---

[24] Richards, *Poetries and Sciences*, p. 45.
[25] Richards, *Principles of Literary Criticism*, p. 20.
[26] Ibid., p. 15.
[27] See ibid., pp. 76 and 120, and also *Practical Criticism*, p. 224.
[28] My PhD thesis highlights similarities in the assumptions made about knowledge by realist literature and *Practical Criticism*, arguing that both assume a world 'out there' that we can objectively know. Daniel Cordle, 'Literature and Science Writing in Contemporary Culture: The Challenge to History in Post-Enlightenment Discourses of Literature, Science and Literary Theory', PhD dissertation, University of Leicester, 1996.

It is in this sense that literary criticism operates for Richards as a means of resisting decadence. If decadence offers an escape from both the dominant cultural discourse and the literary responsibility to instruct,[29] then Richards' work operates as a vigilant guard, barring this route of escape. He seeks to maintain the dominant cultural discourse, cementing the place of the established literary greats and denigrating mass culture, and his criticism reinforces literature's instructive function. While it would be wrong to oversimplify the value he places on the instruction literature can offer us (he never suggests that the purpose of reading is to tease out a set of morals or 'messages' from books), his indication that the value of the literary lies in its promotion of order in our lives suggests that it serves a didactic function, albeit one of a rather general nature.

Conclusion

The study of literature is therefore presented, in the three books that Richards published in the 1920s, as a bulwark against two threats. The first is that of science, taking us rapidly into territories of knowledge that we are neither emotionally nor morally equipped to deal with. The second is that of popular culture, diluting and dissipating the positive influence of high culture.

Both these threats are presented as forces of moral chaos. Western culture, as a crumbling order, is therefore depicted in Richards' work as decadent in at least three senses: firstly, it is in a state of decay (due partly, paradoxically, to advances in sciences); secondly, it lacks artistic vigour; and thirdly, as a consequence of these two, it lacks moral vigour.[30] Literary criticism is offered to us by Richards as an active means by which we can resist this decadence.

These forces are also inevitably essential to the definition of literature itself, the object of literary study, that Richards' work produces. Indeed, we might say that three binary oppositions are used to define literature. Two, loudly voiced and closely associated, are those between good and bad literature, and order and chaos. Order is an entirely positive force in Richards' work, and good literature is a means by which order can be disseminated throughout society. Literary criticism helps us to distinguish this 'orderly' literature from the malign influence of that literature which produces a disorderly, chaotic effect; and to refine the influence of that orderly literature upon us.

The third binary opposition, more muted (and at times almost silenced) because it seems so natural, is that between literature and science. Science is associated with rational, verifiable truths, and the 'intellect' of the human mind, while literature is bound tightly to the 'system of interests' which Richards uses

---

[29] As suggested by Professor Martin Stannard at the 1997 Leicester/Pisa colloquium.

[30] *Chambers Concise Dictionary*, 1988 edition, s.v. 'decadence', p. 246.

to explore the emotional aspect of our mental lives. Such a sharp binary distinction between two halves of the human mind has the effect of naturalizing a similar distinction between two halves of human knowledge; between the sciences and the arts.

This therefore provides a framework of knowledge which enables certain ways of thinking and speaking, and disables (or at the very least strongly discourages) others. It invites us to presume that there are essential differences between the sciences and the arts, and it baffles our desire to find bridges between them.

Drawing attention to this, and suggesting that certain rhetorical forms construct a particular framework of knowledge (science against literature) out of which we speak, does not of course mean that the sciences and the arts are essentially the same. However, it does enable us to question whether such a framework is based on well-formulated arguments, or whether it is an assumption that we unthinkingly accept. It also allows us to see how certain forms of literary criticism respond directly to contemporary concerns. Although Richards implies that the critical apparatus he promotes is ahistorical (untainted by passing cultural fads and agendas, and therefore appropriate to the potent conception of the university as unhistoricized, to which Mark Rawlinson draws our attention), it is very clearly a criticism that is rooted in its time. It soon becomes obvious that, for Richards, the value of literary study lies in its ability to hone and focus the regulating influence of great literature, and therefore in the possibility it offers for resisting decadence.

Chapter 14

Blow It Up and Start All Over Again: Second World War Apocalypse Fiction and the Decadence of Modernity

Tristram Hooley

In the late 1930s and early 1940s the people of Europe were struggling to comprehend the implications of a fragmented and decimated urban landscape that was being brought into existence by aerial bombardment. Among them was Graham Greene who was moved to describe what he saw as a 'diseased erratic world' in his October 1940 essay 'At Home'.[1] This pessimistic disillusionment would have resonated with the other stunned sufferers of the Blitz. Greene goes on to speculate that this apocalyptic action could be one of the last of a society the morality of which is founded on violence.

> Violence comes to us more easily because it was so long expected – not only by the political but also by the moral sense. The world we lived in could not have ended any other way.[2]

For the student of the Second World War the ideas of decadence, decay and disintegration take on a far more literal set of connotations than when applied to other periods.[3] The term decadence perhaps sounds inappropriate or flippant in the context of the massive destruction of human life and cultural artefacts which took place during the Second World War. Despite this initial reservation that 'decadence' understates the experience of Europe in the 1930s and 1940s, this essay will seek to demonstrate how it provides a useful starting point for

---

[1]   Graham Green, 'At Home', in *The Lost Childhood and Other Essays* (London: Eyre and Spottiswoode, 1951), p. 190.

[2]   Ibid., p. 189.

[3]   Decadence is described in the *OED* as '1. That is in a state of decay or decline: falling off or deteriorating from a prior condition of excellence, vitality, prosperity etc.'. One might want to question whether British society of the 1930s could be truly said to be excellent, vital and prosperous but the idea of a cultural transformation motivated by decline and deterioration seems to lend itself to a discussion of wartime culture.

contextualizing a series of cultural responses that were generated by the Second World War.

This essay attempts to locate the concept of decadence within a material framework rather than a merely intellectual one. This is not to claim that the actions of the Luftwaffe and Bomber Command render the 1940s *actually* decadent where other periods experienced only *conceptual* decadence. The description and mediation of material circumstances is one of the functions that culture provides in different ways across history. The decaying material circumstances of the Second World War alone are not enough to conclude that the period saw an upsurge in decadence, just as the absence of material decay does not rule out the possibility of a decadent culture. The fact of material decay in 1940s Britain did however provide the raw material upon which an ideological concern with decline and destruction could begin to work.

The fear that civilization was declining and an uneasiness about the frailty of the material basis of society was caused in part by the fear of aerial attack and the realization of the power of modern weaponry. These weapons were capable of levels of destruction that were quite literally apocalyptic by the end of the war. These concerns manifested themselves through a variety of cultural phenomena: in the increased interest in religion and church attendance; in 'the retreat from liberal optimism among the intelligentsia'; in the revival of spiritualism and interest in the occult, and in a different way in the enthusiastic embracing of reconstruction as the mantra of the post-war world.[4] Each of these cultural phenomena in turn is inscribed and worked through in a strange type of novel which it is possible to describe as 'apocalypse fiction'.[5]

Apocalypse fiction, the novel which explores the extremes of destruction, has an obvious and immediate relevance to the world of the Second World War. In a world where immediate death and destruction were constant reality, the production of novels which sought to discuss this issue was inevitable. While the novel of mass destruction is not limited to the Second World War there are two factors which make it possible to argue that during this period it was achieving a relevance that had never before been possible.

The first factor which allowed 'apocalypse fiction' to achieve a new kind of accessibility during the Second World War was the growth of science fiction as a

---

4   See Alan Wilkinson, *Dissent or Conform? War, Peace and the English Churches 1900–1945* (London: SCM Press, 1986) particularly p. 196 for his discussion of the changing political and theological position of the clerical intelligentsia. For a discussion about the rhetoric of reconstruction see Paul Addison, *The Road to 1945: British Politics and the Second World War* (London: Random, 1994).

5   'Apocalypse fiction' is my term for novels which imaginatively render the end of the world or cataclysmic destruction on a global scale. It is important to note that this was not a self-constituted genre and that this essay merely uses the term as a way to group works with similar themes not as an attempt to intellectualize into existence some long-lost literary school.

popular genre.[6] As an awareness of the imaginative and experimental forms associated with science fiction and other related genres grew, science fiction began to provide a model of experience that was uniquely suited to understanding wartime reality. Harry Warner Jr states in his history of science fandom

> Fandom had several reasons for paying some attention to the Second World War. For one thing, it was science fiction turning into reality. Wells' *The Shape of Things to Come* had been the longest and most celebrated of a profusion of stories based on probabilities of the form that would be taken by the successor to the First World War. The public feared that the new war would cause suffering and death beyond imagination, but fans could imagine those results through long experience with stories about them. It made a genuine difference in outlook.[7]

The link between science fiction and technological modernity is obvious and well documented. In the Second World War this link became more pronounced as science fiction and related genres, such as apocalypse fiction and airman stories, were quickly catapulted off the page and into reality. One of the most striking things about accounts of the start of the war is the frequency with which they refer to *The Shape Of Things To Come*. Derek Stanford describes in his memoirs how a thunderstorm on 3 September was construed as the first wave of a German attack after seeing the film:

> Our recognition of this soon led us to construe it as belonging to the actual spear-head of an invasion. If so, the Nazis were acting fast; but that, after all, was what we expected from having seen H.G. Wells' *The Shape Of Things To Come*.[8]

The growth of science fiction meant that an increasing audience was able to read and understand the translated reality that the genre offered. The arrival of the future in so aggressive a way as *blitzkrieg*, the V1, V2 and atom bombs served to speed up and intensify this process.

Apocalypse fiction also took on a new relevance in the Second World War. For the first time humanity had securely placed itself in possession of the means of its own destruction. Even before Hiroshima the destructive power of aerial

---

6   For more information on the growth of science fiction as a genre see Harry Warner Jr, *All our Yesterdays: An Informal History of Science Fiction Fandom in the Forties* (Chicago: Advent, 1969) and Brian Aldiss, *Billion Year Spree: The History of Science Fiction* (London: Weidenfield and Nicolson, 1973).

7   Harry Warner Jr, *All our Yesterdays*, p. 149.

8   Derek Stanford, *Inside The Forties: Literary Memoirs 1937–1957* (London: Sidgwick and Jackson, 1977), p. 5. For further discussion of the way in which the novel and film versions of *The Shape of Things to Come* influenced perceptions of the war see Bernard Bergonzi, *Wartime and Aftermath: English Literature and its Background, 1939–60* (Oxford: OUP, 1993), p. 2.

warfare was quite terrifying to contemplate. Herbert Best attempts to imagine how far the new weapons empower humanity to destroy itself in his novel *The Twenty-Fifth Hour* (1940):

> How it all started was history now, unwritten history for lack of anyone who might write or read. Basically, the preparations for offensive war had been all too efficient, and the peacetime organisation of society had grown too elaborate, too fragile to withstand the shock of such efficient forces of destruction. It was as simple as that.[9]

While his prediction was thankfully incorrect, Dresden demonstrates the potential of mechanized warfare for mass destruction in the pre-nuclear age. For the first time apocalypse fiction was discussing a possible future rather than a hypothetical abstraction.

Matei Calinescu argues that the conception of a decadent society is closely linked to an understanding of linear temporality.[10] Without an awareness that we exist in a period, which Calinescu labels the modern, and which is differentiated from the past, it is impossible to have a perception of the decadent. For Calinescu decadence is an attempt to move away from the modern and to critique it. The existence of a decadent mentality therefore presupposes an unhappiness with the current state of the modern.

It is not difficult to see how a dissatisfaction with the contemporary must have been easy to develop for the average citizen of the world at the end of the 1930s and the beginning of the 1940. The rise of fascism, the bloody totalitarianism of the Bolsheviks, the capitulation of the men of Munich and the rapidly increasing power of weapons of war form only the beginning of the list of the early twentieth century's political, social and technological failures and misdirections. For many it must have felt as if the Wellsian fanfare for modernity, for technological progress, and for social change had led humanity only to the brink of destruction. The development of authoritarian systems of government in German and Russia, for example, often seemed to be paralleled by a growing British state machine fuelled by national government and capitalist crisis. To some it must have seemed that the politicians had become more powerful and despotic than ever, while the poor had starved and the middle classes had huddled in their homes fearing strikes, inflation and war. For contemporary observers this litany of industrial capitalism's failures may have seemed to have reached its climax in the decision to go to war at the end of the 1930s.

Predictions of what form the war would take, like Nevil Shute's *What Happened to the Corbetts* (1939), foresee the approaching conflict as devastating.

---

9   Herbert Best, *The Twenty-Fifth Hour* (London: Jonathan Cape: 1940), p. 17.
10   Matei Calinescu, *Faces of Modernity: Avant-Garde, Decadence, Kitsch* (London: Indiana University Press, 1977).

Shute's novel paints civic and social breakdown as the result of aerial bombardment, graphically detailing the spread of disease and starvation. The novel demonstrates how fragile the civilization of 1930s Britain was, showing how seemingly small amounts of damage, such as the bombing of the water supply, could result in the humiliating degradation of the people of Britain.

> Good class houses have storage tanks, of course – the sort of house that you live in. But some of the poorer parts are in a terrible way for water, really they are. In Chapel and in Northam, down behind, they've been scooping up the water from the gutters where it came up out of the road, and drinking that. If this goes on we'll have to start carting water in from the country.[11]

The authorities are, however, unable to cart water into the towns due to the continuing onslaught. Social disintegration continues with outbreaks of cholera which is presented as a disease of the uncivilized.[12] This kind of fiction only helped crystallize the apocalyptic pictures that were already lodged in the collective psyche. In the inter-war period the understanding of the human cost of the First World War was acute. This combined with the knowledge of more powerful weaponry and the fears inspired by prediction and speculation to open up the possibility that the approaching conflict would require an inconceivable level of sacrifice.[13]

From 1936 to 1942 the Axis gradually gathered up increasing amounts of territory across the globe and the fate of liberal capitalism seemed to hang in the balance. Art and literature looked into oblivion. In the *TLS*, *Horizon* and *Penguin New Writing* pundits discussed whether creativity was possible in the midst of total war.[14] While the political establishment rapidly imploded under the weight of its own foolish inaction and incompetence, sexual and moral licence seemed to abound as people lived hedonistically for the minute.[15]

---

[11] Nevil Shute, *What Happened to the Corbetts* (1939; London: Mandarin, 1993), p. 42.

[12] See ibid., p. 54 for descriptions of cholera as a disease that only 'black men' get.

[13] We can see examples of this awareness of the cost of the First World War revealed in the popularity of First World War related novels during the inter-war period, the existence of the Peace Pledge Union and Chamberlain's reluctance to go to war in 1938.

[14] See for example 'Why not war writers: A manifesto' in ed. Cyril Connolly, *Horizon*, vol. IV, 22 (London: Johnson Reprint Company, Oct. 1941), 236–9; John Lehmann's 'Foreword' in *Folios of New Writing* No. 1 (London: Hogarth, 1940). For more examples see Robert Hewison, *Under Siege: Literary Life in London 1939–45* (Newton Abbot: Readers Union, 1978).

[15] For further discussion of Second World War decadence in terms of personal and sexual morality see John Costello, *Love, Sex and War: Changing Values 1939–45* (London: Collins, 1985).

However, the dominant historical understanding of the period argues that this decadence was not to last long.[16] Out of the chaos of the 1930s would be born the People's War, and out of the One Nationism necessitated by the war would come a new, better and more unified post-war world.

The marriage of a rise in collective solidarity among the people, and the capture of the establishment by the Beveridgite/Keynesian liberal intelligentsia is often used to explain both the way the war was won, and the way the post-war world was built.[17] This is clearly not the whole story but I am not attempting to rewrite the People's War concept in this essay. This has already been extensively questioned by historians such as Angus Calder and Fielding, Thompson and Tiratsoo, who have convincingly argued that the idea of the Second World War as a time of national harmony is at best an exaggeration and at worst a nonsense.[18]

The People's War however, remains a powerful concept around which analyses of the war have been organized. The resonance of this concept is not accidental. It has survived at least in part because of the rhetorical strength of the discourse created to disseminate the People's War idea. Government propaganda, the speeches of Priestley and Churchill, the Army Bureau of Current Affairs and the rhetoric of rationing and the equality of sacrifice all add up to a concerted attempt by various hegemonic forces to sell the war to its participants and to posterity as a democratic war of the common man and woman.[19] This gives the People's War concept a credibility in much of the social commentary from the period and in the memories of people who lived through the war.

A study of high and popular cultural sources therefore reveals a picture of the war which is subtly different from the one produced by more traditional historical sources. Government and trade union records may reveal that there was a continuation of industrial strife, police statistics demonstrate that to many the bombing and disorganization of war was an opportunity to rob their dead, dying, confused or evacuated neighbours, yet the rhetorical strength of the discourse has managed to convince both participants and observers of the war that everyone was pulling together. Nor is it fair to see this as an entirely top-down process. Various political, religious, economic and personal interests used the People's War concept to their advantage, from munitions factories recruiting workers to

---

[16] While the uncritical acceptance of the 'People's War' concept, as characterized by historians from A.J.P. Taylor to Paul Addison, has lost ground in recent years it still underlies many of the assumptions made about the culture of the period. This is particularly true in literary studies such as the work of Alan Munton and Bernard Bergonzi.

[17] This kind of analysis can be found in Paul Addison, *The Road to 1945*, op. cit.

[18] Angus Calder, *The People's War: Britain 1939–45* (London: Cape, 1969) and *The Myth of the Blitz* (London: Pimlico, 1992); Fielding, Thompson and Tiratsoo, *England Arise: The Labour Party and Popular Politics in the 1940s* (Manchester: Manchester University Press, 1995).

[19] For a discussion of how the different sections of the establishment combined to promote the People's War idea see Paul Addison, *The Road to 1945*.

the 'Beauty as Duty' rhetoric used as a selling point by the cosmetic industry.[20]

It is therefore not possible to simply dismiss the People's War as a major component of wartime culture. It remained an essential part of government and hegemonic discourse and is partially responsible for legitimizing the introduction of rationing, the state management and nationalization of industry and the consignment of millions of citizens to their deaths. The People's War may be a crude and controversial term and the communal singing in air raid shelters remains largely mythic, but the People's War was real insofar as it was part of the public discourse. What this essay sets out to show is that there were also public discourses that were oppositional to the People's War concept and that these were often outside the control of the government.

Many students of wartime culture and politics, myself included, begin to study the Second World War with the self-satisfied platitudes of the Labourist New Jerusalem tradition ringing in their ears. The firmly held belief that the swing to the left, as described in *The People's War* by Angus Calder, unproblematically took place leads to a line of enquiry which has proved to be perhaps less fruitful than expected.[21] A dissident left-wing language which was potentially revolutionary can be registered at some levels.[22] However the belief that Britain experienced a near-revolutionary situation in the early 1940s seems to over-estimate the level of politicization that can be assumed from understandable expressions of dissatisfaction with the war effort. What is clear from my examination of speculative fiction from the Second World War is that the People's War and its left critique are only two of a number of different types of personal and political reactions to wartime conditions. The discourse which I have encountered with perhaps the most regularity is one which expresses unhappiness and dissatisfaction in a far less overtly political fashion. It is not necessarily antithetical to the People's War discourse, in that it does not attempt to mount a comprehensive attack on it. What it does do is express a dissatisfaction with the contemporary situation, both in terms of the war and in a wider sense with modernity. This alternative discourse is backwards looking as opposed to the socialist revolutionary analysis which looks forward; it sees a solution, not in the revolution, but in a return to a point in the past before modernity had begun to

---

[20]   For further discussion of the utilization of the People's War rhetoric by the cosmetics industry see Pat Kirkham, 'Beauty as Duty: Keeping Up the (Home) Front', in eds Pat Kirkham and David Thoms, *War Culture: Social Change and Changing Experience in World War Two Britain* (London: Lawrence and Wishart, 1995).

[21]   Fielding, Thompson, and Tiratsoo question the assumption that the Second World War saw a swing to the left in *England Arise*, noting the near halving of Labour Party membership during the war years and the way in which the British electoral system gives an exaggerated impression of the party's success at the 1945 election (p. 68).

[22]   It is possible to find examples of this revolutionary left discourse in the various political circles around the edges of the Common Wealth party, the ILP, the CP and the Labour Left, and also in the publications of the Left Book Club, for example those of George Orwell and Olaf Stapledon.

fail. This discourse sees modernity as stagnating and declining, the war as marking an end rather than a beginning. The contemporary world has become decadent and the apocalypse of war is seen almost in terms of biblical retribution.

The existence of this ideological and emotional interest in defeat and destruction is something that has been ignored too frequently by commentators seeking to emphasize the positive aspects of the Second World War. However, as Raymond Williams observes, ideological conflict is not just fought out between the old and the new, the establishment and the reformers.[23] The pressures for political, social and moral change are more complex. Williams, perhaps still somewhat reductively, offers a model of ideological conflict being fought out between a residual, dominant and emergent ideology. The residual ideology's desire to move backward, away from the contemporary political and economic situation, obviously ties in with the kind of destructive urges that can be found in apocalyptic fiction and elsewhere during the Second World War.

A residual ideology which attempts to move backwards and mounts a battle against the dominant reality of modernity must be closely concerned with the idea of decadence. The fear that society is about to collapse is often couched in terms of a moralistic critique of decadent behaviour and this critique of the decadent forms the basis of much of the discourse and motivation of the residual ideology. Yet the constant attempt to look backwards to a golden age, and to reject the modern also echoes the dynamics of decadence. Answering a fear of decline with the politics of the past is one of the key contradictions in residual ideologies and it is these variant and contradictory understandings of the nature of decadence that provide valuable insights into the culture of a society in obvious material decline like that of the Second World War period.

The decadent obsession with destruction can be seen most clearly in the works of imaginative fiction which see an imminent disaster for humanity. An examination of the apocalyptic literature of the period demonstrates a world picture far removed from the bland progressive certainties of the People's War discourse. While predictive fiction does have a tendency to look towards extremes, either towards destruction or salvation, the fact that over half of the speculative fiction that I have examined depicts an imminent apocalypse, and the other possible future most regularly imagined is Nazi invasion, demonstrates that the defiant hopefulness of the Dunkirk spirit was not universally pervasive.

The urge to imagine a world apocalypse obviously has biblical antecedents and there was perhaps reason for contemporary observers to see the world in pre-diluvian terms.[24] If the world has become morally, socially, artistically and

---

[23]   Raymond Williams, *Culture* (London: Fontana, 1981).

[24]   The fiction of Alfred Noyes and to a lesser extent all other apocalyptic writers are undoubtedly inspired in part by the cultural mythology of the flood '5: And God saw that the wickedness of man was great in the earth, and that every imagination of the thoughts of his heart was only evil continually. 6: And it repented the Lord that he had made man on the earth, and it grieved him at his heart. 7: And the Lord said, I will destroy

technologically decadent it then becomes necessary to destroy it to cleanse the decadence and sin rather than to go into the future on the shaky foundations of the modern.

For this discourse the collective unity of the People's War could only happen once the war had cleansed the planet of modernity. This use of apocalyptic terms to describe the atomizing and alienating aspects of the war can be seen in the statements collected by Mass Observation after the blitz on Coventry. Here people understandably saw the war as very much the end of civic existence, in marked contrast to the idea of the blitz performing its rather questionable but much feted function of bringing people together in a classless unity.[25]

> Mass-Observation volunteers visited Coventry in the two days immediately following the raid on the city of 14 November 1940. Their report caused considerable government alarm since it suggested that civilian morale had disintegrated in the wake of the raid. People were said to be extremely pessimistic, with 'Coventry is finished' and 'Coventry is dead' being typical responses to the attack. It was also claimed that extreme behavioural abnormalities became manifest.[26]

The apocalypse discourse, then, sees war as an end rather than a beginning. The concern with imminent destruction, revealed in the people of Coventry's sense of the finality of their experience, is further developed and explored in apocalyptic fiction.

Apocalypse fiction starts with the end and works backwards to a concern with the idea of modernity and where it has gone wrong, and forwards in a quest for what to put in its place. That a significant number of writers saw a formulaic advantage in advancing their political and personal solutions, after visiting the planet with an apocalypse, perhaps suggests that the current situation was seen by some as beyond salvation. If modernity was perceived as declining into a decadent cesspool, a total apocalyptic solution could have been seen to be necessary in order to be able to talk clearly about its problems and possible solutions.

---

man whom I have created from the face of the earth; both man and beast, and the creeping thing, and the fowls of the air; for it repenteth me that I have made them.' *The Holy Bible: Containing The Old And New Testaments* (Oxford: OUP, 1855) Genesis, VI: 5–7.

[25]   Fielding, Thompson,and Tiratsoo argue in *England Arise* that there are major problems with seeing the Blitz as an experience which fostered social cohesion. They note that even in London only 4 per cent of people used the London Underground as a shelter, 9 per cent utilized other public shelters, and 27 per cent used private shelters, most people stayed in their homes, in bed or under the stairs (p. 25). They also note that the lack of social cohesion was so extreme that 'there were occasions when public shelters were guarded by men with shotguns in an attempt to ensure that only locals come in' (pp. 25–6).

[26]   David Thoms, 'The Blitz, Civilian Morale and Regionalism, 1940–42', in Pat Kirkham and David Thoms, *War Culture*, p. 9

The fear that society was to share the fate of the biblical anteecedents, Sodom and Gomorrah,[27] is summed up most succinctly by the maverick poet and author Alfred Noyes in his novel *The Last Man* (1940). In this novel he argues that declining morality has been the result of modernity and that the ultimate destruction of the race will be the inevitable result of modernity's cycle of hedonism and war:

> But, as the war went on, our enemies imposed their own totalitarian views on us in other forms. We began to talk almost with contempt of the value of individual life and to squander it almost as recklessly as we squandered material treasure, despite all the efforts that were made to counteract it. The gospel of 'eat and drink for tomorrow we die' sprang up amongst us, and inevitably, led to other kinds of squandering too.[28]

He paints a picture of a modernity crippled by an inability to prioritize and an intellectual and moral irresponsibility. *The Last Man* depicts a secular anarchy, where the new is fetishized at the expense of the wisdom and morality of tradition.

> For nearly half a century, the literature and art of western civilization had succumbed (partly out of intellectual snobbery) to the subtle propaganda of the new atheism. They had been glorifying the breaking of the pledged word in the most sacred relationships of the individual human life; they had been revelling in the analytical destruction of all the foundations of morality; and sneering at those who defended them as 'out-of-date', while the most leprous stigmata of degeneracy had again and again been upheld as a vital proof of new and advanced thought and original aims.[29]

Noyes' critique of modernity is sweeping in its scope, targeting aesthetic modernism, military and technological innovation, art and philosophy as well as politics and international relations. For Noyes' hero Mark Adams, the whole package of modernity is a disaster that is leading humanity only to further catastrophe.

> He saw clearly how the new intellectual and spiritual incompetence had contributed to the modern chaos, and eventually to the catastrophic end of civilisation.[30]

---

[27]   The destruction of Sodom and Gomorrah engages with the idea of decadence as they are destroyed because 'their sin is very grievous', Genesis 18: 20. It also provides a vivid literary model for the writers of apocalypse fiction, 'Then the Lord rained upon Sodom and Gomorrah brimstone and fire from the Lord of heaven; And he overthrew those cities, and all the plain, and all the inhabitants of the cities, and that which grew upon the ground.' Genesis 19: 24–5.

[28]   Alfred Noyes, *The Last Man* (London: John Murray, 1940), p. 141.

[29]   Ibid., p. 80.

[30]   Ibid., p. 106.

It would be easy to dismiss Noyes as the last bearer of a high Victorian faith in religion and tradition as the touchstones of morality, but while Noyes was blowing up the world, many other writers also felt the need to cleanse the world of modernity's failings by visiting it with an apocalypse.

We can pick up this feeling of decadence and stagnation in many of the other novels of the period. J.D. Beresford's *A Common Enemy* (1942) comes from a slightly different political position from Noyes' book, offering agrarian socialism rather than high Christianity as the solution to society's problems, but essentially the problems that it identifies are the same: too much mechanization, too much sexual license, drinking, jazz music, and modern dancing and not enough hard work and collective endeavour. Beresford is unhappy with the modern world; his critique is not just of a particular system, but of modernity in all its guises.

> And were all the shifts and devices of the twentieth century, Communism, Fascism, Democracy, anything more than attempts to plant new designs on old structures, by the imposition of elaborate economic and social facades upon a civilisation the members of which were still thinking fundamentally in the old way? Nationalism, the doctrine of force, the restriction of individual liberty, still remained as the essential fabric.[31]

The solution for the world of *A Common Enemy* is not a more technical, more affluent society, it is a simpler, more egalitarian but essentially retrospective society. A deurbanized, deindustrialized society practising an idyllic common cultivation of land would seem to be an eccentric solution to the problems of the 1940s. However, as Beresford's hero Mr Campion notes,

> Here we were, you know, in the depths of the most widespread, purposeless, destructive, debasing war ever known, apparently sinking deeper and deeper into a horror and misery from which we could see no escape except by a complete reconstruction of our social system.[32]

This message that society has run itself out, that the war is merely the culmination of all of the mistakes of modernity, that the decadent slide to immorality and mutual destruction is beginning, comes through again and again in these novels, and it is not difficult to understand why. The appalling devastation caused by the Blitz was only a fraction of what some civil service experts had predicted and for many it must have seemed that a world in the process of turning its back on God was to be visited with a disaster of biblical proportions.[33]

---

[31]   J.D. Beresford, *A Common Enemy* (London: Hutchinson and Co., 1942), p. 105.

[32]   Ibid., p. 102.

[33]   Richard M. Titmuss, "'The Expected Attack', in *Problems of Social Policy* (London: Longmans, 1950).

It is perhaps this sense of being in the middle of a biblical disaster that generated so much apocalyptic fiction in the period, and it is why apocalypse fiction is useful for examining the most extreme personal and political responses to the war. If the People's War rhetoric describes how the people of Britain felt at the highest points of morale, then the rhetoric of apocalypse, decadence and biblical devastation represents them at their lowest. By looking forward, all that could be seen was war, so it is hardly surprising that many authors decided to blow it all up and start again, or to look backwards for solutions from the past.

Herbert Best's novel *The Twenty-Fifth Hour* (1940) puts together the apocalyptic form with an attempt to look forwards into the future after the Second World War. As with Noyes there is a pacifist strain running through his writing; the apocalyptic form is not just a way to wipe the slate clean and begin the creation of a new and better society as it is in Beresford's work. For Best and Noyes the vision of the onrushing apocalypse represents if not a prediction, then at least a final warning to turn aside from the mechanized and militarized path pursued so ruthlessly by modernity. *The Twenty-Fifth Hour* imagines humanity visiting itself with appalling degradation, degradation comparable with the events that were beginning to unfold in central Europe while Best wrote. In this critique of industrialized modernity we see humanity reduced to the level of cannibalism by an over-reliance on technology. As the fragile balance of supply and demand is disrupted by war, modernity, especially in the West, is increasingly unable to meet the basic needs of the populace. Eventually as all industrialized and mechanized processes break down completely, in an extreme extrapolation of the kind of problems that Shute imagines in *What Happened To The Corbetts*, civilization collapses altogether.

> People couldn't have been such idiots! Each nation building up its population until only the most elaborate and delicate organisation of supplies and communication could allow the land to support such hordes of people; and blindly at the very same time, getting ready to blast to bits the delicate organisation of a neighbouring nation. Hadn't they ever heard that people in glass houses should not throw stones? Oh, men can't have been so mad![34]

Like Noyes and Beresford, Best saw the problems that civilization was undergoing as the result not of one political system, but of modernity. Only by returning to a society based more clearly on morality and less on material possession could humanity hope to be saved.

In *The Twenty-Fifth Hour* the solution is shown to be a peculiar combination of an intellectualized and liberalized Islam and an economy centred on agriculture. Best is perhaps trying to inject the secularity of the modern with a

---

[34]   Herbert Best, *The Twenty-Fifth Hour*, op. cit., p. 217.

spirituality untainted by contact with the decadent West. Learning is to be encouraged, but the new society will avoid developing the level of mechanization that allowed civilization to be destroyed so easily.

> The great men of our land must rid themselves of riches, or none will esteem them great. Bribery, extortion, even theft, unless of the simplest necessities, will bring shame and humiliation upon the man who shows himself enriched, even though the crime itself is hidden. Charitable gifts have ever been encouraged by Islam, but yearly it becomes more difficult to find one who will accepts such gifts, lest they enrich and shame him. So public services benefit, knowing neither the honour of poverty, nor the shame of wealth. Schools and colleges will flourish under their endowments, and process will be discovered and rediscovered in everything from mathematics to pottery, agriculture to astronomy.[35]

Religious charity and individual morality are being used to supplant complex state machinery and the modern welfare system. Best ensures that his ideal society improves by encouraging the individual to consume less while denying the state the power to assume any control over the individual. Liberty is equated with simplicity, decadence and oppression with sophistication and material possession.

All three writers imagine such distinctly different solutions to what they identify as modernity's problems that it would be quite wrong to try to claim that they belonged to any kind of mutually supportive movement. For one thing it is quite possible that they were unaware of each other's work. However, it is possible to contend that they were attempting to work through similar concerns and to represent the problems of wartime society in a way that allowed them freedom from the constraints imposed on pacifist, anti-government or pro-fascist works that could be seen as directly relating to the wartime situation.

It is also wrong to represent these novels as coherent ideological blueprints for future societies. The speculative nature of fiction means that it operates within a profoundly different political space from an equivalent set of ideas articulated as a political manifesto or a newspaper editorial. It seems unlikely that even Noyes believed that his utopian solution to the problems of modernity, of placing communities under the leadership of Franciscan monasteries, was workable. The level at which it can be said to represent an alternative to the more credible political positions of the Second World War is in its desire to correct problems that mainstream politics chose to ignore or embrace.

For the reader the impact of these novels could not have been simply to convey their rather ill-thought-out ideas for better world government. J.D. Beresford's anti-democratic advocacy of liberal oligarchy would have been problematic for much of his readership.

---

[35] Ibid., p. 283.

> A nominal democracy had been tried and had failed. The new rule would
> be government by the few, avoiding the dangers of Dictatorship by a single
> mind.[36]

Even if Beresford believed that the country really needed dictatorship by a benign
middle-class committee, it seems difficult to imagine that a readership so soaked
in rhetoric about defending democracy from Hitler would not have encountered
this idea with a degree of scepticism. Beresford's writing is rich with different
political possibilities and the readers are more likely to engage creatively with the
novel's ideas than to blindly accept everything in it. However the novel does
articulate ideas and experiences that relate imaginatively to readers' experience.
His examination of Britain's attempts to recreate itself positively after an
apocalypse must have conveyed familiar dilemmas to a readership just emerging
from one of the worst periods of Blitz.

> If it taught us all, that lesson of humility I spoke of, there might be a hope.
> It would give us a chance to get together in a common cause, a chance to
> start again with a new programme. I honestly believe that the world is ripe
> for a new beginning.[37]

The transformation of the apocalypse into a positive chance to start again
obviously resonates with the People's War advocation of social democratic
planning as a way to rebuild society. However, for Beresford the entire structure
of modernity must be pulled down; the political possibilities are far more radical
than anything on offer in contemporary Westminster. For the reader the impact is
suggestive rather than convincing: the novel allows the readers to explore new
possibilities and to test their own political assumptions without mounting a
potentially unpatriotic attack on the dominant ideology.

The three authors that I have discussed are not an alternative to Attlee or
Churchill, nor are they even an alternative to Mosley or Sir Richard Acland, the
founder of the Common Wealth party, rather their novels provide an arena for
political experimentation for both the author and the reader. The speculative and
playful nature of these texts is one of the elements that allows them to represent
ideological and emotional possibilities that would normally be suppressed either
overtly through censorship or official disapproval or personally by a belief that
questioning the war was unpatriotic and socially unacceptable.

What this paper has tried to show is that while the public rhetoric which
manifests itself in literature, newspapers, art and other popular culture is
contained to a large extent within the barriers of the dominant ideological
discourse, to understand the cultural and political possibilities of a period it is
necessary to recognize and represent dissenting voices. The People's War concept

---

[36]   J.D. Beresford, *A Common Enemy*, p. 108.
[37]   Ibid., p. 11.

has been correctly challenged and held up as a false depiction of wartime culture, but this has left us without an organizing concept around which to base an understanding of the period. Any attempt to replace it must recognize that culture is composed of a multiplicity of political, ideological, and material circumstances and positions. Our understanding of a historical period's culture should recognize this and avoid simply advancing the dominant ideology or its most credible, or popular, critique as a totalizing representation.

The People's War concept should be understood not as a historical accuracy but as a component of public experience. However, we should also accept that it is not the only axis around which public opinion was seen to fluctuate over the six years of the Second World War. This essay has attempted to suggest one alternative axis around which we can group an understanding of elements of war culture. An examination of a more pessimistic, backwards-looking, retrospective rhetoric is essential in providing some balance to the overly optimistic People's War reading of the Second World War. The war was to many people a wholly or largely horrible experience and one genuine response to this was to throw up hands at the whole of modernity and look back to a period which seemed to promise more. A reactionary response which privileges an unworkable residual ideology and offers it as an answer to a perception of contemporary decadence obviously does not form a logical and legitimate solution to the social and political problems which were being faced during the war. However, it does represent an understandable and strongly felt way in which people interacted with wartime conditions. The attempt by people to salvage what they could out of total war and to get on with their lives was mirrored by the political hegemony's use of these positive and resilient feelings to bolster the feelings of collectivity and patriotism that they sought to encourage.

What has been lost in the commentary of the Second World War that has grown out of the People's War discourse is the understanding that national, personal and political defeat was perceived to be, and actually was, a real possibility in wartime Britain. While the massive destruction and dislocation experienced during the war obviously had some positive aspects, such as the opportunity to rebuild so enthusiastically described in these novels, this has been allowed to obscure the negative elements of experience. The process by which the distressing and alienating experience of a sustained attack on individuals, family and friendship networks, and the buildings and social spaces within which life was conducted, has been obscured, is perhaps an understandable one. It is possible to argue that post-war culture has been complicit in the process of reclaiming the cultural legacy of the Second World War as something positive as a way of affirming and legitimizing the value of personal and social loss. This has had the effective of silencing voices which sought to articulate this loss and examine alternatives to it.

Participants in the war often would have found it difficult to register their concerns and complaints without running the risk of being seen as unpatriotic.

The apocalypse novel provides one possible forum for those grievances to be aired and solutions to be very tentatively suggested. The idea that the British people did not passively accept the onward march of Beveridge and Keynes throughout the war, but also searched for other solutions, should not be forgotten. That these solutions were never taken up is not a good enough reason for us to ignore that they once were offered as possibilities.

Chapter 15

Decadence and Transition in the Fiction of Antonio Tabucchi: a Reading of *Il filo dell'orizzonte*

Marina Spunta

With sixteen published fictional works since 1975 – among which are short and long novels, short stories, two plays for the theatre and a radio play – Antonio Tabucchi is among the most interesting and versatile fiction writers of the late twentieth century. Highly appreciated by readers, and increasingly studied by critics, his distinctive narrative universe conveys the uneasiness, ambiguities and uncertainties of the present period of transition. In this essay I will discuss the nature of decadence and transition of his fiction as postmodern features. My analysis will focus on the short novel *Il filo dell'orizzonte*,[1] and particularly on its abounding signs of decay, death and transition. I shall also consider the central metaphor of perspective, which is integral to the whole novel and which is used to explore the fallibility of the individual's point of view through a postmodern detective device.[2]

Moving from the idea of 'decadence' as a 'state of decaying, a decline from a superior state, standard, or time',[3] I will briefly reflect on decadent and postmodern modes, with a view to highlighting their common traits. Most literature on Decadentism underlines its diffidence for a positivist view of reality,

---

[1]   A. Tabucchi, *Il filo dell'orizzonte* (Milano: Feltrinelli, 1986), trans. Tim Parks as *Vanishing Point* (London: Vintage, 1991).

[2]   In 'the postmodern detective (antidetective novel) [. . .] formulaic expectations are elicited only to be deliberately frustrated or inverted', *The Cunning Craft – Original Essays on Detective Fiction Contemporary Literary Theory*, eds R.G. Walker and J.M. Frazer (Illinois: Western Illinois University, 1990), p. i. Tabucchi subverts the traditional detective device in *Il filo dell'orizzonte*, through metaphysics, as Spino's quest mingles with his own search for identity.

[3]   *The Chambers Concise Dictionary*, eds G.W. Davidson, M.A. Seaton and J. Simpson (Edinburgh: Chambers, 1988), p. 280. Decadent is also defined as: 'a process of falling away or declining from a prior state of excellence, vitality, prosperity', *Oxford English Dictionary*, eds J.A. Simpson and E.S.C. Weiner (Oxford: Clarendon Press, 1989), p. 318, as well as by the overtone of 'lacking in moral, physical or artistic vigour', *The Chambers 20th Century Concise Dictionary*, ed. E.M. Kirkpatrick (Edinburgh: Chambers, 1983), p. 321.

which builds on the paramount faith in a single truth and a solid, geometric notion of space and time. The process of taking apart positive categories causes a sense of angst which is not confined to the period historically labelled as 'Decadentism', but seems to recur at every decline of the century. Yet it is the end of the nineteenth century, Lyotard suggests, with its alterations of the rules for science, literature and the arts, that saw the birth of an underlying sense of decadence, still affecting the present age.[4] The decadent disruption, bringing to the surface the need for a totally new and evocative language, based on an acute sense of the individual, the subconscious and the unknown, results in an art falling back on the 'I', expressing weakness and lack of will, tension and disquiet. All of these traits, which inform many contemporary literary narratives, are central to the fiction of Tabucchi.

Postmodernism can easily be paralleled to the *fin-de-siècle* turbulence of the last century, in its taking apart the categories of modernism, thus continuing the process of disruption with an increased sense of self-awareness and irony. The shared sense of alienation in the relationship between the individual and society results in collapsing hierarchies, including the very existence of literary representation as a category. Its reflection in literature, according to Lucente, brings about a disruption in the narrative closure of the text, which becomes a process instead of a product, a combination of open-endedness and pastiche, fragmentation and 'citationality'.[5] On the same line, in our 'neo-baroque' period,[6] Calabrese detects a loss of wholeness, which is replaced by instability, change, multidimensionality and utter fragmentation.[7] As an ironic revisitation of the past, contemporary narrative builds on the sense of disquiet, transition, weakness and decay, through incessant hybridization. I will consider these parameters in my reading of *Il filo dell'orizzonte*, after introducing the author's view on contemporary literature and art according to the same traits.

The sense of disquiet resulting from a period of cultural transition is an essential ingredient in decadent and postmodern times, and a key to Tabucchi's fiction. The author develops this notion from Pessoa, the Portuguese modernist poet whom he has studied and made known in Italy. In the introduction to Maria José de Lancastre's translation of *Livro do desassossego* Tabucchi defines Pessoa's poetry as an everyday metaphysics, combining the sensitivity of

4   J.F. Lyotard, *La condition postmoderne* (Paris: Editions de Minuit, 1979).
5   G. Lucente, 'Modernism and Postmodernism. Contemporary Italian Fiction and Philosophy', *Annali d'italianistica* 9 (1995), 158–65.
6   O. Calabrese, *L'età neobarocca* (Bari: Laterza, 1987).
7   Similarly, Smyth lists the characters of postmodernism as discontinuity, indeterminacy, plurality, metafiction, heterogeneity, intertextuality, decentring, dislocation, games and alterity ('Introduction' to *Postmodernism*, ed. E. Smyth (London: Batsford, 1991), pp. 9–15 (p. 9).

modernist and decadent modes, which Il filo dell'orizzonte shares.[8] In Tabucchi's words:

> *l'ever-spleen day (la domenica ovviamente) in cui la metafisica si sfilaccia sul greto della quotidianità; la degustazione del Nulla giornaliero che produce un'inquietudine che investe l'universo; i falsi desideri, la notte, l'impossibilità, la solitudine, l'assenza del significato e l'ipertrofia del significante. Insomma, il Decadentismo. Ma a dirla così si tratta di una grossolana semplificazione. Il decadentismo, come il Romanticismo, è un contenitore di grande capienza, ci possono stare dentro comodamente anche Beckett e Montale.[9]*

> [the *ever-spleen day* – Sunday, of course – when metaphysics frays on everyday matters, the savouring of the daily Nothing causing a sense of disquiet which invests the whole universe, fake wishes, the night, impossibility, solitude, the absence of meaning and overabundance of signs. In a word: Decadentism! Yet, such a definition is a gross oversimplification. Decadentism, like Romanticism, is a big box which can easily fit in even Beckett and Montale.]

In conversation with Gaglianone and Cassini on the direction of contemporary novel, the author reflects on the artistic heritage of the twentieth century, with a view to its possible future developments.[10] The sense of imminent evil and transience of existence, resulting from what he claims to be this century's main disasters, the holocaust and the atomic bomb, is reflected in the author's commitment to depicting various forms of evil, as well as 'constructing some very disoriented characters', always 'assailed by gusts of wind'.[11] As the author tells Borsari in another interview: 'without writing an apology of disturbed literature I believe that the more disorientations there are, the better it is'.[12]

Similarly, in the discussion at the Conference in Leuven, the author voices the complexity, fragmentation and sense of absence that is characteristic of contemporary culture:

---

[8]   *Fernando Pessoa. Il libro dell'inquietudine*, intr. A. Tabucchi, ed. M.J. de Lancastre (Milano: Feltrinelli, 1986).

[9]   W. Geerts, 'Il filo dell'orizzonte di Antonio Tabucchi, una lettura della morte', in *Piccole finzioni con importanza*, eds N. Roelens and I. Lanslot (Ravenna: Longo, 1993), pp. 113–24, p. 114.

[10]   *Conversazione con Antonio Tabucchi*, eds P. Gaglianone and M. Cassini (Roma: Ómicron, 1995) (all the translations in square brackets are mine).

[11]   A. Botta, 'An interview with Antonio Tabucchi', *Contemporary Literature* 35, 3 (Fall 1994), 421–40, p. 430.

[12]   A. Borsari, 'Cos'è una vita se non viene raccontata? Conversazione con Antonio Tabucchi', *Italienisch* 13 (1991), p. 6, (*'senza fare l'apologia di una letteratura disturbata, credo che quanti più disturbi ci sono, tanto meglio è'*).

è molto difficile avere uno sguardo totalizzante, unitario su una realtà così
composita e complessa e direi anche piena di buchi come la nostra [. . .]
In questo mondo diventato assolutamente relativo anche la scrittura
diventa relativa e anche la rappresentazione della realtà diventa relativa.[13]

[an all-pervading, unified view on a reality such as ours, so complex and
full of gaps, is very difficult to obtain. [. . .] In this world, which has
become absolutely relative, even writing becomes relative, as well as the
representation of reality.]

From such a realization, it necessarily follows

l'incapacità di esprimere un giudizio forte sul reale, il bisogno di proporlo
come ipotesi, perchè forse a uno scrittore come me, in un momento storico
come il nostro, il reale può apparire del tutto ipotetico. [. . .] *Questo perchè*
nella letteratura odierna [. . .] *la chiarezza non si può fare e quindi*
andiamo a tentoni [*scrivendo una*] *diversa vicenda a seconda dei punti di*
vista.[14]

[the inability to express a strong judgement on reality, the need to present
it as an hypothesis, perhaps because reality can appear utterly hypothetical
to a writer like me, in a historical period such as ours. This is because
modern literature cannot create clarity, therefore we have to feel our way
and write a different story according to different points of view.]

A common denominator to the present sense of disquiet is the 'weakness' of
contemporary thought, according to Italian philosophers such as Gianni Vattimo,
reflecting at the same time the Italian situation of the 1980s, before the advent of
a 'strong' political and media leadership (which directly affects *Il filo
dell'orizzonte*, published in 1986). While realizing the lack of certainties of
contemporary society, this approach has nothing of the passive attitude, showing
instead many traits of a 'strong' and active outlook in the determination to
continue the search, despite the awareness of the target being unattainable. Linda
Hutcheon has interestingly defined it as a 'paradoxically potent weak thought',
whereby, as Renate Holub explains, the philosopher retains a strong presence, by
means of adhering to the traditional logic of cause and effect.[15] In portraying the

---

[13] 'Dibattito con Antonio Tabucchi', in *Piccole finzioni con importanza*, eds N.
Roelens and I. Lanslots (Ravenna: Longo, 1993), pp. 146–66, p. 155.
[14] A. Spinette, 'Incontro con Antonio Tabucchi', *Gli spazi della diversità, Atti del
convegno internazionale, Rinnovamento del codice narrativo in Italia dal 1945 al 1992*
(Roma: Bulzoni, 1995) II, pp. 651–68, p. 656.
[15] R. Holub, 'Weak Thought and Strong Ethics: the Postmodern and Feminist
Theory in Italy', *Annali d'italianistica* 9 (1995), 125–43, p. 133. 'Weak thought', she
claims, is at the same time modern and postmodern, as it is linked to the Italian tradition,
while extensively borrowing from foreign influences.

contradictions of the present period of transition and 'positive' decadence, Tabucchi still maintains the specific nature of Italian philosophical culture, in his interest in the hermeneutical and dialogical approach.

Tabucchi's dialogical inclination clearly emerges in the hybrid nature of his fiction, which mirrors the state of cultural transition of contemporary narrative. Among the major Italian interpreters of our times, both Calvino and Tabucchi continuously step out of their native culture to assume their 'adopted' French and Portuguese identities. This is both a decadent and postmodern trait, for the need to escape the present boundaries of space and time, such condition of 'otherness' could be a secret of their art, as well as of Italian literature in general: the ability to decentre an already very dispersed culture, which can only be grasped by further displacing oneself. The implosion of all boundaries between literary genres, one of the main characteristics of late twentieth-century Europe, determines the independence of literary texts from any labels, except that of 'narrative texts', which our author advocates.

Tabucchi's repeated use of the phrase 'narrative texts' underlines the high degree of hybridization of his fiction, while derogatively commenting on the miswritings of contemporary literature. In the above-cited interview with Gaglianone and Cassini, the author presents late twentieth-century fiction as being deserted by all the muses but one, ironically defined as an association, a trade union muse, perhaps somewhat lame.[16] This postmodern version of the mythic figure is comically pictured in the introduction of *I volatili del Beato Angelico* (*The Flying Creatures of Fra Angelico*),[17] a collection of prose works revolving around the question of perspective like *Il filo dell'orizzonte*. The subversion of categories of high and low, earthly and divine, which in the title story stages the comical encounter between Fra Giovanni (Fra Angelico) and a 'divine' bird, is introduced in the author's note to the novel, where he calls upon the muse figure of a lame chicken (*'pollo zoppo'*).[18] Contemporary literature, the author seems to imply, cannot aspire to a single truth anymore, but has to resort to the inspiration of a sick postmodern muse that can only suggest questions to be asked, riddles to be posed, puzzles to be left in the hands of the reader. Despite the vagueness and weakness of this position, leading to an increasingly self-centred and individual search, the quest the character undergoes is striking in its determination, as the secret of searching is in not finding.[19] The contemporary

---

[16] *Conversazione con Antonio Tabucchi*, pp. 11–12.

[17] Tabucchi, *I volatili del Beato Angelico* (Palermo: Sellerio, 1987), p. 10; trans. Tim Parks as *The Flying Creatures of Fra Angelico*, in *Vanishing Point* (London: Vintage, 1991).

[18] The image of the lame muse also serves the author to express his fear for the risk of globalization in the arts, which, in the worst outcome, becomes what he defines the 'plastic literature' of today (in *Conversazione con Antonio Tabucchi*, p. 15).

[19] 'Le secret de la Recherche c'est qu'on ne trouve pas' (F. Pessoa), in J.A. Seabra, *Fernando Pessoa ou le poétodrame* (Paris, José Corti, 1988), p. 7.

reader needs to make up for the 'lameness' of the present muse by means of their increasing empowerment with the task of finding their own truth in the text.

Having set the framework by discussing decadent and postmodern features common to our age, as the very author discusses in various interviews, I will now focus on the signs of decay and transition in *Il filo dell'orizzonte*. The first of Tabucchi's short novels, published in 1986 and translated into English in 1991, *Il filo dell'orizzonte* is an interesting instance of open narrative text. The novel is centred on the metaphor of seeing, common to much of Tabucchi's narrative (along with that of many of his contemporaries), particularly in the form of impaired seeing, clearly implying a state of intrinsic decay and malaise, as well as the inability to focus on one single truth. The very title postulates the centrality of the metaphor of vision and point of view, together with the basic notion of physical, temporal and cultural transition, affecting everything and everyone in the novel, but especially Spino, the protagonist. His quest for the identity of a dead young man who is delivered to him at the mortuary where he works, soon turns out to be a search for his very self, leading to no definite answer. As a 'reverse detective' story,[20] decadent in its abundance of signs of death, illness, past and decay, this novel can be considered a realistic and metaphysical picture of the constant instability of contemporary culture.

The metaphor of perspective needs here some further discussion as an intrinsic element of Tabucchi's fiction, which is considerably influenced by visual art in a broad sense. The 'edge of the horizon' (as the novel's title would be translated literally), the author explains in the end note, is a geometric place, which moves together with the observer, who bears it in his eyes.[21] Spino, the protagonist, like the Sephardi philosopher Spinoza to whom he declaredly owes his name,[22] is a modern version of the 'Wandering Jew', searching for rational explanations in a third dimension. Like Bernardo Soares, one of Pessoa's heteronyms, he is a man at the window who is learning to see.[23] The metaphor of the edge of the horizon is already evident in the visual resolution in the cover

---

[20] I use the term 'reverse detective' since the protagonist is increasingly compelled to search for his own identity rather than the cause of the boy's death.

[21] The author tried to distance himself from the subjectivity of this view by shifting the initial first person to a third person narrator, after following Calvino's advice.

[22] Baruch Spinoza spent his life trying to solve Cartesian dualism by means of a metaphysical principle (identifiable with God) that could guarantee rational order and individual freedom.

[23] The author nears B. Soares's '*desassossego*' to Rilke's disquiet: '*Io imparo a vedere. Non so perché tutto penetra in me più profondo e non rimane là dove, prima, aveva fine e svaniva. Ho un luogo interno che non conoscevo. Ora tutto va a finire là. Non so cosa vi accada*', in *Fernando Pessoa. Il libro dell'inquietudine*, p. 9 (from R.M. Rilke, *Die Aufzeichnungen des Malte Laurids Brigge*) [I'm learning to see. I don't know why everything falls more deeply into me and does not remain where before it came to an end and vanished. I have a place inside I didn't know. Now everything ends up there. I don't know what happens there.]

picture of the novel's Italian paperback edition – Hopper's *Room by the Sea* presenting an open door overlooking the open sea. The visual component of the paratext immediately places the reader in the same position as Spino, that is looking out, but also inside himself, while underlining the horizontal antithesis of earth/sea and sky, phenomenon and noumenon. In a different yet equivalent metaphor, in the English translation, Tim Parks favours the idea of '*vanishing point*', displacing binary oppositions by means of the metaphor of single focalization. This shift of perspectives is maintained in the graphic solution of the English cover in the form of De Chirico's *The Mystery and the Melancholy of the Street*, which conveys a 'metaphysical' view of a single vanishing point, a focused view. It is interesting to notice that in both pictures the actual vanishing point falls outside the frame, as if to suggest the idea of an unattainable target, an illusion. From the book's very cover, the novel appears as a study in perspective (the art to represent depth on a bi-dimensional surface) by staging Spino's attempt to come to grips with a third dimension, the metaphysics of the unknown.

The novel opens with a striking image of death, as the third-person narrator portrays the protagonist, Spino, during his night shift at the mortuary, while filing away dead bodies. The perfect automaticity and geometry of the filing system, which is described in detail, is soon disrupted by the enlarged shapes of the bodies that have not yet undergone autopsy. The attention to the obstructed mechanics of the drawers, while presenting a first sign of decay, anticipates Spino's obsessive concern for the 'mechanics of facts' (12)[24] (or better its misfunctional mechanics, a common theme in Tabucchi), as the protagonist takes up the role of the detective, after the case is soon filed by the police. The morgue, where the action originates, is a clear image of the 'store of life', as the narrator himself remarks. This variation on the metaphor of archives, recurring also in other works, is paralleled by the image of '*bamboloni*' (big dolls), referring to the corpses (1), and later to mannequins in the tailor's shop (45). Such an abundance of signs of decay and death sets the key and images of the whole novel, building towards a picture of a dead city, an underworld society. Among these inanimate presences, the protagonist eventually emerges as an equally impersonal absence, an 'impassible and objective' guardian, yet a sympathetic tutor ('*tutore*') (10). His quest for identity starts as he is unable to answer his own question on the actual distance between dead and living people.

Continuing on the same theme of decay, the outside scene is striking in terms of its physically declining environment: a worn-out city, almost certainly Genoa (where Tabucchi taught for some time at the local university), which lives on past glories and postpones measures of urbanistic reform. The author is clearly ironic with regard to 'this old part of town, otherwise referred to as the historic centre,

---

[24]　All the references to page numbers are drawn from the English translation of *Il filo dell'orizzonte* cited above.

[. . . which] grows more and more decrepit' (3). The city centre is in no better state, as

> *Qui invece è un'agonia diffusa, una lebbra lenta che ha invaso muri e case, la cui fatiscenza è sorniona e inarrestabile, come una condanna.*[25]

> Here in the centre, on the other hand, the agony is diffuse, a slow leprosy that has invaded walls and houses whose decay is stealthy and irreversible, like a death sentence.

The structures of the city and its inhabitants, with its mixture of pensioners, prostitutes and street vendors in 'damp, dark shops' (3) among other marginalized groups, evoke an atmosphere of a flourishing past that is now long gone, replaced by decadent modern examples of 'second-class humanity', such as drug-addicts. The opening chapter reaches the climax of decadence with an image of aggressive rats of nearly unimaginable size, which adds another suggestion of transition, in the form of the fantastic dimension, to the initial crude realism.

After the quasi-apocalyptic vision of the opening, the second chapter continues the description of the physical decay of the city, with its stairways worn by use and its 'pitted walls invaded by tufts of caper plants obscuring faded graffiti' of 'things from years gone by' (5). This 'untidy geometry' is paralleled by Spino's obsession with reading the meaning of every sign. Street names also contribute to multiplying the memories of transition and past. Windswept Lane (Vico Spazzavento) suggests the unstable condition of those who search, while Carbonari Lane (Vico dei Carbonari), carries associations of a clearly outdated job, together with an equally old-fashioned ideal of political unity. All these signs build up to create an oppressive sense of nostalgia and cosmic grief, as Spino feels the world's indifference to its inhabitants:

> *E allora lui ha sentito una stanchezza opprimente, come se gli pesasse sulle spalle la stanchezza di tutto ciò che lo circondava, è uscito nel cortile e ha sentito che anche il cortile era stanco, e le mura di quel vecchio ospedale erano stanche, e anche le finestre, e la città, e tutto; ha guardato in alto e gli è parso che anche le stelle fossero stanche, e ha desiderato che ci fosse un'eccezione per tutto ciò che è, come un differimento o una dimenticanza.*[26]

> At which Spino felt an oppressive tiredness, as though the exhaustion of everything around him were bearing down on his shoulders. He went outside and sensed that even the courtyard was tired, and the walls of this old hospital were tired, the windows too, and the city, and everything. He

---

[25]   Ibid., pp. 11 and 3.
[26]   Ibid., pp. 21 and 13.

looked up and had the impression that even the stars were tired, and he wished there were some escapes from this universal tiredness, some kind of postponement or forgetting.

The sense of decadence grows into a world image of loneliness and decay, as Spino realizes that:

quel morto a cui pensava non importava a nessuno, era una piccola morte nel grande ventre del mondo, un insignificante cadavere senza nome e senza storia, un detrito dell'architettura delle cose, un residuo.[27]

the dead man he was thinking of meant nothing to anybody; it was one small death in the huge belly of the world, an insignificant corpse with no name and no history, a waste fragment of the architecture of things, a scrap-end.

The narration continues in the pattern of clear transition from chapter to chapter, from a decaying external setting to the decadent interior of the *kitsch* Hungarian 'trattoria', linking past and present with the oneiric dimension. The metaphor of transition continues in the allegoric representations of disasters and miraculous interventions on the paintings of the village church, whose priest Spino has come to ask about the dead young man (who in the meantime has acquired the suggestive name of Carlo Nobodi). The church paintings are compared to tarots, suggesting chance as the theme of Spino's search, as his belief in the logic of the signs he encounters is soon defeated.

Like the 'formality and sadness' (43) of terraced houses built under fascism whose 'meagre, inert charm makes [them] feel almost unreal' (44), the series of characters Spino encounters on his quest, more functional to the plot than all-round protagonists, are all figures of the past, sharing elements of decadence, in the form of illness, tiredness and melancholia and in their various physical impairments in seeing. I will note just one example: Mr Faldini, the accountant, who has 'the face of someone who has spent his entire life addressing letters to distant countries while looking out across a landscape of derricks and containers' (48) and prefers to live in dreams, as 'belongings, [he claims] they're always so slippery [. . .] they move about, they even get the better of our memory' (51). Apart from these figures of 'mannequins', the characterization of Spino and Sara, and the portrayal of their relationship, best reflects the general decadent mode of the novel. Sara emerges as a plain character with her main function to induce Spino's reaction against the general inertia and nostalgic mood. She is immediately characterized as suffering from arthrosis, which causes her to be perpetually cold and to assume a regular posture of 'defence'. With her legs drawn in and her shoulders covered by a shawl, she appears as a picture of old

---

[27]   Ibid., pp. 35 and 24.

age, both physically and psychologically, given her nostalgia for an unachievable future, which is best conveyed by one of her few utterances: 'How nice it would be to get away [. . .] wouldn't it?' (6). Sara and Spino's relationship can easily be read as decadent in terms of its repetitiveness, its claustrophobic nature, its impregnation with death, and its displacement in the cinematic dimension, the only reality where they are happy and successful. As Geerts points out, every stage of their life is perceived as conclusive, offering no open perspective, as they find themselves in a permanent state of transition between a reminisced past and a dreamed future.[28] Their distinctive nostalgic mood stems from Tabucchi's favourite state of *saudade*, a Portuguese term indicating a sense of 'nostalgia' for both past and future, a kind of Dantesque *disio* and Baudlerian *spleen*.

The novel ends in an increasingly metaphysical mode, as things start coming together for Spino when he faces the epigraphs and the hyper-real statues in the cemetery. He finally organizes all the clues he has encountered in his quest on his own 'edge of the horizon', a washing line on his balcony on which he actually pins his drawn conclusions, bridging together the realms of the inside and the outside, the past and the present, fantasy and reality. In his final attempt to understand the mechanics of facts, which is also the most evident sign of his 'Hamlet-like' madness, he seems to win over chance by identifying with his other self and similarly presenting himself to his silent interlocutor, death. As with most postmodern detective stories, Spino's reverse search is left open, as he walks in the dark towards the sea.

In this reading of *Il filo dell'orizzonte* I have highlighted a number of decadent elements in the physical decay of the setting, which is reflected in the 'weakness' of its inhabitants, among whose presences Spino's quest tentatively advances. His disoriented state of failed life, both professionally and socially, caught in the unreal dimension of cinema, and between past memories and future dreams, is reversed by his determination to search for an unattainable all-encompassing truth, which leads him to experience a state of perpetual transition, ultimately bringing him to share the destiny of his alter-ego in his annihilation. Spino's state of change in his search for otherness is his drama of the present perfect, of '*l'essere stato*' (the state of having existed), as the epigraph from Jankelevitch recites. As a '*giallo* (detective story) *sui generis*', which, in the author's words, is perhaps 'the best way to ask questions today', the novel is an interesting realization of postmodern decadence in its playing with games of reversal and cultural transition of which Tabucchi is a master.

---

[28]   W. Geerts, in *Piccole finzioni con importanza*, p. 118.

Chapter 16

Beyond Decadence: Huysmans, Wilde, Baudrillard and Postmodern Culture

Nicholas Zurbrugg

To what extent can one identify parallels between the modernist and postmodern 'decadent' mentalities, and to what extent do these mentalities inhibit our understanding of technological cultural mutations? Pursuing this question still further, it seems evident that the blindspots of both modernist and postmodern 'decadent' mentalities inform and *deform* such seemingly quintessentially contemporary accounts of postmodern culture as the writings of Jean Baudrillard – or at least, do so up to those turning-points at which they advance 'beyond decadence', towards more pragmatic approaches to media culture.

Reconsidered with hindsight, the modernist 'decadent' mentality is perhaps best understood as a somewhat fearful, technophobic pathology preceding the more comprehensive cultural revolution brought about by the modernist technological *avant-garde*. In turn, the postmodern 'decadent' mentality ressurects a needlessly apprehensive mindset, preceding, and in many respects refusing, the still more comprehensive cultural revolution precipitated by such postmodern technological *avant-gardes* as the work of the video and computer artists of the last decades.

Some century after the last *fin de siècle*, most mainstream theoretical accounts of the early twentieth century now effortlessly jettison the myths of the late nineteenth century's decadent poetics, freely acknowledging the positive potential of the modernist 'cultural order'. By contrast, most mainstream and 'postmodern' theoretical accounts of the late twentieth century still complacently reflect the alarmist prejudices of the postmodern 'decadent' mindset, reflecting the positive potential of the postmodern 'cultural order'.

Defending James Joyce's *Work in Progress* in his essay 'Dante . . . Bruno. Vico . . . Joyce' (1929), Samuel Beckett memorably warned: 'Here is direction expression – pages and pages of it. And if you don't understand it, ladies and

Gentlemen, it is because you are too decadent to receive it.'[1] Judged by such standards, most contemporary accounts of postmodern culture are doubly 'decadent', both as mindsets still informed by the 'decadent' phase of the modernist mentality, and as sensibilities 'too decadent to receive' the affirmative creative of the late twentieth-century postmodern *avant-garde*. Certain key exceptions to this rule, such as the writings of Jean Baudrillard, fascinatingly refine – and then to some extent refute – the claims of such 'doubled' decadence.

But first let me define my general frames of reference. By 'modernist', I refer to the general cluster of cultural innovations associated with cultural modernism's responses to processes of social modernization during the period from the 1880s to the 1930s, and by 'postmodern' I refer to those more recent, ongoing cultural practices responding to the forces of social postmodernization from the 1930s to the present day. How, then, are these two cultural periods informed or animated by 'decadent' mentalities, and more particularly, by 'decadent' forms of creative and theoretical practice? As Renato Poggioli's *The Poets of Russia 1890–1930*, observes 'the modern idea of Decadence' is best defined in terms of those moments 'when the vision of impending catastrophe merges with the expectation that another culture will be built on its ruin'.[2]

This initial definition prompts three further hypotheses. Firstly, Poggioli argues that the decadent mentality reflects a dialectic of exhaustion and annunciation insofar as it witnesses both the end of an old regime and the birth of the kind of new mentality, new practices and new theoretical mindset that he associates with a subsequent 'cultural order'. In this respect,

> An old, tired and sophisticated society may at least in part turn the very object of its fears into objects of hope. The last heirs of a dying tradition may be willing to prepare the ground for the builders of another cultural order, who will be at once their successors and destroyers; the representatives of the series already closing may even delude themselves that they may become the first representatives of the series not yet begun.

But what kind of cultural rebirth does the decadent mentality envisage? According to Poggioli's second general hypothesis, new kinds of cultural innovation following the decadent artist's ecstatic agony are likely to be a hybrid of present and past values, or a compound of the now and the then. The decadent crisis, Poggioli suggests, inoculates or contaminates recently entropic traditions with the twin viruses of past and present discourse; with restorative 'shots', one might say, of antiquity and contemporaneity. Accordingly,

---

[1]   Samuel Beckett, 'Dante . . . Bruno. Vico . . . Joyce', in *Our Exagmination Round his Factification for Incamination of Work in Progress* (1929) (London: Faber and Faber, 1972), p. 13.
[2]   Renato Poggioli, *The Poets of Russia 1890–1930* (Cambridge, Massachussetts: Harvard UP, 1980), p. 80

> Modern Decadence derives its essence and meaning from the antinomy of
> such contrasting concepts as civilization and barbarism, from the very
> antithesis of the ideas of decay and re-birth. This implies the fusion, as
> well as the cleaving, of the old and the new . . . [3]

Poggioli's third general hypothesis proposes that the Decadent mentality's
simultaneous appeal to old and new values effects a curious fusion of old and new
values, both displacing the empire of recently rejected orthodoxies, and at the
same time neutralizing the general sense of crisis peculiar to what one might
think of as the initial panic mode of the Decadent mentality. As Poggioli explains:

> The final outcome of such a rift is the reconciliation within the Decadent
> outlook of two extremes which at first sight seem to deny equally the
> Decadent principle, even though from contrary ends. These two extremes
> are the opposite cultural polarities generally named primitivism and
> modernism.[4]

Poggioli's distinctions can perhaps be developed still further, particularly in terms
of his claim that the Decadent artist's critique of 'a dying tradition' implies
commitment to 'another culture [. . .] built on its ruin'. What exactly does
Poggioli mean by 'another culture'? And in what ways might the 'last heirs of a
dying tradition' be said to substantially 'prepare the ground for the builders of
another cultural order'?

If Decadent art merely reinvigorates ailing orthodoxies with homeopathic
injections of 'primitivism and modernism', then in many respects it does not so
much build 'another' culture 'on' the ruins of the present (thereby adding to the
present), as build an aesthetically bricollaged alternative to present cultural ruin
from the ruins and the energies of the present, and *from* the ruins and the energies
of the past. Such art certainly effects a 'reconciliation' and 'fusion' of available
materials but, as Poggioli hints, while the makers of this kind of aesthetic
bricollage may see themselves as 'the first representatives of the series not yet
begun', their efforts at best perhaps merely 'prepare the ground for the builders
of another cultural order', rather than inaugurating any distinctively new cultural
order.

Indeed, as Poggioli observes, the decadent mentality's strategies for
distancing itself from preceding 'cultural orders' simultaneously isolate and
inhibit its proponents from active commitment to those still more radical
'builders of another cultural order' whom he distinguishes as both 'successors' to
and 'destroyers' of their decadent precursors. Firstly, as Poggioli notes, the
decadent artist's commitment to aestheticism 'implies the supremacy of art, on
the one hand over nature, and on the other, over life'.

---

[3]   Ibid., pp. 80–81.

[4]   Ibid., p. 81.

More generally, decadent tendencies prompt the cult of 'artificiality' and the impulse 'to fashion life after the pattern of art'. More generally still, they prompt attitudes of *nihilism*, with its 'rejection of ethos and conscience' and its 'indifference and apathy'; of *hedonism*, with 'its exaltation of pathos and the senses'; of *immoralism*, or the idea that 'there is a tie between beauty and evil'; of *extreme individualism*, or the 'religion of the creative personality'; and of *amoralism*, or the refusal 'to choose between foul and fair'.[5] For Poggioli, then, 'the task of Decadence', consists firstly in 'a denial of culture' (or the assertion of an entropic culture's ruin), and secondly, in a kind of re-cultivation of – or from – such ruins, in terms of what he calls 'a culture of negation, a flower of both evil and ill'.[6]

As Poggioli implies, the Decadent mentality is perhaps most interesting as a symptom of moments of crucial transition between cultural orders; moments of anguished aesthetic adolescence, one might say, between intolerable past orthodoxies and a sense of 'no future', or at least of no clear future. Considered in such terms, both the modern and the postmodern decadent mentalities advantageously close the door upon stagnant intellectual and cultural traditions, but disadvantageously obscure those new doors opening upon subsequent creative innovation inaugurating examples of genuinely 'modern' or 'postmodern' cultural orders.

Comparison of early modernist responses to the trauma of social modernization, and early postmodern responses to the trauma of social postmodernization, reveal surprisingly similar solutions to surprisingly similar complaints. In each instance one confronts clear examples of the classic symptoms that Poggioli attributes to the decadent dilemma; a celebration of creative individualism – or at least, a celebration of poetically inflected theory, increasingly informed by a turn from social and natural reality to the domain of art, artifice and simulation; and by subsequent impulses towards nihilism, hedonism, immoralism and amoralism.

Both the modernist and the postmodern decadent mentalities denigrate mass values, mass culture and mass-media, and both mentalities usually retreat from the 'now' of social and technological innovation, to vaguely defined variants of an imaginary 'then', far away from the dynamics of disturbing technological and cultural change. Briefly, both modern and postmodern decadent mentalities frequently evince a kind of conceptual agoraphobia, or a fear of new and unfamiliar open spaces (especially new technological open spaces), and tend to retreat to imaginary or artificial delights, in order to evade the perils of more threatening, more impoverished, or perhaps, more enthralling forms of nouvelle cultural cuisine.

---

5   Ibid., p. 84–6.
6   Ibid., p. 88.

Paradoxically, the central arguments of writers such as Mallarmé, Huysmans, Baudelaire, Pater and Wilde not only fairly predictably confirm the general accuracy of Poggioli's diagnoses of the modernist decadent mindset, but also rather unexpectedly suggest the curiously *modernist* decadent quality of many of the pillars of allegedly *postmodern* theory. In this respect, reconsideration of the modernist decadent mindset of the 1890s frequently illuminates the surprisingly old-fashioned *poetic rationale* informing many of those writings allegedly affording the most revolutionary exegeses of the 1990s.

As Mallarmé indicates in his essay 'Crisis in Poetry' (1895), one of the most striking features of the modernist decadent imagination is its alchemical ambition to transform base materials into magical essences. Describing his poetic ambition as a quest for the 'true condition' of 'free and individual' expression, Mallarmé complains that 'Languages are imperfect because [. . .] the supreme language is still missing', and proposes that, 'The ideal would be a reasonable number of words stretched beneath our mastering glance, arranged in enduring figures, and followed by silence'.[7]

With this ideal in mind, Mallarmé places language in 'two different categories'; 'first for vulgar or immediate, second, for essential purposes', and argues that if 'Language, in the hands of the mob, leads to the same facility and directness as does money', language in the poet's hands 'is tuned, above all, to dream and song'.[8] Accordingly such qualities arise from 'evocation, allusion, suggestion' as opposed to logical 'description', and offer 'the magic charm of art', 'beyond the book itself', in the realm of 'Spirit' and 'universal musicality'.[9] Finally aligning himself with 'The decadent or Mystic School', Mallarmé concludes that poetry should commemorate 'the suggestiveness of things' by establishing 'a careful relationship between two images, from which a third element [. . .] will be distilled and caught by our imagination', thereby revealing poetic 'essence in all purity'.[10]

Making similar distinctions between vulgar and poetic reality, Des Esseintes, the hero of Huysmans' *Against Nature* (1884), deplores 'the tyranny of commerce with its narrow-minded, venal ideas', sensing that it is 'all over now' as 'waves of human mediocrity' threaten Paris with 'the negation of all honesty, the destruction of all art', as though 'America' were 'transported to the continent of Europe'.[11] Withdrawing 'further and further from reality and above all from the society of his day, which he regarded with ever-growing horror', Des Esseintes shuns 'as far as possible pictures and books whose subjects were confined to

---

[7]   Stéphane Mallarmé, 'Crisis in Verse' (1895), in ed. William W. Austin, *Debussy's Prelude to 'The Afternoon of a Faun'* (New York: Norton: 1970), p. 118.

[8]   Ibid., p. 122.

[9]   Ibid., p. 120.

[10]   Ibid., pp. 120 and 122.

[11]   Joris-Karl Huysmans, *Against Nature* (1884), trans. Robert Baldick (Harmondsworth: Penguin, 1968), pp. 217, 219 and 218.

modern life', and seeks 'intellectual friendship' with earlier writers sharing 'a state of mind analogous to his own'.[12] In turn, astutely diagnosing the consequences of the decadent artist's retreat from the mediocrities of modernity, Huysmans' narrator comments:

> The fact is that when the period in which a man of talent is condemned to live is dull and stupid, the artist is haunted, perhaps unknown to himself, by a nostalgic yearning for another age.
>
> Unable to attune himself [. . .] to his environment [. . .] he bursts out of the prison of his century and roams about at liberty in another period, with which, as a crowning illusion, he imagines he would have been more in accord.
>
> In some cases there is a return to past ages, to vanished civilizations, to dead centuries; in others there is a pursuit of dream and fantasy . . .[13]

What seems most striking here is the emphasis upon the predominantly retrospective quality of the decadent imagination, an imagination which either travels back in time, or, as the narrator of *Against Nature* subsequently remarks, dwells upon artificial paradises and paradoxes.

> As a matter of fact, artifice was considered by Des Esseintes to be the distinctive mark of human genius.
>
> Nature, he used to say, has had her day . . .
>
> There can be no shadow of doubt that [. . .] the time has surely come for artifice to take her place whenever possible.[14]

Yet at the same time, *Against Nature* ends with a kind of apocalyptic agnostic prayer, both asserting and regretting the loss of past illumination, and one discovers an almost subliminal nostalgia for spiritual value in Des Esseintes's final utterance:

> Lord, take pity on the Christian who doubts, on the unbeliever who would fain believe, on the galley-slave of life who puts out to sea alone, in the night, beneath a firmament no longer lit by the consoling beacon-fires of the ancient-hope! [15]

---

12   Ibid., pp. 180 and 181
13   Ibid., pp. 181–2.
14   Ibid., pp. 36–7.
15   Ibid., p. 220.

Baudelaire's *Intimate Journals* similarly equate the decadence of late nineteenth century Paris with the impact of mechanical progress and the increasing 'coarseness of [. . .] perceptions' deriving from the materialism of the American mentality.[16] 'So far will machinery have Americanized us', Baudelaire writes, 'so far will Progress have atrophied in us all that is spiritual.'[17] Like many other critics of social modernization, Baudelaire condemns the bombardment of media culture, or what we might now think of as *paparazzi* culture, regretting that:

> It is impossible to glance through any newspaper [. . .] without finding on every line the most frightful traces of human perversity, together with the most astonishing boasts of [. . .] charity, and [. . .] the progress of civilization.

> Every journal, from the first line to the last, is nothing but a tissue of horrors [. . .] an orgy of universal atrocity. [18]

Yet despite these complaints, Baudelaire also identifies a certain distinctive poetry within modern life, remarking in his essay on 'The painter of Modern Life' (1859), that modernity evinces the 'mysterious beauty' of 'the transient, the fleeting, the contingent', qualities which he finds particularly evident in 'the dress of the day'.[19] It is with this distinction in mind that Baudelaire praises dandies as 'a new kind of aristocracy' evincing 'the last flicker of heroism in decadent ages'.[20] For Baudelaire, dandies are 'the last champions of human pride', in an age levelled by 'the rising tide of democracy, which spreads everywhere and reduces everything to the same level'.[21] Dandies, Baudelaire claims, 'all share the same characteristic of opposition and revolt, of that need, which is rare in the modern generation, to combat and destroy triviality'.

Employing similarly apocalyptic imagery to Huysmans' evocation of a *fin de siècle* 'no longer lit by the consoling beacon-fires of ancient hope', Baudelaire finally characterizes 'Dandyism' as something 'like a setting sun; like the declining star, it is magnificent, without heat and full of melancholy'.[22] Opposing a society that has 'lost sight of the notion of the differences that mark [. . .] the physical and the moral worlds, the natural and the supernatural',[23] the dandy's

---

[16] Charles Baudelaire, *Intimate Journals*, trans. Christopher Isherwood (Hollywood: Marcel Rodd, 1947), p. 58.

[17] Ibid, p. 56.

[18] Ibid., p. 101.

[19] Charles Baudelaire, *Selected Writings on Art and Literature*, trans. P.E. Charvet (London: Penguin, 1992), p. 403.

[20] Ibid., p. 421.

[21] Ibid., p. 422.

[22] Ibid., pp. 421–2.

[23] Ibid., p. 121.

contrived composure, Baudelaire implies, reflects an attitude 'close to spirituality and to stoicism'.[24]

Walter Pater's *Studies in the History of the Renaissance* (1873) offers yet another alternative to the 'stereotyped world' of superficial perception. Defining essential reality as variants of 'exquisite passion' transcending 'theory, or idea, or system',[25] Pater proposes that art should register 'the highest quality' of moments of 'quickened, multiplied consciousness', 'as they pass', and 'simply for those moments' sake'.[26] Dismissing the 'flood of external objects' offering 'unstable, flickering, inconsistent' impressions, Pater commends the more lasting 'stirring of the senses' of 'strange dyes, strange flowers, and curious odours, or work of the artist's hands, or the face of one's friend'.[27] Once again, the decadent sensibility prioritizes the 'strange', the 'aesthetic', as well as signs of interpersonal communication, cultivating those sensations from a more or less familiar world which also afford a greater intensity than habitual experience.

Taking Pater's argument one step further, Wilde's *Intentions* (1891) argues that culture 'at the close of this wonderful age' is at once 'too cultured and too critical, too intellectually subtle and too curious of exquisite pleasures' to consider any other value system than that of art.[28] Contending that 'religious ecstasy is out of date', and that 'To be good according to the vulgar standard of goodness' merely requires 'a certain lack of imaginative thought', Wilde concludes that 'Aesthetics are higher than ethics', and that 'a colour-sense is more important in the development of an individual, than a sense of right and wrong', insofar as it is 'through Art only, that we can shield ourselves from the sordid perils of actual existence'.[29] Here too, the decadent mentality retreats from 'actual' existence to 'aesthetic' existence; from the realm of vulgar 'goodness' to the realm of those 'exquisite pleasures' made available by imaginative thought.

As the first stanzas of Wilde's 'Les Ballons' (1885) and 'Symphony in Yellow' (1889) suggest,[30] his articulations of this ideal culminate in a curiously atemporal, partially oriental, partially impressionist, poetics, transforming modernity into pre-modernity, as omnibuses transmute into butterflies, and balloons transmute into 'satin' moons and 'silken' butterflies; a poetics of artifice and simulation sharing Des Esseintes's enthusiasm for the 'copy', 'almost miraculously executed in indiarubber and wire, calico and taffeta, paper and

[24]   Ibid., p. 420.

[25]   Walter Pater, *Studies in the History of the Renaissance* (1973), in ed. Gordon S. Haeight, *The Portable Victorian Reader* (Harmondsworth: Penguin, 1972), p. 631.

[26]   Ibid., p. 632.

[27]   Ibid., pp. 629–31.

[28]   Oscar Wilde, *Intentions* (1891), in *Plays, Prose Writings and Poems* (London: Dent, 1965), p. 41.

[29]   Ibid., p. 63.

[30]   Oscar Wilde, 'Les Ballons' (1885) and 'Symphony in Yellow' (1889), in ed. Edward Engelberg, *The Symbolist Poem* (New York: Dutton, 1967), pp. 236–7.

velvet'.[31] 'Les Ballons' and 'Symphony in Yellow' respectively begin:

> Against these turbid turquoise skies
> The light and luminous balloons
> Dip and drift like satin moons
> Drift like silken butterflies;

and:

> An omnibus across the bridge
> Crawls like a yellow butterfly,
> And, here and there, a passer-by
> Shows like a little restless midge.

In both stanzas urban reality is transformed into fanciful ornamentation; into a timeless, pre-modern iconography, light years away from the self-consciously contemporary variants of 'the transient, the fleeting, the contingent', that Baudelaire associates with the experience of 'Modernity'.[32]

But even Baudelaire's city poems perhaps only partially prepare the way for what Poggioli might call the truly modernist cultural order explored by subsequent, far more radical modernist artists such as the Italian Futurist leader, Marinetti, whose manifestos both denigrate the symbolist aesthetic of the decadent poets and celebrate the new-world machine culture deplored by Baudelaire. Marinetti's *War, the World's Only Hygiene* (1911–15), for example, triumphantly declares: 'today we hate our glorious intellectual fathers [. . .] the grand Symbolist geniuses', explaining:

> Our Symbolist fathers had a passion that we consider ridiculous: a passion
> for eternal things, a desire for immortal, imperishable masterworks. [. . .]
> To the tears of beauty brooding tenderly over tombs, we oppose the keen,
> cutting profile of the pilot, the chauffeur, the aviator. [. . .] We cooperate
> with Machines in destroying the old poetry of distance and wild solitudes
> . . .[33]

In somewhat the same way, Marinetti's manifesto 'The Variety Theater' (1913) celebrates new kinds of performance, 'born as we are from electricity' and 'lucky in having no tradition' which, he proposes, should: 'In every way encourage the type of the eccentric American, the impression he gives of exciting grotesquerie, of frightening dynamism [. . .] (making) [. . .] the world's face

---

[31] Huysmans, *Against Nature*, p. 97.

[32] Baudelaire, *Selected Writings on Art and Literature*, p. 403.

[33] F.T. Marinetti, *War, the World's Only Hygiene* (1911–15), *Selected Writings*, trans. R.W. Flint and Arthur A. Coppotelli, ed. R.W. Flint (London: Secker and Warburg, 1972), pp. 66–7.

young again.'[34] Dismissing the decadent mentality's symbolist aesthetic, embracing social modernity, envisaging social and cultural modernity as inseparable mutually sustaining forces, and anticipating many of the aspirations of postmodern multimedia art, such Futurist manifestos boldly enunciate the new technological 'cultural order' of modernism.

To be sure, many of Marinetti's projects remained unrealized for half a century until subsequent technological innovations allowed their realization. But as Walter Benjamin observes in his essay on 'The Work of Art in the Age of Mechanical Reproduction' (1936),[35] the most vital energies of modernist culture frequently share this quality of precocious prescience. Indeed, reconsidered from the mid-1930s, the apparent 'extravagances and crudities' of such heroic modernist *avant-gardes* as Futurism and Dadaism could be re-evaluated as aspirations to 'effects which could be fully obtained only with a changed technical standard, that is to say in a new art form'. Put very simply, whereas the *fin de siècle* or decadent modernist mentality breaks away from realism, but rebounds backwards from techno-modernism, subsequent more radical modernist movements such as Futurism and Dadaism break into techno-modernism, and, as Benjamin argues, anticipate new effects attainable only with the new technologies of techno-postmodernism.

At this point, we may now consider the surprising similarities between the decadent mentalities of the 1890s and of the 1990s, particularly in terms of certain striking correspondences between the writings of Mallarmé, Huysmans and Baudelaire and Jean Baudrillard – the postmodern theorist whose writings perhaps most clearly suggest the overlaps between these two technophobic responses to cultural revolution. Like Mallarmé, Huysmans and Baudelaire (and like any number of other recent cultural theorists deploring the 'postmodern condition') Baudrillard appears convinced of the incompatibility between technology and poetic utterance. His essays in *The Perfect Crime* (1995), for example, repeatedly assert that new forms of technology typify a conspiracy to neutralize the vitality of radical thought:

> They are trying to persuade us that technology will inevitably produce good [. . .] They are trying to wipe out all the supernatural reflexes of thought . . .[36]

Like the modernist decadent poets before him, Baudrillard contrasts the negative impact of new technologies 'extirpating all the magic from thought', with language's positive capacity to generate a vaguely defined quality of 'magic',

---

[34] F. T. Marinetti, 'The Variety Theater' (1913), ibid., pp. 116 and 121.

[35] Walter Benjamin, 'The Work of Art in the Age of Mechanical Reproduction', in *Illuminations*, trans. Harry Zohn, (Glasgow: Collins, 1979), p. 239.

[36] Jean Baudrillard, *The Perfect Crime* (1995), trans. Chris Turner (London: Verso: 1997), p. 18.

and, in an interview of 1983, he characteristically explains that he feels most fulfilled when able to 'cause' provocative arguments to exist by a more or less alchemical process:

> At a given moment [. . .] you cause things to exist, not by producing them in the material sense of the term, but by defying them, by confronting them. Then at that moment it's magic.[37]

But like many modernist 'decadent' poets, Baudrillard seems persuaded that new technologies will neutralize the 'supernatural' and that 'magic' itself is now gradually becoming extinct. For example, somewhat as Baudelaire suggests that the dandy's stoicism evinces a 'last flicker' of heroism, and might be likened to a 'setting sun' or a 'declining star' – to an entropic force which still seems 'magnificent' but which is now 'without heat', Baudrillard discusses his concept of 'the scintillation of being' in similarly apocalyptic terms. Asked in an interview of 1993 whether this term implied confidence in the possibility of positive revelation, Baudrillard revealingly replied:

> I use the term 'scintillation' in terms of the way that it is used with reference to stars – for very different stars which perhaps have died, but which still seem to scintillate or shine. In other words, there are two alternatives, there seems to be light, but perhaps there isn't any light, and perhaps it's just an apparition.[38]

Like Wilde's wittiest writings, Baudrillard's finest paragraphs frequently refine elegantly apocalyptic paradox. For example, somewhat as Wilde posits that 'We cannot go back to the saint. There is far more to be learned from the sinner',[39] Baudrillard proposes that 'Since it is no longer possible to base any claim on one's own existence, there is nothing for it but to perform an *appearing act* without concerning oneself with *being* – or even with *being seen*'.[40]

On other occasions, Baudrillard's phrasing elegantly emulates the apocalyptic extravagance of both his modernist masters and such early postmodern precursors as Samuel Beckett. If Huysmans' Des Esseintes (like Beckett's Estragon)[41] posits

---

[37] Jean Baudrillard, 'The Power of Reversibility That Exists In The Fatal' (1983), interview with D. Guillemot and D. Soutif, *Baudrillard Live: Selected Interviews*, trans. Mike Gane and G. Salemohamed, ed. Mike Gane (London: Routledge, 1993), p. 44.

[38] Jean Baudrillard, 'The Ecstasy of Photography' (1993), interview with Nicholas Zurbrugg, trans. Nicholas Zurbrugg, in ed. Nicholas Zurbrugg, *Jean Baudrillard: Art and Artefact* (London: Sage, 1997), p. 41.

[39] Wilde, *Intentions*, p. 41.

[40] Baudrillard, *The Transparency of Evil* (1990), trans. James Benedict (London: Verso, 1993), p. 23.

[41] See Samuel Beckett, *Waiting for Godot* (1956; London: Faber and Faber, 1977), which begins with Estragon's complaint 'Nothing to be done', p. 9.

that 'there was nothing to be done, nothing whatever, that it was all over',[42] Baudrillard argues that: 'The maximum in intensity lies behind us; the minimum in passion and intellectual inspiration lie before us'.[43]

Nevertheless, like modernism's decadent poets (and to a large extent, like Beckett), Baudrillard finally places his aesthetic confidence in his capacity to re-orchestrate and re-energize available language in order to effect what he calls 'the resolution of the infelicity of meaning by the felicity of language'. So far as Baudrillard is concerned, content, or ideas, are far less important than felicitous or magical form. Accordingly, *The Perfect Crime* advises:

> As for ideas, everyone has them. More than they need. What counts is the poetic singularity of analysis. That alone can justify writing, not the wretched critical objectivity of ideas. There never will be any resolving the contradictoriness of ideas except in the energy and felicity of language.[44]

Clearly then, Baudrillard's general poetics and the underlying technophobia of his most influential writings share many of the less attractive traits of the modernist decadent mentality. But this is not the whole story. Fascinatingly illustrating the rather more illuminating process of what Beckett called 'a great mind in the throes',[45] Baudrillard's most recent writings increasingly manifest what one might think of as a 'post-decadent' flexibility, both reassessing his initial unqualified dismissal of contemporary media culture, and reaffirming the validity of the (r)evolutionary techno-poetics enunciated by modernism's historical *avant-gardes* and consolidated by the video art and computer art *avant-gardes* of the postmodern decades. Introducing this shift of perspective in an interview of 1993, Baudrillard memorably observes,

> Yes, of course, I offer a very critical account of technology and of technology's impact on the world. I'm not the only one to do this – everyone speaks of technology in this way. But now [. . .] I'm beginning to formulate another hypothesis [. . .] Let's say that the rather critical or pejorative vision of technology represents a first position. Now, from a second position, I'm more interested in seeing technology as an instrument of magic . . .
>
> Up to now I think that technology has been analyzed in too realistic a way. Accordingly, it has been typecast as a medium of alienation and

---

[42]   Huysmans, *Against Nature*, p. 219.
[43]   Jean Baudrillard, 'The Anorexic Ruins', trans. David Antal, in eds Dieter Kamper and Christoph Wulf, *Looking Back at the End of the World* (New York: Semiotext(e), 1989), p. 40.
[44]   Baudrillard, *The Perfect Crime*, p. 103.
[45]   Beckett, Samuel, 'Proust in Pieces', review of Albert Feuillerat's *Comment Proust a composé son Roman*, *The Spectator*, 22 June 1934, p. 915.

depersonalization [. . .] But I now sense that a sort of reversal of focus is taking place [. . .] it's also necessary to identify another form of analysis – a more subtle form of analysis . . .[46]

As these lines indicate, Baudrillard still invokes those cultural practices which most interest him as variants of 'magic' rather than offering them more specific terminology. Contemporary cultural theory, one discovers, often confronts contemporary cultural practices with the most general and most metaphorical 'theory tales', and more specific insights into the dynamics of multimedia culture are best sought in the work of contemporary practitioners, such as Doug Hall and Sally Jo Fifer's anthology *Illuminating Video: An Essential Guide to Video Art* (1990), or Bill Viola's *Reasons for Knocking on an Empty House, Writings 1973–1994* (1995),[47] rather than in academia's misreadings of the present *fin de siècle*'s media culture.

That most accounts of postmodern culture still experience 'delay' in addressing present technological practices typifies the extent to which mainstream cultural theory and postmodern cultural theory remain substantially blinkered by the 'decadent' mentality. As the following diagram suggests, striking parallels inform both the synchronic and diachronic phases of modernist and postmodernist culture as they slowly evolve from techno-denegration to techno-celebration.

---

[46]   Baudrillard, 'The Ecstasy of Photography', *Jean Baudrillard: Art and Artefact*, pp. 38–9.
[47]   Doug Hall and Sally Jo Fifer, eds, *Illuminating Video: An Essential Guide to Video Art* (New York: Aperture, 1990); Bill Viola, *Reasons for Knocking at an Empty House, Writings 1973–1994* (Cambridge, Mass.: MIT Press, 1995).

19th-century realist mentality	Mid-20th-century late modernist mentality
1880s Early social modernization	1930s Early social postmodernization
Fin de siècle decadent mentality (Mallarmé, Baudelaire, Huysmans, Wilde, etc.)	Mid-20th-century decadent mentality (Baudrillard, etc.)
(Technophobia and cult of artificial and exotic)	(Technophobia and cult of artificial and exotic)
Early modernist symbolist aesthetic ('magic')	Early postmodern symbolist aesthetic ('magic')
Pre-First World War Mature modernist mentality and (r)evolution of techno-*avant-gardes* (Futurism, Dadaism)	Post-1950s Mature postmodern mentality and (r)evolution of techno-*avant-gardes* (video/computer art)
Post-First World War/1930s Delayed critical recognition of the modernist techno-*avant-garde*'s 'new demands'	1960s–1970s–1980s Delayed critical recognition of postmodern techno-*avant-garde*'s 'new demands'

Chapter 17

Translation: Decadence or Survival of the Original?

Amir Ali Nojoumian

This paper is a comparative study of the ideas of translation and the original text in the writings of Walter Benjamin and Jacques Derrida in order to explicate the curious relation of the original to the translation and ask the following question: does translation help towards developing the 'kinship of languages', giving the original an after-life and enabling it to survive, or does it instead 'kill' the original and substitute it with a decayed text?

The traditional view of language contends that translation is a decadent act since it corrupts the pure 'innocence'[1] of the original language. This widely accepted view has its roots in Greek thought and religious traditions. For instance, Herder believed that when a text guards itself from all translations it retains its vital innocence.[2] This exemplifies the long-standing religious and mystical perspective George Steiner refers to as 'seeking to protect the holy texts from traduction'.[3] The mystical text seeks to protect itself from translation by inscribing itself as irreducibly singular. Like Rousseau's account of the 'origin of languages', the mystical is situated in an essentially undivided point of linguistic 'innocence'.

I would argue that we need to re-read the postulate of 'translation as decadence' in the light of Walter Benjamin's theory of language. I choose Benjamin's argument for three reasons. Firstly, because Benjamin's writings on the theory of language and translation have been seminal in many respects and after more than eighty years have not lost their importance in the discussions of literary theory. Secondly, I would argue that Benjamin's text inaugurates a new status to the act of translation as I will show. Thirdly, I would argue that Derrida's theory of translation and meaning is greatly indebted to the thought of Benjamin. In fact,

---

[1]   See George Steiner, *After Babel: Aspects of Language and Translation*, 2nd edn (Oxford: OUP, 1992), p. 82. 'Innocence' is a term Steiner uses to suggest the original uncorrupted status of language.

[2]   Johann Gottfried Herder (1744–1803) contends that thought and language are inseparable in that a study of culture and thought should always return to language. He also argues that all languages have a common root.

[3]   Steiner, *After Babel*, p. 82.

this study is the first attempt to create a stronger correspondence between
Benjamin's postulate and Derrida's ideas on the notion of translation.

Benjamin, in his 1923 essay 'The Task of the Translator', in brief argues that
the translator's task can be even more significant than the role of the writer of the
original text. He believes that the translator, through the decayed barriers of his
own language, releases 'the pure language'. The translator, in his view, liberates
the language imprisoned in a work in his re-creation of that work.[4] Benjamin
compares the process of translation and poetic writing when he writes: 'The
intention of the poet is spontaneous, primary, graphic; that of the translator is
derivative, ultimate, ideational. For the great motif of integrating many tongues
into one true language is at work.'[5] For him, the 'task' of the translator is far more
important than, and different from, that of the poet:

> It is the task of the translator to release in his own language that pure
> language which is under the spell of another, to liberate the language
> imprisoned in a work in his re-creation of that work. For the sake of pure
> language he breaks through decayed barriers of his own language.[6]

Therefore, I would argue that Benjamin overturns the hierarchy and views the
original text, as well as the translated text, as overcoming the 'decayed barriers'
of the respective languages as a means of both survival and revival. As Benjamin
says, '[i]n translation the original rises into a higher and purer linguistic air, as it
were'.[7] Before I explain this thesis in detail and draw conclusions through
Derrida's reading, I shall put forward an outline of Benjamin's general
understanding of translation theory.

In order to outline Benjamin's thought regarding the translation, we need to
return to the story of Genesis. Genesis is indeed the story of language as well as
the creation of the world. Three of the main events ('narratives') in Genesis point
to three stages in the theological history of language: (a) man's act of naming or
appellation; (b) the tree of knowledge and man's fall from Eden; and (c) the tower
of Babel and the dispersion of both man *and* language. It is indeed through re-
reading Genesis that Benjamin gives the term 'translation' other significations of
transference (apart from its immediate references such as translation among
multiple languages and translation within a single language in its different
stages). Benjamin sees a process of translation in the way things created by God
enter into man's vocabulary in the shape of naming (appellation). He calls
'naming' the first stage in the story of language and regards 'name' as the

---

    4   Walter Benjamin, 'The Task of the Translator', in *Illuminations*, trans. Harry
Zohn (1955; London: Fontana/Collins, 1982), p. 80.
    5   Ibid., pp. 76–7.
    6   Ibid., p. 80.
    7   Ibid., p. 75.

'original language' or 'pure language' (a recurrent phrase throughout his work).[8] He then sees a second stage of transference from the realm of names into the realm of knowledge through his reading of the story of the 'tree of knowledge'. At this stage, for Benjamin, language declines to become a tool to affect ideas giving them 'value' and 'judgement'.

Benjamin in his 1916 paper, 'On Language as Such and on the Language of Man', argues that language starts to *mediate* after the fall. It becomes a means of communicating, a mere sign. This in turn lays the foundation for the plurality of languages reflected in the story of Babel. Man having 'injured the purity of name'[9] turns away from the contemplation of 'things' that are the basic concepts and natural objects created by God in Genesis and named by man:

> *Signs* must become confused where things are entangled. The enslavement of language in prattle is joined by the enslavement of things in folly almost as its inevitable consequence. In this turning away from things, which was enslavement, the plan for the tower of Babel came into being, and linguistic confusion with it.[10]

Benjamin's notion of the multiplicity of language and language as a means or sign are important background ideas for a study of his theory of translation, because, for Benjamin, the loss of the original is the very emblem of decadence, which translation in a sense resists and reverses. Here, I use Jacques Derrida's outline of Benjamin's views towards translation, as later I shall place Benjamin's theory in the context of Derrida's postulate concerning translation. According to Derrida, Benjamin believes that in translation neither *reception*, nor *communication*, nor *representation* or *reproduction* is intended.[11] Derrida, here, points to and challenges three widely accepted criteria of translation – reception, communication and representation – that I will now go on to clarify in more detail.

Benjamin, at the very beginning of 'The Task of the Translator', claims that a work of art is not intended for the reader: 'In the appreciation of a work of art or an art form, consideration of the receiver never proves fruitful. [. . .] No poem is intended for the reader, no picture for the beholder, no symphony for the

---

8   At this time in the biblical context, language is not thought of as communicative. Instead of this, meaning is immanent and pure. It is only after the Fall that language starts to adopt a communicative function.

9   Walter Benjamin, 'On Language as Such and on the Language of Man', in *One-Way Street and Other Writings*, trans. Edmund Jephcott and Kingsley Shorter (London: Verso, 1985), p. 120.

10   Benjamin, 'On Language as Such and on the Language of Man', p. 121.

11   Jacques Derrida, 'Des Tours de Babel', trans. Joseph F. Graham, in ed. Joseph F. Graham, *Difference in Translation* (Ithaca and London: Cornell University Press, 1985), p. 180.

listener'.[12] Thus, he initially problematizes both the notions of *reception* and *communication*. Benjamin, in the same paragraph, also states that even the concept of an 'ideal' receiver is detrimental.[13] Therefore, I would argue that what Benjamin criticizes about the concept of reception is the *singularity* of intention and communication. In other words, if a work of art is intended to create a single communicative relationship with its audience, its horizon of meanings and interpretations will be channelled and therefore it dies. In Benjamin's view, the original text is, therefore, beyond communication.

Now, if we accept that a literary text is not intended towards reception and therefore communication, what happens when it is translated? Benjamin claims that both reception and communication are not happening in the translating process, either. In translation, while we see a struggle to channel the meaning process of the original, what remains is a 'complementary' process between two languages. In other words, the two languages affect one another. The first language intrudes into the second one and the second language rephrases the language of the original text. This reciprocal relation points towards 'kinship' or the 'complementary' characteristic of languages. This is part of the process whereby translation counteracts the decadence of pure language because of the Fall. I will return to this later in more detail.

The final point about Benjamin's thought on translation is that *representation*, or *reproduction*, is not intended in translation. To understand this point, we need to return to the notion of mimesis. Benjamin believes that likeness should not be the final goal of the translator. It has been argued repeatedly in the history of translation theory that translation cannot achieve likeness simply because it is impossible, even in one single language.[14] Benjamin is not interested in the possibility of this act; rather he is interested in the idea that the translator should achieve something much higher. Benjamin's postulates concerning the notion of mimesis in relation to the original and the act of translation seem to be contradictory. While Benjamin argues for mimesis in some places, he stages a critique of mimesis in his other writings. For instance, in his 1933 paper, 'On the Mimetic Faculty', Benjamin argues that 'language may be seen as the highest level of mimetic behaviour'.[15] Andrew Benjamin, in his 'Walter Benjamin and the Translator's Task', distinguishes the relation between the word and the representation from that of the translation and the original:

---

12 Benjamin, 'The Task of the Translator', p. 69.
13 Ibid.
14 As an example Shelly argues that the 'curse of Babel' makes the act of translation impossible; Susan Bassnett, *Translation Studies*, revised edn (London and New York: Routledge, 1991), p. 67. See Bassnett, *Translation Studies*, p. 29 for more examples.
15 Walter Benjamin, 'On the Mimetic Faculty', in *One-Way Street and Other Writings* (London: Verso, 1985), p. 163.

> For Benjamin mimesis refers to what he calls 'non-sensuous similarity' between language and what is signified. It is not however the case that the relationship posited between language and the signified is the same as the relationship between the translation and the original. The difference between the 'mode of intention' and the 'intended object' can be understood in mimetic terms, the relationship between the translation and the original cannot.[16]

In the mimetic representation of things, Walter Benjamin postulates a 'non-sensuous' relationship between the word and the representation. By contrast, the relationship between a translation and its original operates on the basis of the intimate and reciprocal exchange of self and other. This relation is not that of 'likeness'. Instead, in structural terms, the process is analogous to the relation of 'kinship'.[17] 'Kinship of languages' is the concluding statement in Benjamin's theory of translation and the starting point for the argument of this paper. In 'The Task of the Translator', Benjamin argues that there is a complementary process in operation between the translation and the original text. In other words, he claims that the translation instead of rendering meaning, communicating something, or resembling the meaning of the original, should make the original and the translation recognizable as 'fragments' of a greater language.[18] For Benjamin, translation expresses the intimate relation among languages; it 'reflects the great longing for linguistic complementation'.[19] A good translator 'touches lightly'[20] on the poetic elements of the original text and 'promises a kingdom to the reconciliation of languages' towards the 'language of the truth'.[21] A good translation is a transference of language so that the original can be kept alive. The original, if sealed off, will effectively die, since its language cannot act in an interplay with the broad realm of 'original language'. Benjamin believes that 'Languages are not strangers to one another, but are, a priori and apart from all historical relationships, interrelated in what they want to express'.[22]

Translation, in Benjamin's view, unfolds the inexplicable essence of language and brings that essence back to language.[23] Therefore, as Benjamin contends, to

---

16   Andrew Benjamin, 'Walter Benjamin and the Translator's Task', in *Translation and the Nature of Philosophy* (London and New York: Routledge, 1989), p. 186.

17   In 'The Task of the Translator', Benjamin writes: 'Translation thus ultimately serves the purpose of expressing the central reciprocal relationship between languages.' This is the 'central kinship of languages'(p. 72).

18   Ibid., p. 78.

19   Ibid., p. 79.

20   Ibid., p. 80.

21   Derrida, 'Des Tours de Babel', p. 200.

22   Benjamin, 'The Task of the Translator', p. 72.

23   Hent de Vries, 'Anti-Babel: The "Mystical Postulate" in Benjamin, de Certeau and Derrida', *Modern Language Notes* 107, 3 (April 1992), p. 456.

say that a translation reads as if it had originally been written in the second ('target') language is not a high praise: 'A real translation is transparent; it does not cover the original, does not block its light, but allows the pure language, as though reinforced by its own medium, to shine upon the original all the more fully.'[24] In other words, Benjamin says that the original should not and could not affect the translation in a mimetic gesture. It is the translation that should be affected by the original.[25] For Benjamin, a good translation, instead of domesticating the original language into the second language, in fact gives a 'foreign' sense to the second language: 'the basic error of the translator is that he preserves the state in which his own language happens to be instead of allowing his language to be powerfully affected by the foreign tongue'.[26]

Derrida and the paradox of decadence and survival

It is now necessary to clarify Derrida's point of departure from Benjamin while arguing that Derrida's account is more closely allied to Benjamin's theory than the theories of the other post-structuralists.[27] Derrida in fact takes two main themes from Benjamin's essay and gives these terms a more generalized meaning: Derrida examines the notions of the 'kinship of languages' and 'survival' in the act of translation and then situates them within his new definition of the 'text'. Whereas Benjamin regards translation as a univocal performance, one that reveals true meaning, Derrida in fact criticizes this idea as a 'metaphysical' attempt. In his view, a metaphysical way of thinking first distinguishes and privileges the 'signified' over the 'signifier' in a text assuming the signifier as the vehicle for the signified. For him, translation is impossible if we want to transfer the 'sense' of the original text, simply because there is no single 'sense' in the text. Thus if translation stabilizes the text, then the text will die. And it is here that we find a connection between Benjamin's theories and

---

24   Benjamin, 'The Task of the Translator', p. 79.
25   Ibid., pp. 80–81.
26   Ibid., p. 81.
27   A very different attitudes towards translation is expressed by Paul de Man, who provides a 'deconstructive' reading of Benjamin's theory. Despite his philosophy of negation towards 'the original', de Man takes the translation to be a failure. He believes that the translator could never achieve what the original text does. Any translation is always secondary in relation to the original and the translator has lost the game from the very beginning. De Man thinks that 'translation', as performed in a general sense in 'critical philosophy' or 'literary theory', kills 'the original by discovering that the original was already dead'. In fact, de Man, by taking the 'translation' as a kind of 'reading', reiterates his understanding of deconstruction as a form of reading of the text which is found to be always already disarticulated and alienated. See Paul de Man, 'Conclusions: Walter Benjamin's "The Task of the Translator"', in *The Resistance to Theory* (Minneapolis: University of Minnesota Press, 1986), p. 84.

Derrida's deconstruction of metaphysics. As we saw, for Benjamin, translations create a reciprocal relationship among languages towards the 'greater language'. Derrida, however, does not subscribe to the notion of totality in language. He sees a limiting force at work upon language when the translator in effect reduces the meaning of the text to a singular interpretation.[28] For instance, in his book, *Dissemination*, he argues that translators have missed one 'sense' of the double bind of *pharmakon*.[29] On a more general level, they have also ignored one aspect of the paradox of 'writing' as *pharmakon*:

> All translations into languages that are the heirs and depositories of western metaphysics thus produce on the *pharmakon* an *effect of analysis* that violently destroys it, reduces it to one of its simple elements by interpreting it, paradoxically, in the light of the ulterior developments that it itself has made possible.[30]

In other words, subsequent versions permit and encourage an analysis of the former text that reduces it to some simple message or possible meaning that it seemed to contain, thereby preventing other potential meanings from ever emerging. However, Derrida simultaneously takes an opposite turn and acknowledges Benjamin's findings when stating that every *inevitable* translation always helps a text to 'live on', provoking new 'senses' within the original text.[31]

Derrida, then, destabilizes the text, seeing it as a multiplying phenomenon. Though not believing in the notion of an 'origin' or a 'true' language in the 'beginning', Derrida nevertheless sees a mutual indebtedness between the translation and the original text. The original demands translations and the translation is an 'origin' for re-translations: 'the structure of the original is marked by the requirement to be translated. [. . .] The original is the first debtor,

---

[28] Derrida always returns to the texts which are written in more than one single language or texts in which more than one language is implicated. He explains how any translation betrays the text even if the target language is the same as one of the languages embedded in the original text. For in this case the significance of the presence of that language will be effaced ('Des Tours de Babel', p. 171).

[29] *'Pharmakon'* is a Greek term used in Plato's *Phaedrus* that means both 'poison' and 'remedy' or 'cure'. Derrida argues that both these senses of the word are in operation in the text. Therefore, writing becomes both poison and cure, 'on the one hand, a threat to the living presence of authentic (spoken) language, on the other an indispensable means for anyone who wants to record, transmit or somehow commemorate that presence'; Christopher Norris, *Derrida* (London: Fontana Press, 1987), pp. 37–8.

[30] Jacques Derrida, *Dissemination* (London: Athlone Press, 1993), p. 99.

[31] I would like here to make a personal observation and suggest that there are two existing movements in two opposite directions when translating a text. First, the original, a text which can be engaged in the infinite process of 'reading', is being univocalized through translation into a closed form (the translated text). This is in contrast to Derrida's argument that translation is a multiplying performance. In fact, it is in the act of reading the translation that the reader can turn this closed form into more possible 'readings'.

the first practitioner; it begins by lacking and by pleading for translation.'[32] Derrida relates this to the position of God and the Shem – the builders of the tower of Babel. There, it is not only the 'translators' – the builders – who strive to 'found a universal tongue translating itself by itself; it also constrains the deconstructor of the tower: in giving his name, God also appealed to translation'.[33] And this is why Derrida argues that, for Benjamin, translation is guaranteed in 'the thought of God' as a debt.[34]

In short, Derrida does not subscribe to the possibility or impossibility of translation. Derrida believes that if we can transfer the sense of the original work into the translation, we have already chosen one sense among many other senses of the original text. As a result, the translation of the original becomes impossible if this means retaining multiple possibilities of meaning. However, Derrida does not see this as the task of the translator. For him, the translator only helps in multiplying the senses of the original. If the translator attempts to unify the senses, this is not called translation in Derrida's terms. A translation that grants a unitary original sense to the text as if it has a single meaning deep inside is a contradiction in terms. It declares the untranslatability while pretends to be a translation itself. If a unique single meaning in fact exists within the text how can the translator claim that it can be repeated?

I would argue that Derrida sees translation as inevitable, instead, in the sense

---

[32]   Derrida, 'Des Tours de Babel', p. 184.

[33]   Ibid., p. 184. At this point, it is necessary to give a brief discussion of Derrida's reading of the story of Babel as emblematic of the act of translation. Derrida argues that man in his endeavour to 'make a name of himself' (Genesis 11: 4) tries to regain the lost glory in paradise. But God destroys the tower and man's aspiration to 'touch the heavens' (Genesis 11:4) becomes frustrated. The Babel incident multiplies the number of languages among man and therefore creates more distance between the language of man and God's Word. This movement in the two falls of language (the fall of man from paradise and later the fall of Babel) makes translation more and more necessary and impossible.

In other words, God chooses a proper name for the tower, Babel, yet simultaneously by destroying the tower creates the very need for translation by multiplying languages. To Derrida, the story of Babel is 'an epigraph for all discussions of translation' (*The Ear of the Other*, p. 100) and hints to the internal limits and aporias of translation, and more generally of language. Derrida argues that God imposes a double command in the Babel story: translate me and don't translate me. He concludes that every proper name (that part of language which is untranslatable and unique, which Derrida calls an 'outcast' of language) is caught in this dilemma: respect me as a proper name yet also preserve me within the universal language – i.e. translate me into the reiterable realm of common noun (*The Ear of the Other*, p. 102). Derrida's answer to 'how can a proper name be translated?' ('Living On / Border Lines', p. 143–4) is that a proper name, an outcast of language, *cannot be translated* in a conventional essentialist sense but *should only be translated* in the post-structuralist sense of redefinition of the singular proper name, in order for it to survive and this consequently makes the proper name a common noun ('Des Tours de Babel', p. 172). He concludes that translation therefore becomes a necessity and an impossibility ('Des Tours de Babel', p. 170).

[34]   Jacques Derrida, 'Des Tours de Babel', p. 182.

that the translation preserves the multiple meanings of the original text and in turn demands more translations to create more multiple meanings. Translation as interpretation makes every text prone to multiple translations, none more authoritative than the other, but the texts demand translation as it is the secret to their survival. Single authoritative translation is like non-translation. This totalizing approach which claims to protect the text from 'misreadings' will in effect kill the text.

But do Benjamin, Derrida and de Man agree on the possibility of re-translations? The answer to this question will reveal further differences between their views. De Man reminds us that, for Benjamin, while the original asks for translation, the translation of the translation is impossible:

> That the original was not purely canonical is clear from the fact that it demands translation; it cannot be definitive since it can be translated. But you cannot, says Benjamin, translate the translation; once you have a translation you cannot translate it any more. You can translate only an original.[35]

Benjamin maintains that 'translation, ironically, transplants the original into a more definitive realm since it can no longer be displaced by a secondary rendering'.[36] In other words, a good translation does not fix or restore the 'original' meaning (if there is any) but it strives to preserve the ambivalent nature of the meaning of the original in the translated text. Therefore, for Benjamin, translations themselves are untranslatable 'because of the looseness with which meaning attaches to them'.[37]

Derrida, in contrast to Benjamin, thinks that re-translations are possible and even necessary. The notion of 'iterability' which is repeated in different forms in Derrida's texts points to the same theory. For instance, 'the proper name', 'the signature', and 'the postcard' are all caught in the same paradox of the necessary repetition of a singular event. For Derrida, translation as a form of reading and interpretation (and indeed repetition) needs to be repeated since every reading is a signifier for later readings. (I will return to this below when I discuss Derrida's theory of the 'text'.)

I would point out that this position is justified even in the light of de Man's theory. As I discussed above, de Man argues that translation kills and stabilizes the original. I would argue that stabilizing the original will make the re-translation even more possible, simply because it is much easier to interpret (or translate) based on a definitive 'stabilized' text with a single meaning. On the other hand, if every translation is only one of the many readings of the original,

---

[35] De Man, 'Conclusions: Walter Benjamin's "The Task of the Translator"', p. 82.

[36] Benjamin, 'The Task of the Translator', p. 75.

[37] Ibid., p. 81.

any single reading can result in re-readings. To Benjamin and Derrida, this is the secret to 'the survival' of the text.

Translation as the survival of the original

Benjamin believes that the original can have an afterlife only if it becomes translated. Therefore, for Benjamin, translation helps the original to overcome the forces of decay. The original undergoes 'a maturing process', 'a transformation', and 'a renewal' when being translated.[38] Derrida, I believe, elaborates and generalizes this point in many of his writings.

In 'Des Tours de Babel', Derrida writes that Benjamin sees the task of the translator as 'to redeem in his own tongue that pure language exiled in the foreign tongue, to liberate by transposing this pure language captive in the work'.[39] Derrida concludes from this remark that, for Benjamin, translation is a poetic transposition that liberates the 'pure language'. It does not render the meaning of the original but extends the body of languages and puts languages into symbolic expression. Eventually, the translation and the original complement each other to form a larger tongue in the course of a 'sur-vival' that changes them both. The translated text, like a child, is not simply a product of reproduction; it becomes bigger, and complements its original parent text.[40]

The relationship of the original to the translation is like the relationship of life to survival.[41] Elsewhere, Derrida says, for Benjamin, 'the structure of the original text is survival', what he calls 'uberleben'.[42] The word 'uberleben' means 'to live beyond your own death in a sense'.[43] Therefore translation seeks to exhibit its own possibility, and not just communicate meaning which 'is subjected to a permanent "drifting"'.[44] Since the original 'lives on and transforms itself'[45] and engages in an act of 'postmaturation',[46] the translation does not and should not copy or provide restitution for an original but rather becomes a moment in 'the holy growth of the original'.[47]

In order to grasp fully what the process of 'survival' and 'living on' is according to Derrida's thought, it is necessary to examine the essay 'Living On /

---

[38]   Benjamin, 'The Task of the Translator', p. 73.
[39]   Derrida, 'Des Tours de Babel', p. 188.
[40]   Ibid., pp. 189–91.
[41]   Ibid., p. 182.
[42]   Jacques Derrida, *The Ear of the Other – Otobiography, Transference, Translation: Texts and Discussions with Jacques Derrida*, ed. Christie McDonald, trans. Peggy Kamuf (Lincoln and London: University of Nebraska Press, 1988), p. 121.
[43]   De Man, 'Conclusions: Walter Benjamin's "The Task of the Translator"', p. 85.
[44]   De Vries, p. 474.
[45]   Derrida, 'Des Tours de Babel', p. 188.
[46]   Ibid., p. 183.
[47]   Ibid.

Border Lines' in which this idea is elaborated. The essay opens with an account of the signification of the term 'text' in Derrida's thought. 'Text' in Derrida's terminology has a distinct significance. It is widely claimed that deconstruction argues that the 'text' is a piece of writing in which the process of signification does not take place. In contrast, the text is a space with multiplying significations. Derrida argues that a text is not a closed entity. He therefore problematizes the boundaries of the text – boundaries such as 'the supposed end and beginning of a work, the unity of a corpus, the title, the margins, the signature, the referential realm outside the frame, and so forth'.[48] The text multiplies and 'overruns' all the limits. It is no longer

> a finished corpus of writing, some content enclosed in a book or its margins, but a differential network, a fabric of traces referring endlessly to something other than itself, to other differential traces. Thus the text overruns all the limits assigned to it so far (not submerging or drowning them in an undifferentiated homogeneity, but rather making them more complex, dividing and multiplying strokes and lines) . . .[49]

The text is not totally absent or present. It is caught in a suspended life-in-death state. It is simultaneously translatable and untranslatable and this is how Derrida relates the concept of translation to the notion of 'survival':

> A text lives only if it lives on {sur-vit}, and it lives on only if it is at once translatable and untranslatable. [. . .] Totally translatable, it disappears as a text, as writing, as a body of language {langue}. Totally untranslatable, even within what is believed to be one language, it dies immediately. Thus triumphant translation is neither the life nor the death of the text, only or already its living on, its life after life, its life after death.[50]

Derrida, then, relates the notion of 'survival' to 'living on'. He asserts that the term 'survivre' or 'living on' does not mean maintaining oneself in a 'life-less' state. For him, it is rather a case of arresting the process of decaying and dying.[51] What is happening in a text to make it live on is that 'one text reads another' or, in other words, a text translates another one.[52] For 'each "text" is a machine with multiple reading heads for other texts'.[53]

Interestingly Derrida presents the same paradoxical argument elsewhere but replaces 'survival' with 'meaning'. In his view, the process of signification is only

---

48   Jacques Derrida, 'Living On / Border Lines', trans. James Hullbert, in eds Harold Bloom et al., *Deconstruction and Criticism* (London and Henley: Routledge & Kegan Paul, 1979), pp. 83–4.
49   Ibid.
50   Ibid., 102–3.
51   Ibid., p. 107.
52   Ibid., p. 147.
53   Ibid., p. 107.

possible when we face a text in which language is acting in a two-way movement from translatability to untranslatability. For him, 'understanding is no longer possible when there are only proper names, and understanding is no longer possible when there are no longer proper names'.[54]

In a roundtable on the question of translation and Benjamin, Derrida recapitulates his reading of Benjamin's theory of language. He speaks of a 'mutual contract' between the translation and the original in general terms. The translation and the original not only demand one another and suspend each other's decay but they also enable language to survive through this symbiotic relationship. Derrida, in short, translates/redeems Benjamin's theory from a discourse of metaphysics while maintaining distance from de Man's negative deconstruction:

> Translation augments and modifies the original, which, insofar as it is living on, never ceases to be transformed and to grow. It modifies the original even as it also modifies the translating language. This process – transforming the original as well as the translation – is the translation contract between the original and the translating text. In this contract it is a question of neither representation nor communication; rather, the contract is destined to assure a survival, not only of a corpus or a text or an author but of language.[55]

Translation brings 'the past' to 'life'. However, for Derrida, translation *remains* a 'promise'. The story of translation is the story of that 'kingdom' which is at once 'promised and forbidden where the languages will be reconciled and fulfilled'.[56]

---

[54] Derrida, 'Des Tours de Babel', p. 167.
[55] Derrida, *The Ear of the Other*, p. 122.
[56] Derrida, 'Des Tours de Babel', p. 191.

Chapter 18

The Decadent University: Narratives of Decay and the Future of Higher Education

Mark Rawlinson

'Almost single-handedly, the professors [. . .] have destroyed the university as a centre of learning and have desolated higher education, which no longer is higher or much of an education.'[1] In the past decade, populist jeremiads like this one by Charles Sykes have portrayed a US higher-education system ruined by 'tenured radicals', affirmative action, political correctness, multiculturalist curricula and research-obsessed professors absenting themselves from the classroom, with standards falling as fast as charges rise.[2] The accusation that the university is a 'sclerotic and even decadent'[3] institution has provoked a high-profile public debate the terms of which reflect both the advanced state of the economic and demographic development of American higher education, and the weakening of its boundaries. However, it has only intermittently registered the real conditions of most of the system's 3,000 institutions and 600,000 faculty. The scale and diversity of post-secondary education is at once a measure of extraordinary success, and of the internal and external forces which have transformed conceptions of the university. In Britain, the relatively belated and underfunded expansion to a mass system confronts us with different questions about the size and function of the academic profession. Growth has been accompanied by a largely unreflective commitment to homogeneity of institutional function (in

---

[1]   Charles J. Sykes, *ProfScam: Professors and the Demise of Higher Education* (New York: St Martin's, 1990), p. 4.

[2]   See, for instance, Dinesh D'Sousa, *Illiberal Education: The Politics of Race and Sex on Campus* (New York: Free Press, 1991); Roger Kimball, *Tenured Radicals: How Politics Has Corrupted our Higher Education* (New York: HarperCollins, 1990); Allan Bloom, *The Closing of the American Mind: How Higher Education Has Failed Democracy* (New York: Simon and Schuster, 1987); Lynne V. Cheney, *Tyrannical Machines: A Report on Educational Practices Gone Wrong and Our Best Hopes for Setting Them Right* (Washington DC, 1990); Robert Hughes, *Culture of Complaint* (New York: OUP, 1993).

[3]   'Preface to the Issue "The American Academic Profession"', *Daedalus* 126, 4 (Fall 1997), p. vii.

contrast to the greater explicitness of the stratification of US higher education). The vaunted democratization of access to the cultural and economic capital associated with the title 'university' – for students, teachers and researchers, and institutions alike – reinforces traditional values while putting those values under stress.

At the turn of the century Britain had fourteen universities with 20,000 students. By the time of the expansionist Robbins report (1963) there were around 20,000 academic staff in twenty-four institutions.[4] Three quarters of today's universities have been established since then: '[a]lmost everything about higher education – system, institutions, students – is new'.[5] The emergence of the 'system' was made possible by the post-war concept of large-scale central government financing of higher education, a perspective which needs to be kept in mind when reflecting on levels of funding since the late 1970s. Perceptions of change, I will suggest, are regulated by narratives of decline. They are complicated and contradictory because that to which decadence is ascribed is at once of long standing ('the idea itself of the university' is the most important legacy of the medieval foundations)[6] and contemporaneously emergent (the university system).

It is no accident that David Damrosch opens his recent diagnosis of the failure of the university as community with a reading of a classic *fin-de-siècle* text, *Jude the Obscure* (*We Scholars* in fact takes its title from Nietzsche's 1886 reflections on the threat of specialization to thought). In Hardy's novel Jude's conclusion that his scholarly aspirations are too early is balanced by the speculation that his son's generation are too late. Father Time's suicide is a metonym of an incipient decadence, a 'universal wish not to live'. Damrosch contends that this 'archetype of modern youth has proved to be the type of the modern *scholar*': the isolating tendencies of disciplinarity have stifled scholarly community. The decadence of the university is registered here in the correlation of an exponential proliferation of knowledge production and the 'eclipse of genuine intellectual life'.[7] Institutional values and structures reproduce the isolation which tempts academics to desire an end to academic life, a wish confirmed by more than half of the respondents to a recent AUT survey: 'if they had the chance to start afresh, [. . .they] would choose a different profession'.[8] Damrosch cites Father Time's laconic suicide note to suggest a connection between the growth of the academic profession and the behaviour and beliefs of its members. But a different emphasis

---

4 A.H. Halsey, *The Decline of Donnish Dominion: The British Academic Profession in the Twentieth Century* (Oxford: OUP, 1992), p. 62.

5 Peter Scott, *The Meanings of Mass Higher Education* (Buckingham: SHRE and Open University Press, 1995), p. 11.

6 Peter Scott, *The Crisis of the University* (London: Croom Helm, 1984), p. 26.

7 David Damrosch, *We Scholars: Changing the Culture of the University* (Cambridge, Mass.: Harvard University Press, 1995), pp. 1–3.

8 *The Independent*, 30 April 1998, *Education +*, p. 2.

– '*Done* because we are too menny' – raises a more controversial perspective. Is the university done, finished, because there are too many of us? Has the post-war economic and demographic development of the university sector brought about the ruin of its functions and character, and a radical discontinuity in its history?

In the discourses of Marxist-Leninism, Nazism, or British Francophobia, the ascription of decadence is denunciatory, a form of 'political or social abuse'.[9] The US higher-education debate has frequently collapsed into unreflective oppositional name-calling, and exhibits a proclivity to characterize disagreement as conflict. Academics, retaliating against neo-conservative ideology and policy in books with titles like *Beyond the Culture Wars*, *Loose Canons*, *PC Wars* and most recently Lillian S. Robinson's *In the Canon's Mouth: Dispatches from the Culture Wars*, are not immune to this rhetoric.[10] It has turned inter-faculty incommunicado into warmongering, for instance where controversy over the constructionist or relativistic claims of the sociology of science is verbally escalated into 'science wars' between postmodernists in the humanities and laboratory-based researchers.[11] The rigid binarism of these conflictual structures belies the complexity of the late twentieth-century university. Drawing a line between science and the rest of the university is a defensive response to boundary weakening, for instance the fact that scientific research is not predominantly located in the university.[12] We might ask whether or not the sociological and hermeneutic critique of scientific method (a monolithic projection of that critique) reflects nostalgia for the conditions of the university prior to the explosion of scientific research funding by state and industry.

The ascription of decadence often involves temporal comparison; it diagnoses a state of decay or decline or falling off from an anterior condition of excellence,

---

9 Robert M. Adams, *Decadent Societies* (Berkeley, Calif.: North Point Press, 1983), p. 1.

10 Gerald Graff, *Beyond the Culture Wars: How Teaching the Conflicts can Revitalize American Education* (New York: Norton, 1992); Henry Louis Gates, Loose Canons: Notes on the Culture Wars (New York: OUP, 1992); Jeffrey Williams, ed., *PC Wars: Politics and Theory in the Academy* (New York and London: Routledge, 1995).

11 See Paul R. Gross and Norman Levitt, *Higher Superstition: The Academic Left and Its Quarrels with Science* (Baltimore, MD: Johns Hopkins University Press, 1994); Paul R. Gross, Norman Levitt and Martin W. Lewis, *The Flight from Science and Reason* (New York: New York Academy of Sciences, 1997); Christopher Norris, *New Idols of the Cave* (Manchester: Manchester University Press, 1997). For the latest public instalment, see the adversary reactions to Alan Sokal's unmarked parody of theoretical writing in the humanities from *Social Text* 46/47 (1996), more broadly disseminated in the 'two-cultures' rhetoric of the reception of Alan Sokal and Jean Bricmont, *Impostures Intellectuelles* (Paris: Editions Odile Jacob, 1997)/*Intellectual Impostures* (London: Profile Books, 1998).

12 Jay S. Labinger, 'The Science Wars and the Future of the Academic Profession', *Daedalus* 126, 4 (Fall, 1997), p. 202; Roger L. Geiger, 'Science and the University', in eds John Kriege and Dominique Pestre, *Science in the Twentieth Century* (Amsterdam: Harwood Academic, 1997), p. 159.

vitality, prosperity.[13] To speak of decadence is to invoke both new conditions and notions of tradition or of ancestry, though the comparison is almost invariably an incomplete one. This asymmetry is reflected in the anecdotal character of much that is written to promote images of the decadent university, notably a preoccupation with localized and short-term phenomena.[14] But living and working in the university creates both long- and short-term indentifications. The university has been described as the second oldest institution with a continuous history in the Western world, but that history is also an aggregation of diverse accommodations with the universities' social, economic and political environments.[15] The image of the decadent university draws on an often profoundly unhistorical consciousness of change and tradition, making it a potent professional and anti-professional myth, and an apt starting point for assaying the impact of concepts of the temporality of the university on current thinking about higher education.

The discrepancy between ideas of the university and the practical conditions of academic work is a source of both vitality and inertia. Whether self-consciously or not, academics (traditionally the non-transitory fraction of the university community) reproduce accommodations and dissonances between concepts of higher learning and the reality of their institutions and their locations within them. Despite Oxbridge's declining numerical significance in British higher education this century (from 1900 to 1971 its proportion of staff and students fell, respectively, from 40 per cent to less than 10 per cent, and from 32 per cent to around 12 per cent, a pattern accelerated dramatically in the last twenty-five years), it continues to dominate the system as a model.[16] But the conceptual power of ideas of the university is not coincident with their (compromised) incarnation in the most prestigious national institutions. Not only are the leading institutions sites of struggle to transcend local conditions of failure and accommodation, but their hegemony produces contestation as well as mimicry. Ideal types, such as that of the liberal university identified with its community of disinterested scholars, are also significant determinants of academic consciousness.

The narrative of the university's decadence appeals to such ideal-types but rarely addresses the adequacy of their correspondence to the historical conditions of universities' boundaries and their internal and external relations. Funding conditions are now the chief reference point of academic perceptions of the decadence of the university, but thinking hard about the economics of higher education has little appeal to those, especially in the humanities, whose professional identity is dependent on the notion of academia being external to a

    [13]   *Oxford English Dictionary*, 2nd edn.
    [14]   See Francis Oakley, 'The Elusive Academic Profession: Complexity and Change', *Daedalus* 126, 4 (Fall 1997).
    [15]   Sheldon Rothblatt and Bjorn Wittrock, eds, *The European and American University Since 1800: Historical and Sociological Essays* (Cambridge: CUP, 1993), p. 1.
    [16]   See Halsey, *The Decline of Donnish Dominion*, fig. 3.3, p. 64.

system of exchange values.[17] These attitudes feed into academic antipathy to the idea of non-governmental funding as a means to resolve the crises resulting from the straitjacket of state financing of higher education. If lack is the economic language that academics are most likely to talk as a result of the funding climate of the last twenty years, they are in a double-bind created by the myth of scholarly transcendence of material interests. Individual academics are poorer (in job satisfaction as well as monetary terms), less secure in their employment, and harder worked, but there are also more of them, a fact that cannot be ignored in assessing perceptions of the shift from an elite to a mass university system. At the end of the 1980s, before the binary divide was breached, British universities employed 30,000 full-time academic staff: a decade later the higher education sector (158 institutions) numbers 96,000 academics among nearly a quarter of a million staff.[18]

Higher education in the US is a 'mature industry': with 67 per cent of high school graduates in post-secondary education, it is no longer a funding priority.[19] As Arthur Levine has noted, change must now occur by substitution of activities rather than expansion.[20] In Britain, the growth of higher education has been constrained by the exclusionary conviction that there should be parity of standards across the system. Until the 1980s, expansion was pegged by the UGC's defence of the unit of resource as a mechanism for preserving what now seem luxurious staff-student ratios.[21] The Conservative government's higher-education cuts of the early 1980s, selectively imposed by the UGC under the guise of pruning lower-quality provision, only temporarily reversed growth in student numbers, but had by 1985 resulted in a 10 per cent reduction in full-time staff in five years.[22] There followed 'expansion under adverse conditions' in the late 1980s and 1990s, driving down the unit cost of graduates by instituting internal markets for 'fees only' students.[23] But in the thirty years to the Higher and Further Education Act of 1992, from the Robbins principle of demand-led expansion to a newly unified system of over one hundred universities, public expenditure on higher education had risen twentyfold (ten times as many

---

[17] See, for instance, Stanley Fish, 'The Unbearable Ugliness of Volvos', in *There's No Such Thing as Free Speech and its a Good Thing, Too* (New York and Oxford: OUP, 1994), pp. 273–9.

[18] Noble's *Higher Education Financial Yearbook 1998*, reported in *THES*, 19 June 1998, p. 3.

[19] 'US breaks student record', *THES*, 22 May 1998, p. 10.

[20] Arthur Levine, 'How the Academic Profession is Changing', *Daedalus* 126, 4 (Fall, 1997), pp. 2–3.

[21] See Martin Trow, 'Academic Standards and Mass Higher Education' (1987), in ed. Michael Shattock, *The Creation of a University System* (Oxford: Blackwell, 1996), p. 205.

[22] Halsey, table 4.1, p. 93.

[23] Ibid., p. 9.

students), and 'much faster than public spending overall'.[24] The per capita costs
of the pre-Robbins system were not sustainable at the levels of access achieved
towards the end of the century. Even a democratized higher education system
cannot justify a privileged claim on public expenditure in competition with
universal provisions like health, and primary and secondary education. Twenty
years of real-term reductions in the unit of teaching resource have left the
universities dramatically underfunded: 'But though the university system may be
worse off than it was a generation ago, it is certainly far better off than it was two
generations ago.'[25] These words of the last chairman of the UGC (replaced by the
less-independent UFC in 1989) are cold comfort to the contemporary academic
profession and their students, but they serve nevertheless to bring to light the
distortions that accrue with short-term perspectives.

While the universities cannot be held solely responsible for failing to supply
the direction absent from the ever-changing financial controls of their increasingly interventionist paymasters, the system remains locked ideologically into the
pursuit of uniformity, stifling the innovation both necessitated and made possible
by the changing constituency of academics and students. Funding mechanisms
reinforce this institutional and professional goal of elite status, with the effect that
the facts of expansion are more often represented as a threat to business as usual
(reproducing historical differentials of resourcing and prestige, rather than
eroding them), as opposed to a new responsibility for rethinking the meaning and
function of higher education. Visible evidence of institutional decay presses upon
academics, in sharp contrast to the optimism expressed in the campus-building
programme of the 1960s (though few in the existing universities were
enthusiastic about the UGC's rival foundations).[26] The Baedecker foundations of
the 1960s – well-appointed non-urban residential campuses which materialized
spatially the social and intellectual boundaries of the university conceived as an
introspective and disinterested community – embodied assumptions about higher
education that have been negated by the expansionist ideas that created them, and
the lack of will to pay for them. But consciousness of the university's decadence
works against a critical understanding of these conditions when, as it so often
does, it projects the recent past as a norm or inviolable tradition.

The interchangeable use of the terms 'university' and 'higher education' (the
removal of the binary divide seems to have reinforced the gap between HE and
FE) masks another source of the idea of decadence. Despite their collocation in
institutions, higher education, viewed as an instrument of the economic and social
policies of the state, and critical learning, viewed as the defining function of the
university, are widely perceived as being in conflict. This opposition may be

---

24   Scott, *The Meanings of Mass Higher Education*, pp. 24–5.
25   Peter Swinnerton-Dyer, 'Policy on Higher Education and Research' (1991), in
Shattock, ed., p. 239.
26   Shattock, ed., p. 7.

objectified in the relations of faculties, but more likely it is to be found in the concurrent functions of many British institutions as both sites of the production of knowledge (the modern, Humboldtian university) and of processes of knowledge (the liberal university of Newman or Jaspers). While this duality is downplayed in the ideal of the teacher-scholar (the mutual reinforcement of good pedagogy and good research is currently a default argument in defending parity of function across the system), the notion that 'students and knowledge are competitors' has developed from a symptom of multiplicity of institutional function into a metric of academic identity and prestige.[27] But the threat of the demands for higher education to ideals of the university is just one description of a persistent and irresolvable conflict between the institutions of intellectual life, which demand freedoms and privileges, and 'the populace and the powers' whose suspicions persist however 'serviceable' the university is 'to material production or civilized consumption'.[28] It is irresolvable because the 'institutions of intellectual' life are not, and never have been, a separate sphere. However we identify the university's boundaries, which may be thought of as physical (defensible precincts), legal or precedential (ordinances, rituals and customs), social (the community of its students and scholars) or cognitive (practices for the transmission or production of critical knowledge), it is also necessary to note their permeability. Conceptualizations of the university in terms of its defining processes or products (or indeed personnel), by reifying these boundaries for heuristic purposes, reinforce local perceptions that compromised autonomy is a recent event, rather than a condition of historical development.

The significance of decadence as a regulatory trope in reflection on the university is not confined to an unhistoricized rhetoric of imminent demise. Narratives of decadence have themselves been used to bring the idea of the university into crisis in the root sense of a decision or judgement. Jacques Derrida's account of the progressive 'orientation' of the knowledge produced by the university – a common-enough perception among the liberal cadre of the 'multiversity' – reads decadence as deconstruction. The university's boundaries are erased as it becomes impossible to 'distinguish between technology on the one hand, and theory, science and rationality on the other' and to 'distinguish programs that one would like to consider "worthy" or even technically profitable for humanity, from programs that would be destructive'.[29] The expansion of the modern university was abetted by its *not* calling to question the grounds of the reason which supposedly grounded the autonomy of its intellectual activities. As that autonomy withers – these activities, from basic science to literary theory, have been progressively 'oriented' to the requirements of the state and the

---

27 See Scott, *The Crisis of the University*, p. 46 and passim.
28 Halsey, p. 57.
29 Jacques Derrida, 'The Principle of Reason: The University in the Eyes of its Pupils', trans. Catherine Porter and Edward P. Morris, *Diacritics* (Fall 1983), p. 12.

military – so the possibility opens up that autonomy may come into its own in the free play of thought on thought.

> The chance for this event is the chance of an instant, an *Augenblick*, a 'wink' or a 'blink,' it takes place 'in the twinkling of an eye,' I would say, rather, 'in the twilight of an eye,' for it is in the most crepuscular, the most westerly situations of the Western university that the chances of this 'twinkling' of thought are multiplied. In a period of 'crisis,' as we say, a period of decadence and renewal, when the institution is 'on the blink,' provocation to think brings together in the *same* instant the desire for memory and exposure to the future, the fidelity of a guardian faithful enough to want to keep even the chance of a future, in other words the singular responsibility of what he does not have and of what is not yet.[30]

The 'event' of which Derrida was speaking at Cornell fifteen years ago was a reflection 'on the very conditions of reflection',[31] on reason's reason. The university's crisis was also its hope. The most far-reaching of Derrida's conclusions is the idea that the rethinking of the university may not be of the university: 'It is not certain that such thinking can bring together a community or found an institution in the traditional sense of these words. What is meant by community and institution must be rethought.'[32] But the association of Derrida's deconstruction of the university with a foundation that 'exists' (Derrida's description of the Collège International de Philosophie) reveals some of the limits of this rethinking. The desire 'to displace and to question the dominant model [. . .] of the western University' is not compatible with such a foundation: 'the idea of a *project* is incompatible with deconstruction. Deconstruction is a situation.'[33] The Collège takes part in the 'deconstruction at work everywhere', but as an enterprise it can only reproduce institutional structures, as Derrida's insistence on its legal existence and status suggests:

> the legal status of this institution is that of a private association supported by the government, but as a free, private and autonomous institution [. . .] it has to be a liberal institution. Which implies that it should be totally autonomous and totally free with regard to its relation to the state on the one hand and on the other to – let's call it civil society.[34]

---

30   Ibid., p. 20.
31   Ibid., p. 19.
32   Ibid., p. 16.
33   Jacques Derrida with Geoffrey Bennington, 'On Colleges and Philosophy', *Postmodernism: ICA Documents*, ed. Lisa Appignanesi (London: Free Association Books, 1989), p. 222.
34   Ibid., pp. 209–10, 212.

By contrast with his earlier remarks about orientation, the conceptual boundaries made explicit here appear positively utopian. Rethinking the traditional university is dependent on its being in a decadent state, 'on the blink', rather than on any practical remodelling of it.

This idea of the decadent university as a site of rethinking which is not a rebuilding is developed in Bill Reddings' *The University in Ruins*. For Reddings it is necessary to recognize that the university is ruined, but those ruins 'must not be the object of a romantic nostalgia for a lost wholeness but the site of an attempt to transvalue the fact that the University no longer inhabits a continuous history of progress'.[35] The contemporary university is 'post-historical', having outlived the era in which it could define itself 'in terms of the project of historical development, affirmation, and inculcation of national culture'.[36] This project was metonymically represented in the professor or student, but these heroes or subjects of the university's narrative of development have been displaced in the triumph of the administrator of the contemporary 'corporate' institution. Reddings' analysis is at once a penetrating re-interpretation of the history of the ideas of the university, and a response to more immediate changes in the practical governance of the university. His theorization of the concept of excellence as a non-referential principle permitting the maximum of uninterrupted internal administration articulates the fears of many in the British university sector, which is becoming a world-leader in the elaboration of academic audit mechanisms. Resistance to this administrative logic is a matter of keeping open the acts of evaluation which the discourse of excellence forecloses because its emptiness 'masquerades as an idea'.[37] The empty quantifications of the excellent university – for example completion times, and other delineations of the proper duration of study – are to be opposed with the 'empty name of Thought', which functions not as an answer but as a question.[38] Thought, with a capital T, is not a metalanguage which translates everything into an idea: it 'throws those who participate in pedagogy back into reflection upon the ungroundedness of their situation'.[39] This programme replaces the modern university's work of identification with an ethical obligation, and the *telos* of the self-unveiling subject with the open-ended activity of 'listening to Thought'.

The Ruins of the University is addressed to the pessimism associated with the commonplace of the university's loss of integrity, autonomy and cultural authority, in particular as these are correlated with limitations on the state's underwriting of expansion. The fruits of historical consciousness of institutional history are to be borne out in strategies for inhabiting the ruins of the university,

---

[35] Bill Reddings, *The University in Ruins* (Cambridge, Mass.: Harvard University Press, 1996), p. 129.
[36] Ibid., p. 6.
[37] Ibid., p. 160.
[38] Ibid.
[39] Ibid., p. 161.

not fleeing them in bouts of nostalgia or in the defensive and illusory demarcation of a private sphere, 'my work', within the compromised community. As with Derrida, the history of the institution is the motor of its deconstruction, not the encoding of its future. In both cases, the university is envisaged as the possibility of thinking that exceeds the way the university incarnates certain models of thought ('philosophy is the university', says Derrida).

For Derrida and Reddings the decadence of the university is recuperable as a critical moment which has the potential to issue in new responsibilities informed by an awareness of the shaping force of the very institutional norms (particularly those associated with the pretence of being 'the institution that is not an institution') that are coming apart.[40] Derrida's 'guardian' (who is faithful to what is temporally absent – a past and an as-yet-unrealized future) and Reddings' post-historical teachers and students inherit a situation in which the undermining of the unifying idea of the university (respectively reason and culture) and the de-differentiation or dereferentialisation of its disciplines opens up the question of 'whether and how thoughts fit together'.[41] For Reddings, the university of excellence is the home of an unreflective disciplinarity, where questions of integration are unnecessary because all that matters is excellent performance which helps 'the aim of total quality'. But the flip side of a situation where any kind of belief is 'simply [. . .] fodder for evaluation in terms of excellence' is 'room for manoeuvre', so long as questions are kept open. Derrida also identifies disciplinarity as a resistance to reflection on the order of knowledge in the university:

> the approach I am advocating here is often felt by certain guardians of the 'humanities' or of the positive sciences as a threat. It is interpreted as such by those who most often have never sought to understand the history and the system of norms specific to their own institution: the deontology of their profession. They do not wish to know how their discipline has been constituted, particularly in its modern professional form.[42]

Of course, disciplines *are* historically self-conscious. But the particular histories which are constructed as disciplinary communities articulate and contest their ideological and methodological identity may be seen as both a counterweight to the narrative of the decadent university, and contributing factors in the dissolution of unifying ideas of the university. Their presentist teleology may foster a communal sense of progress at the same time that it obscures the larger institutional frameworks which have determined the evolutions or revolutions that they posit as the engines of development. But the buoyancy of intra-disciplinary history is counteracted by an ideology which figures the authority

---

40   Ibid., p. 183.
41   Ibid., p. 191.
42   Derrida, 'The Principle of Reason', p. 15.

and societal necessity of academia ironically, in proportion to its precariousness. As Bruce Robbins argues in *Secular Vocations*, the professional rights of the critic are established in lamentation, and 'vocation obtains the progress it requires [. . .] safely surrounded by a narrative of remorseless decline'.[43] Matthew Arnold's response to modernity, in which Robbins locates criticism's effort to 'ensure professional autonomy by clinging to culture-as-failure', has its parallels in the identification of the university as a terminally sick institution.

The two inflections of decadence I have discussed, which might conveniently be labelled the nostalgic and the deconstructive, are both responses to the increasing permeability of the university, whether in demographic, political, economic or bureaucratic terms, and to the explosion of activities undertaken within and across its weakened boundaries. With respect to both versions of the ruin of the university, it is the unprecedented inclusiveness of the higher education sector in the developed world which has thrown into question the serviceability of earlier models of the university's institutional character and function.

The nostalgic and the deconstructive narratives of decadence share a rhetoric of crisis, though the meanings they read off this putative event are radically different. In each case, drawing attention to the condition of the university by conceiving it as precarious, on the cusp of radical transformation into something else, promotes hypostasis and begins to militate against the kind of historical consciousness that would enable us to comprehend the university as a thoroughly contingent matrix of institutions. What is called for now, but not only now, is an awareness of the mutability of the formations represented by our ideal types, one that is neither disablingly mournful nor facilely apocalyptic, alongside a capacity to recognize the settlements of the last few decades as temporary or transitional, rather than as defining and essential. The chief among these passing and mutating factors is state funding of the universities and of their personnel. Understanding the forces that have determined the contemporary nature of our academic institutions will not in itself guarantee that we can shape their future to our various ends, but it is a prerequisite for taking some responsibility for them.

---

[43] Bruce Robbins, *Intellectuals, Professionalism, Culture* (London: Verso, 1993), p. 122.

Chapter 19

The Lateness of the World, or How to Leave the Twentieth Century

Martin L. Davies

Le présent est en perdition.

Edgar Morin[1]

The weight of this sad time we must obey;
Speak what we feel, not what we ought to say.
The oldest hath borne most: we that are young
Shall never see so much, nor live so long.[2]

These lines from the end of the last act of *King Lear* encapsulate a defining experience of European consciousness: the feeling – ominous in the extreme – of living at a late stage of the world. They evoke a conviction which the late twentieth century – in which 'much more is real than is possible' – recognizes only too well: a sense of the sheer surfeit of eventuality, of burdensome plenitude which preempts, hence inevitably involves the foreclosure of, existence in time to come.[3] They intimate a sense of destitution, both historical and personal, comparable, perhaps, to one of the most dreadful thoughts in European philosophy, itself the product of late reflection: Hegel's assertion that 'world history is not the ground of happiness'; 'periods of happiness are empty pages in it, since they are periods of harmony, suspensions of its dialectical movement' – and confined (it might be surmised by extending the metaphor) to the fly-leaves front and back, before the whole enterprise begins or after the whole business is finished.[4]

---

[1]   'The present is in a state of perdition': Edgar Morin, *Pour sortir du XXe siècle* [*To Leave the Twentieth Century*], Coll. Points (Paris: Seuil, 1984), p. 341.
[2]   *King Lear*, V.iii, 323–6, in *William Shakespeare: The Complete Works*, ed. P. Alexander (London: Collins, 1978).
[3]   Hans Jonas, quoted in Emil Fackenheim, *To Mend the World. Foundations of Post-Holocaust Thought* (Bloomington and Indianapolis: Indiana University Press, 1994), p. 233.
[4]   G.W.F. Hegel, *Vorlesungen über die Philosophie der Geschichte* [*Lectures on the Philosophy of History*], with an introduction by Theodor Litt (Stuttgart: Reclam, 1961), pp. 70–71.

The age is the problem. But, just because they are taken from early seventeenth and early nineteenth-century sources, these illustrations are no pretext for resorting to historical explanation by asserting that this experience is 'nothing new', or for indulging purely antiquarian interests by claiming that it has 'a long tradition'. It speaks volumes for the prevailing cognitive value of the human sciences, that their commonest cognitive conventions – procedural tropes such as traditions, legacies, precedents, transitions, and influences – turn on such redundant formulations, themselves obvious symptoms of the cultural psychopathology of lateness.

The age is always the problem. Inherent in consciousness, in its material, temporal situation, is a sense of it arriving afterwards – a sense of delay. Let us recall that the owl of Minerva always takes flight as darkness gathers. Painting its figures *en grisaille*, when the social process of reality has run its course, philosophy – as the attempt to grasp the world in thought, to reveal how the world ought to be – 'comes in any case always far too late' [*so kommt dazu ohnehin die Philosophie immer zu spät*].⁵ The human creature, 'projected into existence', discovers in and through the process of becoming self-conscious traces which the world's previous inhabitants have already left behind them – such as the abandoned megaliths and menhirs of the Armorican peninsula, their sublime, uncompromising presence now transfigured by incomprehension and forgetfulness. Not without consternation it discovers, particularly through constant historical revision, the prior existence of other times and peoples. Resentfully even, it finds itself constrained to concede priority to its precursors, to understand itself as always in a state of being additional after the event [*Nachträglichkeit*], of constantly having to reassess and reposition itself in the light of subsequent remembrances, or deferred reconstructions, of past events.⁶

In particular, the psychopathology of lateness compulsively generates the anxieties, which sustain it, creates – self-indulgently almost – its typical sense of destitution, of impending foreclosure. 'Thereafter, would that I were not among the men of the fifth generation, but either had died before or been born afterwards. For now truly is a race of iron, and men never rest from labour and sorrow by day, and from perishing by night'; so runs Hesiod's lament for a long-distant 'golden race of mortal men who lived in the time of Cronos when he was reigning in heaven' and who 'lived like gods without sorrow of heart, remote and free from toil and grief': for now, by contrast, in a world bereft of the gods, of

---

    ⁵ G.W.F. Hegel, *Grundlinien der Philosophie des Rechts* [*Basic Outlines of the Philosophy of Law*], ed. Johannes Hofmeister, *Philosophische Bibliothek*, 4th edn (Hamburg: Felix Meiner, 1967), p. 17.

    ⁶ Cf. the explanation of '*Nachträglichkeit*' in J. Laplanche and J.-B. Pontalis, *Vocabulaire de la psychanalyse* [*Vocabulary of Psychoanalysis*], 10th edn (Paris: P.U.F., 1990), pp. 33–6.

Aidôs and Nemesis, 'bitter sorrows will be left for mortal men, and there will be no help against evil'.[7]

> *Aber Freund! wir kommen zu spät. Zwar leben die Götter,*
> *Aber über dem Haupt droben in anderer Welt.*
> *Endlos wirken sie da und scheinens wenig zu achten,*
> *Ob wir leben, so sehr schonen die Himmlischen uns.*

Thus, the unmistakable voice of this late age, of this 'night time of the world' [*Zeit der Weltnacht*] (to use Heidegger's phrase): Hölderlin's – in his lament of a disorientated self left behind in a disenchanted world, in a destitute age [*in dürftiger Zeit*].[8]

It is not, however, a foregone conclusion that the idea of the lateness of the world entails destitution or disenchantment. A sense of the past is frequently synonymous with the enjoyment of wealth and abundance: for Francis Bacon, who regarded himself as living in 'the autumn of the world', it was self-evident that 'a more advanced age of the world' would be 'stored and stocked with infinite experiments and observations'.[9] This sentiment is found too in the works of other thinkers of the seventeenth and eighteenth centuries such as Pascal, Hume, Lessing, Condorcet and Herder, for whom the growth and development of the human race through history was analogous to the process of maturation in the individual human being. The apparently liberal features of this analogy need to be offset by the reflection that it in effect establishes a social-psychological coordinating matrix which permits individual differentiation within a controlling political or economic structure. Following Foucault, Jochen Schulte-Sasse points out that

> the Enlightenment's concept of time and its narratological ramifications emerged [. . .] in an age in which the citizens of Western European nations internalized their own supervision. The 'disciplinary methods' established during this age 'reveal a linear time whose moments are integrated, one

---

    [7]   Hesiod, *Works and Days*, in *Homeric Hymns, Epic Cycle, Homerica* with an English translation by Hugh G. Evelyn-White, Loeb Classical Library (Cambridge, Mass. and London: Harvard University Press, 1995), pp. 3–65 (pp. 15–17).

    [8]   Friedrich Hölderlin, 'Brot und Wein' [Bread and Wine], in *Sämtliche Werke* [*Collected Works*] (Leipzig: Insel Verlag, n.d.), pp. 185–201 (pp. 199–200): 'But my friend! we have come too late. True the gods still live / But far above us in another world./ There they endlessly go about their work and seem to care little / whether we live, so far removed from us are these divine beings.' Cf. Martin Heidegger, 'Wozu Dichter?' [What are poets for?], in *Holzwege* [*Paths through the Woods*], 5th edn (Frankfurt am Main: Vittorio Klostermann, 1972), pp. 248–95 (p. 248).

    [9]   Francis Bacon, *The New Organon*, ed. with an Intr. by Fulton H. Anderson, *The Library of the Liberal Arts* (Indianapolis and New York: Bobbs-Merril, 1960), p. 81, §LXXXIV.

upon another, and which is oriented towards a terminal, stable point; in short, an "evolutive" time'.

Schulte-Sasse continues:

> The Enlightened citizen managing his affairs does so on the basis of temporalizing his 'world' and individual life: he imagines that he designs his actions by projecting an improvement of his state of affairs into the future. Thus Thomas Henry [. . .] writes in 1791 that the 'Merchant and Manufacturer' must also be a 'philosophical historian' since he cannot be satisfied 'with the mere relation of facts.' Henry sees very clearly that the predominant dimension of the analytic approach of the merchant or manufacturer is not spatial, as in the case of the scientist, but temporal. The businessman must discover 'how the various interests, situations and connections of different countries should lead to different kinds of traffic'.[10]

This analogy, between the individual and history which in ideological terms facilitates acceptance of a coordinating matrix of social action, makes historical knowledge a precondition for the accumulation of personal and social goods.

'Heritage' is the term now applied to this accumulated, and still accumulating stock of historical knowledge, to the multifarious artefacts it has produced 'down the ages', and now associated with the aesthetic spectacle provided by the display and experience of it (in museums, for example). 'Heritage' is itself a term redolent of lateness: by definition an inheritance passes to those who survive its previous, now departed custodian; the very process of succession enables its value and the interest in it to mature. The wealth generated by heritage, by the past's added value (so to speak), along with the amount of material investment necessary to sustain the antiquarian affinities required to appreciate and manage it, indicates how obsessed the social imagination is with its sense of lateness.

Consequently, following an old-fashioned inclination towards taking the 'total view', one would, therefore, want to examine how the social obsession with history's heritage fits with a society intoxicated with being up-to-date, how history can be the dominant idea – Marx's *herrschende Idee* – of a postmodern socio-economic system of production, of the age of *late* capitalism.[11] One forgets: lateness is dialectical (logically speaking), and ambivalent (in psychological terms). On the one hand, the psychopathology of lateness must express itself in the traditional conventions of academic historical study, in tropes of deference, gestures of deferral, mental complexes generating intricate patterns of sequentiality, and – last but not least – the ultimate nostalgia dependency: the

---

[10]   Jochen Schulte-Sasse, 'Paradoxes in the Narratological Foundation of the Enlightenment', in eds W. Daniel Wilson and Robert C. Holub, *Impure Reason. Dialectic of Enlightenment in Germany* (Detroit: Wayne State University Press, 1993), pp. 129–30.

[11]   Cf. Karl Marx, *Manifest der kommunistisches Partei* [*Manifesto of the Communist Party*] (1848), in *Die Frühschriften* [*Early Writings*], ed. Siegfried Landshut (Stuttgart: Kröner, 1968), pp. 525–60 (p. 546).

infatuation with origins. On the other hand, the same psychopathology compels the social individual as consumer to project his or her desires onto brand-new commodities (for example, up-to-the-minute designer fashions, the current cinema sensation, the newest chart-topping album, the most recent computer software); these are, after all, the *latest things*.

What binds these apparently contradictory affinities together is the underlying process by which society reproduces itself. To sustain itself society must repetitiously produce the commodities it requires; the raw material has invested in it, and is transformed by, the value it acquires in the production process: its use-value, its exchange-value, and what might be called its 'interest value', intrinsic qualities of material, design, workmanship, together with its 'fetishistic' connotations. From this standpoint, history as a means both of structuring time and understanding human development is the production process *par excellence*, the production process in its sublimated, if not to say ideal form. Take anything, some piece of detritus, a defunct implement, a scrap of manuscript, an unrecognized heirloom: it has only to be 'historical', redolent of a now vanished social practice, or characteristic of an extinguished personality, to be valued, to be a realizable asset – and not just prized by scholars, but, crucially, redeemable by collectors in the market for cash.[12]

What other production process can start with a 'raw material' which is so cheap, so ubiquitous, so heterogeneous, so inexhaustible (since each passing age generates its own historical interests and values)? What else can produce such added value, generate such a dividend of interest, especially since everyone is either a producer or almost inevitably a consumer and principally since the media (including theatre, film and advertising), tourism, institutions of higher education – history's management structure (so to speak) – have between them a virtual monopoly on what really matters: the financial return?

Media and commercial interests may well exploit the culture of lateness and remain the chief beneficiaries of the past's legacy; but they do not create it. This task falls to education, specifically to the scholarship which sustains it. For example: there is no justification for a miniature replica of the Rosetta Stone, available from the British Museum shop (itself virtually replicating in miniature the museum in which it is situated) to be a desirable commodity; unless, beyond its function as a souvenir of London or as a paper-weight, it triggers in its owner a purely academic moment of recognition; unless it elicits a degree of intellectual interest fostered by a higher education. The study of the humanities in general, let

---

12 Geraldine Norman, 'In the Right Frame. Why Would Anyone Pay £33,000 for a Frame without a Picture?', *Independent on Sunday Magazine*, 9 July 1995, p. 78: 'Compared to other stylish old furnishings, picture frames are also pretty cheap. The oldest in Tuesday's sale, a 15th-century tabernacle frame – a plain, 10in carved rectangle with a stepped base – is valued at £500–£700. The most spectacular in the auction, a Venetian 16th-century carved and gilded cassetta (box-like) frame almost 3ft high, is valued at £15,000–£20,000.'

alone history in particular, culminates primarily in the production of more discriminating and informed consumers: those who, having been trained in objectivity, accuracy and the testing of evidence, will become connoisseurs of the historial simulacrum, predisposed towards synthetic verisimilitude (for example, the latest Jane Austen film adaptation, living museums and so on), and, equipped with skills for promoting the *latest things*, will in turn reinforce the social-psychopathological lateness complex.

Precisely because in this information society historical knowledge, assimilating popular memory and parochial recollection, now constitutes the social memory, the academy has never been able to monopolize it, least of all now, in this late stage of the world, when the heritage industry plays such a large role in mass entertainment (cf. the TV show *Gladiators*) and the study of the humanities – like DIY or aerobics – has itself become a widely accessible leisure pursuit. The cultural implications of the general raising of educational standards, of the social dissemination of received historical learning, is to be found in the social environment as a whole when it is represented, even celebrated, as 'theatres of memory' (in the late Raphael Samuel's words).[13] To appreciate the naivety of this historical mentality, to recognize it as an expression of decadence in its purest form, as an unmistakable symptom of the psychosis of lateness, involves recalling Nietzsche's blistering attack on the promiscuous, parodic character of European culture, as exemplified by its sense of history.[14]

If lateness – failing to turn up at the right time – is an expression of dysfunctionality, then one of its most common behavioural tropes involves self-incrimination. It may take several forms.

1. There is the sense of being in debt to the past – for social and moral values, in particular – which is the source of all reactionary politics, a reflex reaction to the alleged decadence of the present for apparently falling short of past ideals and expectations. There is, for example, Prime Minister Stanley Baldwin in 1924 invoking 'the sounds of England [. . .] the tinkle of hammer on anvil in the country smithy, the corncrake on a dewy morning, the sound of the scythe against the whetstone'. For him, 'these things strike down into the very depths of our nature and touch chords which go back to the beginning of time and the human race'.[15]

---

[13] Raphael Samuel, *Theatres of Memory. Vol. 1: Past and Present in Contemporary Culture* (London: Verso, 1994), p. 25.

[14] Friedrich Nietzsche, *Jenseits von Gut und Böse* [*Beyond Good and Evil*], in *Kritische Studienausgabe* [Critical Paperback Edition], eds G. Colli and M. Montinari, 2nd and rev. edn, 15 vols (Munich and New York: DTV/de Gruyter, 1988), V, pp. 9–243 (p. 157), §223.

[15] Quoted from Patrick Wright, 'England as Lost Idyll. Tory Fantasies of a Forsaken Past Are No Way to Address the Present', *Independent on Sunday*, no. 332, 16 June 1996, p. 21.

2. There is, further, a sense of being obligated to the past, to what went before, which is the product of a late inferiority complex and a compensating desire to 'make good' – demonstrated in the national obsession with conservation and renovation. Thus the myth of a golden age generated from our own flawed lateness, permeates the very reflexes of current actions, the very synapses of contemporary judgement.

3. But there is also a form of lateness in which the past itself lays its incriminating charges before a present which would deny or repress the past delinquencies from which it profits. Those who come afterwards are by definition guilty: that one arrives late is reason enough to have a guilty conscience (even if, in mitigation, one has a legitimate excuse). Hindsight, of itself, produces better, alternative courses of action that might or ought to have been followed: if only one had known. The surviving victims look to posterity for recognition, atonement and compensation.[16]

4. There is also the conviction that justice – the justness of a defeated cause – may be recognized subsequently, by a later world. This demand invokes the metaphor – found, for example, in Montesquieu and Hegel – of history as the court of last appeal.[17] Except that history cannot be both judge and plaintiff: when historical events eventually do come before a court of law, as Arendt found in the case of Eichmann and Finkielkraut in the case of Barbie, the issues have proved to be confused, the evidence disputable, and memory itself unreliable.[18] Indubitably, late knowledge is inconsequential knowledge.

---

[16] In August 1995, on the 50th anniversary of the end of hostilities in the Far East, there was considerable outrage in the British press over the reluctance of the leaders of contemporary Japan – an economy which has boomed in the intervening post-war period – to apologize for the atrocities committed by its armed forces during the Second World War. It was recognized that the issue of an apology mediated both in Japan and in the international community a wider sense of ambivalence about its current world economic rôle as much as it apparently confirmed a lack of contrition about its national past. cf. 'Sorry Seems to be the Hardest Word', *The Independent*, 12 August 1995, p. 14; Richard Lloyd Parry and Will Bennett, 'Japanese PM Accused of Double-speak', *The Independent*, 16 August 1995, p. 1.

[17] Hegel, *Rechtsphilosophie* [*Basic Outlines of the Philosophy of Law*], pp. 288–9, §§340–2 ; Montesquieu, 'Mes Pensées' [My Thoughts], in *Oeuvres complètes*, ed. Roger Caillois, 2 vols, Éditions de la Pléiade (Paris: Gallimard, 1949), I, p. 1133.

[18] Cf. Hannah Arendt, *Eichmann in Jerusalem. A Report on the Banality of Evil*, revised and enlarged edn (Harmondsworth: Penguin, 1983), p. 19: 'For it was history that, as far as the prosecution was concerned, stood in the center of the trial'; p. 81: 'Eichmann's memory, jumping with great ease over the years [. . .] was certainly not controlled by chronological order, but it was not simply erratic. It was like a storehouse, filled with human-interest stories of the worst type'; cf. Alain Finkielkraut, *La mémoire vaine. Du crime contre l'humanité* [*Remembering in Vain: The Klaus Barbie Trial and Crimes against Humanity*], folio/essais (Paris: Gallimard, 1992), p. 12: 'Avec le procès Barbie, [. . .] Nous avons vu, nous, un passé déjà historique transmué en présence judiciaire.'

5. Hence the psychosis of lateness involves a sense of fatalism. History is driven by human dysfunctionality on a phylogenetic scale, as Reinhart Koselleck remarks: 'What characterizes history is that the foresight human beings have, the plans they then conceive, and the way in which they are subsequently carried out always diverge in the course of time.'[19] Dealing with the finished product, confronting the done deed, sublimating vital interests into dead things, history is the management system of this fatalistic culture of the death-drive.

The development of civilization inevitably entails the stress of neurosis as desires are channelled into abstract or reified investments (for instance, into work, money, possessions), sublimated (for example, into art, leisure pursuits), or repressed (for example, via narcotics, self-abuse). These pressures of the reality principle visit the social individual in the form of self-inflicted psychopathological snares, the dysfunctionalities [*Fehlleistungen*], of everyday life. They also show up (as Elaine Showalter has argued in her recent book *Hysteries. Hysterical Epidemics and Modern Culture* (London: Picador, 1997)) as mass psychogenic disorders produced by the contagious influence of pathological syndromes (she discusses *inter alia* ME, Gulf War Syndrome, fixations on crop circles, UFO sightings, reports of alien abduction). To this nosology of cultural psychopathology needs to be added the mass psychogenic disorder of lateness, the neurosis *par excellence* of the postmodern condition, a neurosis so easily ignored because it constitutes the very fabric of normality. Moreover, of all the symptoms it displays, its most obvious, its most 'normal' has yet to be mentioned: its infatuation with speed. After all, if one is late, one cannot help rushing in order to be in time, to get things done in time, and – after all – to save time.

What characterizes the culture of lateness is the acceleration [*Beschleunigung*] of time: from the eighteenth century time ceases to be simply the metaphysical framework in which history happens, but becomes a dynamic factor in history itself.[20] Time becomes a factor in, and product of, social processes, hence splits into various asynchronous strata. The symptoms of acceleration are various.

1. There is the exponential growth and intensity of information relating to a given period of time which reaches saturation point (one might think) with the establishment of twenty-four-hour televized global news networks. As a result all information has an ephemeral appearance, the perspective for judgement

---

[19]   Reinhard Koselleck, *Vergangene Zukunft. Zur Semantik geschichtlicher Zeiten [Futures Past: On the Semantics of Historical Time]*, 4th edn (Frankfurt am Main: Suhrkamp, 1985), p. 272: '*Geschichte zeichnet sich dadurch aus, daß menschliche Voraussicht, menschliche Pläne und ihre Durchführungen im Ablauf der Zeit immer auseinandertreten.*'

[20]   Koselleck, *Vergangene Zukunft [Futures Past]*, pp.77, 88 and 321.

is radically foreshortened, so that (as Paul Virilio has remarked) 'actuality itself is made obsolete' [*l'actualité est déjà passée*].[21]

2. There is the economic pressure to make time more productive. In the process of the manufacture, distribution and marketing of goods, this time-space compression is achieved by organizational shifts (such as vertical disintegration and 'delayering', small-batch production monitored by new techniques of economic control), by 'parallel accelerations in exchange and consumption' (driven by sophisticated techniques of inventory control and market feedback), by the development of arenas of consumption beyond the ultimately limited sphere of physical goods (such as the mobilization of fashion in mass markets, leisure and life-style activities and products, and the consumption of ephemeral services), and – where the employee is concerned – by the frenetic ethos of 'hyperwork'.[22]

3. Time thus becomes a precious commodity, to be saved, to be used cost-effectively, to be managed by time and labour-saving instruments, as the scientific ability to manipulate time is transferred to society as a whole by a whole range of electronic appliances and artefacts involved in the process of social reproduction. This intoxication with speed, with the latest development, means that those who have little access to the various technologies of time-management become marginalized by their slowness, or socially disqualified for being wasteful of time. But a further effect is, paradoxically, that for all this time management, few people feel that they have any time of their own.[23]

4. This late rush of all things produces ultimately a sense of suspension, an information culture the aim of which is to produce and market events as a 'visual psychodrama' unfolding in the void of actuality.[24] Helga Nowotny uses the term 'extended present' [*erstreckte Gegenwart*] to describe the conception of the future in a culture of lateness: in a culture obsessed with lateness nothing unprecedented will emerge from time to come.[25] Time will instead have already been colonized by the managerial strategies for producing the *latest things* – statistical projections, computer modelling, forward scheduling, etc., etc., etc.

[21] Paul Virilio, *L'espace critique* [*Critical Space*] (Paris: Christian Bourgois, 1984), p. 105.

[22] David Harvey, *The Condition of Postmodernity. An Enquiry into the Origins of Social Change* (Oxford: Basil Blackwell, 1990), pp. 240ff., 284ff.; Neil Ascherson, 'You Don't Need a Watch to Tell You That Your Time's Not Your Own', *Independent on Sunday*, 30 July 1995, p. 24.

[23] Helga Nowotny, *Eigenzeit. Entstehung und Strukturierung eines Zeitgefühls* [*Time: The Modern and Postmodern Experience*], suhrkamp taschenbuch wissenschaft, 2nd edn (Frankfurt am Main: Suhrkamp, 1995), pp. 19, 28ff., 42ff., 81ff.

[24] Jean Baudrillard, *L'illusion de la fin ou La grève des événements* [*The Illusion of the End or the Standstill of Events*] (Paris: Éditions Galilée, 1992), p. 31.

[25] Nowotny, *Eigenzeit* [*Time: The Modern and Postmodern Experience*], pp. 52ff.

* * *

It is late in the world: we shall leave the twentieth century and it will be later still. Perhaps it has left us already, this wretched era which, arguably, began late (in 1914?) and finished early (in 1989?) so that the shadow of the latest age, the third millennium – invoked and appropriated for some time now in sound-bites by spin doctors - falls upon us the sooner. To leave the twentieth century properly would mean recovering from the mentality of lateness, even though at present what this might involve is unclear. As Stephen Toulmin remarks: 'The most we can hope to foresee is the limits within which "available" human futures lie. Available futures are not just those that we can passively forecast, but those we can actively create.' This involves knowing what 'intellectual *posture* to adopt' and 'what capacity [. . .] we have to change our ideas about available futures'. Certainly, (as Toulmin goes on to argue) we know it means the end of the universal, 'value-free' rational explanation of human action, inaugurated by Descartes and Leibniz and exposed as discreditable by the cultural and philosophical revolution of the 1960s.[26] It would mean the end of history, because (as Edgar Morin points out) it would be superseded automatically in a phylogenetic drive towards a form of hypercomplexity in both society and the human cortex which the creatively destructive or destructively creative, but increasingly volatile, processes of historical change could no longer deliver.

It would also mean a new intellectual ecology: reaffirming the autonomy of thinking, distanced from being implicated in what is conventional or traditional, wary of being seduced by ideological or simplistic formulations, alert to the propensity for ideas and attitudes to drift [*dérive*]. As Edgar Morin has argued at length, it would mean, finally, vindicating attitudes currently anathema to the institutions of society but which are creative and vital in cultural terms: a predilection for uncertainty, a taste for contingency [*aléa*], a sense of reservation towards the prevailing practices of knowledge.[27]

In the meantime, let us at least forget the earnest postures of our late learning, dishabituate ourselves for historical scholarship. By contrast, reflection is stimulated by words and texts, a musical cadence, impasto images, provocative forms, the prismatic effects of light: that is what turns the spotlight on the enduring shabbiness of this late world, that is what exposes the fundamental diremptions of our ancient society. There are suggestive, multifaceted texts to be turned and turned again in the mind's eye like fragments of translucent amethyst or misty quartz held against the morning light: 'The century moves forwards; but

---

[26]   Stephen Toulmin, *Cosmopolis. The Hidden Agenda of Modernity* (Chicago: University of Chicago Press, 1990), p. 2, passim.

[27]   Cf. Morin, *Pour sortir du XXe siècle* [*To leave the Twentieth Century*], pp. 86, 136, 148, 153ff., 158ff., 168ff., 256ff.; Morin, *Le paradigme perdu*, Coll. Points (Paris: Seuil, 1989), pp. 226ff.

each individual person still starts from the beginning' [*Das Jahrhundert ist vorgerückt; jeder einzelne aber fängt doch von vorne an*] (Goethe); 'It is in my own mind, then, that I measure time. I must not allow my mind to insist that time is something objective. I must not let it thwart me because of all the different notions and impressions that are lodged in it' (St Augustine).[28] As midnight steals inexorably over the world on the last day of 1999 many will surely have had the time of their lives – hardly, though, in their own time.

---

[28] J.W. von Goethe, *Maximen und Reflexionen* [*Maxims and Reflections*], in *Werke* [*Works*], Hamburger Ausgabe, eds Erich Trunz et al., 14 vols , 8th edn (Munich: C.H. Beck, 1978), XII, pp. 364-547 (p. 544; no. 1348); Saint Augustine, *Confessions* (Harmondsworth: Penguin, 1966), p. 276 (Book XI, §27).

Bibliography

Aarne, Antti, *The Types of the Folktale. A Classification and Bibliography* (1928) trans. Stith Thompson (Helsinki, Suomalainen Tiedeakatemia: Academia Scientiarum Fennica, 1964).

Adams, Robert M., *Decadent Societies* (Berkeley, Calif.: North Point Press, 1983).

Addison, Paul, *The Road to 1945: British Politics and the Second World War* (London: Random, 1994).

Alain, Finkielkraut, *La mémoire vaine. Du crime contre l'humanité* [*Remembering in Vain: The Klaus Barbie Trial and Crimes against Humanity*], folio/essais (Paris: Gallimard, 1992).

Aldiss, Brian, *Billion Year Spree: The History of Science Fiction* (London: Weidenfeld and Nicolson, 1973).

Antongini, Tom, *D'Annunzio* (London: Heinemann, 1938).

Arendt, Hannah, *Eichmann in Jerusalem. A Report on the Banality of Evil*, revised edition (Harmondsworth: Penguin, 1983).

Aristotle, *The Politics*, trans. T.A. Sinclair and Trever J. Saunders (Harmondsworth: Penguin, 1981).

Arnold, Matthew, *Selected Poems and Prose*, ed., Miriam Allott (London: J.M. Dent, 1978).

———, *The Complete Prose Works of Matthew Arnold*, ed. R.H. Super, 11 vols (Ann Arbor: University of Michigan Press, 1960–77).

Artaud, A., 'Theatre and the Plague' in *The Theatre and its Double* (London: Calder and Boyars, 1970).

Ashcraft, Richard, 'Latitudinarianism and toleration: historical myth versus political history', in *Philosophy, science, and religion in England, 1640–1700*, eds Richard Kroll, Richard Ashcraft and Perez Zagorin (Cambridge: C.U.P., 1992), pp. 151–77.

Ashley, Maurice, *Charles I and Oliver Cromwell: A Study in Contrast* (London: Methuen, 1987).

Augustine, Saint, *Concerning the City of God against the Pagans*, trans. Henry Bettenson (Harmondsworth: Penguin, 1984).

———, *Confessions*, trans. R.S. Pine-Coffin (Harmondsworth: Penguin, 1966).

Austin, William W., ed., *Debussy's Prelude to 'The Afternoon of a Faun'* (New York: Norton: 1970).

Aytoun, William Edmondstoune, *Firmilian: or the Student of Badajoz. A Spasmodic Tragedy* (Edinburgh: William Blackwood and Sons, 1854).

———, *Poems of William Edmondstoune Aytoun*, ed. F. Page (Oxford: Humphrey Milford/O.U.P., 1921).

Bacon, Francis, *The New Organon*, ed. Fulton H. Anderson, The Library of the Liberal Arts (Indianapolis & New York: Bobbs-Merril, 1960).

Bailin, Miriam, *The Sickroom in Victorian Fiction: The Art of Being Ill* (Cambridge: C.U.P., 1994).

Baldick, Chris, *The Concise Oxford Dictionary of Literary Terms* (Oxford: O.U.P., 1990; paperback edn 1991).

Barron, Stephanie, *'Degenerate Art' :The Fate of the Avant-Garde in Nazi Germany* (Los Angeles and New York: published jointly by Los Angeles County Museum of Art and Harry N. Abrams, Inc., 1991).

Bassnett, Susan, *Translation Studies*, revised edition (London & New York: Routledge, 1991)

Baudelaire, Charles, 'Notes nouvelles sur Edgar Poe', Nouvelles histoires extraordinaires (1857) ['New notes on Edgar Poe', New Strange Stories] in *Baudelaire, Oeuvres complètes*, Claude Pichois ed., Bibliothèque de la Pléiade, 2 vols (Paris: Editions Gallimard, 1975–6), II, pp. 319–37.

——, *'The Painter of Modern Life'*, *Baudelaire: Selected Writings on Art and Literature*, trans. P.E. Charvet (London: Penguin, 1992).

——, *Intimate Journals*, trans. Christopher Isherwood (Hollywood: Marcel Rodd, 1947).

——, *Oeuvres complètes*, 4 vols (Paris: Michel Lévy frères, 1868–9).

——, *Selected Writings on Art and Literature*, trans. P.E. Charvet (London: Penguin, 1992).

Baudrillard, Jean, *Baudrillard Live: Selected Interviews*, trans. Mike Gane and G. Salemohamed, ed. Mike Gane (London: Routledge, 1993).

——, *L'illusion de la fin ou La grève des événements* [The Illusion of the End or the Standstill of Events] (Paris: Éditions Galilée, 1992).

——, *The Perfect Crime*, trans. Chris Turner (London: Verso: 1997).

——, *The Transparency of Evil*, trans. James Benedict (London: Verso, 1993).

Beal, Rebecca S., 'Grace Abounding to the Chief of Sinners: John Bunyan's Pauline Epistle', *SEL*, 21 (1981), 147–60.

Beaumont, Agnes, *The Narrative of the Persecution of Agnes Beaumont* (1760) reprinted in *Grace Abounding with other Spiritual Autobiographies*, ed. John Stachniewski with Anita Pacheco (Oxford: O.U.P., 1998).

Beckett, Samuel, 'Dante.. Bruno. Vico.. Joyce', in *Our Exagmination Round his Factification for Incamination of Work in Progress* (1929) (London: Faber and Faber, 1972).

——, *Waiting for Godot* (1956) (London: Faber and Faber, 1977).

Belsey, C., *The Subject of Tragedy: Identity and Difference in Renaissance Drama* (London: Methuen, 1985).

Benjamin, Andrew, *Translation and the Nature of Philosophy* (London and New York: Routledge, 1989).

Benjamin, Walter, *Illuminations*, trans. Harry Zohn, (Glasgow: Collins, 1979).

——, *One-Way Street and Other Writings* (London: Verso, 1985).

Beresford, J.D., *A Common Enemy* (London: Hutchinson and Co., 1942).

Bergonzi, Bernard, *Wartime and Aftermath: English Literature and its Background, 1939–60* (Oxford: O.U.P., 1993).

Best, Herbert, *The Twenty-Fifth Hour* (London: Jonathan Cape, 1940).

Birken, Lawrence, *Consuming Desire: Sexual Science and the Emergence of a Culture of Abundance, 1871–1914* (Ithaca, N.Y: Cornell University Press, 1988).

Bloom, Allan, *The Closing of the American Mind: How Higher Education Has Failed Democracy* (New York: Simon and Schuster, 1987).

Bloom, Harold, *Anxiety of Influence: A Theory of Poetry* (London: Oxford U.P., 1973).

——, ed., *Deconstruction and Criticism* (London and Henley: Routledge & Kegan Paul, 1979).

Boccaccio, Giovanni, *Teseida*, trans. S. Battagua (Firenze: Garzanti, 1958).

Bonaventure, Saint, *The Life of St. Francis*, trans. Ewert Cousins (New York: Paulist Press, 1978).

Botta, A., 'An interview with Antonio Tabucchi', *Contemporary Literature*, vol. 35, 3 (Fall 1994), 421–40.

Bottrall, Margaret, *Every Man a Phoenix: Studies in Seventeenth Century Autobiography* (London: John Murray, 1958).

Bourget, Paul, 'Charles Baudelaire' (1881), in Paul Bourget, *Oeuvres complètes de Paul Bourget*, 9 vols (Paris: Plon and Nourrit, 1899–1911), I, pp. 3–25.

Boyd, Charles W., ed., *Mr Chamberlain's Speeches*, 2 vols (London: Constable, 1914).

Brooks, Chris, and Faulkner, Peter, eds., *The White Man's Burdens: An Anthology of British Poetry of the Empire* (Exeter: University of Exeter Press, 1996).

Brown, Emerson, 'Priapus and the Parlement of Foulys', *Studies in Philology* 72 (1975).

Brown, Peter, *The Body And Society: Men Women and Sexual Renunciation in Early Christianity* (London and Boston: Faber and Faber, 1989).

Bunyan, John, *Christian Behaviour* (1663), in *The Miscellaneous Works of John Bunyan*, ed. J. Sears McGee, 13 vols (Oxford: Clarendon Press, 1987), III.

————, *Grace Abounding to the Chief of Sinners*, ed. Roger Sharrock (Oxford: Clarendon Press, 1962).

————, *The Holy War*, eds James F. Forrest and Roger Sharrock (Oxford: Clarendon Press, 1980).

————, *The Life and Death of Mr. Badman*, eds James F. Forrest and Roger Sharrock (Oxford: Clarendon Press, 1988).

————, *The Pilgrim's Progress*, ed. N.H. Keeble (Oxford: O.U.P., 1984).

Burnet, Gilbert, *Some Passages of the Life and Death of Rochester* (1680), in *Rochester: The Critical Heritage*, ed. David Farley-Hills (New York: Barnes and Noble, 1972), pp. 47–92.

Calabrese, O., *L'età neobarocca* (Bari: Laterza, 1987).

Calder, Angus, *The Myth of the Blitz* (London: Pimlico, 1992).

————, *The People's War: Britain 1939–45* (London: Cape, 1969).

Calinescu, Matei, *Faces of Modernity: Avant-Garde, Decadence, Kitsch* (London: Indiana University Press, 1977).

Camden, Vera, 'Blasphemy and the Problem of the Self', *Bunyan Studies: John Bunyan and his Times*, 1 (1989), 5–21.

Cassese, Giovanna, 'Niccolò Colantonio', in Jane Turner, ed., *The Dictionary of Art*, vol. 7 (London: Macmillan 1996).

Chadwick, Henry, *Augustine* (Oxford: O.U.P., 1986).

Chaucer, Geoffrey, *The Riverside Chaucer*, gen. ed. Larry D. Benson (Oxford and New York: O.U.P., 1987).

Cheney, Lynne V., *Tyrannical Machines: A Report on Educational Practices Gone Wrong and Our Best Hopes for Setting Them Right* (Washington D.C., 1990).

Chernaik, Warren, *Sexual Freedom in Restoration Literature* (Cambridge: C.U.P., 1995).

Clarendon, Edward Hyde, Earl of, *Clarendon: Selections from The History of the Rebellion and The Life by Himself*, ed. G. Huehns (Oxford: O.U.P., 1978).

Cocker, Mark, *Loneliness and Time: British Travel Writing in the Twentieth Century* (London: Secker and Warburg, 1994).

Combe, Kirk, *A Martyr for Sin: Rochester's Critique of Polity, Sexuality, and Society* (Newark: University of Delaware Press, 1998).

Connolly, Cyril, ed., *Horizon: A review of literature and art*, vol. I–V: no. 1–30 (London: Johnson Reprint Company, Jan 1940–June 1942).

Costello, John, *Love, Sex and War: Changing Values 1939–45* (London: Collins, 1985).

Cowgill, B.K., 'The Parlement of Foules and the Body Politic', *Journal of English and Germanic Philology*, 74 (1975), 315–35.

Crowley, Tony, 'The Return of the Repressed: Saussure and Swift on Language and History', in *New Departures in Linguistics*, ed. George Wolf (New York and London: Garland, 1992), pp. 236–49.

D'Annunzio, Gabriele, 'The Virgin Orsola', trans. Raymond Rosenthal, in *Nocturne and Five Tales of Love and Death* (London: Quartet, 1993).

————, *Di me a me stesso* [*From Me To Myself*], ed. Annamaria Andreoli (Milan: Mondadori, 1990).

————, *The Child of Pleasure*, trans. Georgina Harding (Sawtry, Cambs.: Dedalus, 1991), p. 302.

————, *The Flame*, trans. Susan Bassnett (London: Quartet, 1992).

————, *The Triumph of Death*, trans. Georgina Harding (Sawtry, Cambs.: Dedalus, 1990).

————, *La Gioconda* in *Tutto il Teatro di Gabriele D'Annunzio, Tragedie, Sogni e Misteri* (Milan: Mondadori, 1939).

————, *The Virgins of the Rocks*, trans. Agatha Hughes (London: Heinemann, 1899).

Damrosch, David, *We Scholars: Changing the Culture of the University* (Cambridge, Mass.: Harvard University Press, 1995).

Davidson, Angus, *The Romantic Agony* (Oxford: 1933).

De Insulis, Alanus, *De Planctu Naturæ*, trans. Douglas M. Moffat (New Haven, Conn., 1908).

De Krey, Gary S., 'Reformation in the Restoration Crisis, 1679–1682', in *Religion, Literature, and Politics in Post-Reformation England, 1540–1688*, eds Donna B. Hamilton and Richard Strier (Cambridge: C.U.P., 1996), pp. 231–52.

————, 'Rethinking the Restoration: Dissenting cases for Conscience, 1667–1672', *Historical Journal*, 38 (1995), 53–83.

De Lancastre, M.J., ed., *Fernando Pessoa. Il libro dell'inquietudine*, intr. A. Tabucchi (Milan: Feltrinelli, 1986).

De Man, Paul, *The Resistance to Theory* (Minneapolis: University of Minnesota Press, 1986).

De Quincey, Thomas, *The Collected Writings of Thomas De Quincey*, ed. David Masson, 14 vols (London: A. and C. Black, 1896–7).

De Sola Pinto, Vivian, *Enthusiast in Wit: A Portrait of John Wilmot, Earl of Rochester, 1647–1680* (London: Routledge and Kegan Paul, 1962).

De Vries, Hent, 'Anti-Babel: The "Mystical Postulate" in Benjamin, de Certeau and Derrida', *MLN* 107: 3 (April 1992), 456.

Deak, Frantisek, *Symbolist Theatre. The Formation of an Avant-Garde* (Baltimore and London: The Johns Hopkins University Press, 1993).

Derrida, Jacques, 'The Principle of Reason: The University in the Eyes of its Pupils', trans. Catherine Porter and Edward P. Morris, *Diacritics* (Fall, 1983).

————, *Dissemination*, trans. Barbara Johnson (London: Athlone Press, 1993).

————, *The Ear of the Other – Otobiography, Transference, Translation: Texts and Discussions with Jacques Derrida*, ed. Christie McDonald, trans. Peggy Kamuf (Lincoln & London: University of Nebraska Press, 1988).

———— with Geoffrey Bennington, 'On Colleges and Philosophy', *Postmodernism: ICA Documents*, ed. Lisa Appignanesi (London: Free Association Books, 1989).

Descartes, René, *Discourse on Method and Other Writings*, trans. F.E. Sutcliffe (1637; Harmondsworth: Penguin, 1968).

Dickens, Charles, *David Copperfield* (1849–50), ed. Trevor Blount (Harmondsworth: Penguin Books, 1966).

————, *Hard Times* (1854), ed. Kate Flint (Harmondsworth: Penguin Books, 1995).

————, *Our Mutual Friend* (1864–65), ed. Stephen Gill (Harmondsworth: Penguin Books, 1971; repr. 1985).

Dollimore, Jonathan, *Sexual Dissidence: Augustine to Wilde, Freud to Foucault* (Oxford: Clarendon Press, 1992).

Dowling, Linda, *Hellenism and Homosexuality in Victorian Oxford* (Ithaca and London: Cornell U.P., 1994).

————, *Language and Decadence in the Victorian Fin de Siècle* (Princeton: Princeton U.P., 1986).

D'Sousa, Dinesh, *Illiberal Education: The Politics of Race and Sex on Campus* (New York: Free Press, 1991).

Durham, Mary Edith, *High Albania* (1909) (London: Virago Press Ltd, 1985).

Eco, Umberto, *The Search for the Perfect Language*, trans. James Fentress (London: HarperCollins, 1997).

Elam, Keir, ' "In what chapter of his bosom?": Reading Shakespeare's Bodies', in *Alternative Shakespeare* 2, ed. Terry Hawkes (London: Routledge, 1996).

Elfenbein, Andrew, *Byron and the Victorians* (Cambridge: C.U.P., 1995).

Elias, Richard, 'Political Satire in Sodom', *SEL*, 18 (1978), 423–38.

Elleke, Boehmer, ed., *Empire Writing: An Anthology of Colonial Literature 1870–1918* (Oxford: O.U.P., 1998).

Elliott, Alison Goddard, *Roads to Paradise: Reading the Lives of the Early Saints* (Hanover: Brown University Press, 1987).

Ellis, Henry Havelock, 'A Note on Paul Bourget' (1887), in Ellis, *Views and Reviews, First Series: 1884–1919* (London: Harmondsworth, 1932), pp. 48–60.

Ellman, Maud, *The Poetics of Impersonality: T.S. Eliot and Ezra Pound* (Brighton: Harvester, 1987).

Emerson, O.F., 'Legends of Cain, Especially in Old and Middle English', *PMLA* XXI (1906), 831–929.

Emmerson, Richard K. and Ronald B. Herzman, *The Apocalyptic Imagination in Medieval Literature* (Philadelphia: University of Pennsylvania Press, 1992).

Engelberg, Edward, ed., *The Symbolist Poem* (New York: Dutton, 1967).

Fackenheim, Emil, *To Mend the World. Foundations of Post-Holocaust Thought* (Bloomington & Indianapolis: Indiana University Press, 1994).

Falkner, John Meade, *The Lost Stradivarius* (London and Edinburgh: Blackwood,1895; Oxford and New York: O.U.P., 1991. ed. Edward Wilson).

Fermor, Patrick Leigh, *Between the Woods and the Water* (Harmondsworth: Penguin, 1988).

Fielding, Thompson and Tiratsoo, *England Arise: The Labour Party and Popular Politics in 1940's Britain* (Manchester: Manchester University Press, 1995).

Fisch, Harold, 'The Puritans and the Reform of Prose Style', *ELH*, 19 (1952), 229–48.

Fish, Stanley, 'The Unbearable Ugliness of Volvos', in *There's No Such Thing as Free Speech and it's a Good Thing, Too* (New York and Oxford: O.U.P., 1994).

Fleming, John V., *From Bonaventure to Bellini: An Essay in Franciscan Exegesis* (Princeton: Princeton University Press, 1982).

Ford, J., *'Tis Pity She's a Whore*, ed. D. Roper (London: Methuen, 1975).

Foucault, Michel, *The Use of Pleasure*, trans. Robert Hurley (London: Penguin, 1985).

Fowler, Edward, *A Defence of the Doctrine of Justification by Faith* (London: 1672).

————, *The Design of Christianity* (London: 1671).

Fowler, Roger, 'Polyphony and Problematic in Hard Times', in *The Changing World of Charles Dickens*, ed. Robert Gittings (London: Vision Press, 1983), pp. 100–101.

Freud, Sigmund, *Art and Literature*, ed. Albert Dickson, *The Penguin Freud Library*, gen. ed. James Strachey, 15 vols (London: Penguin, 1956), XIV.

Friedman, John Block, *The Monstrous Races in Medieval Art and Thought* (Cambridge Massachusetts: Harvard University Press, 1981).

Friedmann, Herbert, *A Bestiary for Saint Jerome: Animal Symbolism in European Religious Art* (Washington D.C.: 1980).

Fussell, Paul, *Abroad: British Literary Traveling Between the Wars* (New York, Oxford: O.U.P., 1980).

————, *Wartime: Understanding and Behaviour in the Second World War* (Oxford: O.U.P., 1989).

Gaglianone, P., and Cassini, M., eds, *Conversazione con Antonio Tabucchi* (Rome: Ómicron, 1995).

Garnett, Richard, *The Age of Dryden* (1895), in *Rochester: The Critical Heritage*, ed. David Farley-Hills (New York: Barnes and Noble, 1972).

Gates, Henry Louis, *Loose Canons: Notes on the Culture Wars* (New York: O.U.P., 1992).

Geerts, W., 'Il filo dell'orizzonte di Antonio Tabucchi, una lettura della morte', in *Piccole finzioni con importanza*, eds N. Roelens and I. Lanslot (Ravenna: Longo, 1993), pp. 113–24.

Geiger, Roger L., 'Science and the University', in John Kriege and Dominique Pestre, eds, *Science in the Twentieth Century* (Amsterdam: Harwood Academic, 1997).

Gide, André, *The Immoralist*, trans. Dorothy Bussy (London: Penguin, 1960).

Goldie, Mark, 'The Theory of Religious Intolerance in Restoration England', in *From Persecution to Toleration: The Glorious Revolution and Religion in England*, eds Ole Peter Grell, Jonathan I. Israel, and Nicolas Tyacke (Oxford: Clarendon Press, 1991), pp. 331–68.

Goldman, Harvey, *Max Weber and Thomas Mann: Calling and Shaping the Self* (Berkeley: University of California Press, 1988).

Graff, Gerald, *Beyond the Culture Wars: How Teaching the Conflicts can Revitalize American Education* (New York: Norton, 1992).

Graham, Joseph F., *Difference in Translation* (Ithaca and London: Cornell University Press, 1985).

Greaves, Richard L., ' "Let Truth be Free": John Bunyan and the Restoration Crisis of 1667–73', *Albion* 28 (1996), 587–605.

————, 'Amid The Holy War: Bunyan and the Ethic of Suffering', in *John Bunyan and English Nonconformity* (London: Hambledon Press, 1992), pp. 169–83.

————, 'The Spirit and the Sword: Bunyan and the Stuart State', in *John Bunyan and English Nonconformity* (London: Hambledon Press, 1992), pp. 101–26.

————, *John Bunyan and English Nonconformity* (London: Hambledon Press, 1992).

Greenblatt, S., ed., *The Forms of Power and the Power of Forms in the English Renaissance* (Norman: University of Oklahoma Press, 1982).

Greene, Graham, *The Lost Childhood And Other Essays* (London: Eyre and Spottiswode, 1951).

Griffin, Dustin H., *Satires Against Man: The Poems of Rochester* (Berkeley, Los Angeles and London: University of California Press, 1973).

Gross, Paul R. and Norman Levitt, eds., *Higher Superstition: The Academic Left and its Quarrels with Science* (Baltimore, MD: Johns Hopkins University Press, 1994).

————, Levitt, Norman and Lewis, Martin W., eds, *The Flight from Science and Reason* (New York: New York Academy of Sciences, 1997).

Guerard, Albert J., *André Gide* (Cambridge MA: Harvard U.P., 1969).

Guzman, Gregory G., 'A Growing Tabulation of Vincent of Beauvais' Speculum Historiale Manuscripts', *Scriptorium: International Review of Manuscript Studies* XXIX (1975), 122–5.

Haeight, Gordon S., ed., *The Portable Victorian Reader* (Harmondsworth: Penguin, 1972).

Hall, Brian, *The Impossible Country: A Journey Through the Last Days of Yugoslavia* (London: Minerva, 1996).

Hall, Doug and Fifer, Sally Jo, eds, *Illuminating Video: An Essential Guide to Video Art* (New York: Aperture, 1990).

Halsey, A.H., *The Decline of Donnish Dominion: The British Academic Profession in the Twentieth Century* (Oxford: O.U.P., 1992).

Harbord, R.E., ed., *The Reader's Guide to Rudyard Kipling's Works*, 8 vols (Canterbury: privately printed, 1970).

Haren, Michael, *The Western Intellectual Tradition from Antiquity to the 13th Century* (London: Macmillan, 1985).

Harris, Tim, ' "Lives, Liberties, and Estates": Rhetorics of Liberty in the Reign of Charles II', in *The Politics of Religion in Restoration England*, eds Tim Harris, Paul Seaward and Mark Goldie (Oxford: Blackwell, 1990), pp. 217–41.

Harvey, David, *The Condition of Postmodernity: An Enquiry into the Origins of Social Change* (Oxford: Basil Blackwell, 1990).

Haskin, Dayton, 'Bunyan, Luther, and the Struggle with Belatedness in Grace Abounding', *University of Toronto Quarterly*, 50 (1980–81), 300–13

Hawkins, L.M., *Anecdotes, Biographical Sketches, and Memoirs* (London: F.C. and J. Rivington, 1822).

Hayles, N. Katherine, *Chaos Bound: Orderly Disorder in Contemporary Literature and Science* (Ithaca: Cornell U.P., 1990).

Hayward, Jennifer, *Consuming Pleasures: Active Audiences and Serial Fictions from Dickens to Soap Opera* (Lexington: University Press of Kentucky, 1997).

Hegel, G.W.F., *Grundlinien der Philosophie des Rechts* [*Basic Outlines of the Philosophy of Law*], ed. Johannes Hofmeister, Philosophische Bibliothek, 4th edn (Hamburg: Felix Meiner, 1967).

————, *Vorlesungen über die Philosophie der Geschichte* [*Lectures on the Philosophy of History*], mit einer Einführung von Theodor Litt (Stuttgart: Reclam, 1961).

Heidegger, Martin, *Holzwege* [*Paths through the Woods*], 5th edn (Frankfurt am Main: Vittorio Klostermann, 1972).

Heilbut, Anthony, *Thomas Mann* (London: Macmillan, 1996).

Henderson, Heather, 'The Travel Writer and the Text: "My Giant Goes With Me Wherever I Go," ' in *Temperamental Journeys: Essays on the Modern Literature of Travel*, ed. Michael Kowalewski (Athens, Georgia and London: The University of Georgia Press, 1992).

Henderson, John A., *The First Avant-Garde 1887–1894. Sources of the Modern French Theatre* (London: Harrap, 1971).

Henley, W.E., *For England's Sake: Verses and Songs in Time of War, The Works of W.E. Henley*, 8 vols (London: David Nutt, 1908).

Hewison, Robert, *Under Siege: Literary Life in London 1939–45* (Newton Abbott: Readers' Union, 1978).

Hill, Christopher, *A Turbulent, Seditious, and Factious People* (Oxford: O.U.P., 1988).

————, *The Collected Essays of Christopher Hill*, 3 vols (Brighton: Harvester Press, 1985), I.

————, *The World Turned Upside Down: Radical Ideas During the English Revolution* (Harmondsworth: Penguin, 1972).

Hobsbawm, E.J., *The Age of Capital 1848–1875* (1975; London: Abacus, 1995).

Holmes, George, *The Good Parliament* (Oxford: Clarendon Press, 1975).

Holub, R., 'Weak thought and strong ethics: the postmodern and feminist theory in Italy', *Annali d'italianistica*, 9 (1995), 125–43.

Hoppé, E.O., *In Gipsy Camp and Royal Palace: Wanderings in Rumania* (London: Methuen and Co. Ltd, 1924).

Hughes, Robert, *Culture of Complaint* (New York: O.U.P., 1993).

Hutton, Ronald, *Charles the Second: King of England, Scotland, and Ireland* (Oxford: Clarendon Press, 1989).

Huysmans, Joris-Karl, *Against Nature* (1884), trans. Robert Baldick (Harmondsworth: Penguin, 1968).

Jacobs, Carol, 'The Monstrosity of Translation', *MLN* 90 (1975), 755–66.

Jacobus of Voragine, *The Golden Legend of Jacobus of Voragine*, trans. Granger Ryan and Helmut Ripperger (New York: Arno Press, 1941).

Jerome, Saint, *Life of Malchus*, trans. Sister Marie Liguori Ewald, in Roy J. Deferrari, ed., *Early Christian Biographies, The Fathers of the Church*, vol. 15 (Washington D.C.: The Fathers of the Church, 1952), pp. 281–97.

———, *Life of St. Paul the First Hermit*, trans. Sister Marie Liguori Ewald, in Roy J. Deferrari, ed., *Early Christian Biographies, The Fathers of the Church*, vol. 15 (Washington D.C.: The Fathers of the Church, 1952), pp. 217–38.

———, *Select Letters of St. Jerome*, ed. and trans. F.A. Wright (London: Heinemann, 1933).

Johnson, Lionel, 'A Note Upon the Practice and Theory of Verse at the Present Time Obtaining in France', *Century Guild Hobby Horse*, vol. 6, no. 22 (April, 1891), 61–6.

Jolly, Penny Howell, 'Jan Van Eyck and St. Jerome: A Study of Eyckian Influence on Colantonio and Antonello da Messina in Quattrocento Naples' (University of Pennsylvania, PhD thesis, 1976).

Jones, J.R., *Charles II: Royal Politician* (London: Allen and Unwin, 1987).

Jung, C.J., *Dreams*, trans. R.F.C. Hull (1900; London: Ark Paperbacks, 1985).

Kamerbeek, J., 'Style de Décadence', *Revue de littérature comparée*, vol. 39 (1965), 268–86.

Kamper, Dieter and Wulf, Christoph, eds, *Looking Back at the End of the World* (New York: Semiotext(e), 1989).

Keeble, N.H., *The Literary Culture of Nonconformity in Later Seventeenth-Century England* (Leicester: Leicester University Press, 1987).

Kelly, Ann Cline, *Swift and the English Language* (Philadelphia: University of Pennsylvania Press, 1988).

Kelly, J.N.D., *Jerome: His Life, Writings, and Controversies* (London: Duckworth, 1975).

Kennedy, Liam, *Susan Sontag: Mind as Passion* (Manchester: Manchester U.P., 1995).

Kimball, Roger, *Tenured Radicals: How Politics Has Corrupted our Higher Education* (New York: HarperCollins, 1990).

Kipling, Rudyard, *The Five Nations* (London: Methuen, 1903).

———, *The Seven Seas* (London: Methuen, 1896).

Kirkham, Pat, and Thoms, David, eds, *War Culture: Social Change and Changing Experience in World War Two Britain* (London: Lawrence and Wishart, 1995).

Knight, Philip, *Flower Poetics in Nineteenth-Century France* (Oxford: Clarendon Press, 1986).

Knowlson, James, *Universal Language Schemes in England and France, 1600–1800* (Toronto: University of Toronto Press, 1975).

Koselleck, Reinhard, *Vergangene Zukunft. Zur Semantik geschichtlicher Zeiten [Futures Past: On the Semantics of Historical Time]*, 4th edn, (Frankfurt am Main: Suhrkamp, 1985).

Kristeva, Julia, *Powers of Horror*, trans. Leon S. Roudiez (New York: Columbia U.P., 1982).

———, *Strangers to Ourselves (Etrangers à nous-mêmes, 1988)*, trans. Leon S. Roudiez (New York: Columbia U.P., 1991).

Labinger, Jay S., 'The Science Wars and the Future of the Academic Profession', *Daedalus* 126, 4 (Fall, 1997).

Laidlaw, G. Norman, *Elysian Encounter: Diderot and Gide* (New York: Syracuse U.P., 1963).

Lamb, Jeremy, *So Idle a Rogue: The Life and Death of Lord Rochester* (London: Allison and Busby, 1993).

Lane, Rose Wilder, *The Peaks of Shala: Being a Record of Certain Wanderings Among the Hill-Tribes of Albania* (London and Sydney: Chapman and Dodd Ltd, 1922).

Laplanche, J. and Pontalis, J.-B., *Vocabulaire de la psychanalyse* [*Vocabulary of Psychoanalysis*], 10 edn (Paris, P.U.F., 1990).

Lawrence, C.H., *The Friars: The Impact of the Mendicant Movement on Western Society* (London: Longman, 1994).

Leavis, F.R. and Yudkin, Michael, *Two Cultures? The Significance of C.P. Snow with an Essay on Sir Charles Snow's Rede Lectures* (London: Chatto and Windus, 1962).

————, *The Great Tradition* (1948; London: Chatto and Windus, 1962).

Ledger, Sally, 'In Darkest England: The Terror of Degeneration in *fin de siècle* Britain', *Literature and History*, 4.2 (1995), 75.

Lehmann, John, ed., *Folios of New Writing I–IV* (London: Hogarth, Spring 1940 – Autumn 1941).

————, ed., *New Writing 1–3* (London: Hogarth, Autumn 1938–Christmas 1939).

————, ed., *Penguin New Writing*, No. 1–25 (Middlesex: Penguin, 1940–45).

Levine, Arthur, 'How the Academic Profession is Changing', *Daedalus*, 126, 4 (Fall, 1997).

Loewe, Raphael, 'The Medieval History of the Latin Vulgate', in ed. G.W.H. Lampe, *The Cambridge History of the Bible*, Vol. 2 (Cambridge: C.U.P.), pp. 102–54.

London, Jack, *The People of the Abyss* (London: Isbister and Company Limited, 1903).

Lowry, H.F., ed., *The Letters of Matthew Arnold to Arthur Hugh Clough* (1932; Oxford: Clarendon Press, 1968).

Lucas, John, *Charles Dickens: The Major Novels* (Harmondsworth: Penguin Books, 1992).

Lucente, G., 'Modernism and Postmodernism. Contemporary Italian fiction and philosophy', *Annali d'italianistica*, 9 (1995), 158–65.

Lyotard, J.F., *La condition postmoderne* (Paris: Editions de Minuit, 1979).

Macaulay, Lord, *The History of England from the Ascension of James the Second,* ed. Charles Harding Firth, 6 vols (London: Macmillan, 1913–15).

Macaulay, Thomas Babington, 'John Bunyan', in *Critical and Historical Essays*, 2 vols, ed. A.J. Grieve (London: J.M. Dent, 1907), II, pp. 399–410.

Mallarmé, Stéphane, *Oeuvres complètes*, eds H. Mondor and G. Jean-Aubry (Paris: Gallimard, 1945).

————, *Divagations* (Paris: Bibliothèque Charpentier, 1897).

Mandel, Barrett John, 'Bunyan and the Autobiographer's Artistic Purpose', *Criticism*, 10 (1968), 225–43.

Mann, Thomas, *Death in Venice and Other Stories*, trans. David Luke (London: Minerva, 1996).

Marinetti, F.T., *Selected Writings*, trans. R. W. Flint and Arthur A. Coppotelli, R.W. Flint, ed. (London: Secker and Warburg, 1972).

Marsden-Smedley, and Klinke, Jeffrey, eds, *Views from Abroad: The Spectator Book of Travel Writing* (London: Paladin Grafton Books, 1989).

Marvell, Andrew, *Selected Poetry and Prose*, ed. Robert Wilcher (London and New York: Methuen, 1986).

————, *The Rehearsal Transpros'd and The Rehearsal Transpros'd the Second Part*, ed. D.I.B. Smith (Oxford: Clarendon Press, 1971).

Marx, Karl, *Manifest der kommunistisches Partei* [*Manifesto of the Communist Party*] (1848), in *Die Frühschriften* [*Early Writings*], ed. Siegfried Landshut (Stuttgart: Kröner, 1968).

Mayor, J.B., 'Decadence, *Journal of Philology*, vol. 3 (1871), 347–8.

McGregor, J.F. and Reay, B., *Radical Religion in the English Revolution* (Oxford: O.U.P., 1984).

Miller, D.A., *The Novel and the Police* (Berkeley: University of California Press, 1988).

Miller, John, *Charles II* (London: Weidenfeld and Nicolson, 1991).

Money, Chiozza, *Riches and Poverty* (London: Methuen and Co., 1905).

Montesquieu, *Oeuvres complètes*, ed. Roger Caillois, Éditions de la Pléiade, 2 vols. (Paris: Gallimard, 1949).

Morin, Edgar, *Pour sortir du XXe siècle* [*To Leave the Twentieth Century*], Coll Points (Paris: Seuil, 1984).

Nietzsche, Friedrich, *Jenseits von Gut und Böse* [*Beyond Good and Evil*], in *Kritische Studienausgabe* [*Critical Paperback Edition*], eds G. Colli & M. Montinari, 2nd rev. edn, 15 vols (Munich & New York: DTV/de Gruyter, 1988), V.

————, *Twilight of the Idols*, trans. R.J. Hollingdale (London, Penguin, 1990).

Nisard, Désiré, *Etudes de moeurs et de critique sur les poètes latins de la décadence* [*Moral and Critical Investigations into the Latin Decadent Poets*], 3 vols (Brussels: Louis Hauman, 1834).

Norris, Christopher, *Derrida* (London: Fontana Press, 1987).

————, *New Idols of the Cave* (Manchester: Manchester University Press, 1997).

Nowotny, Helga, *Eigenzeit. Entstehung und Strukturierung eines Zeitgefühls* [*Time: The Modern and Postmodern Experience*], suhrkamp taschenbuch wissenschaft, 2nd edn (Frankfurt am Main: Suhrkamp, 1995).

Noyes, Alfred, *The Last Man* (London: John Murray, 1940).

Nussbaum, Martha C., *Love's Knowledge: Essays on Philosophy and Literature* (New York: O.U.P., 1990).

O'Neill, John H., *George Villiers, Second Duke of Buckingham* (Boston: Twayne, 1984).

Oakley, Francis, 'The Elusive Academic Profession: Complexity and Change', *Daedalus* 126, 4 (Fall 1997).

Oliver, Kelly, *Reading Kristeva: Unravelling the Double-Bind* (Bloomington: Indiana U.P., 1993).

Olson, P.A., 'The Parlement of Foules: Arisfotle's Politics and the Foundations of Human Society', *Chaucer Review*, 24 (1990), 53–69.

Owst, G.R., *Literature and Pulpit in Medieval England* (Oxford: Blackwell, 1961).

Packe, Michael, *Edward III* (London: Routledge and Keegan Paul, 1983).

Pagels, Elaine, *Adam, Eve, and the Serpent* (London: Penguin Books, 1988).

Parker, Samuel, *A Discourse of Ecclesiastical Politie* (London: 1670).

Parry, Ann, *The Poetry of Rudyard Kipling: Rousing the Nation* (Buckingham: Open University Press, 1992).

Parry, Graham, *The Seventeenth Century: The Intellectual and Cultural Context of English Literature, 1603–1700* (London: Longman, 1989).

Pater, Walter, *Marius the Epicurean: His Sensations and Ideas* (London: Macmillan, 1885; Oxford and New York: O.U.P., 1986. ed. Ian Small).

————, *The Renaissance: Studies in Art and Poetry* (London: Macmillan, 1873).

Pearsall, Derek, *The Life of Geoffrey Chaucer* (Oxford: Blackwell, 1992).

Pepys, Samuel, *The Diary of Samuel Pepys*, eds Robert Latham and William Matthews, 11 vols (Berkeley and Los Angeles: University of California Press, 1970–83).

Perkin, J. Russell, 'Religion, Language, and Society: Swift's Anglican Writings', *English Studies in Canada*, 15 (1989), 21–34.

Phipps, Christine, ed., *Buckingham: Public and Private Man – The Prose, Poems and Commonplace Book of George Villiers, Second Duke of Buckingham (1628–1687)* (New York and London: Garland, 1985).

Pinney, Thomas, ed., *The Letters of Rudyard Kipling*, 5 vols, (Basingstoke: Macmillan, 1996).

Pocock, J.G.A., 'Within the margins: the definitions of orthodoxy', in *The Margins of Orthodoxy: Heterodox Writing and Cultural Response, 1660–1750*, ed. Roger D. Lund (Cambridge: C.U.P., 1995).

Poggioli, Renato, *The Poets of Russia 1890–1930* (Cambridge Massachusetts: Harvard U.P., 1972).

Pooley, Roger, 'Language and Loyalty: Plain Style at the Restoration', *Literature and History*, 6 (1980), 2–18.

Pratt, R.A., 'Chaucer's Use of the Teseida', *Publications of the Modern Language Association of America*, 62 (1947), 598–621.

Praz, Mario, *La carne, la morte e il diavolo nella letteratura romantica* (Milan, Rome: La Cultura, 1930; Florence: Sansoni, 1966).

Pritchard, Allan, 'A Defense of His Private Life by ·the Second Duke of Buckingham', *Huntington Library Quarterly*, 44 (1981), 157–71.

Propp, Vladimir, *The Morphology of the Folktale* (Leningrad: Academia, 1928), trans. Laurence Scott, second edition ed. Louis A. Wagner (Austin and London: University of Texas Press, 1968).

Quillard, P., 'La Fille aux Mains coupées', *La Pléiade, Revue littéraire, musicale et dramatique* (April 1886), 33–41.

Raimondi, Ezio, *Il D'Annunzio e il simbolismo in D'Annunzio e il simbolismo europeo*, ed. Emilio Mariano (Milan: Il Saggiatore, 1976).

Reddings, Bill, *The University in Ruins* (Cambridge Mass.: Harvard University Press, 1996).

Reed, Joel, 'Restoration and Repression: The Language Projects of the Royal Society', *Studies in Eighteenth-Century Culture*, 19 (1989), 399–412.

Rennie, Neil, *Far-Fetched Facts: The Literature of Travel and the Idea of the South Seas* (Oxford: Clarendon Press, 1995).

Rice, Eugene F., *Saint Jerome in the Renaissance* (Baltimore: Johns Hopkins University Press, 1985).

Richards, I.A., *Practical Criticism: A Study of Literary Judgement* (1929) (London: Routledge, 1964).

———, *Poetries and Sciences: A Reissue of Science and Poetry* (1926, 1935) with Commentary (London: Routledge, 1970).

———, *Principles of Literary Criticism* (1924) (London: Routledge, 1989).

Ring, Grete, 'St. Jerome Extracting the Thorn from the Lion's Foot', *Art Bulletin* XXVII (1945), 188–96.

Rivers, Isabel, 'Grace, Holiness, and the Pursuit of Happiness: Bunyan and Restoration Latitudinarianism', in *John Bunyan: Conventicle and Parnassus, Tercentenary Essays*, ed. N.H. Keeble (Oxford: Clarendon Press, 1988).

———, *Reason, Grace, and Sentiment: Studies in the Language of Religion and Ethics in England, 1660–1780* (Cambridge: C.U.P., 1991).

Robbins, Bruce, *Intellectuals, Professionalism, Culture* (London: Verso, 1993).

Robinson, I.S., *The Papacy 1073–1198: Continuity and Innovation* (Cambridge: C.U.P., 1990).

Roelens, N. and I. Lanslots, I., eds, *Piccole finzioni con importanza* (Ravenna: Longo, 1993).

Rothblatt, Sheldon and Bjorn Wittrock, eds, *The European and American University Since 1800:Historical and Sociological Essays* (Cambridge: C.U.P., 1993).

Ruskin, John, 'Of Queens' Gardens', *Sesame and Lilies* (1865), (London: Cassell, 1909).

Salmon, Vivian, *The Works of Francis Lodwick: A Study of his Writings in the Intellectual Context of the Seventeenth Century* (London: Longman, 1972).

Samuel, Raphael, *Theatres of Memory. Vol. 1: Past and Present in Contemporary Culture* (London: Verso, 1994).

Sarton, George, *Introduction to the History of Science*, Vol II (Baltimore: Williams & Wilkins, 1931).

Sava, George, *Donkey Serenade: Travels in Bulgaria* (London: Faber and Faber, 1940; The Travel Book Club, 1941).

Schochet, Gordon J., 'From Persecution to "Toleration" ', in *Liberty Secured? Britain Before and After 1688*, ed. J.R. Jones (Stanford: Stanford University Press, 1992), pp. 122–57.

————, 'Between Lambeth and Leviathan: Samuel Parker on the Church of England and political order', in *Political Discourse in Early Modern Britain*, ed. Nicholas Phillipson and Quentin Skinner (Cambridge: C.U.P., 1993), pp. 189–208.

Schulte-Sasse, Jochen, 'Paradoxes in the Narratological Foundation of the Enlightenment', in *Impure Reason: Dialectic of Enlightenment in Germany*, eds W. Daniel Wilson and Robert C. Holub (Detroit: Wayne State University Press, 1993).

Scott, Peter, *The Crisis of the University* (London: Croom Helm, 1984).

————, *The Meanings of Mass Higher Education* (Buckingham: SHRE and Open University Press, 1995).

Seabra, J.A., *Fernando Pessoa ou le poétodrame* (Paris: José Corti, 1988).

Searle, G.R., *The Quest for National Efficiency: A Study in British Politics and Political Thought, 1899–1914* (Oxford: Basil Blackwell, 1971).

Sedgwick, Eve Kosofsky, 'Homophobia, Misogyny, and Capital: The Example of Our Mutual Friend', in *Charles Dickens*, ed. Steven Connor (London: Longman, 1996), pp. 178–96.

————, *Between Men: English Literature and Male Homosocial Desire* (New York: Columbia University Press, 1985).

————, *Epistemology of the Closet* (Berkeley and Los Angeles: University of California Press, 1990).

Semmel, Bernard, *Imperialism and Social Reform: English Social and Imperial Thought 1895–1914* (London: George Allen and Unwin, 1960).

Sensabaugh, G.F., *The Tragic Muse of John Ford* (New York: Benjamin Blom, Inc., 1965).

Shanks, Edward, *Rudyard Kipling: A Study in Literature and Political Ideas* (London: Macmillan, 1940).

Shires, Linda M., 'Literary Careers, Death, and the Body Politics of David Copperfield', in *Dickens Refigured: Bodies, Desires and Other Histories*, ed. John Schad (Manchester: Manchester U.P., 1996), pp. 117–35.

Shute, Nevil, *What Happened To The Corbetts* (1939) (London: Mandarin, 1993).

Smiles, Samuel, *Self-Help, With Illustrations of Conduct and Perseverance* (1859) (London: John Murray, 1908).

Smith, M., *The Darker World Within* (Newark: University of Delaware Press, 1987).

Smith, Nigel, ed., *A Collection of Ranter Writings from the 17th Century* (London: Junction Books, 1983).

Smyth, E., *Postmodernism* (London: Batsford, 1991).

Snow, C.P., *The Two Cultures and the Scientific Revolution* (Cambridge: C.U.P., 1959).

Sontag, Susan, *Illness as Metaphor/AIDS and its Metaphors* (London: Penguin, 1991).

Spackman, Barbara, *Decadent Genealogies* (Ithaca and London: Cornell University Press, 1989).

Spargo, Tamsin, *The Writing of John Bunyan* (Aldershot: Ashgate, 1997).

Sparks, H.F.D., 'Jerome as Biblical Scholar' in P.R. Ackroyd and C.F. Evans, eds, *The Cambridge History of the Bible*, Vol. 1 (Cambridge: C.U.P., 1970), pp. 510–41.

Spinette, A., 'Incontro con Antonio Tabucchi', *Gli spazi della diversità, Atti del convegno internazionale, Rinnovamento del codice narrativo in Italia dal 1945 al 1992* (Rome: Bulzoni, 1995), II, pp. 651–68.

Spurr, John, ' "Rational Religion" in Restoration England', *Journal of the History of Ideas*, 49 (1988), 563–85.

————, ' "Latitudinarianism" and the Restoration Church', *Historical Journal*, 31 (1988), 61–82.

————, 'Religion in Restoration England', in *The Reigns of Charles II and James VII & II*, ed. Lionel K.J. Glassey (London: Macmillan, 1997), pp. 90–124.

Stanford, Derek, *Inside The Forties: Literary Memoirs 1937–1957* (London: Sidgwick and Jackson, 1977).

Starkie, Walter, *Raggle-Taggle: Adventures with a Fiddle in Hungary and Roumania* (1933) (London: Edward Arnold, 1935).

Steiner, George, *After Babel: Aspects of Language and Translation* (Oxford: O.U.P., 1992).

Stewart, Walter, 'Der Tod in Venedig: The Path to Insight', *Germanic Review*, 53 (1978) 50–4.

Sutcliffe, E.F., 'Jerome' in ed. G.W.H. Lampe, *The Cambridge History of the Bible*, Vol. 2 (Cambridge: C.U.P., 1969), pp. 80–101.

Swift, Jonathan, *A Proposal for Correcting, Improving, and Ascertaining the English Tongue* (1712), in *The Prose Works of Jonathan Swift*, ed. Herbert Davis et al., 14 vols (Oxford: Blackwell, 1939–68), IV.

————, *Satires and Personal Writings*, ed. William Alfred Eddy (London: O.U.P., 1932).

————, *The Complete Poems*, ed. Pat Rogers (Harmondsworth: Penguin, 1983).

————, *Gulliver's Travels*, ed. Peter Dixon and John Chalker (Harmondsworth: Penguin, 1985).

Swinnerton-Dyer, Peter, 'Policy on Higher Education and Research' (1991), in Shattock, ed., *The Creation of a University System* (Oxford: Blackwell, 1996).

Sykes, Charles J., *ProfScam: Professors and the Demise of Higher Education* (New York: St Martin's, 1990).

Symons, Arthur, 'The Decadent Movement in Literature', *Harper's New Monthly Magazine*, vol. 87, no. 522 (November, 1893), 858–67.

Tabucchi, A., *I volatili del Beato Angelico* (Palermo: Sellerio, 1987).

————, *Il filo dell'orizzonte* (Milano: Feltrinelli, 1986)

Talon, Henri, *John Bunyan: The Man and his Works*, trans. Barbara Wall (London: Rockliff Publishing, 1951).

Taylor, A.J.P., *English History: 1914–45* (Oxford: O.U.P., 1965).

Taylor, Henry, *Philip van Artevelde: A Dramatic Romance* (London: Edward Moxon, 1834).

Thickstun, Margaret Olofson, 'The Preface to Bunyan's Grace Abounding as Pauline Epistle', *Notes and Queries*, 32 (1985), 180–2.

Thomas of Celano, *Tractatus de Miraculis Beati Francisci*, in *Analecta Franciscana X* (Quaracchi: Collegii a S. Bonaventura, 1928).

Thompson, Roger, *Unfit For Modest Ears: A Study of Pornographic, Obscene and Bawdy Works Written or Published in England in the Second Half of the Seventeenth Century* (London: Macmillan, 1979).

Thormälen, Marianne, *Rochester: The Poems in Context* (Cambridge: C.U.P., 1993).

Thornton, R.K.R., *The Decadent Dilemma* (London: Edward Arnold, 1983).

Titmuss, Richard M., *Problems of Social Policy* (London: Longmans, 1950).
Toulmin, Stephen, *Cosmopolis: The Hidden Agenda of Modernity* (Chicago: University of Chicago Press, 1990).
Tremain, Rose, *Restoration* (London: Hamish Hamilton, 1989).
Trotter, David, 'Wanton Expressions', in *Spirit of Wit: Reconsiderations of Rochester*, ed. Jeremy Treglown (Oxford: Blackwell, 1982), pp. 111–32.
Trow, Martin, 'Academic Standards and Mass Higher Education' (1987), in Michael Shattock, ed., *The Creation of a University System* (Oxford: Blackwell, 1996).
Turner, James G., 'The Properties of Libertinism', *Eighteenth-Century Life*, 9 (1985).
Ulmann, Walter, *Principles of Government and Politics in the Middle Ages* (London: Methuen, 1961).
Underwood, T.L., ' "It pleased me much to contend": John Bunyan as Controversialist', *Church History*, 57 (1988), 456–69.
Van Wyk Smith, M., *Drummer Hodge: The Poetry of the Anglo Boer War (1899–1902)* (Oxford: Clarendon Press, 1978).
Velay-Vallentin, Catherine, *L'histoire des contes* (Paris: Fayard, 1992).
Vickers, Brian, *'The Royal Society and English Prose Style: A Reassessment'*, in *Rhetoric and the Pursuit of Truth: Language Change in the Seventeenth and Eighteenth Centuries* (University of California, Los Angeles: William Andrews Clark Memorial Library, 1985).
Vieth, David M., *Attribution in Restoration Poetry: A Study of Rochester's Poems of 1680* (New Haven: Yale University Press, 1963).
Viola, Bill, *Reasons for Knocking at an Empty House, Writings 1973–1994* (Cambridge, MA: MIT Press, 1995).
Virilio, Paul, *L'espace critique [Critical Space]* (Paris: Christian Bourgois, 1984).
von Goethe, J.W., *Maximen und Reflexionen [Maxims and Reflections]*, in *Werke [Works]*, Hamburger Ausgabe, ed. Erich Trunz, 14 vols, 8th edn (Munich: C.H. Beck, 1978), XII.
Vonnegut, Kurt, *Breakfast of Champions* (London: Jonathan Cape, 1973).
Walker, David, ed., *André Gide* (London: Longman, 1996)
Walker, R.G. and Frazer, J.M., eds., *The Cunning Craft – Original Essays on Detective Fiction Contemporary Literary Theory* (Illinois: Western Illinois University, 1990).
Walsingham, Thomas, *Historia Anglicana*, ed. H. Riley, 2 vols, Rolls Series, 1863–4, I.
Warner, Harry Jr, *All our Yesterdays: an informal history of science fiction fandom in the forties* (Chicago: Advent, 1969).
Warner, Marina, *From the Beast to the Blonde* (London: Vintage, 1995).
Warren, Kenneth, *John Meade Falkner, 1858–1932: A Paradoxical Life* (Lewiston, Queenston and Lampeter: Edwin Mellen Press, 1995).
Waters, Catherine, *Dickens and the Politics of the Family* (Cambridge: C.U.P., 1997).
Watts, Michael R., *The Dissenters: From the Reformation to the French Revolution* (Oxford: Clarendon Press, 1985).
Weinstein, M.A., *William Edmondstoune Aytoun and the Spasmodic Controversy* (New Haven: Yale U.P., 1968).
Wellek, René, *A History of Modern Criticism, 1750–1950*, 5 vols (London: Jonathan Cape, 1970), III, *The Age of Transition*.
Wells, H.G., *Anticipations* (London: Chapman and Hall, 1902).
West, Rebecca, *Black Lamb and Grey Falcon: The Record of a Journey Through Yugoslavia in 1937*, 2 vols (London: Macmillan, 1942).
Whistle, Jeremy, *Deux Pièces symbolistes* (Exeter: University of Exeter 'textes littéraires', 1976).

White, Arnold, *Efficiency and Empire* (Brighton: Harvester Press Limited, 1973).

White, Barrie, 'John Bunyan and the Context of Persecution', in *John Bunyan and his England, 1628–1688*, eds Anne Laurence, W.R. Owens, and Stuart Sim (London: Hambledon, 1990), pp. 51–62.

White Jr, L., 'Death and the Devil', in R. Kinsman, ed., *The Darker Vision of the Renaissance* (Berkeley: University of California Press, 1974).

Wilcoxon, Reba, 'Rochester's Sexual Politics', *Studies in Eighteenth-Century Culture*, 8 (1979), 137–49

Wilde, Oscar, *The Picture of Dorian Gray* (1890) (New York: Airmont, 1964)

Wilkinson, Alan, *Dissent or Conform? War, Peace and the English Churches 1900–1945* (London: SCM Press, 1986).

Williams, Jeffrey, ed., *PC Wars: Politics and Theory in the Academy* (New York and London: Routledge, 1995).

Williams, Raymond, *Culture* (London: Fontana, 1981).

————, *The Country and the City* (London: Paladin Books, 1973).

Wilmot, John, Earl of Rochester, *The Letters of John Wilmot, Earl of Rochester*, ed. Jeremy Treglown (Oxford: Blackwell, 1980).

————, *The Poems of John Wilmot, Earl of Rochester*, ed. Keith Walker (Oxford: Blackwell, 1988).

Winston, Richard, and Winston, Clara, eds. and trans., *The Letters of Thomas Mann, 1889–1955* (Harmondsworth: Penguin, 1975).

Wintle, Sarah, 'Libertinism and Sexual Politics', in *Spirit of Wit: Reconsiderations of Rochester*, ed. Jeremy Treglown (Oxford: Blackwell, 1982), pp. 133–65

Woodhouse, John, *Gabriele D'Annunzio: Defiant Archangel* (Oxford: Clarendon, 1998).

Wordsworth, William, 'Essays Upon Epitaphs' (1810), in W.J.B. Owen and J.W. Smyser, eds, *The Prose Works of William Wordsworth*, 3 vols (Oxford: Clarendon Press, 1974), II, pp. 84–5.

Webster Newhold, ed., *The Renaissance Imagination*, vol. 15 (New York and London: Garland Publishing Inc., 1986).

Yardley, Bruce, 'George Villiers, Second Duke of Buckingham and the Politics of Toleration', *Huntington Library Quarterly*, 55 (1992), 317–37.

Zipes, Jack, *Fairy Tales and Fables from Weimar Days* (Hanover and London: University Press of New England, 1989).

Zurbrugg, Nicholas, ed., *Jean Baudrillard: Art and Artefact* (London: Sage, 1997).

Zwicker, Stephen N., *Lines of Authority: Politics and English Literary Culture, 1649–1689* (Ithaca and London: Cornell University Press, 1993).

Index

Aarne, Antii 119
Ackroyd, P.R. 3
Adams, Robert M. 237
Addison, Paul 184, 188
aestheticism (*see* decadence: *fin-de-siècle*)
AIDS 162
Alain De Lille 18–21
Aldis, Brian 185
Alexander, P. 246
Allestree, Richard 51
Allot, Miriam 143
Ambrose, St xiii
Anderson, Fulton H. 248
Andreae, Joannes 6
Andreoli, Annamaria 128
Antal, David 220
Anthony, St 10, 15
Antoine, André 121
Antongini, Tom 130
Apocalypse xvii, 15, 150, 185–98, 206
Appignanesi, Lisa 242
Aquinas, St Thomas 18, 31
Arendt, Hannah 252
Aristotle 2, 18–21, 31
Arnold, Matthew 91, 92, 94, 95, 143
Ashcraft, Richard 53
Ashley, Maurice 29
atomic bomb (*see* Hiroshima) 201
Augustine, St xii–xvii, 1, 2, 169, 256
Austin, William W. 213
Autard, A. 28, 30,
avant-garde ix, 121, 125, 186, 209, 210, 220
Aytoun, William Edmondstoune 91, 92

Babel xvii, 224, 230
Bacon, Francis 248
Bailey, P.J. 91
Bailin, Miriam 78
Bakhtin, Mikhail 37
Baldrick, Chris 64
Baldrick, Robert 213
Baldwin, Stanley 251
Balkans xvii, 141–53
Barron, Stephanie ix
Bassnett, Susan 226
Battagua, S.
Baudelaire, Charles 84, 67, 90, 94, 157, 213–21, 254

Baudrillard, Jean 209–21
Beaumont, Agnes 52
Beckett, Samuel 209, 219, 220
Beckmann, Max x
Belsey, C. 28
Benjamin, Andrew 227
Benjamin, Walter xvii, 218, 223–34
Bennett, Will 252
Bennington, Geoffrey 242
Benson, Larry D. 20
Beresford, J.D. 193
Bergonzi, Bernard 185, 188
Best, Herbet 186
Bettenson, Henry xiii, 1
Bible 41, 190; (Genesis) xvii, 1, 192, 224, 230; (Ezekiel) 15; (Galatians) 15; (Revelation) 2; (Vulgate) 3
Birken, Lawrence 96
Birkenhead (Lord) 111, 116
Bloom, Allan, 235
Bloom, Harold 157, 233
Blount, Trevor 66
Boccaccio 24, 25
body xiv
Boehmer, Elleke 114
Boer War 108–17
Bonaventure, St 15
Borsari, A. 201
Botta, A. 201
Bottrall, Margaret 49
Bourget 88
Boyd, Charles W. 111
Bricmont, Jean 237
Britt, David x
Brooks, Chris 116
Brown, Emerson (Jr) 24
Brown, Peter xiii, xv
Bunyan, John 45, 48–63
Burnet, Gilbert 48, 58
Bussy, Dorothy 156
Butler, Samuel 43

Calder, Angus 189
Calinescu, Matei 186
capitalism 186
Cassese, Giovanna 3
Chadwick, Henry xii, xvi
Chalker, John 43
Chamberlain, Joseph 108

Charles II 49–63
Charvet, P.E. 215
Chaucer xvi, 17–26
Cheney, Lynne V. 235
Chernaik, Warren 47
Chiaromonte, Isabella (Queen) 3
Christianity xii
Chrysostom, John xiii, xv
Church Fathers xiii, 6, 31
Churchill, Winston 188, 196
Cicero xii, 17
Civil War (English) 40
Clare, St 15
Clarkson, Laurence 44, 49
class xvi, 51, 77, 79, 80, 82, 108–17, 147
classical culture 2, 13, 86, 95
classicism 86
Clifford, Martin 59, 62
Clough, Arthur Hugh 93
Cocker, Mark 142
Colantonio, Niccolò xvii, 3–16
Cold War 152
Combe, Kirk 63
communism 193
Connolly, Cyril 187
Connor, Steven 69
Cook, Eliza 78
Coppe, Abiezer 44, 49
Coppotelli, Arthur A. 217
Costello, John 187
courtly love 20, 24
Cousins, Ewert 15
Cowgill, B.K. 18
Cowper, William 72
Cromwell, Oliver 41
Crowley, Tony 39
culture 171–82 (European) xvi

D'Annunzio, Gabriele xvii, 118–40
D'Sousa, Dinesh 235
Dadaism 218
Damrosch, David 236
dandyism 215
Darwinism (social) 109
Daves, Charles W. 43
Davidson, Angus 118
Davidson, G.W. 199
Davis, Herbert 39
De Krey, Gary S. 54
De Man, Paul 228, 231
De Quincy, Thomas 83

De Vries, Hent 227
Deak, Frantisek 122
decadence (politics of) ix–xvi 17; (social) xvi, 18, 45, 107 144 185 205; (fin-de-siècle) xvii, 64, 83–94 96–106, 142 155, 164, 200, 209, 215, 218, 236; (urban) 1, 107, 205 (of royal courts); 17–26, 39–63; (and French criticism) 83–94; (decadent novel) 97; (resistance to) 171–82; (of translated texts) 223–34
decadent subject xiii
Deferrari, Roy J. 9
Derrida, Jacques xvii, 223–34, 241, 242, 244
Descartes, René 172–4, 204, 255
Dickens, Charles xvii, 64–82
Dickson, Albert 120
Dix, Otto x
Dixon, Peter 43
Dobell, Sidney 91
Dollimore, Jonathan, 169
Dowling, Linda 84–9, 95, 99, 100
Dryden, John 58
Dundes, Alan 119
Durham, Mary Edith 143–5, 151–3
Duse, Eleonora 124, 128, 139

Earl of Clarendon 41
Eddy, William Alfred 40
Edward III xvi, 17, 21–6
Elam, Keir 27
Elfenbein, Andrew 65
Elias, Richard 58
Eliot, T.S. 97, 166
Elizabethan period 29
Elliott, Alison Goddard 9
Ellis, Henry Havelock 84
Ellman, Maud 166
Emerson, O.F. 1
Emmerson, Richard K. 16
Engelberg, Edward 216
Enlightenment 173
Entartete Kunst (Degenerate Art) x–xii
Etherege, George (Sir) 43
eugenics 109
Europe, European 185; (medieval) xvii; (philosophy) 246
Eustochium 11
Evans, C.F. 3
Evelyn-White, Hugh G. 248
Ewald, Sister Marie Liguori 9

Exclusion Crisis 55

Fabian Society 109
fairy-tales 118, 119, 120, 123, 126
Falkner, John Meade xvii, 95–106
Fall, of man xiii, xvii, 6, 225
Farley-Hills, David 46
fascists, fascism ix, 130, 153, 186, 193,
    195
Faulkner, Peter 116
feminism 110
Fentress, James 44
Ferdinand I, (King) 3
Fermor, Patrick, Leigh 143, 147–8, 151
Feuillerat, Albert 220
Fifer, Sally Jo 221
fin-de-siècle (*see* decadence)
Finkielkraut, Alain 252
First World War 129, 145, 185, 187
Firth, Charles Harding 42
Fisch, Harold 54
Fish, Stanley 239
Fiume episode 128
Fleming, John V. 16
Flint, Kate 64
Flint, R.W. 217
Foot, Michael 43
Ford, J. 27–38
Forrest, James F. 50
Fort, Paul 121–2
Foucault, Michel 105, 158, 169, 248
Fowler, Edward 45
Fowler, Roger 65
Francis, St (Franciscans) xvii, 3, 13, 15,
    16, 195
French criticism 83–94
Freud, Sigmund 119–20, 163, 169, 178
Friedman, Herbert 6
Friedman, John Block 1
Fussell, Paul 146
Futurism 218

Gaglianone, P. 201
Gallienne, Richard Le 148
Gane, Mike 219
Garnett, Richard 46
Gates, Henry Louis 237
Gautier, Théophile 84, 88, 94
Geerts, W. 201, 208
Geiger, Roger L. 237
Gerasimus, St 5

Gide, André xviii, 154–70
Gilbert and Sullivan 96
Gill, Stephen 74
Glanvil, Joseph 51, 53
Glassey, Lionel K.J. 55
Goldie, Mark 55
Goldman, Harvey 160
Good Parliament xvi, 17, 18–26
Graff, Gerald 237
Graham, Joseph F. 225
Greenblatt, S. 30
Greene, Graham 149, 185
Gregory the Great 5
Grell, Ole Peter 55
Griffin, Dustin H. 48
Gross, Paul R. 237
Grosz, George x
Guerard, Albert 154
Guillemot, D. 219
Guzman, Gregory C. 6
Gwynn, Nell 61

Haeight, Gordon S. 216
Hall, Brian 143
Hall, Doug 221
Halsey, A.H. 236
Hamilton, Donna B. 54
Harbord, R.E. 112
Harding, Georgina 133
Hardy, Thomas 236
Haren, Michael 31
Harley, Robert 40
Harris, Tim 56
Harvey, David 254
Haskin, Dayton 49
Hawkins, L.M. 83
Hayles, N. Katherine 173
Hayward, Jennifer 79
Hazlitt, William 27
Hegel, G.W.F. 246–7, 252
Heidegger, Martin 248
Henderson, Heather 143
Henderson, John A. 121
Henley, William Ernest 116
Herder, Johann Gottfried 223
Herzman, Ronald B. 16
Hesiod 248
Hewison, Robert 187
Hichens, Robert 96
Hill, Christopher 44
Hiroshima 185

history xiii, 184, 249–56
Hobsbawn, E.J. 78
Hofmeister, Johannes 247
Hölderlin, Friedrich 248
Hollingdale, R.J. 155
Holmes, George 21
Holub, Renate 202
Holub, Robert C. 249
Homer 86
homoeroticism 69, 99–106, 156–70, 161, 164
Hoppé, E.O. 143, 147–8, 151–3
Hovis, Jacques F. 122
Huehns, G. 41
Hughes, Agatha 136
Hughes, Robert 235
Hull, R.F.C. 120
Hullbert, James 233
Hutcheon, Linda 202
Hutton, Ronald 57
Huysmans, Joris-Karl 94, 99, 162, 209–21

imperialism 107–17
individual perspective, xvii, 199, 205
Isherwood, Christopher 215
Isidore of Seville 5
Islam 194, 195
Israel, Jonathan I. 55

Jacobean 27–38
Jacobus of Voragine 6
Jean-Aubry, G. 122
Jephcott, Edmund 225
Jerome, St xiii, 1–16
John of Gaunt 21–2
John, St 6
Johnson, Samuel 48, 178
Johnson, Lionel 84
Johnson, Samuel 48
Jolly, Penny Howell 3
Jonas, Hans 246
Jones, J.R. 55
Joyce, James 152, 170, 209
Jung, C.J. 120

Kamerbeek, J. 88
Kamper, Dieter 220
Kamuf, Peggy 232
Keats, John 93
Keeble, N.H. 46
Kelly, Ann Cline 40

Kelly, J.N.D. 3
Kennedy, Liam 167
Kimball, Roger 235
Kinsman, R. 29
Kipling, Rudyard xvi, 107–17
Kirchner, Ernst Ludwig x
Kirkham, Pat 189
Kirkpatrick, E.M. 199
Klinke, Jeffrey 148
Knight, Philip 123
Knowlson, James 44
Koselleck, Reinhard 253
Kowalewski, Michael 143
Kristeva, Julia 156, 158–70
Kroll, Richard 53

Labinger, Jay S. 237
Laidlaw, G. Norman 157
Landa, Louis 40
Landshut, Siegfried 249
Lane, Rose Wilder 143, 145
Lanslot, I. 201, 202
Laplanche, J. 247
Latimer, William 22
Lawrence, C.H. 13
Lawrence, D.H. 142
Le Gallienne, Richard 84
Leavis, F.R. 172, 175, 179
Ledger, Sally 110
Leibniz, Gottfried Wilhelm 255
Leonardo da Vinci 138
Levine, Arthur 239
Levitt, Norman 237
libertines xvi, 39–63
linguistics 83–94
Litt, Thodor 246
Loewe, Raphael 3
London, Jack 116
Lowry, H.F. 93
Lucan 83, 86
Lucas, John 64–7, 69
Lucente, G. 200
Lund, Roger D. 52
Lyons, Richard 22–3
Lyotard, J.F. 200

Maccubin, Robert P. 47
Macke, August x
Malchus the monk 9, 10
Mallarmé, Stéphane 121–2, 213
Mallock, W.H. 96

Mandel, Barrett John 49
Mann, Thomas xviii, 154–70
Manning, Gillian 52
Mariano, Emilio 125
Marinetti, F.T. 217, 218
Marsden-Smedley 148
Marston, J.W. 91
Marvell, Andrew 56, 61
Marx, Karl 101, 237, 249
McDonald, Christie 232
McGee, J. Sears 50
McGregor, J.F. 44
media xviii, 250, 253
metaphor 162, 199, 252 (sexual) xi
metaphysics 223–34
Migne, Jacques Paul 5
Mill, J.S. 95
Miller, D.A. 69, 73
Milton, John 66, 75
mimesis 226
Minnis, Alastair J. 25
modern xviii; (-ism) 166, 184–98; (post-)
    199, 200, 209, 210
modernism 152
Moffat, Douglas M. 18
Mondor, H. 122
Money, Chiozza 108
Montale, Eugenio 124
Morin, Edgar 246
Morris, Edward P. 241
Moschus, John 5
Mosley, Oswald 196
Moxon, Edward 91
Müller, Max 85
Munton, Alan 188
Mussolini, Benito 130–1
mysticism 213, 223
myth 119, 142, 203, 252

National Socialist Party ix
naturalism 131–2
Nature (personification of) 17, 18, 20;
    nature 18–21, 35
Nazis ix, 149, 151, 190, 237
Neville, John 22
Newhold, Webster W. 32
Nietzsche, Friedrich 136, 155, 160, 236,
    251
Nisard, Désiré 83–94
Nolde, Emile x
non-conformists xvi

Norman, Geraldine 250
Norris, Christopher 237, 229
Norton, Charles Eliot 110
Norwood, Richard 49
Nowotny, Helga 254
Noyes, Alfred 190
Nussbaum, Martha C. 69

O'Neill, John H. 59
Oakley, Francis 238
Oliver, Kelly 163
Olson, P.A. 18
Olympic Games xi
original sin xv
Orwell, George 189
Osborn, Thomas (Sir) 59
Ottoman Empire 143, 150
Ovid 127
Owen, John 56
Owst, G.R. 22

Pacheco, Anita 52
Packe, Michael 22
Page, F. 92
Pagels, Elaine xv, xvi
Parker, Samuel 55
Parks, Tim 199
Parliament (Cavalier) 55–9
Parry, Graham 42
Parry, Richard Lloyd 252
Parson, Robert 49
Pater, Walter 83, 95, 97, 104, 167, 216
Paterson, A.B. 113
Patrick, Simon 53
Patterson, J.D. 47
Paul the hermit 9
Paul, St xiii, 9
Paulson, Kristoffer F. 62
Pearsall, Derek 23
People's War 187–91
Pepys, Samuel 42
Perkin, J. Russell 40
Perrers, Alice 22–6
Pessoa, F. 203
Peter de la Mere (Sir) 21–2
Peter, St 9
pharmakon 229
Phillipson, Nicholas 53
Phipps, Christine 59
Pichois 87
Pinney, Thomas 110

Plato xii, 21, 31, 35, 168, 229; (neo-
  Platonism) 98, 99, 103
Pocock, J.G.A. 52
Poggioli, Renato 210–11
politics (see Decadence) ix–xvi, 2, 17,
  150, 192 195–6; (Aristotelian theory)
  18–26; (Restoration) 39–63; (reformist
  politics) 108, 187
Pontalis, J.-B. 247
Pope, Alexander 90
Porter, Catherine 241
positivism 199, 203
postmodern (see modern) xviii
Pound, Ezra 166
Pratt, R.A. 26
Praz, Mario 118
Pritchard, Allan 59
Propp, Vladimir 119
psychology 173
Puritanism 28, 44, 49

Quakers 54
Quehen, Hugh 62
Quillard, Pierre xvii, 118–19, 121–4

Raimondi, Ezio 124–5
Ralph, Julian 111
Ranters 54
rationality, rationalism xiv, 173
reason (see rationality)
Reay, B. 44
Reddings, Bill 243
Reed, Joel 44
Renaissance 27–38, 131, 143, 168
René, D'Anjou 3
Rennie, Neil 142
Restoration 40–63
Revolution 54
Rhodes, Cecil 117
Rice, Eugene F. 5
Richards, I.A. xviii, 171
Richardson, Samuel 66
Rilke, R.M. 204
Ring, Grete 6
Ripperger, Helmut 6
Rivers, Isabel 46
Robbins, Bruce 245
Roberts (Lord) 111
Robinson, I.S. 8
Roelens, N. 201, 202
Rosenthal, Raymond 132

Rothblatt, Sheldon 238
Roudiez, Leon S. 156
Ruskin, John 80
Ryan, Granger 6

Salemohamed, G. 219
Salmon, Vivian 44
Samuel, Raphael 251
Sarton, George 9
Saunders, Trever J. 2
Sava, George 143, 149
Schad, John 69
Schmidt-Rottluff, Karl x
Schochet, Gordon 53
Schopenhauer, Arthur, 155
Schulte-Sasse, Jochen 249
science xviii, 171–82
science fiction 185
Scott, Peter 236
Seabra, J.A. 203
Searle, G.R. 115, 108
Seaton, M.A. 199
Seaward, Paul 56
Second World War xvii, 149, 153, 185–98,
  252
secularization xvii
Sedgwick, Eve Kosofsky 69, 81, 99, 102
Semmel, Bernard 108
Sensabaugh, G.F. 33
Sérusier, Paul 122, 124
Severus, Sulpicius 5
sexual politics xviii
sexuality, sexual desire xiii, 17, 132, 187
Shakespeare 35, 93, 120, 127, 178, 246
Shanks, Edward 116
Sharrock, Roger 50
Shattock, Michael 239
Shaw, George Bernard 109
Shires, Linda M. 69
Shorter, Kingsley 225
Showalter, Elaine 252
Shute, Nevil 187
Sibellato, Ercole 131
Simpson, J. 199
Sinclair, T.A. 2, 19
Skinner, Quentin 53
Smiles, Samuel 80
Smith, Alexander 91
Smith, D.I.B. 61
Smith, Molly 29, 37
Smith, Nigel 44

Smith, Van Wyk 113
Smyth, E. 200
Snow, C.P. 172, 175
Sokal, Alan 237
Sontag, Susan 162, 167
Soutif, D. 219
Spackman, Barbara 126
Spargo, Tamsin 52
Sparks, H.F.D. 3
Spasmodic poets 91–2
Spinoza, Baruch 204
Sprat, Thomas 43, 53
Spurr, John 53, 55
squalid argument 108
Stachniewski, John 52
Stanford, Derek 185
Stapledon, Olaf 189
Starkie, Walter 143, 147–8
Steinner, George 223
Stephens, A.G. 114
Stevens, Wallace 97
Stewart, Walter 155
Stillingfleet, Edward 51, 53, 61
Strachey, James 120
Strier, Richard 54
Super, R.H. 93
Superman 128, 136
Sutcliffe, E.F. 3
Swift, Jonathan xvi, 39–63
Swinburne, Algernon Charles 116, 134
Swinnerton-Dyer, Peter 240
Sykes, Charles J. 235
symbolism 121–2, 127, 151, 161–2, 168, 217
Symonds, J.A. 95
Symons, Arthur 64, 84, 94, 144

Tabucchi, Antonio xvii, 199–208
Talon, Henri 49
Taylor, A.J.P. 188
Taylor, Henry 91
technology xviii, 212
theatre 122–4
theology xii, xvi, xvii
Thickstun, Margaret Olofson 49
Third Reich x
Thomas of Celano 15
Thompson, Roger 42
Thompson, Stith 119
Thoms, David 189
Thornton, R.K.R. 84, 96, 141

Tillotson, John 53
Titmus, Richard M. 193
Tosi, Guy 125
Toulmin, Stephen 255
translation 223–34
Trapnel, Anna 49
travel writing xvii, 142–53
Treglown, Jeremy 47
Tremain, Rose 42
Trevor-Roper, Hugh 41
Trotter, David 47
Trow, Martin 239
Trunz, Erich 256
Turner, Chris 218
Turner, James G. 47
Turner, Jane 3
Tyacke, Nicolas 55

Ulmann, Walter 18–21
Underwood, T.L. 46

Van Eyck, Jan 3
Vanbrugh, John (Sir) 43
Vattimo, Gianni 202
Velay-Vallantin, Catherine 120, 123
Venus (goddess) 23-25
Vieth, David M. 57
Villiers, George 58
Vincent of Beauvais 6
Viola, Bill 221
Virgil 86
Virilio, Paul 254
Vivian de Sola Pinto 48
Von Goethe, J.W. 256
Vonnegut, Kurt 179

Wagner, Louis A. 119
Wagner, Richard 138
Walker, David 154
Walker, Keith 45
Walker, R.G. 199
Wall, Barbara 49
Walsingham, Thomas 26
Warner, Harry (Jr) 185
Warner, Marina 120
Warren, Kenneth 97
Waters, Catherine 77
Watts, Michael R. 55
Waugh, Evelyn 142, 147, 149
Webb, Sidney 109
Weber, Carl Maria 155

Weber, Max 160
Weiner, E.S.C. 199
Weinstein, M.A. 92
Wellek, René 86
Wells, H.G. 109, 186
West, Rebecca 143, 149, 152–3
White, Arnold 109–10, 114–15
White, Barrie 60
White, L. (Jr) 29
Wight, Sarah 49
Wilcoxon, Reba 47
Wilde, Oscar xvii, 90, 92, 94, 96–106, 160, 169, 209
Wilders, John 62
Wilkinson, Alan 184
will xiv–xv, 19, 103
Williams, Jeffrey 237
Williams, Kathleen 40
Williams, Raymond 2, 74, 190
Wilmot, John, Earl of Rochester 45–8, 51–63

Wilson, Daniel W. 249
Winstanley, Gerrard 52
Winston, Clara 155
Wittrock, Bjorn 238
Woodhouse, John 118
Wordsworth, William 88, 89, 90, 93, 94
Wright, F.A. 11
Wright, Patrick 251
Wright, Thomas 32
Wulf, Christoph 220

Yardley, Bruce 59
Yudkin, Michael 172

Zipes, Jack 120
Zogorin, Perez 53
Zohn, Harry 218, 224
Zola, Emile 121
Zwicker, Stephen N. 42